Migration and Vodou

New World Diasporas

Florida A&M University, Tallahassee
Florida Atlantic University, Boca Raton
Florida Gulf Coast University, Ft. Myers
Florida International University, Miami
Florida State University, Tallahassee
University of Central Florida, Orlando
University of Florida, Gainesville
University of North Florida, Jacksonville
University of South Florida, Tampa
University of West Florida, Pensacola

New World Diasporas
Edited by Kevin A. Yelvington

This series seeks to stimulate critical perspectives on diaspora processes in the New World. Representations of "race" and ethnicity, the origins and consequences of nationalism, migratory streams and the advent of transnationalism, the dialectics of "homelands" and diasporas, trade networks, gender relations in immigrant communities, the politics of displacement and exile, and the utilization of the past to serve the present are among the phenomena addressed by original, provocative research in disciplines such as anthropology, history, political science, and sociology.

Migration and Vodou

Karen E. Richman

University Press of Florida

Gainesville · Tallahassee · Tampa · Boca Raton · Pensacola · Orlando · Miami · Jacksonville · Ft. Myers

10 09 08 07 06 05   6 5 4 3 2 1

A record of cataloging-in-publication data is available from the Library of Congress.
ISBN 0-8130-2835-3

All photographs were taken by the author except where noted.

The University Press of Florida is the scholarly publishing agency for the State University
System of Florida, comprising Florida A&M University, Florida Atlantic University, Florida
Gulf Coast University, Florida International University, Florida State University, University
of Central Florida, University of Florida, University of North Florida, University of South
Florida, and University of West Florida.

University Press of Florida
15 Northwest 15th Street
Gainesville, FL 32611-2079
http://www.upf.com

In memory of Min and Ti Chini

Contents

Figures

Compact Disc

Foreword

In his book *The Social Construction of What?* (1999), philosopher of science Ian Hacking is concerned to show how simplistic notions of "the social construction of reality"—certainly a central concept in the social sciences, history, cultural and literary studies and beyond—can leave us confused as to just what is being constructed and what is not or cannot be constructed, and, when we are even aware of it, the *consequences* of depicting something as socially constructed or not. Hacking comes up with "indifferent kinds" of phenomena, and "interactive kinds." Indifferent kinds are not aware of, indeed can't be aware of, human classificatory schemes, even if humans are responsible for the creation of these phenomena and affect their existence. One example Hacking gives is plutonium. Interactive kinds, by contrast, refer to classifications that, "when known by people or by those around them and put to work in institutions, change the ways in which individuals experience themselves—and may even lead people to evolve their feelings and behavior in part because they are so classified. Such kinds (of people and their behavior) are 'interactive kinds.' This ugly term has the merit of recalling actors, agency and action. The *inter* may suggest the way in which the classification and the individual classified may interact, the way in which the actors may become self-aware of being of a kind, if only because of being treated or institutionalized as of that kind, and so experiencing themselves in that way" (104).

That diaspora is an interactive kind of phenomenon, an interactive kind interacting with other interactive kinds, can be seen in this fine book by anthropologist Karen Richman. *Dyaspora* is now a category of analysis in the Kreyòl language of Haiti, used when referring to individuals who have returned to visit or those of

Haitian descent born abroad (and it is not always a flattering term or a term of endearment). Before he even became president, since-ousted President Jean-Bertrand Aristide paid special attention to the Haitian diaspora, and once elected he created a cabinet-level post responsible for the affairs of Haitians and their descendants abroad that also tried to secure investments, facilitate remittances, and ensure political loyalties. Richman properly starts from these cultural and political conceptions of diaspora. If we should not falsely substantialize or reify diaspora but should, as Rogers Brubaker recently argues (in "The 'Diaspora' Diaspora," *Ethnic and Racial Studies* 28(1) [2005]:1–19), conceive of diaspora as "a category of practice, project, claim and stance, rather than as a bounded group" (13), it is also the case that diaspora-as-interactive kind is defined by counter-practice, counter-project, counter-claim and counter-stance. This is Richman's other starting point. Thus, academic and popular categorizations mix and intermingle and mutually shape (but of course not on equal footing nor with equal power), reinforce, and contradict each other as concepts and the behavior of those deemed to be Haitian and in/of the Haitian diaspora while, at the same time, power relations from the inside and outside enter at all levels.

Indeed—and this is part of the politics of representation Richman confronts—the image of "Haiti" itself is certainly an interactive kind, from the height (or depths) of the notoriously racist and primitivist travel writing of the 1920s and 1930s on Haiti that served to help justify the long U.S. occupation of Haiti (1915–34), to the subsequent ideological edifices justifying foreign domination and exploitation in the form of a narrative of decadence, exoticism, primitivism, sensuality, barbarism, and racialized notions of political immaturity, among many other negative allusions, with certain key representations such as "Race" and "Vodou" recurrent and recurrently powerful, made to stand for particular features of the Haitian social formation over time. Works such as Paul Farmer's *AIDS and Accusation: Haiti and the Geography of Blame* (1992) and *The Uses of Haiti* (1994), J. Michael Dash's *Haiti and the United States: National Stereotypes and the Literary Imagination* (1988), Alex Dupuy's *Haiti in the World Economy: Class, Race, and Underdevelopment Since 1700* (1989), Robert Lawless's *Haiti's Bad Press: Origins, Development, and Consequences* (1992), Brenda Gayle Plummer's *Haiti and the United States: The Psychological Moment* (1992), Mary A. Renda's *Taking Haiti: Military Occupation and the Culture of U.S. Imperialism, 1915–1940* (2001), and *Getting Haiti Right This Time: The U.S. and the Coup* by Noam Chomsky, Paul Farmer, and Amy Goodman (2004) all richly document a topography of power relations, while works such as Alex Stepick's *Pride Against Prejudice: Haitians in the United States* (1998), *Diasporic Citizenship: Haitian Americans in Transnational America* by Michel S. Laguerre (1998), Anthony V.

Catanese's *Haitians: Migration and Diaspora* (1999), and Flore Zéphir's *The Haitian Americans* (2004), as well as the 1997 film *Black and White in Exile*, which shows Haitians' differential treatment at the hands of U.S. immigration laws and practices, all reveal that the violence of dislocation undermines the easy celebratory acceptance of the diaspora-as-travel trope.

As Richman is at pains to show, neither representations of Haiti nor the diasporic consciousness of Haitians abroad or in Haiti simply hang in the air, but are materially constituted by multiple and myriad relationships of unequal exchange at many levels, as well as by ubiquitous state and political structures. Her long-term, ethically conscious, and politically committed ethnographic fieldwork in Florida, Virginia, and Haiti was with vulnerable, super-exploited farmworkers who sent remittances back to their families in Haiti, as well as with villagers in the Plain of Léogane who made their family members abroad present in their everyday and religious ritual lives.

In attending closely to the textures of diasporic processes, Richman keys in on the communications to their families these workers record on audio cassettes in the Kreyòl language. These recordings convey the workers' thoughts and feelings via the language's proverbs and sayings, speech events that are part of what might be called subaltern diaspora rites. These performances construct and reconstruct what it means to be Haitian in Haiti and in *dyaspora*. Luckily, we can hear and appreciate these on the compact disk that accompanies Karen Richman's wonderful book.

Richman utilizes as a concept-metaphor the *pwen* (a perhaps untranslatable Kreyòl word that refers to the distillation of complex concepts or events through familiar and simple images and symbols) in order to talk about the dialectics and dialogics of diaspora. Revealing essential meanings via reproducing what it reduces, *pwen* comes to assume many forms, most often manifested in antiphonal, indirect speech and song that can include biting social commentary. The *pwen* is used with religious ritual overlays in the Vodou complex to effect a moral stance, a way of talking about taking care of the homestead and community and resisting involvement in the capitalist system of commodity production. This talk is directed at migrants, who in turn insist that what they are doing is neither antisocial nor immoral but rather a necessary evil. Instead of adopting a kind of culturalist stance that holds that things change so that they can remain the same, Richman is attuned to how what she sees as a widespread ambivalence to capitalist encroachment and proletarianization becomes transformed within Vodou as a central counterpoint between "Guinea" or "Africa" (*Ginen*) and "Magic" (*Maji*), where *Ginen*, laden with authenticity, represents community and communal interests, and *Maji* the self-seeking and selfish forces. *Ginen* and *Maji*, each entailing its opposite, are in a dialectical relationship. They provide the changing frame through which the accusations and the rebuttals of *pwen* are made. They serve as an idiom through which an understanding and control of the contradictions of the material social relationships are affected. And they also provide reference for the ritual processes of long-distance worship engaged in by the farmworkers in Florida. Through these cassette communications they are able to listen to services—with ritual drumming, prayers, and possession—for the ancestors and spirits of local descent groups inhabiting the sacred lands back in Haiti. There are now *lwa* (Vodou gods) concerned with migrants and their ability to produce and exist abroad, as well as their obligation to provide for those left behind. All of this occurs in what Richman calls a "transnational ritual circuit and performance space."

Influential proscriptive pronouncements about the future of anthropology, that it should be concerned with the appreciation of cultural diversity along with the critique of social and representational inequality (Bruce M. Knauft, *Genealogies for the Present in Cultural Anthropology*, 1996), and that it needs to be based on "multi-sited" ethnography rather than research territorially and conceptually chained to the idea of bounded cultures existing in one location (George E. Marcus, "Ethnography in/of the World System: The Emergence of Multi-Sited Ethnography," *Annual Review of Anthropology* 24 [1995]:95–117), equally apply to the social scientific efforts to chart diaspora processes. And it is Richman who, through her principled research and clearly articulated arguments, already anticipates these ideals while showing us how anthropologists and others should pursue the dialectics and dialogics of diaspora.

Kevin A. Yelvington
Series Editor

Acknowledgments

*You tell me that you'd be pleased if I would do things with you, with the people you are
associated with—you'd like it if I would do things the way I do them with you so you could
explain these things to other people, no problem. As long as you'd like me to do it, to work
with you to help you, no problem. I have no reason to be embarrassed. Why would I be
embarrassed? Neither do I have anything to fear. And, you told me that you would put my
name in the project, in the book, and you would change my name if I were afraid. I'm not at
all. Do you know—is there something you know of about it that would get me in trouble? If
you knew that something would get me in trouble, you would never get me involved in it. You
would never get me involved in it. In the same way, I wouldn't do that to you either. . . .
Whatever you do, it's fine. However you can do it, do it. You understand? However you can
do it, do it. No problem. . . . Whatever you want to do that would please you, you may do it
for me and you.*

Pierre "Ti Chini" (Little Caterpillar) Dioguy "wrote" these words in a cassette
letter to me. I had asked his permission to publish his letters and songs in a book
I was writing about Haitians' religion and migration. I had also inquired about
publishing his identity and his interest in talking to audiences with me about the
project.

The seeds of this book were unintentionally planted when I met Little Caterpillar and other newcomers from Léogane, Haiti, on a wretched farm labor camp
in Tasley, Virginia. I had heard about a summer internship with a small legal aid
program for the indigent that was looking for someone who could communicate with the new group of vegetable pickers in their Kreyòl (Creole) language.
Though I had no legal background, I did what I could to help them defend their
rights not to be abused and not to be cheated out of their wages. For my own part

and for the farmworkers, I thank the intrepid public lawyers who took up their cause: George Carr, Rob Williams, Garry Geffert and, especially, Gregory Schell. Yves Pont-du-Jour and Edwin Dimitri Stephen, paralegals in Maryland and North Carolina, also deserve our gratitude.

Little Caterpillar and the Dioguy and Dedine families, the D'Haïti siblings, and members of the Dediscar and Clairant families warmly welcomed me into their transnational households, stretched between South Florida, where East Coast migrant farmworkers generally live for seven months of the year, and Ti Rivyè, a coastal village in Léogane. My gratitude to them is profound. I especially thank Pierre D'Haïti, my foster son and constant source of help, his eloquent sister, Mercina, and the lay philosopher Joseph "Malgre Sa" Météllus, who called me his "mother" for helping him through his convalescence and legal battles, but who deserves my thanks for his generosity of insight on virtually any epistemological concern to me. I also am grateful to Gasby Alexis, Yvon Daniel, and Jean Fritz Altidor, entrepreneurs who help migrants adjust to United States society and connect them to their families back home.

I am indebted to many people for the Ti Rivyè phases of my research, especially my "mother," Germina Amilcar, my "uncle" Faustin, who was my history teacher and companion, their siblings, Gwe and Marc, and many of their children, nieces, and nephews, including Immaculat Riché, Mireille Amilcar, Yves and Ti Mafi Mehu, Nason Alèrte, Tata Marthurin, and Tinoufi Philibert. Yves Watermann was my energetic and able field assistant. Kanès Pierre added his dedication and good humor to our interviewing team. The late Camolien Alexandre, Clotilde Worral, and Mozart Desmesmin generously shared their recollections of Ti Rivyè's history. The virtuoso musicians Zo Guerrier, Bobine Moïse, and Archange Calixte were immensely generous. I thank Eve and Se Byen Dioguy and Germaine and Andréline Bien-Aimée for their hospitality. Bonheur Calixte, Pepe Michel, Leda Dorsainville, Joiecius Mehu, and Emile Clairant taught me about ritual practice in Ti Rivyè. Because everyone I would like to recognize from Ti Rivyè cannot be named here, I will respectfully invoke the last stanza of "The Guinea Prayer": "To all of those I know and all of those I do not know," I acknowledge your generous gifts to me.

I was introduced to Haitian religion in college by Karen McCarthy Brown, and her compassionate teaching and writing kindled an interest that still burns strong. Alex Stepick took me under his generous wing as I was beginning my research on Haitian migrants and he has been a source of inspiration and unwavering support ever since. Sidney Mintz, whose analysis of Caribbean slavery and peasants had a profound effect on my thinking, was a kind shepherd over the years. Gerald Murray deserves my profound gratitude. His ethnography provided a direction for this research project, for which he was a generous reader. My research might not have been attempted, though, were it not for Ira Lowenthal, who insisted that I put aside my vague ambition to go to East Africa and return to Haiti. I am grateful to Ira's intellectual brother, Drexel Woodson, for his friendship, challenging questions, and confidence in my work, which he demonstrated by playfully addressing me as "Dr. Richman" well before I earned the title. I thank another pair of academic age-mates, Paul Farmer and Paul Brodwin, whose comments and writing have also pushed me to refine my approach.

Port-au-Prince has been the home of a convivial community of local and foreign students of Haitian society, many of whom have been involved in development. Shelagh O'Rourke, the patron spirit of this community, took me under her able wing when I first arrived and occasionally came to visit me in the village. John and Faith Lewis's dining room table frequently was the setting of stimulating seminars covering everything from Haitian politics to sugarcane production. John appointed himself my professor in the field; the success of my fieldwork in Ti Rivyè owes much to his counsel and occasional visits. Jacques Bartoli, for whom medical expertise is one of many talents, was a reliable friend and healer not only for me but also for several residents of the village where I lived. Donna Plotkin and Hermann Lauweryson freely shared ideas and bibliographic sources. I am grateful to Jeff Liteman and Jim Allman. I also thank Robert Maguire, formerly of Inter-American Foundation, which sponsored my dissertation research along with Organization of American States.

Bernard Ethéart taught me much about Haitian political-economy and offered invaluable logistical support, including arranging my affiliation with the State University, and ultimately my official permission from the state to carry out field research. The Usine Sucrière Nationale de Darbonne (Léogane) offered many resources. I am especially indebted to Herbert Docteur, director, and Nicolas Guy Jules, cartographer. I also appreciate the help of Albert Hill, director of the Haitian American Sugar Company.

I wish to express my gratitude to my undergraduate teachers at Wesleyan, Johannes Fabian, Mark Slobin, Elizabeth Traube, and Willard Walker, and Leslie Desmangles, of nearby Trinity College, for shaping my intellectual development and stewarding my first ethnographic research in Haiti. The University of Virginia's Department of Anthropology created a challenging and humane environment for its graduate students. I had the privilege of being a student of the late Victor Turner, who guided this study in spirit. I owe a great debt to Frederick Damon, the chairman of my dissertation committee, a true and steadfast mentor and friend. Roy Wagner has a well-known and remarkable capacity for discovering and articulating, in penetratingly simple terms, the motivating essence of any ethnographic example or problem set before him. I thank him for showing a struggling graduate student the "point," or *pwen*, of her data. I am grateful to the other members of my dissertation committee, Virginia Young and Benjamin Ray.

I have benefited from the ideas, suggestions, and support of many colleagues and friends. I fortuitously met Nina Glick-Schiller at a point when I was endeavoring to interpret the making of a transnational ritual circuit and performance space and she, along with Linda Basch and Cristina Szanton Blanc, was elaborating an approach to the transnational social fields of new migrants. Her long championship of my work began with encouraging me to pursue my interest in how President Aristide's discourse reformulated the growing consciousness of transnationalism in Haitian society. During the same period, David Griffith involved me in ambitious comparative ethnographic research in South Florida studying immigrant incorporation, inter-ethnic relations, and transnationalism, projects funded by National Science and Howard Heinz Foundations.

I have been fortunate to have been in supportive academic environments surrounded by kind and stimulating colleagues. I would like to thank James Arnold and University of Virginia's New World Studies Program for granting a postdoctoral teaching and research fellowship. While I was at University of Chicago for a postdoctoral teaching fellowship, there were many whose interest and insights were especially meaningful, including John and Jean Comaroff, Ray Fogelson, Daniel Wolk, Leslie Balan-Gaubert, Moishe Postone, Bert Cohler, John MacAloon, and Andrew Abbott. Jim Grossman and Bruce Calder deserve my thanks for their comments and conviviality during my semester at the Newberry Library. In addition, I am grateful to the Social Science Research Council for awarding a fellowship to study religion and migration in South Florida. Josh Dewind of the Social Science Research Council deserves enormous thanks for inviting me to contribute to fascinating interdisciplinary conferences and publications. In those contexts, I was fortunate to work with Liza McAllister, Sarah Mahler, Manuel Vasquez, Albert Raboteau and Karen Leonard.

The University of Notre Dame's Anthropology Department sets the standard for collegiality. I am especially grateful to Roberto DaMatta, Patrick Gaffney, and Jim McKenna for their support and insightful comments on my scholarship. Notre Dame's Haiti Program, headed by the indefatigable Thomas Streit, deserves my thanks. Generous funding from the University of Notre Dame's Institute for Scholarship in the Liberal Arts, College of Arts and Letters, and Graduate School have made this book possible.

I am grateful to my editor, John Byram, and to my series editor, Kevin Yelvington, for their enthusiastic support for this work. I owe a huge debt to Edith

Turner and an anonymous reader who reviewed the manuscript. I thank Katharine Liegel for her careful editorial assistance.

Finally, I wish to thank my extraordinary family, for whom anthropology is a mode of communication. George and Rosalind Richman extended unswerving support of my education and zealous interest in my writing. I am grateful to my sister, Amy, for her insights into my research and practical help designing and coding my questionnaires, my brother Ted, who visited me in the village, for his astute observations and essential medical advice, and my brother Neil, who also came to Ti Rivyè to conduct his own study of healing, which influences his practice of orthopedics today. My deepest gratitude is to my partner, Mark Kruger, whose fleeting "doctor's visits" in Ti Rivyè delighted everyone, and me most of all. I thank him for his patience and loving support through this prolonged and intimate migration.

A Note on the Text

All translations of Creole are mine, unless otherwise noted. Creole orthography has undergone changes in the past fifty years. In some instances, I have used updated spelling (for example, *petwo* instead of *petro*) in discussions of earlier works, rather than revert to the earlier spelling.

1

The Pwen of Transnational Haitian Migration

1.1. Little Caterpillar at Farmex labor camp in Tasley, Virginia, July 1985.

Pierre Dioguy's family and close friends call him by his childhood nickname: Little Caterpillar (Ti Chini, pronounced Tee Sheenee) or Caterpillar (Chini), for short. He was a larva-sized baby, one of a triplet birth, the only who survived. The name certainly matched the grown man. Little Caterpillar was compact, wiry, and composed. He was a witty and eloquent master of Creole, the French-derived vernacular spoken by the subordinate masses of Haiti. (Only the educated minority know French.) He was especially adroit in a prized genre of sacred song whose double-entendre renders verses oriented to the spirits into interpersonal weapons of persuasion and authority. He was also known for his command of forms of divination, healing, and worship, and his power to embody and direct the forces of the divine. He had long been expected to succeed his elder brother as the one who "drives" (*kondi*) their lineage's spirit house.

Little Caterpillar grew up in a peasant homestead in a rural section along the northern coast of the sugar-producing Plain of Léogane, Haiti. Of his parents' ten children who reached adulthood, he was the youngest son. Six of his siblings are alive today. Three sisters reside in Guadeloupe; a brother and sister live in Léogane. None of them ever had the opportunity, as he says, to "sit on a school bench." (Caterpillar, who is not literate, marks a cross when required to sign his name.) Most of the adult men in Caterpillar's settlement farmed or fished; the women marketed. Caterpillar sharecropped several postage-stamp-sized plots. Maxia, his wife, conducted a barely profitable food trade.

In June 1980, when Little Caterpillar was thirty-four, he and twenty cousins and neighbors left for the United States. They embarked to *chache lavi pou fanmi yo*, to "search for a livelihood for their families." Caterpillar's group braved the 700 miles of sea in a motorless "canoe" (*anòt*) christened in their best mimesis of the colonial language, "Confiance en Dieu" (Confidence in God). Their voyage was one of a flotilla of boats that transported about 70,000 primarily male, young, peasant Haitian natives to South Florida between 1979 and 1981.

The only "life" opportunity available to Little Caterpillar in the United States was in the lowliest of occupations: migratory farm labor. Caterpillar likened the toil to a losing battle against the fire of the sun: the sun eats up the laborer's body and turns it into water. Squalid, isolated labor camps, decrepit but expensive tenement houses, crooked crew bosses, worksite accidents, pesticide poisoning, and violent crime are all routine conditions of migratory farmwork. Immediately off the boat in Florida, he embarked on his first migratory farm labor job, which took him by bus to Michigan. The labor contractor abandoned his crew. While walking down a road to look for help, Caterpillar was accosted by a gang of white men spouting an English word he would later recognize as "nigger." They beat and stabbed him, then left him for dead in a woods.

As he lay there, he saw the image of the beautiful spirit Ezili Freda. She came to him to comfort him and gave him a sign that he would not die. He awoke in a hospital, unable to communicate with the medical staff. A Creole interpreter eventually arrived at his bedside. The mulatto woman's questioning soon led to the happy discovery that they were from the same locale in Léogane, though from very distant social places. Her father was a prominent Léogane landowner and proprietor of a mill and distillery. She asked him on behalf of an American official if he wanted to be sent back home to Haiti. He declined, saying he hadn't yet "sent to do" (*voye fè*) anything for his family back home.

Three years later, his index finger was severed between two orange crates, leaving him with chronic nerve pain. Caterpillar nevertheless managed, despite long periods when he could not work, and trifling pay when he could, to "find some life" for his siblings and for his wife. A quarter of the money from his measly workman's compensation claim he sent to them.

I first met Little Caterpillar at a desolate labor camp on the Eastern Shore of Virginia in June 1981. I was serving as an advocate for Peninsula Legal Services' farmworker assistance program between semesters of graduate school, hired to reach out to the new and, therefore, particularly vulnerable Haitian population. Little Caterpillar made sure I knew him among the scores of Haitian cucumber pickers at the Farmex camp. He would stop me, never to ask for my help or counsel, but to quiz me about my interest in Haitian culture and language. He eventually discovered that I had some familiarity with Haitian ritual music. I had studied ritual performance at cult centers in Port-au-Prince, the subject of my undergraduate honors' thesis in anthropology and music.

Once, when I was standing in the compound besieged by workers all simultaneously soliciting my aid, Caterpillar appeared holding a portable cassette player. Surprising me, he queried in Creole, "Excuse me, Miss Carline, can you identify this rite?" Suddenly all was quiet except for the recorded sounds of multimeter ritual drumming. With all eyes on me, I tried to listen carefully to the esoteric rhythm. Having dabbled in Haitian ritual drumming, I believed I recognized the pattern as one deriving from West Africa, which in Haitian ceremonies is beaten to honor a pantheon of "Guinea" spirits known as Ogoun. I timidly ventured, "It sounds to me like Nago Zepol" (Nago Shoulders Style). Little Caterpillar howled and cavorted and nearly fell down. "The American woman knows Nago Zepol!" he yelled at the growing crowd. "The American woman knows Nago Zepol!" "Nago Zepol," he greeted me, grinning, the next time I entered the labor camp.

After Nago Zepol, Caterpillar and I had our first real chat. He invited me into the cabin he shared with two other men. He again surprised me by not talking at all about ritual music nor grilling me further about my knowledge of his religious traditions. He wanted to tell me, rather, about the people for whom he was "searching for life": his wife, Maxia, his oldest brother and surrogate parent, Se Byen, Adam (Adan) and Eve, his twin brother and sister, his nieces and nephews, and others. All of them, he said, depended upon him. He described in a gratified tone the nice cement and tin-roofed house he was having built back home (in his absence), financed by his remittances. Erecting such a house was expected of everyone who left, a conspicuous signifier of the migrant's success abroad and the strength of his bonds to the home. Caterpillar did seem to be "living" back home (*lakay*), while just toiling over here. He remained actively involved in his home family's experience, and they in his.

Considering the formidable material, linguistic, and financial barriers to communication between poor, unlettered people in the remote Haitian countryside and their relatives in isolated farm labor camps and slums in the United States, the vitality of their intimacy was remarkable. They maintained their relationship in creative ways that entirely bypassed formal channels of communication. Independent entrepreneurs who specialized in the business of "coming and going" afforded the vital connections between home villages and their satellites abroad. A trusted man named Antoinne Edouard traveled biweekly between Caterpillar's village in Léogane and Palm Beach County carrying money, letters, and gifts. While the migrants were away "on contract," between June and September, however, they did not have regular access to Antoinne. Apart from the occasional opportunity to send mail through a trusted person who happened to be traveling between "the contract" and Antoinne's bases in Palm Beach County, they were obliged to suspend correspondence with their home relatives until they returned to Florida.

Their primary medium of correspondence was audio cassette-tape. Recorded tape offers poor Haitians, whose domination has long been reproduced by illiteracy in the colonial language, a creative way of "writing" in their own beloved vernacular, Kreyòl (Creole). But even if people were literate, the tapes are far more congenial for extending their emphatically oral Creole aesthetic—one that prizes proverbs, figurative language, indirection, antiphony, and fluid shifting between speech and song. Corresponding by cassette has become so normal that the term "to write [a letter]" (*ekri*) means recording a cassette rather than the epistolary form. There is now a distinctive genre of cassette-discourse, including formulaic greetings and salutations. Both recording and listening to a cassette-letter are "performance events" (Bauman [1977] 1984).

Affordable, portable cassette-radios coincidentally appeared in stores around the same time as the Haitians' boats began arriving in Florida. The migrants quickly appropriated them to their long-distance lives. Powered by batteries, the devices afford migrants and their home kin a way to transcend unequal access to electrical current, one of the "patterned differences" in technological development across the world-system.[1] The portable cassette-radio stands as an epitomizing symbol, or "a model of and a model for" their long-distance society (Geertz 1973:93). Likely to be prominently displayed in both the migrants' quarters and the home family's dwelling, the device radiates the vitality of the dispersed family's intimacy and the migrant's success abroad.

Little Caterpillar and I also corresponded by the universal medium of "letter writing" between families in rural Haiti and their members living abroad. We "wrote" cassettes in between our meetings at this same Virginia Eastern Shore camp during subsequent summers and in South Florida, where the farmworker crews lived and worked between December and June. On his cassette letters to me, Little Caterpillar has defined himself as my teacher—of Creole, of ritual songs, of intercropping sugarcane and sweet potatoes—anything "Haitian." I did not actively try to learn or record what he gave me, though, until more than a year after we met. I thought of myself as an advocate for a better life for Haitian immigrant farm workers, rather than as a student of their experience. I was, in fact, planning to conduct dissertation research among a pastoralist society in East Africa. Once I realized I wanted to research what I had been increasingly lured to defend, I designed a bilateral research project to explore the experience of transnational migration and its relationship to religious change, both for those who left and those who remained behind, beginning with ethnographic research in the home site for 18 months.

Caterpillar was delighted that I wanted to go to his home in Léogane, as were several other Léogane emigrants whom I had tried to help. Among them was a sibling group and their spouses and babies. My partner and I were foster parents for their teen-aged brother. I asked several of the Léogane emigrants to contact their families at home to apprise them of my desire to live in their village. Little Caterpillar told me that he would gladly write to Se Byen (his eldest brother) and his family about me. Caterpillar did eventually record a florid cassette-letter compelling his family to load me with food and other gifts whenever I visited and, if necessary, to go out and buy the presents and send him the bill. But the tape reached Se Byen and his relatives after I did. My arrival was totally unannounced.

In July 1983, I followed Caterpillar's directions to the settlement in Ti Rivyè (Little River) of Ka Piti (Petit's House; Petit was the name of the colonial owner of the plantation). I was accompanied by my partner and a young man from a nearby settlement. We parked our borrowed car on the dirt road and stopped the first person we saw to ask directions to the home of Se Byen Dioguy. He did not respond but summoned another man to talk to us. The second man appeared, dressed in tattered shirt and frayed pants, a hoe balanced on one shoulder. He looked familiar. I asked again for Se Byen Dioguy. I asked for the twins, Adam and Eve Dioguy; I asked for relatives of other young men from the village. The man's face was ice. I said something to the effect that "Little Caterpillar told me that I could find his family here." The ice melted. A friendly, trusting face looked back and said, "I'm Adam Dioguy, Pierre Dioguy's brother. Come with me and I'll introduce you to Se Byen." Adam led us from the road into a shaded, residential yard. He invited us to sit down under a thatched arbor, which ran the length of a large tangerine colored shrine. Se Byen soon appeared and introduced himself. His sister, Eve, came. Se Byen's two wives, cousins, nieces and nephews greeted us, one by one engulfing us in an unforgettably tender and warmhearted welcome.

Adam later described our meeting to Little Caterpillar. He "wrote" on a taped letter:

> We were sitting here and a car appeared over there. Se Byen wasn't here. I got up; I was going to work in my garden. I met Yvon who said, "There are two Americans here asking for every single member of the Dioguy family and the first person they asked for was Se Byen Dioguy." I went to talk to them; then I sent for Se Byen. When the Americans came in they sat under the arbor. They asked us questions about every single one of the men who left here and went to the U.S. They got along well with them over there. They started to mention names, this person, that person. All of the people they asked for—whole families—we had them all come before them. It was a beautiful thing. Everybody saw that it wasn't a trick because—look, how else could they have known the business about the name, Little Caterpillar? When they came and talked about the business of the name, Little Caterpillar, everyone, truly, saw that you and the Americans must live in the same place. I'm not going to pretend that everybody wasn't a little worried at first—but then they relaxed.

This beautiful moment was nonetheless sullied by Se Byen and Adam's baffling accusations against their brother. They felt utterly abandoned by him. Until we got there, they said, they feared that their younger brother might have been dead. Little Caterpillar? The migrant who drudged and endured for the sake of loved ones back home? The migrant who, for all intents and purposes, "lived" back home in Léogane? I had expected his relatives to be singing their hero's praises. Se Byen declared that he had not heard from Caterpillar for three years. Three years was exactly how long Caterpillar had been away. How could that be? Could Little Caterpillar have been lying to me about his remittances to his home?

Se Byen told me he wanted to "write" to Caterpillar. He requested that I help him record the letter, leading me to believe that he either did not own a radio-cassette player or know where to borrow such an appliance, let alone know how to operate one. I promised to return later that week.

Se Byen was waiting for us when we came back, his ample frame wedged between the narrow bench and the tangerine wall of "the [spirit] House." He is the

1.2. Se Byen Dioguy, Ti Rivyè, June 2003.

priest and healer at the House. He was wearing the same wide-brimmed straw hat with the tall cylindrical crown and loud, wilted polyester long-sleeved shirt as when we met him. Se Byen's glance as we approached conceded his mild approval that we had kept our promise to return with the cassette-recorder. He got up and asked that we follow him. He walked around the side of the House, unlocked a door and gestured for me to enter. We went inside an eerie, dark chamber. The door stayed open. Frankel, his first cousin, carried in two more chairs and lit a tiny gas lamp. I set the recorder on the smooth cement of an altar, in between two vessels decorated with red and black cloth. Se Byen announced that he was ready to commence the recording (CD, track 1).

After a perfunctory greeting to Little Caterpillar, Se Byen launched into his oration. Adroitly manipulating proverb, rhyme, and rhythm, this master orator designed a pathetic portrait of his devastation since his "child" had abandoned him.

> Hello, Pierre Dioguy. Se Byen Dioguy is speaking to you, your big brother. I haven't heard from you at all. We started out communicating just fine. But it's been three years since I got any news from you and because of it, I am not managing at all. Our mother had seven children; my man, you were the one here with me. You looked out for me; I looked out for you. But I never thought you would do this to me. After all, you left merely to pursue a livelihood. Well my man, I'm letting you know that I haven't heard from

1.3. The House in Ti Rivyè, 1983.

you and I'm wasting away. The way you remember me is not how I look today. I haven't seen you; I can't live, I can't drink. When I think about you, I don't know how I am. I'm hungry; I don't see you. I'm bare naked; I don't see you. You are hungry; I don't see you. You are bare naked; I don't see you. My man, I'm letting you know that I'm dirty; I'm torn; the work doesn't go the way you remember it—in Haiti. But when you're down, you take what comes, if nothing comes your way, you accept it.

Se Byen proceeded to conclude. Suddenly, he interrupted the letter's closing to add a postscript: "But there is just one more thing I'll tell you. I repeat, there is just one thing, and as soon as I say it, you will understand my message." His voice effected a seamless modulation into song. The only signal of this shift was a sudden cry of "genbo!"—a soloist's call to ready the chorus and drummers to respond in this particular ritual style. Accompanying himself with a ritual rattle, Se Byen lined out the verses; Frankel sang the choral refrain.

The House falls down;
Ti Jean doesn't fall down.
The House falls down;
Ti Jean doesn't fall down.
Brother Chini, my friend,
It's for their big mouths, true.

Little Caterpillar falls down;
Se Byen doesn't fall down.
Little Caterpillar falls down;
Se Byen doesn't fall down.
Brother Caterpillar, my friend,
It's for their big mouths, true.

The House stumbles;
The House is mad;
Ti Jean sits there.
The House goes on;
Ti Jean sits there.
Little Caterpillar, my friend,
It's for their big mouths, true.

First verse repeats

Kay la tonbe;
Ti Jean pa tonbe.
Kay la tonbe;
Ti Jean pa tonbe.
Frè Chini, monchè,
Se pou dyòl yo, vre.

Ti Chini tonbe;
Se Byen pa tonbe.
Ti Chini tonbe;
Se Byen pa tonbe.
Frè Chini monchè,
Se pou dyòl yo, vre.

Kay la bite;
Kay la fache;
Ti Jean chita la.
Kay la ap mache;
Ti Jean chita la.
Ti Chini, monchè.
Se pou dyòl yo, vre.

The song contradicted his previous masterfully scored, verbal harangue. It was as if he were saying, "the story of my suffering over your abandonment was a ruse.

1.4. Nelio Dediscar, Zo Guerrier, and Frankel Dedine drumming at the House, August 1983.

My real message to you is, I don't need you anyway." The song's refrain conjured up the image of a beleaguered, crumbling spirit House (where we were recording the tape). Yet Ti Jean, the defiant spirit who dwells there, stood firm. Ti Jean is Se Byen's patron spirit. In other words, Se Byen also stood strong. In the second verse, Little Caterpillar "falls down" while Se Byen endures. The last line of the refrain challenges any "big mouth" gossip who would say otherwise.

As these verses unfolded through Se Byen and Frankel's call-and-response exchange, Zo, the father of one of the migrants, appeared with a drum and started playing along with a clipped, ebullient rhythm. Zo's wife surfaced, then Se Byen's wife, and then more kin until we had to move into the large performance space in the center of the House to accommodate the growing "letter-writing" team. Two more drummers joined in to complete polyrhythmic drum battery. Se Byen passed the lead-singer role to several equally impressive soloists who lined out song after song improvising phrases aimed at the rascal who departed and abandoned his family. Se Byen acted as narrator, identifying the soloists and drummers. And, as if Little Caterpillar needed to be reminded of my conspicuous participation in the irreverent chorus, Se Byen shouted into the microphone over the chorus's refrain to one of the songs, "The woman is sitting here listening to this! She is ashamed to find out that her friend doesn't write to his family!"

When the hour-long tape was full, one of the drummers supplied another. They filled up that one, too. About thirty-five men and women were dancing and singing the choral refrains and an equal number of children were parodying them. From time to time, people approached the recorder to speak into it, greeting Little Caterpillar or one of the other emigrant men expected to hear the tape. Everyone seemed to be enjoying themselves tremendously. I was, too, even though I hardly grasped the point (or points) of this spectacularly orchestrated and virtuoso correspondence event. Its staging was a vast transnational performance space that included and addressed the migrants absent from the ceremony taking place in the shrine back home.

Little Caterpillar received this extraordinary two-cassette communiqué at the Virginia labor camp a few weeks later. (My partner took it back to the States, and it was delivered to Little Caterpillar by our foster son, who went to the labor camp to visit his family.) Caterpillar immediately taped a response, which was dispatched to Florida and then delivered to Haiti by the courier, Antoinne. In his letter, Caterpillar took up Se Byen's challenge. He proceeded to improvise five poignant ballads based on the same ritual genre used by Se Byen and the others. Although he lacked drummers and a chorus, his astonishing solos clearly outclassed the master singer. The first song was a poignant allegory (CD, track 2). It was set in the same place occupied by Se Byen when he recorded his letter: the spirit House. The anonymous narrator is not inside; he sings from somewhere far off. His kinsmen have scorned him, thrown him away. But one day, he warns, they will invite him in; they will "pick him up."

The first verse portrays what it was like before he was expelled. When he was living with his family—"in the middle of the army"—they ignored him. They did not even "know his name" because, he implies, he was poor and not likely to lift himself or his relatives out of their misery. Since he departed "to search for *their* livelihood," though, those who remain behind have found him of value. "They" busy themselves calculating his "size" and "weight," as if estimating the profits to be skimmed from the labor of chattel. Finally "the day arrives" when they discover they have no one else to turn to. They go searching for him *in the House*. There they confront a painful truth. They weep. When they are ready to accept their emissary and to restore his dignity, he divulges his full name. Then Se Byen picks him up and welcomes him home and into the House.

They forget me.
There is a time
They will remember me.
You throw me away.
I say, contempt.
There is a time, brother Se Byen,
Look, you will need me.

I say, the day is here,
The day is here.
I say the day is here,
The day is here, my brother.
There is a time
You will pick me up
So you won't be in need.

When it's one of your own
My friend, look across from you;
They don't know your worth.
When you are away, yes,
Look, the people will know.
You're in the middle of the army,
Look, they don't need you.
When you go away, boy,
Everyone will know,
Look at how much you weigh.

I say, the day is here,
The day is here.
There is a time, brother,
They will gather me
So they won't need.

They will remember me in the House.
Look, they are searching for me.
Look, they can't even see me.
You will look for me in that House.
Look, you can't see me.
When I was together with them
Look they didn't know my name.

When I truly turn my back on them
You will know my name, brother.
I'm in this country;
Look, the day is here.

I'll turn my back and leave,
Look, when I turn around, brother,
Look, everyone is weeping.
When everyone is weeping
For whom are they asking?
It's Pierre Dioguy
They wanted to see him,
Look, they can't see him.

I say, the day is here, my son.
There is a time
When I appear before them
Everyone will be happy to see me.

They forget me.
There is a time
They will remember me.
You throw me away.
I say, contempt.
There is a time, brother Se Byen,
Look, you will need me.

I say, the day is here,
The day is here.
I say the day is here,
The day is here, my brother.
There is a time
You will pick me up
So you won't be in need.

Yo bilye mwen.
O gen youn tan
Ya sonje mwen.
Adye, nou jete mwen.
M di, lamepriz o.

Gen youn tan, frè Se Byen,
Gade, ou a bezwen mwen.

Mwen di jou a la,
Jou a la o.
Mwen di, jou a la,
Jou a la frè mwen.
O gen youn tan
Ou a ranmase m
Pou ou pa bezwen.

Lè ou gen youn pitit kay ou
Monchè, gade anfas ou;
Yo pan konn valè ou.
Se kan nou deyò, vre,
Gade pèp la ap konnen.
Ou nan mitan lame a,
Gade, yo pa bezwen ou.
Kou ou sòti deyò, ti gason,
Tout mounn ap konnen,
Gade sa ou peze.

Mwen di, jou a la,
Jou a la, vre.
Genyen youn tan, frè
Ya ranmase m
Pou pa bezwen.

Yap sonje m nan Kay la.
Gade, yap chache mwen.
Gade, yo pap sa wè mwen.
Nap chache m nan Kay sa.
Gade nou pap sa wè mwen.
Lè m te ansanm avèk yo
Gade, yo pa konnen non mwen.
Kou m vire do m ba yo vre
Ou a konnen ki jan m rele, frè.
Mwen nan peyi a,
Gade jou a la o.

Map vire do mwen pati,
Gade, kou m vire, frè
Gade tout mounn dlo nan je yo.
Lè tout mounn dlo nan je yo
Pou ki mounn yap mande?
Se Pierre Dioguy o
Yo te anvi wè li,
Gade yo pa sa wè li.

M di, jou a la, ti gason m.
Genyen youn tan
Lè m parèt sou yo
Tout mounn ap kontan wè mwen.

Yo bilye mwen.
O gen youn tan
Ya sonje mwen.
Adye, nou jete mwen.
M di, lamepri o.
Gen youn tan, frè Se Byen,
Gade, ou a bezwen mwen.

Mwen di jou a la,
Jou a la o.
Mwen di, jou a la,
Jou a la frè mwen.
O gen youn tan
Ou a ranmase m
Pou ou pa bezwen.

The Pwen of Caterpillar's Migration

Little Caterpillar's ballad is an elegant example of a complex concept known as *pwen* (or *pwent*), pronounced like and based on the French word *point* (or *pointe*). There is no analogous term in English for the complex concept. Karen McCarthy Brown (1987:151–152), who has provided a subtle interpretation of the concept, describes pwen as "anything that captures the essence or pith of a complex situation." Using aesthetic processes of abstraction, intensification, and exaggeration, a pwen crystallizes a complex reality into "an elegantly simple image," simple enough to be easily grasped and remembered. Pwen are ingeniously underdetermined modes of communication; their meanings are fixed not by those who create them, but by those who perceive them, who, it is said, "pick them up" (*ranmase yo*). Pwen reveal bare truths about persons, situations, powers, and things.

The concept of pwen has to do with the symbolic power of imitation. To use Walter Benjamin's (1968:160) wording, pwen are mimetic ways to "get hold of an object at very close range by way of its likeness, its reproduction." A pwen seizes or stops the power inside the other by reproducing it. Pwen are the work of a mimetic faculty. Michael Taussig's (1993) provocative discussion of the mimetic faculty, which was inspired by the writings of Walter Benjamin, explains that mimesis is a double process involving copying and contact, miming and bodily perception. Echoing Marx's ([1843–44] 1975) critique in the *Economic and Philosophical Manuscripts* of the effect of commodity production and exchange on perception, Benjamin (1968:160) suggested that socialization in "the age of mechanical reproduction" gradually snuffs out our innate mimetic faculty. We recognize this mode of perception in children, who instinctively learn through tactile experimentation, trying things out on their own bodies, learning about the other by becoming and behaving like the other. The work of Durkheim ([1915] 1965), Hocart ([1936] 1970), and other early-20th-century scholars attempting to compare modernity with other forms of society indicates that this faculty remained alive in people who may have been encompassed by capitalism but whose consciousness and perceptual faculties were not converted to rationalist thought.

Artful Haitian performers like Caterpillar and Se Byen engage their mimetic faculty to improvise pwen in a variety of performance frames, including interpersonal dialogue, music, drama, ritual, work, rallies, and broadcast media. A pwen can be a coded message sent to critique an unnamed target. Any song text can become a pwen when its nondirected language is used to capture a truth about an interpersonal situation. It can be a personal nickname like that given to my friend Malgre Sa (In Spite of It), during his infancy after he survived an acute affliction believed to be caused by sorcery. A pwen can be a magical power that symbolically captures the essence of a relation or an entity—a kind of sympathetic magic. A pwen can be a parody like those enacted by the thousands of Haitians who rallied in 1997 in street protests of the sexual torture of Abner Louima in a New York police precinct bathroom. They used mime to redefine and seize control of the grotesque meanings of that violence. They came wearing toilet seats and plungers on their faces, heads, and bodies, portraying torturer and victim (Brown 1997).

Se Byen and Little Caterpillar's hostile exchange typified the genre of indirect, contentious, interpersonal discourse known as "sending" or "throwing points" (*voye pwen*). Analogues to this style of indirect, hostile communication are found throughout the African diaspora, and include the African-American practice of "signifying," the Jamaican style of "throwing words," and the Barbadian routine of "dropping remarks" (Fisher 1976; Mitchell-Kernan 1972). Although pwen may be spoken, singing is the more effective weapon for launching pwen, especially in public antiphonal exchange between leader and chorus (Courlander 1960; Averill 1997). Under the transparent veil of nondirected, public discourse, singing serves as a vehicle for persuasive maneuvering and verbal aggression. The singer can deny any specific aggressive intent because responsibility for interpreting the "meaning" is believed to rest with the unnamed and self-appointed "owner of the pwen." This genre of performance is known as *voye pwen chante*, "sending song pwen" or "singing pwen" (*chante pwen*). Caterpillar in fact identified Se Byen's inauguration of the genre at the outset of his cassette-letter when he acknowledged, "I picked up all of the song pwen you sent [to tell] me. I understood them all." (*M ranmase tout pwen chante ou voye di m. M konprann yo tout.*). Se Byen's deft kickoff of the singing pwen match immediately impressed his relatives and neighbors and seduced them not merely to observe, but also to join in. His audience readily grasped the pwen he aimed at Little Caterpillar. It has taken me years to do the same.

All of the pithy, poignant ritual song texts of this repertoire, known as *makanda*, illuminate some aspect of a sweeping existential conflict. The "point" of Se Byen's songs was to treat the antagonistic relationship between Little Caterpillar and himself as an instance of this struggle. The analogy between this moral contest and Se Byen and Caterpillar's contested relationship was so accessible that when Se Byen and Caterpillar went to throw their respective "points," they found ready fodder in familiar makanda songs. They had only to aim their messages at one another to clarify their "points." What is the analogy? How could these ritual songs so completely apprehend—serve as a pwen for—the relationship between the migrant and the homebody, between the seeker of livelihood and the recipient of livelihood?

The genre concerns the struggle between two moral systems or ways-of-being-in-the-world. Guinea (Ginen) signifies tradition, mutuality, and moral authority. The term Guinea refers to the far off, mythical place "on the other side of the water" from where the ancestors migrated and to which they return at death, and where the lineage's spirits continue to live. The term Guinea is also epitomized by the involved concept known as "inheritance" (*eritaj*), which stands at once for lineal kin's inalienable, inherited land, their peasant ancestors, and their spiritual legacy (Lowenthal 1987).

Magic is Guinea's Other, its ground figure. Magic is associated with wage labor, the outside, unbridled individualism, and, therefore, sorcery. The "work" of

Magic is believed to be executed by a kind of spirit known as pwen. They are called pwen because their Magical powers "capture the (bad) essence" of money and wage labor, animating monetary gain with unnatural, life-giving powers. Pwen are manufactured and sold by sorcerers. One has to travel far away to buy them. They help their masters make money fast, but they inevitably turn on the latter. It is assumed that anyone greedy enough to buy the illicit labor power would be hard pressed to pay the wage slave its due. The disgruntled, or "hungry," pwen consumes its master's most precious "products": children.

In a brilliant article, "The Meaning of Africa in Haitian Vodu," which is based on ethnographic research conducted only a few kilometers from Caterpillar's home in Léogane, Serge Larose (1975a) demonstrated how these illicit powers become the lever in the Guinea-Magic dialectic. Born out of Magic, pwen eventually become incorporated into Guinea as a class of (inferior but nonetheless authentic Guinea) spirit known as *zandò*. The key to Guinea's appropriation of the pwen's vitality is its concealment of the ritual process whereby it transforms these "bad" powers into a class of Guinea spirits.

The narrative in the song Little Caterpillar improvised on the cassette-letter decries the hypocrisy of Guinea's appropriation of pwen. Guinea depends upon its other to give life to itself. Guinea has authority but no power, no pwen of its own. So it must "gather up" the vitality of Magic. Although Guinea repudiates "seeking" (*pwen*), it depends upon absorbing Magic's life-giving contagion. To maintain its facade of authority, Guinea conceals this dependency. A priest-shaman named Pepe, who is a cousin of Caterpillar's, compared this exploitative relationship to a ship. Guinea stands, masterful, at the bow of the ship of morality; pwen, hidden at the stern, furnishes the power.

In Se Byen's songs to his brother, Se Byen situated himself on the morally superior side of Guinea while symbolically placing the migrant, Little Caterpillar, on the illicit side of Magic. He castigated the migrant for going outside the moral community, getting consumed by wage labor and consuming the wages for himself. Little Caterpillar's eloquent rebuttal was, and had to be, set against the same panorama of Guinea against Magic. He improvised upon a ritual song text to critique a process that promotes those who stay behind while it "pwenifies"[2] those toiling hard in distant infernos (where they must also brave racist hostility, intensified by Americans' special hatred of natives of Haiti). Exemplars of Guinea nevertheless find the pwen useful and valuable. They want to harness the pwen's vitality, but they pretend not to need it. His lyrics lampooned the arrogant conduct of those who claim Guinean pedigree. At the song's denouement, the high-handed "Guineans" are shamed into reclaiming and respecting their migrant as one of their own.

The Pwen in Comparative Perspective

Guinea and Magic are the empowering representations of a powerless, "peasant" community. Guinea and Magic are a way of making sense out of and exerting symbolic control over their history. Their African and Creole ancestors freed themselves in violent revolution against the plantation order of colonial Saint Domingue. The swift establishment of a freeholding peasantry undermined efforts by early independence leaders to force them back onto the plantations as wage laborers. But the cosmopolitan elite, supported by the state and European patrons, moved to repossess the peasants' land. Their encroachment, during the late 19th century, upon the peasants' principal weapon in their struggle to stay free made it easier for the new, 20th-century colonial regime, the United States, to commandeer the peasants' labor power, hastening their return to the plantation as dependent wage laborers. During the first half of the last century, Haitian labor power benefited American agribusiness in Haiti, Cuba, and the Dominican Republic; in the latter part of the century displaced Haitian peasants "freely" alienated themselves for capital in the United States itself. Today the vestigial peasantry survives by raising children for export. Since the land tenure system can no longer reproduce itself, it requires the labor of its migrant proletarians—its pwen—in order to remain peasant.

My analysis covers similar ethnographic and analytical terrain to Michael Taussig's (1980) influential *The Devil and Commodity Fetishism in South America*. The Cauca Valley site in Colombia is structurally akin to Léogane: the population is a "reconstituted peasantry" (Mintz 1974a) descended mainly from African slaves; intensive foreign capital penetration violently encompassed the peasantry early in the 20th century. Large-scale sugar plantations today employ "free" mobile laborers who are of peasant origin; they are nominally Catholic. Taussig asserts that this peasant society symbolizes their incorporation as "neophyte proletarians" through their notion of the *muñeco*. Like pwen, muñecos are means of individualistic gain, associated with faceless, migrant wage labor and repudiated by peasants.

Our analyses diverge, however, over the transformation of these illicit powers. Muñecos, in Taussig's scheme, seem to originate and finish in absolute evil. They apparently enrich nothing but their alienated owners, whom they eventually consume, and seem to occupy a fixed place in a rigid dichotomy between use-value and exchange-value, peasants and proletarians, good and evil. I argue that pwen are vilified because of Guinea's need to incorporate them. The laundering of their fast money to vitalize Guinea is the motivating essence of the Guinea-Magic dialectic.

The use of tainted wages, the quintessence of alienation, to energize a system that eschews wage labor seems paradoxical, but it is far from unique. C. A. Gregory's (1980:648) insight in *Gifts and Commodities* that money can "change form and function as an instrument of gift exchange" has been substantiated across a range of colonized societies. These societies have invented ways of ritually purifying tainted money. When migrant workers returned from the coast to Papua New Guinea, they and their products were made to go through a special rite of passage that involved a three-month seclusion in the men's house and culminated with a distribution of the "gifts" they had brought back (Gregory 1980:185). Feeding stands out as a widespread symbolic process of converting money into moral value. Fijians "drink cash"; a Malaysian community "cooks money" (Toren 1989; Carsten 1989). As we will see forthwith, feeding dominates the ritual process of transforming a pwen into a Guinea spirit.

Money and the Morality of Exchange provides a fruitful comparative model for analyzing the transformation of migrants' contaminated labor power into moral, peasant value. In the introduction, Parry and Bloch (1989:25) describe consistent ethnographic evidence of two "organically essential transactional orders." One is a cycle of long-term reproduction; the other is a short-term exchange cycle. The long-term cycle is associated with morality, substance, the social unit, and the inside (1989:25–26). Guinea epitomizes the long-term cycle. The short-term sphere is typified by individual ambition, competition, impersonal contracts and, above all, wages. Magic embodies the short-term (1989:24). Incorporated societies seem obsessed with the problematic articulation of the two cycles. They endeavor to separate the two domains, to keep Magic from contaminating Guinea's authority. Yet they also have to link the domains because, as Parry and Bloch (1989:26) assert, "the long term is sustained by the vitality of the short-term cycle." Because Guinea, the long-term cycle, is all authority and no power, it needs to be vitalized by the contagion of the transient sector. The ability of Magic to animate effete, authentic Guinea is the pwen of the Guinea-Magic dialectic.

Parry and Bloch's comparative discussion applies furthermore to Guinea's anxiety about agents who might exploit their exploitation for their own ends, using the short-term to subvert rather than to vitalize the long-term:

There is always the opposite possibility—and this evokes the strongest censure . . . that individual involvement in the short-term cycle will become an end in itself which is no longer subordinated to the reproduction of the larger cycle; or, more horrifying still, that grasping individuals will divert the resources of the long-term cycle for their own short-term transactions (Parry and Bloch 1989:26).

Guinea's high-handed discipline of pwen issues from this anxiety. An ideological justification for this discipline is the belief that undisciplined pwen (who are not controlled through ritual feeding) become so ravenous they "eat up" Guinea's people.

Is It Voodoo?

It is unfortunately necessary to clarify that this study is not about "Voodoo," even though Voodoo is implicated in the cruel fates of people from Ti Rivyè. "Voodoo" is the quintessential hegemonic construction, representing the dominated as exotic and other. Every Haitian immigrant has painfully confronted this stereotype. The trajectory of Voodoo in hegemonic discourse parallels Haitian resistance to colonial and neocolonial domination. In 1804, the captive African laborers producing for France's most lucrative sugar colony disrupted the world economic order by simultaneously winning independence and eliminating slavery. Dutifully respecting the metropolitan call to censure the dark ulcer in the middle of the colonial Caribbean, popular, scholarly, and political discourses isolated Haiti from its regional, historical and political-economic contexts.

A prolific, self-fertilizing literature about dark, hyper-sexed, primitive "Voodooland" was published during the early 20th century as the United States was consolidating its victories over metropolitan competitors in the Caribbean. During this period, the United States imposed upon Haiti the longest military occupation in the region; Haitian peasants resisting forced, corvée labor for American development projects along with the seizure of their lands for American businesses were the targets of the U.S. military's first experiment with coordinated ground and air attacks. Twentieth-century writers used "Haitian exceptionalism [as] a shield that masks the negative contribution of the Western powers to . . . the longest neocolonial experiment in the history of the West" (Trouillot 1990a:7).

The deeply ambivalent myth of "black" Haiti's exceptionalism has oscillated from romantic enchantment to sinister revulsion, all the while masking the hands of the colonizers in their blundering experiment. As one might expect of any colonial stereotype, Voodoo-ridden Haiti was like, yet different, completely knowable, but mysterious, desired, but feared (Bhabha 1994:76–77). America's romance with the colorful customs of the picturesque nation peaked during the 1950s, when Haiti was a swanky, exotic getaway for jet-setting American and European tourists (Plummer 1990). Among the "little band of Haiti addicts" was the renowned writer Herbert Gold, author of *Best Nightmare on Earth: A Life in Haiti* (1991). His profoundly ambivalent memoir opened to a two-page map of the possessed country called "Herbert Gold's Haiti." He mused that "One comes to Haiti to let anything at all happen" and "Haiti is like everyplace else, except it's Haiti" (Gold 1991:227, 223).

Other writers discovered in the clandestine religion the energizing force of the rebellion against the ruthlessly "civilizing" Occupation. Richard Loederer (1935), for example, published *Voodoo Fire in Haiti* one year after the marines had officially departed. He cited military records in Washington documenting Haitians' practices of slaughtering U.S. marines "for the sake of the ritual cooking-pot," not to mention the Haitians' "demoniacal dances, male drinking orgies and sexual frenzies" (Loederer 1935:17). Speculation about the unholy wedding of Voodoo, human sacrifice and politics continues to captivate contemporary Americans' imaginations of exotic Haiti. For example, Wade Davis's (1985) best-selling book, *The Serpent and the Rainbow*, touted the definitive explanation for the maniacal dictatorship's grip on the nation: its subservience to secret, zombie-producing, paramilitary cults. Wes Craven's (1988) film based on the book, released in the wake of the popular Indiana Jones series, was promoted as the dramatic tale of a dashing anthropologist's true-life adventures in mysterious Haiti.[3]

This study accepts neither the premise of Haitians' exoticism nor their need for taming by a more powerful political entity. It is an ethnography of a ritual praxis that articulates and mediates the experiences of a far-flung society that has become a producer and supporter of migrant labor. The dialectic of Guinea and Magic is a peasantry's representation—and critique—of the encompassment of their moral economy by a system of capitalist production and their incorporation as producers of migrants for export. Their experience and resistance have antecedents in 18th-century Europe (Weber [1905] 1958; Thompson 1967) and numerous parallels in the "developing" world (Mintz 1960; Comaroff 1985; Taussig 1993). In the moral discourse of Caterpillar's community, pejorative cultural constructions of alienated wage labor reinforce the broader structuring of Haitian labor as a low-wage, migrant work force. Their ritual practices reformulate a displaced system of traditional peasant morality, carved out of the very disruptive, monetized processes it tries to conceal.

In Creole, the term Vodou (Vodoun) refers to a genre of ritual music and dance, performed in worship of an important category of Guinea spirits. A legacy of the African cultural past, the term is the Fongbe (Benin) word for spirit. Over time, outsiders applied the term to refer to the religion as a whole, a usage widely accepted, though foreign to many in the countryside. People from Ti Rivyè do not say, "I practice Vodou" or "I believe in Vodou." Rather they speak of being Catholic and "serving their spirits" (*sèvi lwa*). Spirits are called *lwa* (pronounced like French *loi*). Lwa can be thought of as super (in the sense of all-too-human) human beings who are inherited through family lines among land-holding descent groups. Said to be from Ginen (Africa) and to dwell there still, they crystallize a deep historical memory of the violence and displacement of the African ancestors' past. Their iconography and naming blends African and European influences; some are based on Catholic saints, and many have African names. Indeed the term "saint" is used by some rather than the word lwa.

A Haitian man explained to Alfred Métraux ([1959] 1972:323), author of the classic text *Le Vaudou Haïtien,* many decades ago: "you have to be Catholic to serve your spirits (*lwa*)." Thus, despite official condemnation by the Catholic Church of practices oriented to the lwa, Catholicism is fundamental to serving one's lwa. All worship begins with substantial Catholic prayer, led by a lay priest. Attendance at mass and giving alms to beggars gathered at cathedrals are all requirements of serving one's lwa. Ritual action entails enthusiastic, spectacular, multimedia performance involving Catholic prayer (in French), drumming, singing (in Creole), dancing, visual art, parading, spirit possession-performance, and offerings of food, drink, toiletries, and animal sacrifice.

The symbolism of feeding encompasses all ritual discourse and performance. The very term for worship is "to serve" (*sèvi*), as in to offer food. The personalities of lwa are differentiated by their particular tastes in food and drink. Additionally, a lwa's displeasure is cast as hunger, and a ceremony is called a "feeding of the lwa." A successful "feeding" occurs when the spirit, having been enticed to journey all the way from Ginen, arrives personally to "party" with the family and to accept the lavish and copious offerings. The spirit's enjoyment of the music, dance, and food is an implicit signal that s/he has "let go" of the victim and/or agrees not to "take hold" of others, at least not in the immediate future.

Scholarly and popular representations of the lwa or "saints" have created the inaccurate portrayal of universalistic, nature spirits. In fact, lwa are unique to each lineage (Murray 1984). Yet they are also distinct from ancestors, who are worshipped in their own right and whose primary role, in virtue of their proximity to the other world, is to mediate relations between members of kin groups and their inherited lwa. Neither are the lwa nature gods. They do not wield powers to control air, land, or water. Their power is instead primarily confined to afflicting and protecting members of descent groups to whom they belong. The lwa are the protagonists of a cult of affliction and healing.[4] When lwa feel neglected or ignored by the heirs, as they often do in their remote home in Ginen, they retaliate by sending affliction, "seizing" heirs with somatic illness, misfortune, and property loss. Worship by the kin group is a collective effort to ward off illness by enticing the avenging spirits to "release" their victims and to prevent future attacks. Migrants do not escape the mobile lwa's orbit. Indeed migrants are prime "choices" of avenging spirits and they are primary sponsors of rites taking place back home.

Haitian Catholics' overlapping, simultaneous practice of both Catholic and Afro-Creole devotions has puzzled outsiders, especially in the face of the Church's representation of the two as moral and social opposites, Catholicism as the norm and Vodou as the feared and exotic Other. Catholicism is associated with French culture and language, the local elite, and light skin, in contrast to the satanic superstitions of the poor, dark, nonliterate majority. In reality, any given Catholic actor in Haiti falls within the continuum, some as self-described "straight" Catholics (*Katolik fran*) who may know little or nothing of serving the spirits, and some as "lwa fanatics," with the vast middle going through the rites of passage of the Catholic Church while simultaneously maintaining contact with the lwa and ritual specialists/healers in times of crisis. People's involvement ranges from apathy (ignoring their spirits until a crisis looms) to those who are spectators at others' rituals but neither contribute nor worship (through prayer, song, dance), to "servants" (*sèvitè*) of the lwa. The last are often initiated into the ranks of a congregation headed by a professional *oungan* or *gangan* (priest) or *manbo* (priestess).

The practices of the contemporary Haitian Catholic Church further blur its separation from Vodou. In a concerted effort to hold on to its wayward flock, the Church consciously appropriates the captivating styles of Vodou worship in its masses. Melodies that sound more like sacred songs for the lwa are sung in the pews, while a battery of Vodou drums playing West African–derived rhythms accompanies them. Moreover, this fluid, politicized Catholic-Vodou religious culture has an ambiguous relationship to Haitian Protestantism. At least a quarter of Haitians identify as Protestant today, an effect of the postwar spread of North American evangelism throughout the hemisphere. Despite their short history in Haiti, however, the churches are thoroughly creolized: their liturgies are in Creole, and there is a vast native-born clergy. And despite the assertive, separatist stance of the fundamentalists, Protestant practices are also blended ones. Their renunciatory rhetoric notwithstanding, they do appropriate aspects of "the other." Underneath the modern, ascetic cloak worn by the new converts, spiritual healing, sorcery, and magic remain part of their syncretic practices.

Unlike Haitian "Catholic" communities in greater New York, who have established shrines to serve the lwa (Brown 1991), those in the South Florida counties of Palm Beach, Broward, and St. Lucie have not endeavored to serve or feed their spirits in the host society. Rather, these communities practice long-distance worship, anchored in the sacred landscape of the family land back home. The earlier movement to New York involved many migrants from the city of Port-au-Prince who were already a generation (or more) removed from their "inheritance" and may have already been affiliated with urban temple congregations based on voluntary association rather than descent. Yet as Karen McCarthy Brown (1991) describes, people who serve their spirits in New York are nonetheless occasionally enjoined through spiritual affliction to return home to worship as well.

As for communities stretched between rural Haiti and South Florida, creative uses of cassette tape and, increasingly, video recorders have resulted in a reconfiguration of the boundaries of the ritual performance space, allowing migrants to continue to serve their spirits on the inalienable family land. When migrants cannot personally attend the services, they participate indirectly by listening to cassette tapes of the rituals. On these tapes the migrants hear not only the sounds of the performance itself—drumming, singing, praying, and chatter—but also the voices of narrators describing what the listener cannot see: the flow of possessions, offerings, sacrifices, prayers, conversations, etc. (The anthropologist was by no means the only one tape-recording the ceremonies.) Spirits possessing the bodies of ritual actors are not only aware of the recording devices, they often move to the recorder in order personally to address the absent migrant or migrants.

1.5. Service for *lwa* Captain Balendyo on Ti Rivyè Beach in April 1984. The migrant sponsor's stepfather speaks into a cassette tape recorder, narrating the performance of the spirit, who has mounted the sponsor's mother. The sponsor's maternal grandfather, a *gangan ason* (ritual leader) stands holding the *ason* (sacred rattle and bell) in the foreground.

Mobile lwa intervene in the lives of migrants. They reciprocate migrants who send money home to "feed" them by "guarantying" migrants' capacity to alienate their labor power abroad. The lwa take revenge for migrants' negligence by undermining the same. Thus spiritual affliction beliefs, ritual discourse, and performance symbolize and reinforce migrants' role as emissaries of their families' social, economic, and ritual interests. The social norms of mutuality, generosity, and giving to one's capacity encompass migrants. As the kinsmen with the "biggest wrists" (*ponyèt*), migrants are expected to contribute accordingly not just to their own but to their extended family's ever-increasing obligations, ritual and secular alike. The spirits intervene by "holding" a recalcitrant migrant who can, but will not, take responsibility for his or her increased burden. Migrants are frequently the victims of vengeful spirits, which only an expiatory, healing rite performed on the "inheritance" land, by their home family, regardless of the migrant's absence, can assuage.

While some Ti Rivyè migrants attribute their gradual, if modest, success in their host and home societies to the positive interdependence between their home kin, the lwa, and themselves, others have met disappointment as they struggle to survive in the lowest rungs of a hostile, discriminatory South Florida economy and, meanwhile, stay "healthy." The migrants' frustration is further linked to their perceptions that their families no longer look upon them as people but see them rather as insensate beasts of burden, or as pwen. They slave away in hostile, foreign countries for the sake of people who resent them for ever having left. The migrants' perception of insecurity in their home community, to which they expect to return one day, only intensifies their sense of vulnerability in a racist host society. Meanwhile those at home worry that their migrant kin will assimilate to the host society and abandon them. Yet migrants who remain tethered to the home may also incite the latter's resentment. Se Byen, for example, begrudged his dependence upon his devoted junior brother. Many at home sense that migrants condescend toward the folk who stayed behind.

These latent hostilities are among the untoward social costs of their incorporation as producers of low-wage mobile labor, but they can hardly be acknowledged or assuaged in an open discussion. As a result, they are ideal fodder for commentary, contest, and negotiation through sending pwen. The portable tape recorder has also both perpetuated and transformed the esteemed tradition of throwing pwen derived from the informal sacred liturgy representing the contested relation of Guinea and Magic. The pithy, sententious language of the ritual songs provides ample fodder for adept men-and-women-of-words to improvise pwen promoting or contesting their positions across their long-distance, transnational community.

Literature and Lyrics of Dyaspora

Tensions between long-separated home kin and their migrant emissaries are a prevailing theme in the aesthetic expressions of mobile, migrant-producing Caribbean societies (Gmelch 1992). As far back as the 1940s, Haitian writer Jacques Roumain memorialized these latent conflicts in *Masters of the Dew* (*Gouverneurs de la Rosée*), familiar to many English readers through Langston Hughes and Mercer Cook's ([1974] 1978) translation. The novel is set during the first significant wave of Haitian labor migration in the 20th century, which moved tens of thousands of men to work on American-owned sugarcane plantations in Cuba, only to expel them when the sugar economy plummeted in the 1930s.

Even though characters in the novel demonstrate a profound grasp of the collusion of political and economic power undermining their self-determination, they do not refrain from displacing their resentment onto a scapegoat—the migrant. Two elders decry the "sinful" departures of their kin, who leave in shame in the middle of the night. One remarks after a cousin who musters the courage to say good-bye, "Ah, you ungrateful Negroes! This soil has fed you day after day for years. Now you leave it with a few laments for the sake of appearances, and a little water in your eyes as if to wash off your guilty conscience and remorse. Band of hypocrites!" (Roumain [1947] 1978:113). The other likens peasant women's migration to prostitution. She says, "You might say the soles of their feet have been rubbed with pepper. They can't stand still, the shameless hussies! The land is no longer good enough for them. They'd rather go to work as cooks for some rich mulattoes. As if that was the thing to do! A sin, I say, it's a sin, that's what I say" (Roumain [1947] 1978:143).

Roumain applied a subtle understanding of the Creole aesthetics of sending pwen as suitable means for Haitian families to make meaning out of long-term migration. As *Masters of the Dew* opens, Manuel, the doomed protagonist, returns from Cuba to his home village after a 15-year absence. An early omen of his fate appears in the coded language and drama of ritual performance. Manuel's grateful family has sponsored a "feeding" of the lwa to thank them for his safe return. The joyous mood shifts when a spirit unexpectedly "mounts the head" of one participant. The spirit intones a sacred song—a pwen—which Manuel's mother interprets as a foreboding message about her son. Moreover the spirit, an authoritarian "type" known as Ogoun, singles out the self-assured Manuel. Ogoun publicly confronts Manuel in order, no doubt, to objectify local ambivalence toward migrants. Speaking in a conversational style that would be rudely inappropriate in other contexts, Ogoun bears down on Manuel, compelling him to respond to interrogation. Manuel inevitably fails the test. Ogoun judges his answers arrogant and then proceeds to extort the requisite deference from the migrant.

Ambivalence toward migrants is familiar in the fiction, essays, and short stories of Edwidge Danticat, perhaps the leading Haitian-American writer today. She confronts the predicament of long-distance Haitian nationals like herself who feel guilty for having abandoned their home nation and yearn for its acceptance. In her introduction to the edited volume *The Butterfly's Way: Voices from the Haitian Dyaspora* (2001), Danticat recounts her discomfort with being called Dyaspora, in particular the use of the term by friends or family living in Haiti to silence her opposing point of view. "What do you know? You're a Dyaspora," they would say. She describes being caught off-guard by strangers who, wanting to catch her attention, call out, "Dyaspora!" as though it were "a title like Miss, Ms., Mademoiselle, or Madame" (Danticat 2001:xiv).

Wyclef Jean, the popular Haitian-American hip-hop artist, left Haiti when he was nine years old. Like his contemporary, Danticat, his aesthetic work deals with the experience of migration and exile. In a song titled "Yele" (on his first solo recording, *The Carnival* [1997]) he defends his authentic Haitian credentials, reminding his audience that he is Haitian, not a Brooklyn-born American. The cut "Jaspora" (Diaspora) lampoons the social exclusion of Haitian migrants but satirizes even more the migration of class prejudice from Haiti to Haitian settlements in New York, where neighborhoods and boroughs signify Haitian transnational class status, Brooklyn being the lowest. Jean's stinging lyrics echo those of the legendary singer Ti Manno, whom Glick-Schiller and Fouron (1990) identify as the first popular Haitian musical artist to articulate a transnationalist consciousness.

The word *dyaspora* or *jaspora* entered everyday Creole speech during the late 1980s, marking and mirroring an important shift in Haitians' political and social consciousness. Until that moment, French-speaking members of the Haitian elite living in New York and elsewhere were using the term as part of "a narrative of exile that was tied to the politics of return" (Basch et al. 1994:208). The working-class Haitian immigrants in New York interviewed by Nina Glick-Schiller in 1985 were unfamiliar with the word. Neither were the Ti Rivyè migrants I interviewed during the same period using the word. By 1990, dyaspora had entered ordinary Creole speech, but its meaning had changed. Dyaspora now signified Haitians outside who continued to be involved in the affairs of the home, an involvement which no longer required permanent return. Nina Glick-Schiller and Georges Fouron (2001:23) argue that unlike other diaspora populations, these dyaspora were identifying as long-distance nationals, making a claim to a reconstructed Haitian nation-state, a claim that was not dependent upon their location within the boundaries of that nation-state. Ambivalence about these dyaspora or simply, *dyas* (as in "She's a dyas") is nonetheless reproduced in pejorative uses of the term, as recounted by Edwidge Danticat and Wyclef Jean.

The Tenth Province

The transformation of the meaning of dyaspora occurred in the wake of the fall, in 1986, of the twenty-five-year dictatorship of François Duvalier and his son, Jean-Claude Duvalier. Although the series of United States–backed juntas that succeeded the Duvalier regime rivaled its brutality, they could not restrain a grassroots groundswell for change that engaged Haitians at home and abroad. Their mobilization swept into office, if not into lasting power, the outspoken liberation priest, Jean-Bertrand Aristide. (Father Aristide's sermons criticizing alliances between the United States, transnational corporations, and the Haitian dictatorship won him the enmity of all three. His government was violently overthrown in 1991 by the Haitian military, with covert American support, after only seven months in office. He was elected to office again in 2000 but in March 2004 was again forced into exile by American soldiers.)

When Father Aristide became a last-minute presidential candidate in the 1990 elections, he brought his campaign to New York, Miami, Montréal, and elsewhere. He addressed the migrants as a dyaspora, contributing to the growing ubiquity of the term. Having faced suspicion, rejection, and sporadic persecution by the Duvalier dictatorship and the fascist juntas that succeeded it, the migrants suddenly encountered respect and welcome in his eloquent, stirring Creole campaign discourse (Richman 1990a, 1992a). And while the major candidates turned a blind eye to the plight of migrants, even when campaigning among them abroad, Father Aristide alone addressed their specific concerns. The former priest applied his masterful command of Creole oratory, including throwing pwen to crystallize the tensions between home and migrant kin and to admonish those at home about their ambivalent treatment of their migrant emissaries.

One of Aristide's first acts as president was the declaration of a nation-state without borders (Richman 1992a). Haiti now included, in addition to its nine internal provinces, an external Dizyèm Depatman (Tenth Province), divided like the internal ones, into *arrondissements* (districts) and communes, with cabinet-level representation by the "Minister of the Diaspora." The demarcations of the scattered arrondissements corresponded to major outposts of Haitian emigrant settlement while ignoring established geopolitical taxonomies, hence the arrondissements of Guadeloupe, Miami, New York, and Canada. This transnational or "deterritorialized" nation-state affirmed that many of its citizens must live outside the country, but it maneuvered to anchor them to the homeland and benefit thereby from return visits, remittances, and investments.

Like other migrant-sending home nation-states, the new Haitian state has maneuvered to encompass the transnationalism of its dispersed population though its successes have been more rhetorical than substantial. The government of Mexico, the largest contributor to U.S. migration at the time, was similarly intensifying its efforts to harness some of the massive streams of migrants' remittances, to redirect them toward the home state (DeSipio 2000; Orozco 2000). While Aristide was inaugurating the Dizyèm Depatman, Mexico was establishing its Communities Abroad Program to reach out to Mexicans in the United States by sponsoring hometown associations in migrant communities. The United States Agency for International Development (USAID), despite being openly hostile to Aristide, appropriated his Tenth Department politics after his departure. USAID (2004) revealed a new plan formally to involve the diaspora in development, a shift from their previous top-down strategies. The name of the plan was "Leveraging Migrants' Remittances."

Approaches to Transnational Social Processes

Social scientists eventually caught up to the growing transnational consciousness of some contemporary societies and the transnational ambitions of their home nation-states. Having become increasingly aware of the migrations of capital, labor, religious movements, political processes, and the nation-state itself, scholars discovered the inadequacy of disciplinary concepts that assumed an isomorphic relationship among a bounded sociospatial entity, a core population, and an integrated set of ideas, values, and behaviors (Appadurai 1990, 1991; Kearney and Nagengast 1989; Kearney 1991, 1995; Rouse 1991). Scholars studying new immigrant groups from Latin America found that models of ethnic assimilation did not fully explain the adaptations they were observing. Unlike earlier immigrant groups to the United States, who eventually severed their familial and cultural ties to the home and assimilated into mainstream American society, the new migrants seemed to be actively expanding and strengthening their linkages to the homeland (Georges 1990; Grasmuck and Pessar 1991; Smith and Guarnizo 1998; Levitt 2001).

The new focus on the transnational linkages of mobile Caribbean societies was marked by publication of the 1987 volume *Caribbean Life in New York City: Sociocultural Dimensions*, edited by Constance Sutton and Elsa Chaney. The contributors described constant flows of people, money, ideas, and commodities linking New York and the island communities. Constance Sutton (1987:20) defined this phenomenon as "a transnational socio-cultural system, a distinctly unitary though not unified transmission belt that reworks and further creolizes Caribbean culture and identities both in New York and the Caribbean." Linda Basch and Nina Glick-Schiller, contributors to the volume, went on further to refine the concept in light of new theories of the relationships between nation-states, nationalism, and global capital reproduction (Glick-Schiller et al. 1992; Basch et al. 1994). In their formulation, "transnational" meant acting in a social field that extends across national boundaries and implicates migrants in nation-building processes (which they mutually exploit). Nina Glick-Schiller and Georges Fouron's (2001) recent work, *Georges Woke Up Laughing: Long Distance Nationalism and the Search for Home,* interprets Georges' experience as a "cross-border citizen" living between the United States and Haiti, between his incorporation as a professor of education in New York, and his involvement as a long-distance national anchored in his home town of Aux Cayes.

Plan of Book

While my work engages literatures on migration, transnationalism, and global capitalism, at the same time it draws from anthropological perspectives on religion and society and from folklore, ethnomusicological, and sociolinguistic studies of form and communicative aesthetics. Calling upon these widely divergent fields is essential to my approach to understanding how religion, ritual, and performance mediate the historical consciousness and contemporary experience of the mobile, long-distance Ti Rivyè community. The bilateral ethnographic research I undertook in Ti Rivyè and in satellite locations in South Florida, which is described below, grew out of my advocacy for Haitians working on agribusiness farms in the United States. As a result, political and economic policies affecting Haitians and Haitian migrants stay within close sight in these pages, even in descriptions of fine cosmological distinctions or the subtleties of communicative aesthetics.

This book and compact disc present astoundingly creative uses of cassette tapes by Se Byen and his family to mediate relations between the diaspora and home members and to extend the boundaries of rhetorical and ritual spaces. I begin with Little Caterpillar's improvisation of the strikingly poignant song "They Will Remember Me in the House." I pose a simple question. How can this ritual song apprehend the relationship between people who leave and people who stay behind, between the seekers of migrant labor and the recipients of wage remittances? Ensuing chapters explore the question from broader perspectives of society, history, economy, cosmology, aesthetics, and ritual, laying the grounds for recapturing an extraordinary, long-distance rhetorical contest, which was conducted by means of cassette tape.

The next chapter begins with an analysis of the role of labor migration in a global system of capital reproduction. My approach to transnational migration weaves together theories of political economy with local Haitian theories of production, in which feeding is a dominant metaphor. I then explain how the Haitian nation has been transformed from agrarian peasants into producers of unskilled labor for export and consumers of imported food. This broad picture of the movements of Haitian workers within the country, region, and hemisphere then narrows in focus to the sudden and sweeping exodus from Ti Rivyè to Florida around 1980. The tenuous immigration status imposed on the "Haitian boat people" during the 1980s both signified and validated their mistreatment in South Florida. Despite their long separation from their families and their restriction to abusive, low-paying farm work, the migrants continued to send money home.

Chapter 3 deals with how they have remained anchored in Ti Rivyè, where three out of every four households had at least one member living abroad. The consciousness of long-distance community is pervasive. Children internalize early on the inevitability of their own migration to "give a livelihood to their families." The feeling of waiting is overwhelming in Ti Rivyè. They wait for remittances and/or wait to leave in order to live vicariously back home.

In Chapter 4, I examine the salient political-economic trends shaping Ti Rivyè and the Léogane Plain during the early part of this century. I am particularly interested in how the intensified mercantilist exploitation of sugar and coffee at the turn of the century paved the way for "recolonization" of the Plain (and the nation generally) during the second decade. Agrocapitalist penetration disrupted the local economy just enough to incorporate the peasants as producers of low-wage mobile laborers while allowing them to remain peasants. The alienation of the poorer peasants' labor power was concealed in order for the community to retain its traditional peasant character. All parties had interests in perpetuating this facade: transnational corporations, the local elite, peasants, and migrants.

Chapter 5 traces processes of ritual and kinship change in Ti Rivyè in response to the broader demographic and socioeconomic transformations during the early 20th century. The watershed of ritual change introduced new professional ritual leadership, rites of passage for women and spiritual affliction etiologies. I argue that the discourse of "Guinean authenticity" served to legitimize these changes and to ease their integration into the spiritual charters of the descent groups. At the same time that Guinea was being reconstructed, so was its "other."

The 6th chapter explores symbolic constructions of the African Guinea and Magic dialectic and argues that the key to its resolution is in the ritual process known as "picking up" (*ranmase*). The discussion focuses on the most prominent domain for recreating the Guinea-Magic dialectic: ritual food offerings. A careful analysis of the form and contents of ritual food products suggests a consciousness of complex linkages between proletarianization, peasant production, the merchant elite and transnational capital.

The symbolism of feeding is also the point of departure for chapter 7. I explore the construction of ritual reciprocity as an exchange of nurture for "protection." The spirits protect (or "guaranty") the heirs' ability to produce in return for diligent feeding and care. Ensuring the smooth flow of this reciprocity is ever more critical given the exodus of agents of productivity to distant lands. In addition to the threat of losing spiritual protection, migrants face human retribution in the form of sorcery. Migrants' deaths can be blamed on accessible neighbors rather than the remote economic system that uses poor Haitians as its pwen. Through dual narratives of spiritual affliction and sorcery, they reconfigure their natural persecution into symbolic realms they can control.

Chapter 8 explores how the dialectic of Guinea and Magic encompasses relationships between those who stay at home and those who leave to seek a livelihood for them outside. Ritual songs, which capture the Guinea-Magic tension, are used as pwen to capture, contest, and/or advance the "pwenification" of migrants and the "Guinification" of those who stay behind. I return to the two songs introduced above to provide a deeper analysis and present two others that circulated on tapes between Ti Rivyè and "Miami." (The compact disc features these songs in tracks 1–4.)

The migrant finally rebelled against his role as pwen for kin and spirits. Chapter 9 describes Little Caterpillar's strategic use of religious conversion in a bid to reformulate the terms of his relationships to his home kin and spirits. The trenchant cassette letter he sent me in defense of his conversion is included in the text and is on track 5 of the compact disc. The migrant's mutiny brought fleeting relief before he became sick. He was writing to me as he was dying (CD, track 6). He left a searing rebuke of the vast, sorcerous system that turns Haitian peasants into migrants and against one another. The epilogue was written after Caterpillar's agonizing death and my return to Ti Rivyè. I reunited with his home family to come to terms with their migrant's life and death.

The Multisited Research

The research for this project straddles Haiti and the United States. It spans two decades of intimate interaction with immigrants from Ti Rivyè, Léogane, living in South Florida and Virginia, as well as the year and a half I spent residing with their home kin in Ti Rivyè. My acquaintance with Haiti and Haitian ritual, however, reaches back to 1977, when, after learning to speak Creole, I conducted summer research on ritual performance among temple cults of Port-au-Prince. The field-work was supported by Wesleyan University and provided the basis for my senior honors' thesis, jointly submitted to Wesleyan's Departments of Music and Anthropology.

My relationships with Little Caterpillar and other Ti Rivyè immigrants began in squalid labor camps on the Eastern Shore of Virginia in 1981. They were launching their subordinate careers in the migratory agricultural labor stream; I had taken a summer internship, between semesters of graduate school, as a Farmworker Legal Services advocate and interpreter. The other members of my team were law students; my credentials were that I could speak the native language of the new population of migrant farmworkers. My concern and nominal competence in Creole seemingly fostered my role as a one-person, all-purpose social and legal service in the camps.

I subsequently remained involved with advocacy on behalf of Haitian immigrants and farmworkers. My work has ranged from evaluating the case of a Haitian healer of Fort Pierce charged with homicide, a U.S. House investigation and a class-action suit over discrimination against Haitian workers in the Florida sugarcane industry, and testimony in court regarding Haitians' experience with the host legal system. For a wide network of Haitian migrants, my access to the legal and welfare systems remains the practical basis of our reciprocity, as my husband patiently reminded us when he answered our phone with, "Karen Richman's social service." His patient support for the confusion of my advocacy and personal

1.6. Mercina D'Haïti, Little Caterpillar, and Karen Richman, at Farmex labor camp in Tasley, Virginia, July 1985.

1.7. Mercina and Pierre D'Haïti at Farmex farm in Tasley, Virginia, July 1985.

1.8. Laricie St. Fleur, Mercina and Pierre's mother, listens to a letter from her children, Beausant, 1983. Eve Dioguy, Little Caterpillar's sister, listens.

1.9. Laricie St. Fleur with Karen Richman, Beausant, 1983.

life was most palpable, though, when he agreed to my idea to rescue Pierre D'Haïti from a Virginia labor camp and become his foster parents. A native of Ti Rivyè, Pierre was one of the few teenagers at the camp, and he had impressed me with his dignified manner and ambition to read and write English. Over the years, several members of his extended family had come to reside in the town as well.

In the mid-1980s, I conducted continuous fieldwork in Ti Rivyè, sponsored by doctoral research grants from the Inter-American Foundation and the Organization of American States. My dissertation research involved qualitative, quantitative, and archival inquiry (Richman 1992b). I participated in the religious activities of local residents, from services at the town church, to rituals for the ancestors and spirits of local descent groups on their inherited lands, to a pilgrimage festival in the north of Haiti (which some Ti Rivyè residents attend every year). My open-ended interviews were conducted across classes, from the village "little people" (*ti malere*) to town and city-dwelling "big whigs" (*gwo zotobre*)—landlords, politicians, and administrators of the centralized sugar factories. I especially sought out the oldest members of these various sectors in order to reconstruct the important socioeconomic and ritual trends and events of this century.

In contrast to this qualitative work in Ti Rivyè, my multiphased, quantitative research was exclusively focused on the coastal village. With the help of Yves and Yvette Watermann and Kanès Pierre, I conducted a comprehensive census and genealogy of each of the 124 households, which also elicited basic migration, economic, and ritual data. We later conducted more focused, longer interviews on migration and return-migration with selected households. We also conducted a comprehensive land tenure study of all plots in a segment of Ti Rivyè, following the research example of Gerald Murray (1977). (We compared our results with the new sugar factory's cadastral survey of the entire plain.) My archival research in Haiti was aimed at documenting the processes mentioned and implied in the oral histories I collected. Perhaps my most precious finds were local court and tax records dating from 1875, which were disintegrating in a closet in the town Bureau of Contributions. Access to reports written during the second decade on behalf of prospective investors of the Haytian American Sugar Company also proved invaluable (Richman 1992b).

In the mid-1990s I returned to South Florida to collaborate on a comparative research project investigating inter-ethnic relations, immigrant incorporation, and transnationalism headed by David Griffith, with funding from the National Science and Howard Heinz Foundations. Between 2000 and 2002, I researched religious conversion among migrants from Ti Rivyè (and other parts of Haiti) in Palm Beach and Broward Counties. This project was supported by the Social Science Research Council, Notre Dame University's Graduate School, and the Newberry Library. In 2003, I returned to Ti Rivyè with support from Notre Dame's Institute for Scholarship in the Liberal Arts. I traveled with my now grown-up foster son, Pierre D'Haïti, who sailed from Ti Rivyè to Miami in 1980 with his father and siblings. These phases of research have yielded a rich body of detailed, personal, longitudinal data on this single transnational community, from the lives and histories of particular kin units in Ti Rivyè to their migrants' incorporation in the United States, including their patterns of settlement, household formation, work experiences, transnational and local kinship relations, political involvement, inter-ethnic relations, and their religious experience, affiliations and practices.

2

Migrants, Remittances, and Development

Members of the unemployed and partly employed classes, representing various shades from vagabondage to ostensible peasantry, and constituting at the moment the excess population of the country, could be taken care of, at least temporarily and partially, by emigration, by wage employment in Haiti, or by settlement on the land and its more intensive cultivation.

—Arthur C. Millspaugh, Financial Adviser-General Receiver of Haiti, 1927–1929

St. Domingue, the colonial name of Haiti, was France's most lucrative sugar colony. In 1804, the slaves stunned the world economic order by liberating themselves and the colony. During the century following independence, the descendants of slaves "reconstituted" themselves as a freeholding peasantry (Mintz 1974a). By entrenching themselves as small, independent farmers, they were able to resist pressures from the elite and the state to coerce them into plantation labor. It took the economic and military might of a 20th-century colonial power to coerce the Haitian peasants into capitalist agriculture. This chapter will trace how, over the course of the 20th century, the Haitian peasant economy was transformed into one that produces unskilled, wage labor for export and increasingly consumes wage remittances and imported food. Haitian migrant laborers have thus followed and abetted the expansions and declines of North American capital by migrating to Cuba, other parts of Haiti, the Dominican Republic (the eastern side of the island), the Caribbean, and, finally, the United States and Canada.

Labor Migration and the Production of People for Export

In 1980, when Little Caterpillar risked the voyage to the United States, he left behind a household of impoverished peasants. There is a structural linkage among his wage labor in sugarcane fields and cucumber plantations owned by international agribusiness firms, his elder brother planting sugarcane and sweet potatoes on a lilliputian plot he could nevertheless call his own, and his wife trading minuscule single products one would not dream of buying in such particulars here—individual cloves of garlic, single cubes of dried Magui bouillon, one scallion. Their personal struggles to maintain one another across international boundaries contribute to, and are shaped by, the expansion of capital in a "world-system."

Since Wallerstein's (1974, 1980, 1989) comprehensive analysis of the modern "world-system," few would venture to assert that labor migration is merely a relationship within or between individual countries. Movements like Little Caterpillar's migration out of a wretched-poor peasant society must be seen as part of a spatial division of labor taking place on a global scale. Alejandro Portes and John Walton (1981:67), applying Wallerstein's approach to the study of labor migration, have phrased the problem as a "system of capital accumulation on a world scale dependent upon the perpetuation of patterned differences in the conditions of reproduction of the labor force across different political and geographic units."

Wallerstein's (1974:349–351) analytic categories are useful as tools to understand the patterning of these differences in the expansion of the modern world-system. Core nation-states are characterized by strong state machinery and national culture; they produce finished commodities. Peripheral areas (as opposed to states, because they are dependent upon colonial or neocolonial powers) have fascist, authoritarian regimes and coerce labor to produce raw commodities for export. Colonial Haiti produced such basic raw products as sugar and coffee. Neocolonial Haiti today produces raw, or unskilled, peasant labor for export.

A peasantry can be defined as "rural landholders who produce both subsistence and commodities for sale, who are part of a larger social system, and upon whom others of greater power exercise an exaction of productivity in one or another form, which Wolf (1966) subsumes under *rent*" (Mintz 1973:93). Peasant economies are not homogeneous and their internal differentiation permits their linkages to the world-system (Mintz 1973:95). They appear uniform because constituents of transnational capital, merchant elites, and peasantries have vested interests in concealing their internal variation (Mintz 1974b:305).

Heterogeneous peasant communities like Haiti's play a dual role in the contemporary world-system. The forces aligned with capital, including coercive peripheral regimes, destabilize and devalue peasant labor enough to encourage migration into low wage labor (which can be located either inside the territory or in another nation). At the same time, these combined forces leave the peasant economy just viable enough both to pay rent to local elites, and to make up the difference between what capital pays these mobile workers and what they and their dependents need to survive. They make up the difference when they raise, feed, and nurture prospective migrants, when they subsidize the cost of migrants' recruitment, and when they provide care for workers who are sick, injured, or retired. They play the part of both "a nursery and a nursing home" for migrants earning wages abroad (Rouse 1992:28).

As both a nursery and a nursing home for migrants working in wage-labor jobs abroad, "donor" communities subsidize the cost of labor to capital while losing the benefit of that labor at home. Yet the magnitude of this transfer from poor to rich nations remains invisible to most scholars and policy experts. A notable exception is Kindleberger, whose candid assessment is that "if the emigrants were slaves, and raised for the purpose, it would be appropriate to calculate whether it was worthwhile for a poor country to raise slaves for export. . . . The answer would doubtless be 'no'"(Kindleberger 1967, cited in Castles and Kusack 1985:408). Migration represents a net loss for donor societies. As a result, despite the seeming enormity of the monies migrants send home, they do not fully compensate home families for the investments in their upbringing. Their so-called "remittance societies" remain as stubbornly poor as ever.

Few observers of Caribbean and Central American migration have failed to notice the enormous homeward flow of low-wage migrants' wages. More than one development expert in Haiti has told me that remittances, which reached an estimated $800 million in 2004, account for more foreign aid to the country than bilateral lending (USAID 2004). Remittance transmission to Mexico, the largest producer of migrants for export to the United States, grew by more than 20% annually during the 1990s, reaching $9.2 billion in 2001 (Orozco 2000, 2002).[1] If such massive sums enter the rural economy, then why, policy and development experts ask, do these areas remain so desperately poor and undeveloped? Ignoring the contribution of migrants' surplus labor to the accumulation of capital in the core, experts inevitably attribute blame on these peoples' irrational economic motives, especially their fondness for conspicuous consumption of imported commodities rather than capital-generating investments. According to the prevailing view, migrants' and their home relatives' short-sighted waste of vast remittances account for the chronic dependent development and underdevelopment.

Remittances are further vilified, according to this same logic, for "creating envy and eroding work habits" (Keely and Tran 1989:502).

Missing from such scornful appraisals is the recognition that the peripheral location of mobile labor production conditions how migrants spend their wages. Wayne Cornelius (1990), reviewing a decade of studies of Mexican-U.S. migration, including his own significant contributions, concludes that remittances overwhelmingly go toward "family maintenance": "food, clothing, rent, medicines and other everyday needs" (Cornelius 1990:14). The second most frequently cited use of remittances is house construction or improvement, which is another symbolic aspect of producing labor. Ti Rivyè migrants and their families unequivocally view migration as an investment strategy, or a means of "making economy" (fè ekonomi), and, as we will see in more detail in the next chapter, they use remittances when they can to buy land and livestock and to start small businesses run by their relatives. Nonetheless home recipients "eat up" migrants' remittances because of the necessity to make up for the longer-term investments mobile societies make in the production of people for export.

While some economists and migration policy makers may not be fully aware of the feeding costs borne by kin at home, migrants are. When, as a legal advocate, I first worked among Haitian farmworkers, I was struck by how seriously people regarded the obligation to repay these debts. Every child feels duty-bound to one day compensate those who raised her or him and every adult migrant is obligated to "give a livelihood to one's family back home."

Feeding symbolizes these social obligations. Feeding is the epitomizing social process, the essential means to creating, or realizing, relationships. (Because of its salience in constituting relationship, feeding is also the dominant symbol of worship.) Feeding is the encompassing metaphor for worship and for the relationship between persons and lwa. The underlying logic is that feeding symbolizes the production of persons generally, meaning the *making* of persons, from giving birth to supervising to nurturing, as well as to the making of things. Haitian peasants symbolically construct and construe the social production process as feeding. Personal relations and social rank are subtly articulated through exchanging food. Adults are expected to compensate those who "fed" them when they were children. Obligations to the dead are explicitly construed as feeding debts, as are responsibilities to the lwa, spiritual counterparts of human members of the descent group. Serving food is a means of containment or control; a lwa's appetite is a measure of its mood. The inherited land represents, above all, a sacred, inalienable feeding site anchoring members seeking livelihoods in distant lands. In exchange for the food gifts, the spirits, who are quintessential consumers, "protect" the labor power of people abroad.

The morality of feeding is especially evident in attitudes toward infancy. A father's nourishment of the very young child receives higher marks than contributions to his or her conception or the teaching of values and the provision of other material support.[2] Alvarez and Murray (1981:19) further describe how a complex of practices affording the increased nutritional and care requirements of the lactating mother reinforce the highly valued role of lactation in child feeding. They note, for example, that fortifying food is the appropriate "baby-gift" to the post-partum mother. Moreover, childbirth is the only secular occasion for the slaughter of goats (in contrast to purchasing pieces of meat from retailers) for domestic consumption. Customs governing the duration for parental mourning acknowledge these feeding debts, by invoking the period when the mother supported the baby at the breast and the father labored to "take care of" the lactating mother and child (Lowenthal 1987:243). Malgre Sa explained to me that parents will remind children of this debt:

> Your mother will always say to you, she breast-fed you for so many months. My mother nursed me for 20 months. Your father will tell you he worked hard to take care of your mother [and] you, that he did wage labor, that he even did wage labor. He'll say, "I really suffered for you!"

> *Manman ou—tout tan lap di ou sa, li tete ou konbyen mwa. Manman m te tete m 20 mwa. Papa ou ap di ou ke li travay di pou okipe manman ou avèk ou, li fè travay anpeyan, vann jounen. Lap di, "se pa ti mizè m pase pou ou, non!"*

Migrants are expected to compensate those who "fed" them when they were children. Labor migration thus maintains the impoverished means of producing raw labor for export. It does not improve the socioeconomic conditions of peasant societies. Haitians remain, as every journalist seems compelled to announce at the beginning of each news article on Haiti, the poorest, most desperate population in this hemisphere. Its migrant citizens are one of the most coerced work forces in the world.

Incorporating Peasant Producers

The incorporation of Haitian peasants in the world order reached an important turning point at the dawn of the 20th century. At the beginning of the previous century, Haitian ex-slaves used their ownership of land to resist plantation labor (Mintz 1974a). Since the majority could not be coerced into wage labor, they were preyed upon instead when they sold their cash crops of coffee, cacao, and cotton to the cosmopolitan, merchant bourgeoisie who controlled the export and import trade (Dupuy 1990:78, 102; Trouillot 1990b:75).

Mutual exploitation by the weak authoritarian state, European and North American venture capital, and the "parasitic" merchant class eventually led to domination by foreign interests of the import-export trade and of the national debt (Plummer 1988; Trouillot 1990b). American capitalists proved the ultimate spoilers, thanks to a military intervention that lasted two decades, and a World War I victory over its hegemonic rivals in the Caribbean. They had already launched extractive sugar and fruit ventures elsewhere in the Caribbean before penetrating the Haitian lowlands. By confining wages paid to Haitian laborers working for American firms in Haiti to fractions of those paid elsewhere, the Occupation Administration promoted Haiti's "greatest asset" to transnational capital across all of its locations. Haitian wages were one-third to one-fifth the Cuban rate (Castor 1971:80–81; Schmidt 1971:170).

Emigration vastly intensified during the occupation and the U.S. administration reaped an important source of revenue by brokering and organizing the recruitment. The "emigration tax" paid interest on the national debt that preceded the occupation. National City Bank of New York had serviced the debt since 1910, when it pushed out a French bank. National City Bank was the principal warrantor of the American sugar empire in Cuba and the Dominican Republic. Protecting the interests of the National City Bank was also a key factor in the U.S. decision to invade Haiti in 1915. The Haitian government was threatening to default on payment of a hefty loan from National City Bank.

The loan financed an American investor's bogus railroad and banana development project. The government of Antoine Simon had conceded virtually half of arable Haitian land to the American investor, James P. McDonald. McDonald's railway was to connect Port-au-Prince with the northern port and a fifteen-mile stretch on either side for banana plantations feeding his monopoly on the export market (Plummer 1988:156; Schmidt 1971:37). According to Moral (1961:62), the McDonald concession set off the peasant rebellions known as the "second *caco* war," whose harsh containment Simon personally oversaw. The contract furthermore obligated the government to guarantee the success of the railway. The occupation began after a subsequent Haitian government threatened to default on the state's guaranty of the failed project (Schmidt 1971:48–55).

The occupation administration's long neocolonial experiment in Haiti was violent and unsettling enough to achieve the goal of cornering the peasantry just this side of the brink, and harnessing them as a supplier of the most exploitable labor force in the region. These same coercive policies had been tested a century before in Europe to ruin the peasants and give them no recourse but to join a reserve army of mobile wage labor, producing for the new capitalist enterprises (Wolf 1982). The occupation administration was candid about the benefits of

Haitian migration (to other areas of the American sugar empire) in relieving the growing problem of "overpopulation" in the country (Millspaugh 1931:143). Migration was a means of expelling a surplus population rendered superfluous by the devaluation of peasant labor and the decline of domestic food production (Dupuy 1990:137).

The administration aggressively promoted the expansion of capitalized ventures in monocrop, export-oriented agriculture. American firms were granted exclusive export and import monopolies that crushed or thwarted competitors. They received generous concessions of putatively vacant state land—the occupants must have been squatters (Millspaugh 1931:142). The administration also instituted a new policy that further denied peasants access to state lands. To be eligible to lease lands, the farmers had to show proof that they had the capital to develop intensive, monocrop plantations. This policy effectively eliminated all but the large-scale, well-capitalized firms (Dupuy 1990:136).

To improve the infrastructure, the marines seized Haitian men and forced them into migrant road-building gangs. Haitian peasant resistance to the return of brutal corvée labor met with cruel repression. In 1919, the marines conducted the first trial of coordinated air and ground campaigns in the Haitian hills, using bombs to force the "bandits" from the mountains into open areas where the infantry ambushed them. By 1920, the "bandit" leadership had been eliminated. A total of 3,250 Haitians had been killed, compared to 17 marines (Schmidt 1971: 103). After surprising and killing the "bandit" leader Charlemagne Péralte, the marines disseminated photographs of his crucified body to demoralize remaining peasant resistance (Schmidt 1971:102). Péralte immediately became, and remains today, a powerful anticolonial symbol for Haitians. President Aristide embraced the martyr during his first electoral campaign, and greeted audiences with the words, "I salute you in the way of Charlemagne Péralte" (*Mwen salye ou Charlemagnepéraltement*).

Despite enticements to transnational capital in Haiti, most of the foreign firms that started during the occupation failed, but not before upsetting the regional economies of the areas where they displaced peasants and removed land from food production. Two international corporations that endured were the Haytian American Sugar Company and the Haitian-American Development Corporation. The Sugar Company, which operated in Cul-de-Sac, Port-au-Prince, and Léogane, went bankrupt in 1921 and was refinanced by American banks, a pattern of ruin and rescue that beset the company throughout the century. The other firm, which had the prerogative of paying its landless workers in company script rather than cash, planted sisal in the north (Schmidt 1971:174–188; Dupuy 1990:136). As for bananas, whose dubious trade contributed to the United States' decision to invade, the occupation negotiated land concessions and a monopoly banana export contract with Standard Fruit and Steamship Co. of New Orleans (Moral 1961:311). But the "banana salvation" (Moral 1961:311) ended abruptly during the late 1940s when President Estimé moved to confine Standard Fruit's monopoly to the Artibonite, where it directly controlled production, and to allocate regional monopolies in the other banana-growing regions to Haitian-owned firms. Producers' and laborers' prices rose immediately and Standard Fruit left Haiti altogether for more attractive conditions (Saint-Louis 1988:205). The U.S. market subsequently denied access to the Haitian-owned firms. Banana exports plummeted from 19.4% of total exports in 1946–1947 to 0.9% by 1951–1952 (Saint-Louis 1988:206). The Léogane Port of ça Ira, an outlet for banana exports, fell into subsequent decline (Rémy 1969:47).

The withdrawal of the U.S. Marines was forced by increasing strikes and riots, American embarrassment over reports of massacres and indiscriminate killings of protestors, and fear that such news would harm U.S. foreign relations elsewhere in the hemisphere (Schmidt 1971:205). When the marines departed, they left in place a trained Haitian military. This force, armed by the United States, insured that the United States remained firmly in control of its periphery.

The U.S. State Department's strategy for "the experiment" has remained essentially the same since the occupation. During the early 1970s, a shift in the person of the dictator afforded the implementation of a more aggressive State Department policy. In exchange for propping up the government of François Duvalier's more manageable son, Jean-Claude, the State Department enjoyed virtually free development reign. This new phase in Haitian development coincided with major changes in the direction and development of world capitalism. Among them were global contraction, "recomposition" of capital in the center economies and intensified internationalization of production to reduce labor costs (Dixon et al. 1982; Sassen-Koob 1982). Labor in America's backyard was structured to compare favorably with Asia's, the new center of world manufacture (the wage ratio was about 1:3).

The Caribbean Basin Initiative (CBI) of 1980 solicited transnational corporations wanting to relocate phases of production to more "attractive" environments. Exemptions from local taxes and employee benefits and the establishment of a U.S.-Caribbean Free Trade Zone fostered the phenomenon of multiple, simultaneous "subcontracting" across different political entities. Corporations doing business in the Caribbean average 11 different subsidiaries in as many polities (Barry et al. 1984:14). The local government typically built the structures that house the assembly plants, making it easy for phantom corporations to remigrate at whim should the labor become less "attractive" (Barry et al. 1984).

CBI discourse regarding Haiti promoted the country's "comparative advantage" and "the productivity of low-cost labor, proximity to the United States, functioning basic infrastructure, pro-business atmosphere and political stability" (World Bank 1985:3, cited in Hooper 1987:33). The political stability insured by the military dictatorship aided the expansion of "screwdriver" and "sewing machine" assembly operations. What Paul Farmer (1988a:93) calls "operation brastrap," a pun on the controversial Puerto Rican development model known as "operation bootstrap," produced not only women's undergarments but also electronics components, cassette tapes, clothes, sporting goods, stuffed toys, shoes, and leather goods. Three-fourths of the work force was female, a ratio typical of offshore assembly industries because of owners' perception of the greater docility of female labor (Plotkin and Allman 1984; Sassen-Koob 1981).

AIDing Migration, Josh DeWind and David Kinley's (1986) analysis of the relationship between export-oriented agroindustrial "development" and Haitian demographic movements, demonstrated that the industrial plants had a disproportional adverse social and economic impact. The authors showed that while the low-paid assembly workers made "great sacrifices," the firms operated as an "enclave economy" that contributed nothing to the national budget (1986:188). Those sacrificing, of course, involved not only the workers, who totaled only 4% of the working population, but their kinsmen, who "fed" and subsidized their below-subsistence-level wages. Yet, the adverse impact of the export-oriented development policy might have been less severe except for the incursion of imported food into the domestic food market.

Incorporating Peasant Consumers

If the means of production was one way of incorporating the Haitian peasantry, the means of consumption was the other. Peasants not only "produce" laborers, they produce consumers who can be disciplined through the manipulation of their consumption habits. The structuring of consumption on the global scale is the opposite of production. In other words, production is distributed to take advantage of spatial, ethnic, and political differences. Capital expands by increasing markets, hence consumption tends to universalize or homogenize consumers.

The earlier, destabilizing effects of changes in diet on European peasants and the creation of working classes have been described by Wolf (1982) and Mintz (1985). Shifting to consumption of imported food monetized the diet and made consumers more dependent upon obtaining wages to purchase (as opposed to trade) food. This food was, in turn, more subject to inflation in the vagaries of the world market. Moreover, these changes were nutritionally for the worse.

Wages repatriated by Haitian migrant workers are increasingly "consumed" by food purchases. As overburdened and frustrated migrant emissaries complain, their relatives back home use up all of their wage remittances on consumption. "They eat them" (*yo manje yo*), some migrants say. The imports also undercut peasant producers of comparable products and push more of the population into wage labor. These movements include relocation to the very economies exporting the food in question. It is significant that when American grain flooded Europe during the mid-19th century, the crisis it caused sent a stream of "ruined peasants" to America (Wolf 1982:319).

It is revealing to study how the administrators of the occupation construed the experiment with peasant consumption. An important document is the memoir of Arthur C. Millspaugh (1931), the chief financial officer. Millspaugh (1931:166) quotes his own superior to the effect that "as far as the rural population is concerned it can not be denied that the peasant is better clothed, fed and housed than he was five years ago. . . . His standard of living has changed. He demands now something more than mere sustenance." Millspaugh (1931:144) also argued that a benefit of the migration of Haitian workers to Cuba and the Dominican Republic was "the enhanced income of those who returned" to purchase imported goods. The chief advisor nevertheless conceded that the peasants had gotten poorer during the occupation. "The masses are still near the primitive level and there is little reason to think that the slight change in their material circumstances have yet appreciably affected their civic quality" (Millspaugh 1931:166–167). In his estimation, the peasants' intractable "primitive character" was to blame for their chronic poverty, rather than the structuring of peasant poverty in the North American capitalist orbit and the disruptive effects of intensified importation of food that would compete with peasant crops. He regarded as one of his accomplishments the ten-fold increase in the importation of rice, a crop grown by peasants.

Peasant Haiti, heir to a colonial structure ostensibly restricted to monocrop export production, had long imported North American wheat flour and some other foods. The import market was not fully "developed," however, until after the marines landed and the United States strengthened its role as the primary source of Haiti's food imports. Subsidized by the U.S. Department of Agriculture, grain has more recently become the "food for peace" emblem par excellence of U.S. foreign policy in Haiti and elsewhere (Morgan 1979). Market development and subsidization of American agribusiness have invariably superseded third world "humanitarian" or "development" interests in the distribution of food under Public Law 480. According to a president of CARE, the organization responsible for distributing the rest of the "food for [infrastructural] work," developing countries are expected to "graduate" from PL480 to become direct customers of American grain (Barry et al. 1984:179).

By 1985, Haiti was purchasing three-quarters of its wheat imports from commercial sources in North America and Argentina. Since the beginning of the 1970s, Haiti's reliance on North American imports has risen nearly tenfold, from $10.7 million in 1970 to $62.1 million in 1976 to $89 million in 1987. The volume of imported wheat alone has grown at more than 10% a year, and, by 1985, exceeded the value of all agricultural exports (DeWind and Kinley 1986:109). The two state-owned grain enterprises (actually held in partnership with North American corporations) exacerbated the country's foreign debt by $28 million annually because the state purchased most of the wheat on credit, which increased the costs of milled flour by as much as 20% (World Bank 1987:25, 45).

These grain exchanges perpetuate the dependence of the Haitian state upon U.S. food aid. The Haitian state is supposed to use the wheat it receives to support its external debt service and to finance projects that benefit foreign investment and trade (Barry et al. 1984:179) (Between 1993 and 2003, these "commodity grants" amounted to $85 million [USAID 2004]). The Haitian state further enjoys monopolies on the importation, processing, and sale of grain products and refined sugar. State control of these staples artificially boosted the prices of the commodities and the personal fortunes of the Duvalierism. Ever more vulnerable consumers paid the price. Semi-refined soybean oil, pressed at the national factory, became the single most expensive staple food item during the mid-1980s; the price rose 60% between 1983 and 1985 alone (Péan 1985:33). Imported refined sugar, after passing through the state monopoly, sold at several times the world market price. The consumption of imported white sugar in 1985 was about 60,000 tons annually, or about 20 pounds per capita (compared to 32 pounds in Cuba and 30 pounds in Jamaica) (World Bank 1985:20).

Concurrent with USAID's promotion of the Caribbean Basin Initiative in Haiti, the agency unveiled a "new food security" agenda for the country. On the surface the food security plan seemed to counterbalance the overly extractive, export-led program. The plan, however, hardly advanced the cause of food self-sufficiency. "Food security" was to be achieved with imports paid for by earnings from agribusiness and assembly industry exports (DeWind and Kinley 1986: 110). In the course of achieving "food security," AID estimated that as much as 30% of the land cultivated for domestic food crops would be shifted into production of export crops. As Michael Hooper (1987:33) reported, USAID was "surprisingly candid" about the adverse consequences of the food-security strategy for peasants who grow and market food crops: "AID anticipates that such a drastic reorientation of agriculture will cause a decline in income and nutritional status, especially for small farmers and peasants . . . [and] AID anticipates a "massive" displacement of peasant farmers and migration to urban centers" (cited in Hooper 1987:33).

Over the last two decades, I have increasingly heard from Ti Rivyè natives that in Haiti "there isn't any food" (*pa gen manje*). A microstudy of child feeding beliefs and practices during the late 1970s by Maria Alvarez and Gerald Murray (1981:144) already attested to a markedly worsening diet. Alvarez and Murray observed "increasing shortages of food and money, escalation of food consumption debts and a food supply system under stress." While food imports rose, so did "themes of childhood hunger, parental shame and general desperation . . . work their way into the fabric of local life to a degree unknown in the past" (Alvarez and Murray 1981:150). People were learning to palliate their hunger by consuming nutritionally void "mouth passers" (*pase bouch*) because they could no longer afford to purchase fuel or food or to contribute the labor to prepare more than one meal a day. Pressured to return to income-generating activities, however limited, mothers were weaning their infants earlier and starting them earlier on imported "sweet food" (*manje dous*). Even the director of the national sugar factory in Léogane commented to me in 1983 that "Haitian children drink soda with a bread roll *because they are hungry.*"

The soda may have been even less nutritious than my friend imagined. If the information I received from an executive of the Coca-Cola franchise is true, his competitors, makers of the less expensive Haitian *kola* brands, diluted the sugar in their beverages with cheaper artificial sweeteners. Haitians, he claimed, had become unwitting mass consumers of diet soda!

The Ultimate Import Sabotage: North American Pigs

The most noxious step in the food security experiment involved the extermination of the peasants' most valuable livestock: their pigs. The Haitian black pig breed no longer exists. In the early 1980s, the United States (along with Canada and Mexico) moved to protect their domestic swine industries and oversaw, with a sufficiently cooperative Duvalier regime, the extermination of the entire swine population of the island. The black pigs were believed to be infected with a deadly virus whose unfortunate title reveals more about the ideology of the name-givers than the etiology of so-called African Swine Fever. (Haitians who lost their pigs did not adopt this term.) Complete eradication was said to have been necessary despite evidence that the pigs were dying of other diseases, including hog cholera. The disease had reached its peak in the Haitian swine population by 1980 and pigs were no longer dying of the disease by 1982, when the pig slaughtering program began in Haiti, having completed its task in the Dominican Republic on the eastern side of the island (Diederich 1984:16; DeWind and Kinley 1986: 119).

While the United States was conquering African Swine Fever in Hispaniola, it was waging a new war at home against a mysterious human disease: AIDS. Was it inevitable that Americans would blame Haitians—the bothersome "Africans" in the Caribbean—for AIDS, and that they would discover a link between African Swine Fever, Haitian immigrants, and AIDS? During the early 1980s, the Centers for Disease Control singled out Haitians as the only nationality at risk for AIDS (Farmer 1990). Soon there were attempts to link African Swine Fever and AIDS to the migrant Haitian community in Belle Glade, Florida. African Swine Fever had allegedly been discovered in the blood of Haitian AIDS patients. Researchers theorized that the victims ingested raw or undercooked pork (Teas 1983). Long after the damage was done to Haitian immigrants and tourism in Haiti, in particular, the Center for Disease Control quietly admitted that AIDS, unlike the doctors who control public health, does not discriminate by national origin. Neither did they find evidence corroborating the link between African Swine Fever, AIDS, and Haitians in Florida.

Yves Watermann, my field assistant who witnessed the killings of his family's pigs, likened the act to "a rape of the peasantry." Pigs were named pets, they lived in compounds with people, ate their bodily waste, cleaned and fertilized their gardens, and, as is often reported, were self-financing banks (because they required negligible investment and little human labor) (Diederich 1984:41). They were important sources of protein and, even more critically, of fat in the Haitian diet. Pigs were also the primary ritual sacrificial offering to an important pantheon of spirits known as *zandò* or *petwo*. Nelio Dediscar, one very poor Ti Rivyè farmer and a cousin to Little Caterpillar, assessed the effect of exterminating his pigs: "The pig affair," he said, "threw me into total poverty" (*afè kochon an jete m nan malere nèt*).

Although the pig eradication program in Haiti would seem to have signaled the definitive sabotage of the peasantry, the subsequent repopulation effort managed to extend the small farmers' pain. The new porcine population was to be white (or pink) Iowa pigs. The American planners did not seriously consider reserving uninfected, well-acclimated native pigs to use as breeding stock. Nor did they consider importing pigs from nearby islands with similar ecology and practices of rearing livestock.

I discussed the program with staff at USAID and Institut InterAmericain de Cooperation Pour L'Agriculture, the two agencies involved in the repopulation effort. Having arranged to import pigs from U.S. swine producers, the experts were now debating which Haitians should have access to the American pigs: small peasants or the relatively well-off. They framed the debate in "supply-side" economic discourse. They eventually decided to give the Iowa pigs to better-off citizens with the expectation that the piglets would "trickle down" to the poor peasants. The decision was based on the assumption that people of means could more adequately provide for the fair-skinned swine. The requirements were provision of a cement structure, access to running water—a luxury unknown to most Haitian people—and a high-protein vitamin-laced imported grain (Diederich 1984:16). Rearing pigs was thus transformed from a cost-free savings to a risky, debt-generating investment (Dewind and Kinley 1986:122).

Anticipating the market opportunity opened by the vast dip in domestic pork supply, the World Bank meanwhile fostered the expansion of the poultry industry in Haiti. The chicken program was not to redress peasants for the loss of their pigs. It was to support a "fully integrated chicken production plant" owned by the proprietor of the local Kentucky Fried Chicken franchise and by a prominent member of the commercial elite. The emerging poultry and livestock businesses were also important consumers of imported wheat and soybeans processed in Haiti (Dewind and Kinley 1986:124). With the elimination of an important source of dietary fat, consumption of soybean oil also escalated dramatically, as did the price.

Resistance to the killing and repopulation of the pigs helped to spark the "uprooting" (*dechoukaj*) of the Jean-Claude Duvalier regime. Protesters at CARE warehouses decried the wasting of imported grain on the pampered American pigs (Diederich 1984:16). After "the uprooting," grassroots peasant organizations advocated for stopping the flow of grain imports, including agribusiness livestock feed, increasing control over crops produced for export, land reform, and importing pigs from neighboring Caribbean islands (Maguire 1990, 1991). The peasant cooperative groups, along with CARITAS, a Catholic charitable organization, eventually succeeded in reintroducing some Caribbean pigs. The peasant cooperatives found a champion of their interests in Father Jean-Bertrand Aristide, and after the coup d'etat of September 1991 that sent him into exile, the cooperatives became targets of systematic oppression by the American-trained and equipped army. Because "Creole pigs" epitomized the peasant organizations' modest achievements, they, too, were attacked. *Haiti Insight* (1992: 11) reported that "Within the first two weeks of the coup, a group of soldiers . . . in Thomonde [the Central Plateau] slaughtered all the [Creole] pigs that had been supplied to local peasant groups by a Haitian non-governmental organization, the Ecumenical Self-Help Service, in an effort to reintroduce Creole pigs into the country."

Historical Overview of Haitian Transnational Migration

Movements of people between the United States and Haiti reach back to the late 18th century, to the overthrow of European colonial rule and the creation, in 1776 and 1804 respectively, of the first and second independent nation-states in the New World. Opposing ideologies of race and racial slavery undermined potential kinship between the new renegade polities. For North American settlers, winning political and economic autonomy from Britain only compounded racial difference; citizenship presumed whiteness in the new United States. By contrast, the revolution in St. Domingue (the name of the French colony) was a rejection of both racial discrimination (particularly against free persons of color) and chattel slavery, whose resolution ultimately necessitated political independence from France. The first "transnational" migrants between Haiti and the United States sojourned in the racial breach dividing the two nation-states. They were refugees of a race war raging in one and the race-based nation-building of the other.

The 13-year struggle for freedom and citizenship for its African-descended majority was waged in St. Domingue at the same time that plantation slavery was expanding in the new American nation. The thoroughly "free" Haiti that emerged threatened plantation agriculture and slavery in the United States, not to mention the estate of the slave-owning planter president, Thomas Jefferson (Plummer 1992:18). The emergent United States welcomed the fleeing French colonists, many of whom arrived with their slaves, and even provided funds to resettle them (Laguerre 1998:33). The U.S. government refused to recognize the Haitian republic for more than six decades; that is, until the emancipation of black slaves within their own national borders.[3]

The exodus of the colonists and the demise of the plantation system in Haiti at the outset of the 19th century provided openings for descendants of slaves in the newly independent nation to "reconstitute" a freeholding peasantry. Mintz (1974a) has argued that the freed slaves in fact extended their "proto-peasant" experience during slavery. Slaves' control of food production and exchange of products from their provision grounds during slavery provided a crucial foothold such that, once slavery ended, they succeeded in rapidly entrenching themselves as small, independent, land-holding farmers. The peasants were therefore able to resist pressures to coerce them into plantation wage labor by the new state, beginning with the founding president and revolutionary leader, Dessalines. It took the economic and military might of a new 20th-century colonial power—the United States—to push the Haitian peasants into capitalist agriculture. Over the course of the 20th century, the Haitian peasant economy was increasingly weakened and transformed into one that produces unskilled, wage labor for export and consumes more and more imported food. Haitian migrant laborers have thus followed and abetted the expansions and declines of North American capital by migrating to Cuba, other parts of Haiti, the Dominican Republic (the eastern side of the island), the Caribbean, and, ultimately, the United States and Canada. The U.S. occupation of Haiti from 1915 to 1934 consolidated, rather than created, Haiti's emerging role as a source of cheap labor to an expanding American sugar empire. The first important wave of migration to Cuba followed a revolt by native labor, when between 1200 and 1500 Haitians migrated (Lundahl 1983:100–101). Jacques Roumain's (1946) novel, *Gouverneurs de la Rosée*, memorialized this experience in its portrayal of a *viejo* returning from Cuba after a long absence. The rates of migration steadily increased through the mid-1920s, with an annual recruitment by United Fruit and General Sugar of more than 20,000 workers. About one-third of the workers remained permanently in Cuba (Lundahl 1983:101). The flow to Cuba ended abruptly during the depression in the early 1930s when the United States shifted its sugar production to the Pacific and Puerto Rico. Haitian workers were repatriated, exacerbating an already dire employment problem in the home country (Lundahl 1983:106).

The occupation of the western portion of Hispaniola (Haiti) coincided with— and outlasted—the intervention in the eastern side. Between 1916 and 1924, the U.S. Marines occupied the Dominican Republic. While the country was under U.S. political control, the American-owned sugar industry greatly expanded. Haitian workers provided the bulk of the labor. Wages in the Dominican Republic descended to little more than the rate across the border. As a contemporary Dominican observer commented on the 20–30-cents-a-day labor, "the cheap imported seasonal labor digs a pit of subsistence wages at the feet of the Dominican workers in the interest of the sugar business" (cited in Lundahl 1983:122). Lundahl (1983:119) guesses that between 1916 and 1925 at least 150,000 Haitians crossed the border, a migration that had become a "veritable osmosis." Yet, the administration issued only 300 visas in 1918 and 4,100 in 1923, the highest annual amount during the period. The role of the U.S. policy in fostering the undocumented flow during the period is plain.

The huge and vulnerable "illegal" Haitian population were easy scapegoats during the subsequent depression of the Dominican sugar industry. In 1937, between 15,000 and 25,000 Haitian migrants were rounded up and slaughtered. The Haitian government of Stenio Vincent did not only fail to protect them, it also confiscated funds later earmarked to compensate families of victims (Heinl and Heinl 1978:529). I interviewed Richelieu Darius, an elder in the Ti Rivyè hamlet who narrowly escaped the terror in Dominikani. Despite this atrocity and the dreadful conditions there, which are regularly deplored by human rights organizations, the Dominican Republic ultimately became the unwelcoming "host" to the second largest population of diaspora Haitians. The town of Léogane continues to serve as a center of annual recruitment for "the Kongo" in the Dominican Republic. But few men from the village of Ti Rivyè walk the short distance to the town to sign up for the Kongo, which is widely seen as the ultimate symbol of desperation.

As the Bahamas was entering the U.S. economic orbit in the early 1950s, as many as 40,000 Haitians provided the unskilled labor in construction and services (Marshall 1979, 1985). This clandestine migration originated primarily in the north and northwest provinces, the areas within closest reach to these islands. When the Bahamian tourism-driven economic boom ended, Haitian immigrants were subjected to harassment, incarceration, and summary deportations.

While neither the Dominican Republic nor the Bahamas have drawn significant migration from Ti Rivyè, the French départements of Guadeloupe, Martinique, and Quebec have been a magnet for men and women of Ti Rivyè. After South Florida, Guadeloupe hosts the largest number of emigrants from Ti Rivyè. Tens of thousands of Haitians migrated to the French Caribbean, Quebec, and France during the 1970s, leaving on planes with quasilegal status, visa in hand. Indeed a testament to this "legal" movement, which is classified as "leaving with a visa," was constructed near the Ti Rivyè shoreline during the mid-1980s—a new tin-roofed house painted in pink, white, and pastel green, a popular combination during the migration-financed housing boom. Painted on the side of the house was a huge mural of a jet and the words AIR FRANCE, the airline connecting Haiti and the French départements, printed below it.

Haitian workers began migrating to North America in significant numbers during the late 1960s, part of the broad "new" Caribbean migration feeding the restructuring and relocations of U.S. manufacture (Bryce-Laporte 1979). The Caribbean and Central America, as we saw above, were attractive frontiers for the intensified "subcontracting" of phases of assembly-line production. As service industries replaced manufacture in center cities, low-paying, labor-intensive service jobs became a magnet for immigrant workers. Haitian migrants to the United States received ten times as many nonimmigrant tourist visas as they did immigrant visas. Portes (1978) argued that the vulnerability of state-less migrants was structured by the host state. The Immigration and Naturalization Service (INS) fully anticipated that the "tourists" would violate their visas and stay to work. The INS only ever pursued a tiny minority of the undocumented immigrant population, just enough to indirectly harass the nonimmigrant Haitian population as a whole into obedience.

Between 1960 and 1980, a higher proportion of the Caribbean population emigrated than did the peoples of any other world area (Barry et. al. 1984:13). Rates of outmigration ranged as high as 25%. Haiti fell in the middle, with one out of every five or six living Outside (*Deyò*). The annual national emigration rate between 1971 and 1981 was 4.95%, with an estimated 23,240 leaving every year. Port-au-Prince's population of internal exiles from declining rural areas, which had more than tripled during the previous two decades (1950 to 1971), was now growing at only 2% (Haiti, IHSI 1983c, 1984). More Haitian women immigrated to the U.S. cities during this period because women obtained tourist visas more easily than men (Buchanan 1979a). New York was the major destination of emigrés from the capital city, as it was for other Caribbean and Latin American populations.

The mode and destination of Haitian migration to the United States changed at the end of the 1970s, and the number of Haitians living in South Florida today rivals the Haitian population of greater New York.[4] Between 1979 and 1982, a flotilla of sailboats left Haitian waters for the South Florida coast, embarking directly from rural coastal areas and bypassing the capital city of Port-au-Prince, the typical intermediary step for U.S.-bound emigrants. The first detected Haitian refugee boat arrived in Florida in 1963 (Stepick 1987:137). The passengers' asylum requests were denied and they were repatriated. Ten years later, another sailboat reached Florida. As more Haitians became convinced of the possibility of completing the voyage to Florida and of being allowed to stay, the flow increased (Boswell 1982). By 1977, Haitians boats were arriving regularly. Between 1979 and 1981, as many as 70,000 Haitians entered Florida by boat. By 1983, another 10,000–15,000 had entered by plane (Stepick and Stepick 1990:73). The early boat migrants were almost entirely male, but as the flow progressed, more women emigrated. A sample of passengers arriving between January and April 1980, just before the height of the flow, indicated a 70:30 ratio of men to women. The migrants were overwhelmingly young adults: up to 60% were between 18 and 29 years of age and 25–30% were between 30 and 44 years old (Buchanan 1982:iv).

Haitians referred to these voyages as *kanntè*. According to legend, when people started attempting to cross 700 miles of open sea in small, open, motorless "canoe" (*kanòt*) sailboats, someone jested to the effect that, "those crazy people are so sure they will make it to Miami, they would think they were taking a Canter (kanntè)!" Canter signifies power, speed and control—the opposite of the fishermen's "canoes." It is the name of the motor powering the imposing Japanese trucks that transport people, produce, small livestock and other commodities between the central urban market and the provinces. An emblem of internal marketing of peasant products thus became the dominant symbol of ruined peasant laborers risking their lives to sail toward Miami.

The kanntè image was immortalized in the Gemini All Stars de Ti Manno's hit recording of "Canter" in 1981. William Colas, a band member, composed the song. Colas strongly rebuked the impetuous voyagers, who offered themselves as naive prey for smugglers and sharks. The chorus chides,

> You leave for Miami
> You're not sure you'll make it
> You leave your children hungry
> So you can pay the Canter
> When you get to the deep sea
> Captain drops you in the water.

> *Ou ta ale Mayami*
> *Ou pa konn si ou ap rive*
> *Ou kite ti moun grangou*
> *Pou ou ale peye kanntè*
> *Lè ou rive nan fon lamè*
> *Kapiten lag'ou nan dlo.*

Instead, the song exhorts the hopeful migrants to stay in the countryside and put their efforts into farming. The concluding line of the verse shifts to the authoritative register of French to advise the rural poor: trust in providence and patience. The singer cites the French proverb, *Petit à petit l'oiseau fait son nid* (Little by little the bird makes its nest).

> You have to stop cutting down trees
> Farm and god willing we'll eat
> To spend money to go die
> Better to plant the earth with it
> Bit by bit the bird makes its nest.

> *Se pou nou sispann koupe piye bwa*
> *Fè jaden, gras a dye na manje*
> *Pou ou peye lajan pou ou al mouri*
> *Pi bon lage l plante latè*
> *Petit à petit l'oiseau fait son nid*

Ti Rivyè's intense participation in kanntè between 1979 and 1982 partly overlaps with the song's release. The residents of this coastal fishing village certainly "tempted luck" (*tante chans*) by daring to cross 700 miles of open sea in their 15-foot "canoes." Even before they could risk their lives at sea, though, they exposed themselves to arrest for trying to depart illegally by boat. Organizers and passengers of kannte were often arrested, fined, beaten, and imprisoned, though these fates varied in relation to political connections and bribes.

The song's portrayal of vicious smugglers deviates from the experience of coastal Ti Rivyè. Groups of between ten and twenty local relatives and neighbors collaborated to set sail in their own "canoes."[5] They navigated by stars and compass according to instructions sent back by earlier adventurers. They knew what to expect should their boats run aground near Cuba, namely that the Cubans would repair the boats and then pull them out to sea, and they knew what to expect once they arrived in Miami as well. They further anticipated that some boats would reach only as far as the Bahamas with the hope that they could eventually continue to Miami. Many who ran aground in the Bahamas were returned to Haiti, only to attempt the departure again.

These Canter voyages preceded and then coincided with the much larger 1980 flow of 125,000 Cuban refugees from the port of Mariel. The INS extended a warm welcome to the Cuban exiles. It rejected the Haitian refugees. Perhaps the most embarrassing evidence of the disparity in the treatment of the two immigrant groups was the 1979 verdict by Federal District Judge King finding "specific discrimination against Haitians at a high level." Judge King ordered the INS to reprocess 5,000 Haitian asylum applications (*Haitian Refugee Center v. Civiletti* 503 F.Supp. 442 [S.D. Fla 1980]. Benjamin Civiletti was the U.S. Attorney General; see also Miller 1984:94).

The Carter Administration responded to the King verdict by announcing that the INS would henceforth treat the two groups equally (Miller 1984:94; Rocheleau 1984:13; Stepick 1982b:12). In June 1980, the administration created a special temporary Cuban-Haitian "entrant" category, granting the privilege to work and such limited benefits as workman's compensation, food stamps, and public legal services. This policy change probably stimulated increased migrations from both Haiti and the inhospitable host society of the Bahamas (Rocheleau 1984:27).

Almost immediately after taking office, President Reagan moved to garner the growing reactionary and xenophobic mood related to the national economic downturn. The Haitian boat people were a ready scapegoat. The Justice Department led the charge in reformulating an alien threat to the nation that gave the president a mandate to "regain control of the borders" (1981 congressional testimony of Secretary of Justice William French Smith, cited in Miller 1984:72). The coastal invasion of 70,000 black, indigent refugees from the most reviled island nation in the hemisphere was "detrimental to the national interest," even though the coinciding inrush of 125,000 Cubans and 175,000 Indochinese posed no danger to the same (Stepick 1982b:12; Miller 1984:73). Haitians who had already "entered" were consigned to immigration limbo ("status pending") for the better part of the decade, meaning they could not leave the country without jeopardizing their tenuous privilege to work in the United States. Cuban entrants, on the other hand, had their status converted to permanent residents.

Haitians who were still attempting to "enter" were held at the INS detention center in Miami and then dispersed to federal prisons in several other states, ostensibly to await deportation proceedings, but really to coerce them to volunteer to be repatriated. Attorney Cheryl Little of the Haitian Refugee Center told me in 1991 that the INS commonly surprised detainees in the middle of the night and took them to remote federal prisons far away. Isolating them from the support of fellow migrants and legal advocates, and cutting off their ability to communicate with their home succeeded in dissuading many from trying to endure their incarceration. The returned migrants I interviewed in Ti Rivyè who had languished in the prisons told me that the anxiety of not hearing from their families was the key reason behind their requests to be returned.

Haitian prisoners were increasingly being deported until June 1982, when Federal District Judge Spellman ordered all Haitian prisoners released on parole (*Louis v. Nelson* 544 F.SUPP. 973 [S.D. Fla 1982]). Within three months of the Spellman decision, President Reagan and dependent Haitian President-for-Life Jean-Claude Duvalier had signed a treaty to "stop the illegal migration" (letter of U.S. Ambassador to Haiti Ernest Preeg, 23 September 1981). The goal was to keep the refugees from reaching U.S. shores where U.S. courts could enforce their rights under U.S. laws. The accord stipulated placement of U.S. Coast Guard cutters in the windward passage between Cuba and Haiti, interdiction of all Haitian boats, questioning of every passenger to determine valid claims for asylum, and repatriation of those deemed ineligible for refugee status. Between September 1981 and February 1991 a total of 11 Haitians were found to have valid asylum claims and allowed to enter the United States to apply for asylum (*Haiti Insight* 1992 3[6]:4).

For the Haitian state's part, Duvalier vowed to increase surveillance of coasts, to arrest illegal migrants, and not to persecute returnees (with the exception of "traffickers"). In Ti Rivyè, prosecution of those suspected of organizing voyages seemed to correlate with their personal and political connections. I witnessed several cases during my year and a half in Ti Rivyè of men arrested and imprisoned for alleged attempts to organize a boat. None was charged or tried before their relatives purchased their release.

The flow of boats did not resume with any regularity until October 1991, during the violent coup d'etat that ousted the newly elected government of Jean-Bertrand Aristide. The U.S. government immediately dispatched a flotilla of Coast Guard cutters to prevent the refugees from reaching the United States. Two-thirds of the more than 23,000 escapees who had arrived by the end of May were determined to be "economic migrants" and almost immediately repatriated. In response to human rights protests the INS set up a detention camp in Guantanamo Bay (where U.S. laws did not extend) to process their asylum claims. Applying due process, the INS soon found about 10,000 to have valid claims and permitted them to enter the United States.

But the prospect of a new Haitian invasion was politically intolerable. Having no legitimate way to reduce the high rate of acceptance of valid asylum claims, President George H. W. Bush ordered the closing of the Guantanamo camp and reinstated the policy of forced return of all interdictees, without benefit of an interview to determine the validity of their asylum claims (*Haiti Insight* 1992 3[7]:1).[6] A tiny portion of the detention center remained open for an extended period, however, to become the world's first concentration camp for the H.I.V. positive. The INS moved to keep those whom they had already determined to be bonafide refugees from entering the United States by later testing them for H.I.V. The 250 who tested positive languished in the camp's tents for two years before being deported (Richman 1993).

Incorporation into U.S. Society and Economy

Little Caterpillar's experience upon arrival in South Florida was shared by the vast majority of the kanntè migrants: immediate apprehension as their "canoe" approached the Miami coastline, incarceration in the INS Krome detention center in Miami, release "on parole" after several days or weeks into the charge of a sponsoring relative or custodian, and receipt of a 3 x 5-inch I-94 immigration paper with the words "Cuban/Haitian Entrant: Status Pending" stamped diagonally across it.

Profound contempt for Haitian "boat people" as well as the migrants' rural, peasant backgrounds combined to limit opportunities for work. Agribusiness was the one sector that welcomed the new arrivals until they demonstrated their failure to serve as sufficiently docile prey.

Ninety percent of the Ti Rivyè migrants identified in my census settled in farmworker enclaves (the other 10% joined relatives in New York) of Belle Glade, Immokalee, and Fort Pierce. The only lodging they could secure was in dirty, dilapidated buildings: one-room units in tenements (sharing a common bathroom and kitchen), apartments, trailers, and houses. Voracious landlords exploited the migrants, charging Mercina D'Haïti's family of three more to rent a 10 x 10-foot cell in a filthy Belle Glade tenement, for example, than we paid at the time to lease a three-bedroom home in a middle-class neighborhood of Charlottesville, Virginia.

There are few permanent jobs in Florida agriculture. As a result, the enclaves empty out each June and workers migrate north in search of work. During the summer season, which lasts until October, the workers usually live in isolated camps whose fetid conditions, violent and crooked crew bosses, and "company store" systems of credit have been the topics of research, journalism, repeated lawsuits, government sponsored studies, and, occasionally, congressional hearings (Rothenberg 1998). The state-licensed labor camps on the Virginia Eastern Shore (where I met Little Caterpillar) drew the attention of a civil rights commission. They reported that migrants were living in abandoned buses, trailers, chicken coops, and barns, in addition to approved labor camps. Mosquito infestation, overflowing privies and septic tanks, lack of hot water for bathing, rotten ceilings and roofs, and walls with holes were standard conditions in these camps (cited in *Washington Post*, August 28, 1985; cf. Heppel 1982). The only consolation, farmworkers told me, was that this "housing" was usually "free," meaning that rent was not deducted from their pay.

Attorneys Gregory Schell and Robert Williams, farmworker advocates previously associated with Florida Rural Legal Services, estimate that between 30,000 and 40,000 Haitians were employed as farmworkers during the mid-1980s (personal communications). Seventy-five percent of the migrants identified in my

2.1. André Sanon at Farmex labor camp, Tasley, Virginia, August 1981.

2.2. Ti Dyo Bertrand at Farmex labor camp, Tasley, Virginia, August 1981.

2.3. Labor Camp in Atlantic, Virginia, July 1981.

1983–1984 Ti Rivyè survey were working in this inordinately exploitative and poorly regulated industry. Few would dispute that hand-harvesting fruits and vegetables by piece-rate is the most stigmatized and difficult labor in the United States.

Little Caterpillar described what it was like to do farm work on the Virginia Eastern Shore to Hannah Geffert, who had come to the area to collect workers' testimonies for *Tell Them to Stay Home* (n.d.) and her play, *Picking*. I introduced her to Little Caterpillar and served as the translator. Caterpillar told her:

> I want to stop working in the fields. It makes me very tired. It doesn't do anything for me. It's no good. . . . The work that I do in the fields is destroying me; it is completely destroying me. The sun destroys me. People who are rich work; people who are poor work. For example, there is a person who works at a desk job, but he doesn't fight the flames, the flames of the sun, I mean. The sun turns your body into water. You come to this country and this is the only work you find so you have no choice but to work in the fields. (Geffert n.d.)

While the Haitian entrants generally endured the flaming sun and the hard toil of farm work, and even the squalid, unsafe conditions of the labor camps, they were hardly accepting of flagrant and capricious pilfering of their rightful compensation. They regularly challenged—and astonished—their employers, who typically retaliated ruthlessly and violently. While I served with Peninsula Virginia Legal Aid, I interceded for many individual Haitian farmworkers who questioned their employers' payment and were sometimes beaten or simply threatened but always fired. For a migrant farmworker, termination means being stranded in a strange locality without means, and often without enough money, to return home.

A Nelson County, Virginia, labor contractor, for instance, fired every member of the crew who spoke to me and another outreach worker from Legal Aid about their appalling housing in an abandoned school bus in a cow pasture. They also told us of fraudulent payroll deductions, including fees for nonexistent daily meals and a charge of $14.00 for inoculations administered without charge by a public health nurse. The county sheriffs carried all dismissed, and now trespassing, farmworkers to the nearby town of Lovingston and deposited them on the corner where the Trailways Bus passed, regardless of whether they could afford a bus ticket home. Ignacio and Virginia, one of two Haitian couples living in what they called the "cow house" (the abandoned bus), were packing up after being told to leave when the crew leader's sons, wielding axes, approached. They ran to a road and were picked up there by the sheriff, who was coming anyway to evict them.

Attorney Schell has commented to me that Haitians, more than any other ethnic farmworker group he tried to defend, demanded their rights. Schell and other Legal Services and private attorneys filed myriad complaints and lawsuits on behalf of Haitian farmworkers. They sued violently corrupt contractors licensed to recruit, hire, and transport the most invisible workers across state lines. And, after a small but important shift in the language of the federal law known as the Migrant and Seasonal Agricultural Worker Protection Act (MSAWPA) removing growers' ability to deflect all responsibility onto their subcontractors, they sued their agribusiness growers as joint-employers, too. Many of the suits against the contractors have resulted in convictions in federal courts of debt peonage, assault, theft of workers' social security wages, tax fraud, and transporting migrants in unsafe vehicles.[7]

Faced with court fines and stricter state regulation, some agribusiness growers, already in precarious financial shape, sold out to larger agribusiness corporations and to real estate developers. Others shifted to crops harvested by machines. Some improved the labor camps under pressure. Still other planters retaliated against "litigious Haitians" by refusing to hire them again in favor of more docile manual labor forces: guest workers (with H-2 visas) from the English-speaking Caribbean, here only at the discretion of their employers, and undocumented migrants from Mexico and Central America.[8] In 1990, Little Caterpillar's crew went on strike at the Virginia Eastern Shore labor camp in which they had been living every summer since 1981 to protest fetid bathrooms overflowing with sewage. The next year the grower hired an undocumented Mexican crew.

Agribusiness growers responded to Haitian farmworkers' litigation with an intense political campaign against Legal Services at both state and federal levels. Board members of the Legal Services Corporation, who were political appointees, provided a sympathetic ear to growers' complaints. In 1985, the corporation launched a hostile internal assault on Maryland Legal Aid, where Attorney Schell worked from 1984 to 1988, which only ended after a federal district court ordered the corporation to cease (Gouldner 1985). Three years later, the U.S. General Accounting Office conducted an audit that failed to uncover any misuses of funds. President Reagan responded to agribusiness lobbying by denying Legal Services attorneys access to public funds to advocate for noncitizens. Farmworker attorneys, including Schell and Williams, adjusted by collaborating with private law firms and using other sources of funds to cover costs of representing the entrants. Their legal successes did not go unpunished. By 2000, no Legal Services office was allowed to represent noncitizens, even if they secured private sources of funds.

Most of the Ti Rivyè migrants abandoned the irregular and dangerous job of picking vegetables and fruits as soon as they could. Some were of course pushed out by the agriculture industry itself. The 10,000–15,000 Haitians still employed in farm labor tend to be more recent arrivals; for example, many who were admitted as refugees after the 1991 coup d'etat worked in agriculture. The belated receptivity of employers in service sectors to Haitian labor further pulled Haitians away from the greater insecurity of farmwork (Stepick 1998). The migrants from Ti Rivyè relocated therefore from the farmworker slums in Belle Glade, Fort Pierce, and Immokalee to residential areas of Lake Worth, Delray Beach, Palm Beach, Fort Lauderdale, and other cities in Broward and Palm Beach counties. They found jobs in the lower levels of the burgeoning industries of tourism, service, and health care, working in hotels, restaurants, theme parks, landscaping, construction, transportation, cleaning, and nursing homes. Their increasing home ownership in Broward and Palm Beach counties is concrete evidence of their gradual economic success.

Summary

Over the course of the 20th century, American-led development and a dependent nation-state contributed to restructuring Haiti's peasants as a regional supplier of cheap mobile labor and a consumer of migrants' wage remittances. The Haitian peasantry that had emerged in violent struggle against plantation slavery in the early 19th century was gradually coerced into forfeiting their hard-won victory of economic freedom, only to export their sons to serve as free wage-slaves on American-owned plantations in Haiti, Cuba, and the Dominican Republic. Late 20th-century development plans for Haiti reproduced the same strategy of rural displacement, as cynical architects of the "food security" program admitted. At the same time, newly displaced peasants were sailing toward the source of development to face a hostile native population and toil on Florida and East Coast plantations, subsidiaries of some of the same corporations that had exploited a previous generation of Haitian cane cutters in the Dominican Republic.

Even though this new group of Haitians settled in the United States, however, they were simultaneously "living" in Ti Rivyè. At the same time, kin (including ancestors and spirits) located at home regularly inhabited the migrants' new world. Gaining a gradual foothold in America did not therefore require abandoning Ti Rivyè. Creative adaptions of changing technologies of travel and communication, residential concentration, and the movements of trusted couriers fostered their and their family's goals of simultaneous involvement of Inside and Outside, home village and host site. The next chapter describes how migrants stay connected to their home. The culture of migration is ubiquitous among Ti Rivyè families, who organize themselves as producers of people for export, consumers of migrants' remittances and managers of migrants' assets in people and things.

3

Ti Rivyè: Between Home and Over There

To live in Haiti, you have to pursue a livelihood Outside.

—*Lorius "Little Spider" Guerrier, 1984*

Ti Rivyè is the geographical and moral anchor of a mobile community. Since the Canter exodus of 1979–82, nearly every family in Ti Rivyè has at least one member Over There. The consciousness of long-distance community is pervasive. Even young children internalize the interdependence between the village and Over There and the inevitability of their own migration to "give a livelihood to their families." They expect after emigrating to continue to live vicariously back home, irrespective of long separations. This chapter describes life in the home anchor of Ti Rivyè and the multiple ways migrants and their home kin reproduce their long-distance community.

Petite Rivière II, Léogane

The coastal plains of Léogane and Cul-de-Sac meet one another at the central bend in the island's horseshoe-shaped western coast. The 8,166 hectares of the Léogane Plain are bordered on the north by the bay of La Gonâve, which joins the Caribbean Sea; to the south is Jacmel, the southernmost point of the island; to the east is Gressier and beyond it, Port-au-Prince; and to the west is Grand Goâve. The commune of Léogane, with a population of about 250,000, comprises the districts of Léogane, Grand Goâve, and Petit Goâve.

Petite Rivière II (Ti Rivyè), 1 of 13 "rural sections" in the Léogane district, occupies the long, narrow strip of land along the northern coastal margin of the Plain. Petite Rivière II's southern boundary is the national highway that links Port-au-Prince with the south and the southwest peninsula (and divides Petite from Grande Rivière). The eastern end of Petite Rivière II lies about 30 kilometers from the capital, and the western end flanks the town of Léogane. A single dirt road, which the state sugar factory made passable by vehicle during the mid-1980s but has since fallen into disrepair, runs the length of the section. The only significant river, Momance or Grande Rivière/Gran Rivyè, originates in the southern mountains and spills into the bay at the eastern end of this section; a tributary, Petite Rivière, borders the western side of the section. Telephone, electrical, water, and plumbing utilities are mainly confined to the *bourgue*, or to private estates and Christian missions.

The town of Léogane is the administrative center of the commune. Like other formerly active rural centers undercut by centralization, state corruption, and foreign capital penetration, the Léogane *bourgue* has the air of being stuck in *une certaine période de léthargie*—an impression conceded even by the government's official geographer (Haïti, Ministère de L'Information 1983:32). The state report obviously predated the migrant-financed housing boom in the center of town, the one- and two-story cinder block "vacation homes" going up near shells of bygone coffee export houses as well as the plethora of one-room and storefront primary schools educating the children of unlettered emigrants. All but the centralmost streets remain unpaved and are barely passable in the rainy season.[1]

For several days every November, the listless town awakes to—and tries vainly to ignore—the nightmare of violence and confusion of the annual conscription of cane cutters headed for the Dominican Republic. Thousands of desperate single men, mainly from the south, converge on the town. Maurice Lemoine (1983:15–34) captures the cruel ordeal of beatings, psychological torture, and extortion in the opening chapter of his poignant book, *Bitter Sugar: Slaves Today in the Caribbean.*

Among the state administrative services in Léogane are the army post, civil registry, courthouse, tax bureau, and Teleco public telephone station. There is a cathedral, L'Eglise Sainte Rose, an Episcopalian mission and full-service hospital (L'Hôpital St. Croix), the Anacaona Park, named for the martyred 15th-century Arawak queen, a cemetery, a "sport center," half of the county's primary schools, and its two secondary schools. The town has a variety of small retail shops, a branch of Sogebank, two bar/restaurants, a disco, a dry cleaner, a movie house, an ice vendor, pawn shops, tailors' and dressmakers' shops, two bakeries, several funeral parlors, lottery ticket offices, storefront pharmacies, and lawyers' and notaries' offices. Many raw rum distilleries, located in or on the outskirts of town, bestow their distinctive odor on the Léogane *bourgue*. They also contribute to Léogane's high rate of mosquito-borne diseases, including malaria and filariasis, the cause of elephantiasis. (Standing water collecting below pipes during the distillation cooling process provides ideal breeding grounds for mosquitos.) The square in the center of the town becomes a large, regional food market twice a week. Léogane's other two markets are located in Darbonne, an important junction between the plain and the mountain, and at Carrefour Dufour, where highways to the south and west intersect.

Looking at an aerial photograph of the Léogane Plain, two features stand out: the vast inequality of land tenure and the production of sugarcane. More than half of the total land area (8,166 hectares or 20,178 acres) is planted in sugarcane. Most of the sugarcane in Ti Rivyè is cultivated on large, undivided holdings averaging 50 hectares, which are owned by politically powerful absentee landlords who employ wage laborers and sharecroppers. Scattered among these concentrated parcels are the crowded homesteads and lilliputian gardens farmed by local residents. The plots of local residents rarely surpass one "square" (*carreau*), an old French measure equaling 1.29 hectares or 3.19 acres. The land tenure survey we conducted in 1984 of all plots within an area of 8 carreaux (10.3 hectares) indicated that 75% of plots were less than one-tenth of a hectare (one-third acre). A government-sponsored survey carried out in the same area six years earlier showed 78% of cultivators holding 0.65 hectares or less, representing a total of 29% of the cultivated land. Less than 1% of farmers own 32% of the land. On a national scale, the average plot size has declined drastically since the mid-century. In 1950, 60% of cultivators farmed pieces of more than one square of land; only 4.6% of cultivators farmed pieces of less than one-quarter square (0.32 hectare). In 1971, only 30% farmed parcels greater than one square; 50% worked less than one-half square, and 36% were farming less than one-quarter square of land (Haiti, IHSI 1983b:11).

As elsewhere in Léogane and in Haiti, cultivators exploit a variety of tenure arrangements, which place them in relationships of owner, lessor, lessee, sharecropper, gift-holder and/or manager of plots (Raynolds 1986; Woodson 1990). Individual farmers simultaneously maintain an average of five different plots (in various tenure arrangements) in as many locations. Intercropping is the norm: sugarcane is planted with sweet potatoes or, less frequently, corn, while in the food gardens, plantains, peanuts, manioc, peas, pumpkin, and okra are typically cultivated together. Among our survey of 73 plots, 49% were planted in cane, 32% in legumes, etc., and 19% were dormant and used for pasturing cows and goats.

The bay bordering the northern edge of Petite Rivière provides the other means of livelihood for this community: fishing. Groups of three or four men debark in their "canoes" early most mornings to empty traps, pull in nets, and cast lines. When they return in the afternoon, they are met by local residents awaiting fish to cook for the daily meal and by the women traders who will leave before dawn to make their way to the markets in Port-au-Prince (where they also buy provisions for their families). These exchanges link Ti Rivyè traders directly with the capital, bypassing the Léogane markets. Depleted, polluted fishing grounds and lack of access to credit for purchasing gear, storage, and transportation, however, limit their returns. Conch, once plentiful in the waters near Ti Rivyè and the source of livelihood of many local fishermen and traders, have disappeared.

Those who learned trades related to home construction have been succeeding, thanks to the migration-financed housing boom. This construction bonanza includes dwellings for the dead.[2] Since a person's social rank is ultimately established at death by the abundance of children working in the land of opportunity, parents can expect a burial in an elaborate, aboveground, cement and cinderblock tomb. The growth in mortuary businesses in the otherwise sleepy town of Léogane reflects the higher funerary standards for casket, mortuary clothing for the deceased and relatives, photographer, religious services, and reception (which can last a week or more). Indeed some elders who have the migrant-supplied resources build the tomb to their liking while they are still alive.

3.1. Toro's house in Ti Rivyè, 1984. He sent home money to build the first migrant-sponsored house in the compound. The outdoor kitchen is to the side of it.

As for other viable alternatives to farming and fishing, there are few. Most resident families have lacked the resources to finance specialized training or viable trade apprenticeships for their children. Tailoring and dressmaking, once reliable trades, have been rendered nearly obsolete by the importation of ready-made clothes, but sewing school uniforms and ritual garments keeps some professionals afloat. The multitiered internal marketing system has provided some opportunities for women who manage within minuscule profit margins. Young men earn some income selling *borlette* (lottery) tickets and running taxi services for the higglers and other passengers on rented motorcycle taxis or converted pickup trucks. They have few opportunities for steady work and are desperate to find a way out of the country. Said Bo, one out-of-work tailor/cultivator struggling to support his four children, if you stay here "your youth is wasted, you grow old before your time, and you die leaving a heap of dry leaves as your testament."

Straddling Inside and Outside

The peculiar but common experience of spatial dislocation is summed up in Creole by the alienation of "life" from "livelihood." "Life" (*vi* or *lavi*) is inside, but the "means to life" (*lavi*) are outside. This characterization of the separation of life and livelihood brings to mind Marx's early writings on consciousness in capitalist society. Marx ([1843–44] 1975:335) suggested that the opposition between life and work, which arose with capitalism, becomes a taken-for-granted reality; people accept as a given that life begins after work. Migrants and their families, however, view the separation of life from livelihood as unnatural, so unnatural as to merit a struggle to explain it in the form of an adage. "To live in Haiti," Ti Krab (Little Spider), a Ti Rivyè native stated to me, "you have to pursue life Outside" (*Viv an Ayiti; chache lavi Deyò*). Mezye, my co-godparent, expressed the problem this way: "I can't live here; I can't live Over There," in other words, "I can't live in Ti Rivyè without pursuing a living Over There; neither can I live Over There" (*M pa ka viv isit; m pa ka viv Lòt Bò*). His "search for livelihood" had, by 1984, taken him from Ti Rivyè to Guadeloupe, to Miami, and then back to Ti Rivyè.

During the 1980s "Over There" meant "Miami," that is, anywhere in the southeastern United States limited by the expanse of "New York." Miami hosted two-thirds of all the migrants from Ti Rivyè. Over There minimally provides a livelihood for Haitian workers whose "feeding" costs are deflected to the home (in order to furnish maximal surplus value to capital). Over There has only grudgingly invited Haitian migrants "to live."

The perception of dislocation between "life" and "livelihood" is so widespread that even ten-year-old Nason fully comprehended. I lived in the same seven-

3.2. Gérard's house in Ti Rivyè, June 2003. Gérard sent funds to build this house. Construction began in 1984 and the house was enlarged ten years later. Tenten sits in the foreground with children from the yard.

dwelling homestead as Nason, who was named after his paternal great-grandmother and had been living there in the care of his paternal grandmother since the death of his mother two years before. His father, whom he strongly resembles, did not live in the yard, nor any other men of his father's generation, with the exception of his half-brother, Nason's uncle. A fisherman and fish trader based in two other coastal areas (where he also had wives and children), Nason's father occasionally came to visit his family and contribute to Nason's welfare.

Nason's grandmother, Immaculat, immigrated with her daughter to Montréal in 1987, to join the grandmother's youngest son and his wife and their children. (Montréal became a destination point following Immaculat's sister's arrival there. She sponsored her nephew's entrance into the country a decade and a half after she entered, and he, in turn, sponsored the migrations of his mother, sister, and nephew after ten more years.) After Immaculat migrated, Nason was left behind in the care of his uncle and his wife, with whom they had shared the same house. In Montréal, Immaculat takes care of her grandchildren while their parents work. She returns to Ti Rivyè about once a year for an extended stay.

Nason was a gentle, smart child, and I was drawn to him. I indulged his talent for drawing; while I was writing he was often "working" beside me with the paper, crayons, and pens I gave him, drawing pictures of people, including me. During one of our conversations, Nason showed that, already at age ten, he understood how the spatial separation of life and livelihood would determine his future.

K: Nason, what are you going to do when you grow up?
Nason, ki sa ou pral fè lè ou gran mounn?

N: I'm going Over There.
M pral Lòt Bò.

K: Where is that?
Ki kote sa a?

N: Miami.
Mayami.

K: What are you going to do in Miami?
Ki sa ou pral fè Mayami?

N: I'm going to work.
M pral travay.

K: What kind of work?
Ki travay?

N: Cut plantains.
Koupe banann.

K: Why will you go Over There?
Pou ki sa ou pral Lòt Bò?

N: So I can give my grandmother and my family a livelihood.
Pou m bay grann mwen ak fanmi mwen lavi.

K: They don't have a livelihood now?
Yo pa gen lavi kouniyè a?

N: It's so I can give them more livelihood.
Pou m ka ba yo plis lavi.

At age ten, Nason had internalized that the role of the migrant emissaries who took the kanntè to Miami was to send remittances home to provide a livelihood for their families. He also knew that the source of the money flowing home came from the migrants' work in agriculture Over There. He had witnessed the migrants' continued efforts to "live" vicariously at home, irrespective of being unable to return there for years on end.

Migration and Family

Migration is deeply entwined with Ti Rivyè kinship. Extended family units based in Ti Rivyè function as internally differentiated producers of people for export as well as managers and consumers of migrants' wage remittances. A family's long-term strategy for its collective security differentiates those who will migrate from those who will remain (Basch, Glick Schiller, and Szanton Blanc 1994:81–85). A son or daughter seen as selfless and dutiful might be expected to stay behind, even though these qualities would seem to define the ideal migrant, while another perceived as an unreliable burden will be pushed to leave. After migrants start building their "guaranty" at home, they need others willing to stay behind to maintain their investments and mind children left behind until they can emigrate too. And if migrant parents need inexpensive daycare for their American-born children, a grandmother's migration might one day be organized so she can supervise her grandchildren in the host setting.

Although kin units pursue strategies for the migration of some members and the presence of others, they are ready to adjust their plans to changing opportunities (Carnegie 1987:35). Anyone can be a potential migrant. The advent of the Canter boat migrations in the late 1970s offered a new opportunity to send emissaries abroad. Prior to that moment, emigration from Léogane's Ti Rivyè was characterized by the individual, legal, and quasilegal departures of selected members of better-off families to Guadeloupe, Martinique, Montréal, and New York. The opening of an inexpensive, if dangerous route by sea to the United States suddenly made migration tangible even for the poorest families. But even those who could afford visas for their young adult members, including some who had already invested funds in their children's visas, sent them off on boats headed for Miami.

Some young people ignored their elders' projects and left in secret. Fears of capture kept plans for voyages clandestine. As a result, close family members often did not know their relatives had departed, as the Canter song claims. Many of the women I interviewed signified their suffering from the shock of discovering their children had "escaped," by telling me they had to tie their bellies with scarves, an established palliative for duress. Only after they got word of their loved ones did they untie the scarves.

The mass, clandestine exodus of young adults between 1979 and 1982 left behind a population primarily of children and middle-aged and older people. The short-term effects were evident in every residential compound, or *lakou*. The matrilineal, seven-house compound I shared, for example, saw half of its young adult female heirs (between ages 20 and 40) depart along with every male member with two exceptions: a man whose partial blindness made him an unlikely candidate for migration and his elder half-brother, a fisherman and trader who circulated between coastal hamlets. Though short-lived, the boat exodus had a profound longer-term effect on Ti Rivyè's population. The removal intensified and deepened the culture of displacement and long-distance community. Most of the Canter sojourners who reached the United States eventually achieved legal residence there, pursuant to the Immigration Reform and Control Act of 1986—a basis, along with their gradual foothold in employment, for continuing to sponsor the inevitable migration of more family members.

These overlapping and multinational migration strategies are manifest in the experiences of two families from Ti Rivyè. For both kin units, the sudden, short-lived possibility of dangerous but inexpensive escape by boat augmented a longer-range plan for the migration of the younger generation. At the hub of the first family were the couple Filoza and Louis. Filoza was a successful shellfish trader. She commuted between Ti Rivyè and Port-au-Prince, where she maintained a rented residence, until moving back permanently during the late 1970s. Filoza's father was a local supervisor for the American-owned sugar company, a status symbolized by his marriages to 6 women and fatherhood of 42 children. When I met Filoza in 1983, 16 of her full and half siblings were alive. Eight lived in Ti Rivyè, two in the town of Léogane, two in Port-au-Prince, one in Archaie (on the northwest side of Port-au-Prince), one in New York, and two in Montréal. Filoza's husband was a distant relative who also grew up in Ti Rivyè, though not of such prodigious parentage. He remained in Ti Rivyè, supplying her with fish and also farming and managing a sugar mill. Their seven children grew up straddling the capital and the village, going to school in the capital and living in Ti Rivyè in their mother's maternally inherited homestead the rest of the year. Today all of them reside Outside.

Filoza's first child, a son born before she married Louis, left on a boat in 1981. When he departed, he left his two sons behind in Filoza's care. Almost two decades later, the sons, now in their 20s, joined him, his Haitian-born wife, and their American-born children in Pompano Beach.

Komè, the oldest of Filoza and Louis's children, was born in 1951. She worked as a seamstress and an independent, interisland trader of clothes, fabrics, housewares, and toilet articles. She has lived in Guadeloupe and Martinique. She migrated to Guadeloupe with her first husband, a carpenter and native of Ti Rivyè, with whom she had three children. They returned to Ti Rivyè together; after they separated, Komè migrated to Martinique, leaving the three children in her mother and father's care. (The eldest, an epileptic, died in 1986, the second died in infancy, and the third grew up in Ti Rivyè.) Komè later married (and divorced) a Martinican with whom she had twin girls. The girls eventually joined their maternal uncles and aunts in Palm Beach County, Florida. Around the same time as her daughters migrated, Komè moved back to Guadeloupe, where she was soon joined by the daughter who had grown up in her grandmother's yard, along with the daughter's two children. Komè's sister joined her in Martinique in 1982, where she also married a Martinican citizen, and she remains there today.

Filoza and Louis's four other children, two daughters and two sons, all live in close proximity in South Florida. Two left by boat in 1981. The youngest son came by airplane with his wife, also from Ti Rivyè, in 1991. Both sons left behind children in the care of relatives; these children eventually emigrated too. The second daughter, born in 1953, stayed at home. She married a local man of some means and they had three children together. Along with a maternal aunt, she helped care for Filoza when Filoza fell sick and died. Her husband emigrated in 1990. She joined him 11 years later, leaving her aged father behind with her adult daughter in her ample two-story home.

Little Caterpillar was born in 1944 into a family of lesser means than Komè's. Before emigrating, Little Caterpillar had lived all of his life in Ti Rivyè. He never attended school and was a farmer (renter and sharecropper). When he sailed to Florida in 1980, he left behind his wife and her two teenage children. During a return visit in 1990, he fathered a son by another woman, whom he also supported. Both of Caterpillar's parents are long deceased. Five of his siblings are alive today. Three sisters migrated to Guadeloupe during the late 1970s and early 1980s. Se Byen, the eldest, acts as a surrogate parent from their home anchor of Ti Rivyè. His occupations are *gangan*, or priest, owner of a cockfight stadium, and farming. Adam and Eve, fraternal twins, were a farmer and vegetable trader, respectively, in Ti Rivyè. Adam passed away in 1990. Eve's elder daughter migrated to Orlando during the 1990s, and Eve joined her there in 2003. The father of Eve's youngest child migrated to Guadeloupe when she was a baby. She now awaits a visa to the United States.

The Migrants' Guaranty at Home

A new house is the most conspicuous symbol of migrants' success abroad and loyalty to home.[3] In the yard I shared, for example, half of the homes, including the one I leased, had been recently built by emigrants, two of whom would not be able to return to see their dwellings for at least five more years. Three more migrants' "vacation houses" were under construction, a process that, in the absence of mortgages, often takes years to finance and complete. Migrants' new, remittance-financed houses stood out against the older wattle and daub, thatched-roof huts with dirt floors. They were constructed of cinder block, cement floors, and tin roofing; the fancier structures had mosaic tile floors, cement roofs, and forged iron porches.

In addition to enlisting home relatives to supervise the building of their vaca-

3.3. Nason (sitting on chair) and other boys in the yard, Ti Rivyè, 1984.

3.4. Tenten and extended family stand in front of his tomb. June 2003.

tion homes from afar, migrant men and women engage home kin to help them buy land and manage small businesses, including motorcycle-taxis and *tap-tap* (converted pick-up trucks) and retail trades. They take care of migrants' investments in livestock, garden plots, and fruit trees. Little Caterpillar pursued all of these means to "make economy" at home. In addition, he rented a room near the town center to "make a cinema," charging admission to local patrons viewing videos of movies on his television screen.

Before migrants can "guaranty" themselves through investments back home, though, they have to meet more pressing obligations there. Migrants are charged with paying for the educations (fees, uniforms, materials) of children they left behind in others' care and, often, the schooling of consanguines—siblings, nieces, and nephews—as well. As a result of migrants' school remittances, virtually all school-aged children in the hamlet attend schools, which are proliferating in the area. Education is a means of preparing (or producing) a relative for future migration, and sponsorship of their passage is yet another responsibility of migrants.

During their long absences, migrants are expected "to take responsibility for" (*reskonsab*) the life-crises of the family unit. They are called upon to transfer funds to finance treatments for affliction (requiring healing rituals, large "feedings of the gods," biomedical doctors' interventions, and/or hospitalization), funerals and other mortuary rites, and burials in elegant cinder-block mausoleums that may be more expensive and elaborate than were the homes of the people buried inside. Because accumulation is morally suspect in this society, an ambivalence typical of peasantries, the migrants are often themselves the targets of sorcery and spiritual affliction requiring costly ritual therapy at home, regardless of the victims' whereabouts.[4]

When, at the end of the decade of the 1980s, the kanntè migrants' tenuous status as entrants was resolved and they were finally allowed to leave and re-enter the United States without penalty, they extended the scale of "living" in Haiti while "pursuing a livelihood" outside. Men who had been gone for nearly a decade reunited with spouses who had "waited for them." Some of these women eventually joined their husbands in the United States. I helped Malgre Sa fill out forms required by the Immigration and Naturalization Service to allow his wife and their two teenage children to enter the United States, ending a 12-year separation. Alexandre sponsored the migration of his wife 21 years after he first organized the largest kanntè from Ti Rivyè, which carried two of their children in common along with 11 of his children from previous and current unions. Little Caterpillar was reunited with Maxia and applied for her legal immigration.

At the same time, migrant men also established new transnational conjugal unions with spouses who would remain in the village for the foreseeable future. (There are greater socially condoned opportunities in this field for polygynous migrant men than for normatively defined monogamous migrant women.) While he was arranging for his wife's emigration, for example, during one of his visits, Alexandre established a new union with a young woman with whom he now shares a son. Little Caterpillar was similarly reunited with his home wife, Maxia, and applying for her visa through the family reunification law, while he had a child with another woman in the village.

The migrants' repatriation of wages, building of "vacation homes," buying of garden plots, establishment of new, long-distance relationships, and seeking of therapy in the village demonstrate that their strategy is to invest in people and things at home, rather than to leave home for good in order to assimilate completely into the host country. Their aim is to live between host and home locations. A trip back home can be a short "doctor's visit" (*vizit doktè*) or an extended stay that may well appear to be a permanent return until another opportunity to migrate comes along.

Sending Money Home

Through imaginative appropriations of technology, the migrant and host locations of Ti Rivyè stay in constant touch. Relatives use recorded tape to "write" letters in vernacular Creole and to include far-off participants in rituals taking place back home. To exchange money and objects, they apply the same ingenuity to bypass the limitations of their (structured) underdevelopment, exploiting both the latest in communications and computerized banking technology and the most antiquated means of conveyance (mopeds, bicycles, burros, and feet).

Couriers circulate regularly between the home and a few key satellite destinations abroad. During the early 1980s, there were several upstarts in the enterprise of linking Ti Rivyè with its outposts in South Florida, but few lasted. Some mishandled remittances; accusations of diverting U.S. wages were occasionally brought before the local sheriff, or *chef de section*. By all counts, Ti Rivyè's first reliable transnational "postman" (*faktè*) was Antoinne Edouard, whom I first met in Ti Rivyè in 1983. Antoinne was a gentle, unpretentious, and quiet man. He traveled every two weeks between Ti Rivyè and Belle Glade and Delray Beach, carrying cash, letters on cassette tape, and suitcases full of gifts. In the village, residents anticipated his arrival. They would gather in the courtyard of his residence and listen for their names to be read out of a notebook by one of Antoinne's relatives, for he could neither read nor write. Antoinne's impressive cinder-block house with indoor toilet in Mercerie was his base in Ti Rivyè. Apartments rented by his relatives in Belle Glade and Delray Beach served as his "offices" in the U.S.

Antoinne grew up in Ti Rivyè. He migrated to Guadeloupe and spent 12 years there before returning to Haiti. His previous visa helped him to obtain another to the United States in order to start his "coming and going" operation during the early 1980s. Antoinne's warm, honest, disarming character was of course the basis for the community's trust in him. But his success was also the effect of his keen management of informal, personal relations of credit and debt called *pratik* (Mintz 1961). Antoinne secured the loyalty of his clients through his dependable honesty and by extending them informal credit. It was often said, for example, that when a mother in Haiti needed money, she could borrow it from Antoinne and ask him to collect the funds from her son working in Florida when he returned there two weeks later. Conversely, a migrant facing a crisis back home— expenses of an illness, or funeral—could ask and expect Antoinne to front him the money that he would repay when he could.

Evidence of Antoinne's success by the late 1980s was manifest in the construction of two new houses and the purchases of a rum distillery—one of the main economic activities in the town of Léogane—a pick-up truck, and a car. His untimely death in a car accident in Léogane in 1990 jolted both sides of this transnational Ti Rivyè community. Antoinne lost control of his truck on the highway in front of the Léogane cemetery. Sorcery seemed the only possible explanation for the bizarre event. While most narratives I heard attributed the loss of a hero to a jealous rival, one man from Ti Rivyè now living in Fort Lauderdale portrayed the courier as an evildoer, whose death was justifiable revenge for the murder (by sorcery) of a migrant man whose remittance money he stole as well. Several of Antoinne's South Florida clients went back to Haiti for the funeral. Many claimed they would never recover; my friend Malgre Sa, who sent money through Antoinne, said, "I don't think we'll find anyone like him again." But others have inevitably filled in. Yves, a younger affinal relative of Antoinne's, "came and went" for several years in the early 1990s before giving it up to be a supervisor for a construction work crew in Orlando. André, who "took the Canter" to Florida in 1980, became a courier and has since been succeeded by a man whose nickname is To.

At the other end of the lucrative money transfer business are big, licensed, capitalized firms, making profits not only from fees paid by migrants to send money home, which average 8–9% (Orozco 2002:9), but also from interest on the funds and by selling dollars for undervalued Haitian gourdes.[5] Western Union and MoneyGram compete with Haitian-owned transfer houses, including New York–based Hatrexco (now closed) and Boby Express, based in Florida. Ads for

Boby Express boast a toll-free long distance phone number, "money transfers arriving in Haiti by modem every half hour, fourteen offices in the United States and Canada and ten offices in Haiti." Ti Rivyè families can pick up transfers from Boby's location in the center of Léogane.

Working in the middle level between the likes of Boby Express and Antoinne are independent "agents." One is Gasby Alexis, who operates in West Palm Beach, which became host to natives of Ti Rivyè during the mid-1980s as they, along with other kanntè migrants, moved up and out of farmwork into the service industry. Like his counterparts serving poor Haitian clients in Delray Beach, Lake Worth, Fort Pierce, and elsewhere, Gasby offers money transfers, travel arrangements, immigration document translation and preparation, interpreting, notarizing, income tax services, fax, and photocopying. His office is also a music store, selling Haitian records, tapes, and compact discs. In addition, Gasby sells French-language Haitian newspapers and certain French-manufactured products Haitians cannot easily buy in the United States, including vitamins, over-the-counter drugs, and cologne. Gasby employs a Haitian man and woman who work part-time. The shop usually hosts a bustling social scene, anchored by Gasby's engaging personality. One sometimes gets the impression that people go there just to be part of it, and secondarily receive some of the services. Gasby's affability does not seem to have diminished in the face of some severe losses. In 1993, his partner in the food shipment business absconded with funds of his and his clients and he was unable to deliver the food or to pay them back. He has been held up twice. He

3.5. Alexis L'Express in West Palm Beach, July 1992.

3.6. Gasby Alexis at Alexis L'Express, July 1992.

lost everything because he, like his clients, relies on relationships with people, rather than on documents, as his insurance.

Gasby has told me he is from a poor family. He is in his late 50s. As a young man, he was a teacher in the northern city of Port de Paix and later worked for the malaria eradication project. He immigrated to the United States in 1968 and worked in factories in New York and Boston. In 1982 he began managing an office of a money-transfer service in Miami's Little Haiti, owned by his friend. His re-migration corresponds to that of other Haitian immigrants to New York and other northern cities who, as Alex Stepick (1999) has described, moved south in the early 1980s following the migration of tens of thousands of Haitians to south Florida. Like them, Gasby started a small service-oriented business whose market was the new migrants, migrants whose lives straddled and still straddle Haiti and the United States.

Gasby's shop hosted a long-distance telephone service that he called "Teleco," the acronym for the Haitian public telephone company that is a dependable source of graft for the kleptocratic state. The contrasts between the reinvented Florida Teleco and the original Haitian version were staggering. The one was a privately owned, modern, air-conditioned telephone bureau replete with conference call and call-waiting features and remote telephone "beepers." The other was an austere, dilapidated room, representative of "official" Haitian spaces, staffed by a partially competent and cynical worker. He operated an antiquated switchboard and a single black rotary phone. The "service" was pathetic. Many, if not most, calls were frustrated by poor reception and sudden disconnection. These contrasts recapitulated the patterned differences between the two locations in a transnational economy. The one producing and reabsorbing expendable labor (people) is chronically traditional and impoverished. The other, where migrants produce things, is modern and plentiful.

The patrons of Gasby's and his counterparts' Teleco (one competitor's business is called "Teleco Plus") were migrants who could not afford long-distance phone service in their own residences or who could afford the utility but wished to avoid its liabilities. They felt they lacked the self-control to limit phone conversations when talking in the relaxed setting of their own homes; the nouveau Teleco imposed the desired telephone discipline. Moreover, with home telephone service, friends would use the phone but not pay the bills, and relatives back home would called "collect" and they felt obliged to accept. I first visited Gasby's Teleco office, a storefront in the lesser end of downtown West Palm Beach, on a sweltering day in July 1992. Four telephone lines came into his bureau; clients entered one of four air-conditioned booths. Gasby, drenched in sweat in his little office in the back, for which he could not yet afford climate control, acted as operator. Gasby's counterpart on the other end was a state-employed operator in a dilapidated Teleco station, located in Léogane or any other Haitian town. Once the call was connected, each operator summoned the party to enter a booth and pick up the phone. Gasby charged his clients set fees for various intervals; a three-minute phone call to Haiti cost $4.50. He could manage several callers at once. Holding digital stop watches, he interrupted the calls from his phone: "you have 20 more seconds, do you want to double your time?" or "your time is up, kiss your wife good-bye."

Confronted by new technologies and markets for long-distance telephone service, Gasby, like franchisees of Boby Express, responded by dismantling his Teleco cabins, remodeling his office, and selling prepaid international long-distance phone cards. Some "agents" market cellular phones and service. Ads targeting migrants in Haitian newspapers encourage them to give phones to their family members back home. A few cellular phones have found their way to Ti Rivyè.

Gasby and other agents demonstrated similar flexibility in response to new impediments to their clients' transnational linkages after the military junta's overthrow of the Aristide government in September 1991. The international economic embargo imposed upon Haiti the following year threatened the survival of dispersed Haitian families. Ironically, the embargo of basic products headed toward Haiti coincided with the blockade of Haitians trying to flee the violence in their country. In a further paradox, the impoverished Haitian masses bore the brunt of the U.S.-supported embargo while American-owned transnational corporations operating assembly plants in Haiti were exempted from it.

With food prices in Haiti skyrocketing, the migrants were anxious about their remittances being squandered on food alone. In response, Gasby and other agents formed partnerships with Haitian-owned shipping companies based in Miami and began offering migrants food transfer services in addition to wiring money. Migrants placed orders with the agents for bulk quantities of oil, rice, beans, and sugar to be delivered directly to their families back home at costs far below Haitian prices. An outsider unfamiliar with the Haitian peasantry's market orientation might suppose that the food was intended only for immediate consumption; in fact, the migrants expected their relatives both to eat and to resell the food. The migrants endeavored, even during that desperate period, to supply home relatives with stock to start or expand a small trade. Despite the restoration of an elected government in 1994, food costs remain highly inflated, and migrants are still pressed to send food to their families.

The shift from wage to food remittances evinces the resourcefulness of these mobile families and their intermediaries. At the same time it highlights the historical and structural processes encompassing their home nation-state and society analyzed in the last chapter. The illicit movement of these drums of oil and 50-pound sacks of beans, rice, and flour sneaking around a fraudulent international embargo must be understood in the context of the harsh remaking of the Haitian peasantry, since the beginning of the 20th century, as a source of cheap, mobile labor supplying American-owned enterprises in the Caribbean and eventually in the United States itself. The American-led effort—officially termed "modernization and development"—to destabilize the peasant economy enough to encourage wage labor was abetted by oversupplying the internal market with imported, less nutritious food. At the end of the century, the exchange of migrants' wages for imported foods (whether as smuggled food remittances or as purchases in a Haitian market) continues to undermine local food producers, implicating migrants and home families in the very processes that further orient the latter toward out-migration as a survival strategy.

The food remittances thus reflect the structured impoverishment of this labor producing society, for whom producing migrants is a net loss, notwithstanding the magnitude of migrants' remittances to give back to those who produced them. Migrants nonetheless sustain the hope that their remittances will be used for more than consumption, to "make economy" that lifts their families out of misery and guaranties their bifocal life between Ti Rivyè and Mayami.

Waiting in Ti Rivyè

In a village that is "a nursery and nursing home for migrants" (Rouse 1992:28), one waits, just waits. Discouraged, unemployed young adults hold off pursuing local opportunities that, in a moribund peasant economy, are unlikely anyway to yield substantial returns. They expect word to come any day of the next step toward obtaining a visa that is being financed by a migrant relative. They remain in a suspended state of "not yet left" (*poko pati*), a term used to refer to any able person—a potential migrant—living in the village. Their elders are also waiting, waiting for remittances and visitors bearing money and gifts from abroad. "It is just waiting, waiting for money to come in" (*Se annik tann; tann lajan rantre*), I have heard over and over again.

This chapter began with my conversation in Ti Rivyè with cheery, ten-year-old Nason, who confidently predicted his future emigration in order to give life to his family at home. Nason, now a man, waits. He does not work. Still dependable and respectful, he is the chosen contact person between his migrant family and their home. He has the cellular phone paid for by his uncle, whose moped he also uses to transport local and returning relatives on the dirt roads of Léogane. In addition, he has been overseeing the construction of his grandmother's vacation house. Partly because the reliable Nason is most helpful to his migrant relatives if he stays behind, they have no immediate plans to send for him. Desperate to leave, he has been maneuvering to at least get to Bahamas. From there, he hopes that, against great odds, he can somehow cross over to Miami.

Nason's discouragement cast a pall over the first of our conversations during my visit in June 2003. I tried to counter his pessimism, as I recalled the optimistic ten-year-old boy.

> N: There is no work. Farmers [landowners] plant cane to give to the mill. They aren't planting anything else.
> *Pa gen travay. Farmers [landowners] plante kann pou bay nan izinn. Yo pa plante anyen ankò.*

3.7. Nason. Ti Rivyè, June 2003.

K: What about jobs in home construction? Every migrant seems to be
sending back money to build a house.
Ou pa ka jwen travay nan bati kay? Denye mounn ki pati ap voye bati yon
kay.

N: Yes, if you are the contractor. The rest work for $1.75 [a day]. It isn't
worth it. The only thing to do is live off Over There.
Wi, si ou se bòs la. Travay pou senkant goud pa anyen. Se annik viv sou
lòt bò.

I have encountered many young men like Nason who perceive there is no available work. Small cultivators nonetheless complain that because they cannot find
enough labor to plant food crops they resort to growing less profitable sugarcane,
which practically grows by itself. Ti Rivyè's inauspicious labor and land tenure
history, which made emigration in the late 20th century inevitable, are the focus
of the next chapter.

4

Peasants and Hidden Proletarians in Léogane

Powerful men don't sport their money in Haiti. (*Gran nèg pa joui kòb yo an Ayiti.*)

—*Creole proverb*

Sit, sit,
Sit comfortably Jean-Claude.
Jean-Claude, you gave us the factory.
Jean-Claude, you give us the roads, after all.
Sit, sit,
Sit comfortably, Jean-Claude.

—*Marie-Louise Clairant, April 1984*

This chapter traces the history of land tenure and labor in Ti Rivyè from the founding of a Catholic mission that consumed African slaves to produce sugarcane on its vast plantation to Ti Rivyè's contemporary activity as a peasant producer of future low-wage migrants and a consumer of remittances. The slave revolution of 1791, the result of a massive rejection of coerced labor, as opposed to a demand for political independence, gave birth to a freeholding peasantry. The ancestors of the people of Ti Rivyè seized their economic freedom by buying land, which they left for their descendants. Oral histories retold by their descendants implicitly rank economic victory before political triumph, praising heroic settlers rather than brave slave soldiers who vanquished the French.

Beginning around the turn of the last century, elites who were descended from French colonists and wielded state power took back peasant lands. Elders' lurid stories of outsiders commandeering their ancestors' lands are recounted here and are corroborated by evidence I uncovered in archives, company documents, and scholarly publications. The expropriation of these lands, the symbol and instrument of peasants' hard-won liberation, hastened the ultimate betrayal of the revolution. Descendants of people who fought to free themselves from plantation labor returned to the plantation as dependent wage laborers on the very lands their ancestors had purchased and left for them.

Sugarcane production has long shaped economic and social inequality in the Léogane Plain. The production of sugarcane in France's lucrative "pearl" began in the fertile Léogane Plain before expanding into the larger, and ultimately more important, adjoining Cul-de-Sac plain (Debien 1947). The community I studied, located in the center of the rural section of Petite Rivière II, was once part of a colonial sugar plantation founded by six Dominican *frères* who came to Haiti in 1696 by way of the island of St. Croix. The plantation (Fr. *habitation*, Cr. *bitasyon*) of Croix des Pères comprised 156 carreaux (201.34 hectares) and was worked by 180 African slaves (Moreau de St. Méry [1791] 1958:1107). (One square, or carreau, equals 3.14 acres or 1.29 hectares.)

Tangible relics of what residents today call the "foreign period" (*sou blan* or "during the reign of the *blan*") are pieces of foundations, irrigation systems, a water-powered sugar mill, and the ruins of the chapel of Sainte Marie Magdalaine. The site is an important local shrine frequented by pilgrims, who, illuminated candles and braided prayer cords (*kòdon*) in hand, beseech the saint to hear their supplications. What is locally known as Ka (or Kay) Pè, the Father's Residence, today covers an infinitesimal fraction of the colonial plantation. Ka Pè is a residential compound (*lakou*) with adjacent subdivided, minuscule gardens devoted mainly to sugarcane. The ruins of the colonial chapel and sugar mill are part of a 50-carreaux sugar plantation belonging to an absentee landlord from the capital (who grants pilgrims free access to their shrine).

After the war of independence in 1804, ex-slaves and their descendants faced obstacles to freedom as the state, eager to revive the economy, attempted to force them back onto plantations to labor as little better than slaves (Moral 1961:54). Jean-Pierre Boyer (1818–43), the second president of a united Haiti, for example, tried in vain to order rural workers to toil on specific plantations and to enforce harsh punishments for unaffiliated workers in violation of vagrancy laws. After this program failed, Boyer considered securing indentured labor from as far away as India and China, a tactic then being used by British colonists after emancipation of their African-Creole slaves (Nicholls 1979:68). Boyer also encouraged the immigration of African-Americans from the United States to fill the labor void.

After having fought for their freedom from plantation slavery, the Haitian masses were determined to preserve their economic independence. They used the purchase of land to resist Boyer's attempts to force them into plantation wage slavery (Mintz 1974; Murray 1977). It is important to emphasize that the peasants bought lands put up for sale; they were not squatters. The seller was the new Haitian state, at first only indirectly and, later, directly. Short on currency, the government of AlexAndré Pétion compensated military officers and civil servants in land. Active soldiers received the following grants to be held in perpetuity: commanders of battalions and majors: 35 carreaux, captains: 30 carreaux, lieutenants: 25 carreaux, etc. Military and civilian officers of the highest rank received a coffee or sugar estate. These grantees in turn put their concessions up for sale. In addition, the state turned to selling eminent domain to generate revenues. Because the sizes of the parcels were often quite small, many could afford to buy them. Through this legal mechanism the masses moved swiftly to constitute themselves as a smallholding peasantry and to resist pressures to labor on plantations in the name of reviving the national economy.

After 1804, the 156-carreaux Dominican friars' plantation reverted to state property under the principle of eminent domain, setting in motion a similar peasantization process. Charles-Mitan Marie, a colonel from Archaie, became its first private owner. (His tomb is in the town of Léogane. He was buried in the smallpox cemetery. The town sold the land and razed the cemetery, with the exception of Marie's grave, which now sits inside a private yard. His descendants have rights to visit and maintain the grave.)

Camolien AlexAndré was a direct descendant of the colonel. I had the great fortune to befriend Camo when he was in his 90s and the second-oldest living member of the community, still in excellent health. Camolien identified himself as a "Florvil person" (*mounn Florvil*) because he was born during Florvil Hyppolite's presidency (1889–96). He did not know his exact date of birth. Camo was respected for his esoteric knowledge of the long-past "foreigner period" (*lè blan*), and for his competence in the idiom he called "Africa talk" (*pawòl Ginen*)—the old rituals, songs and tales taught to him by the "old time people" (*gran mounn lontan-yo*). Inseparable from these skills was his command of the distribution of land and genealogical links that validated heirs' claims to their parents' lands. Even town-dwelling lawyers and notaries solicited the unlettered Camolien to document the land claims and disputes of their clients.

Camo explained how his ancestor, Charles-Mitan Marie, came to own Croix des Pères.

It was long ago, during the time of the regiment. President Pétion called him. He said, "How did they crush my battalion?" They sent him to a garrison. And then he won, he went, he fought, he won. He won, and by winning

4.1. Camolien Alexandre, Ti Rivyè, May 1984.

he proved to them that he could be one of them. He [Pétion] gave him the land grant, the [Kwa] Pè estate. Of everyone who had land there, only Charles-Mitan had rights, the right to own land.

Se te bagay lontan, afè rejman an. Prezidan Pétion te rele li. Li di, "Koman fè yo kraze batayon mwen?" Yo voye l nan youn ganizon. Epi, tou, li genyen. L ale, li bat, li genyen. Li genyen, nan genyen n, genyen an, li fè vanyan gason n. Li [Pétion] voye bay li don an, bitasyon Pè a. Tout mounn ki te gen tè la a, se Charles-Mitan sèl ki te an pouvwa, ki te an pouvwa proprietè a.

According to Camolien, neither Charles-Mitan Marie nor his heirs desired to maintain the estate. "Everyone sold, they sold over here, sold over there," with the exception of Camolien's maternal grandfather and his mother, who left Camolien and his full sister seven carreaux between them. The remaining 150 carreaux, 95% of the original colonial estate, was divided among those who "came to purchase" from Charles-Mitan Marie's heirs during the second half of the 19th century. Unlike the Dominican monks, Charles-Mitan left no physical remains of his presence in Croix des Pères. Nor did any of Charles-Mitan's direct descendants come to constitute a descent group who might have perpetuated his memory, in particular, through the creation of a mythical charter of their founding ancestor and the establishment of a shrine in a residential yard. Camolien and his sister lived elsewhere and maintained active ties with other descent groups. Their portion of seven carreaux was hardly distinguishable from the identical cane and peanut gardens adjacent to it. The owners never worked the land themselves but instead, as Camolien said, "gave [it] to sharecroppers" (*bay demwatye yo*). In Croix-des-Pères, Charles-Mitan Marie's memory has been obliterated.

Local residents instead remember and regularly consecrate the ancestors who purchased and bequeathed their lands. As one ritual leader explained, "Our first owners of the settlement purchased the land. They alone are our testaments." (*Prenmye mèt bitasyon an achte tè a. Yo menm ki prenmye tèstaman nou.*) The concept of "testament" in Creole is broad enough to encompass several related meanings. It can refer, as the English term does, to a written document providing for the disposition of personal property at death, validated by the signature of its creator and the mark of a notary. Testament can be used to indicate wealth or property bequeathed by a person. In the sense employed by the priest, "testament" approximates what we would call a testator, and this usage is always preceded by a possessive adjective or a pronoun. Regarding the first post-independence owner of Croix des Pères, Charles-Mitan Marie, this priest effectively acknowledged that he might have owned the land before, but he was not *our* first testament and therefore irrelevant to the inheritance group's charter.

> He's not our relative. The first owners of the estate bought the land. They are our first testaments. We invite them to attend our service. Charles Marie is not our family. We cannot invite him. It's the same as if you bought that car. Your children inherit it. It belongs to the descent group.
>
> *Li pa ras nou. Prenmye mèt bitasyon an achte tè a. Yo menm ki prenmye tèstaman nou. Nou envite yo asiste sèvis nap fè a. Charles Marie se pa fanmi nou. Nou pa sa envite li. Se tankou ou menm ou achte machin sa a. Pitit ou eritye li. Se youn bagay lafanmi.*

The concept of purchase by the first testaments is central to their present view of themselves, as Gerald Murray (1977) found when he investigated the history of Kinanbwa (fictive name) in the Cul-de-Sac Plain. Like Croix des Pères, Kinanbwa was once part of a colonial sugar plantation that was conferred in 1812 as a *don national* to a military officer. Murray comments:

> [T]he purchase of land by the *mèt bitasyon* [owner of the estate] was the major theme in the village's history of itself . . . they were unaware of the previous slave status of their ancestors; they never heard of Toussaint, Dessalines, or other giants of the Haitian revolutionary period. What they did know, and pass on to their children, was that the *mèt bitasyon* had come from elsewhere, had married a local woman, and—above all—had purchased land. It was here that local history began (Murray 1977:191–192).

This oral history is re-created during the prelude to virtually every ritual conducted on the former peasant estates located within the former Croix des Pères. Serving as the point of connection between Africa and the estate (deceased and living), the "first owner" is hailed as the source of the "authentic African" (*fran Ginen*) practices, the one who "took" the African lwa to this land and installed them there. The *gangan ason* (initiated priest with the Guinea rattle and bell) leads the kin-group in the meticulous, antiphonal recitation of descent from the African gods, or lwa, to the first owners who purchased the land, and to the ancestors, from most ancient to most recent.

Gerald Murray (1984) has argued that the first century of independence thus culminated in the peasantization not only of rural land tenure but of village ritual and theology as well. As the kin lines established themselves, so did they "install" their own anthropomorphic spirits, or lwa, which their children inherit according to the same model for passing down rights to land. Rather than one descent group inheriting only members of, say, the Danbala Wedo nation and another specializing in spirits of the Ogou (Ogoun) type, all kin-groups inherited the entire, indivisible pantheon whose individual divinities were nevertheless distinct from those inherited by neighboring families (Murray 1984:199). One inherits the lands left by the founder, along with his/her lwa bilaterally, through all four grandparents. The French custom of partible inheritance was thus carried over into Haitian laws governing the transmission of property.

Croix des Pères' "first testaments" established their estates between 1860 and 1890. The plantation was divided among smallholders whose estates averaged fewer than ten carreaux (13 hectares or 32 acres). The property bought by a man informally known as Tonton Ogoun (1830–75), for example, was one of the smallest: three carreaux. His father-in-law's land covered 12 carreaux, and between it and the beach lay another parcel of five carreaux (owned by his affines). Next to Tonton Ogoun's land was the largest estate, originally covering about 25 carreaux. Purchased in 1866 from one of Charles-Mitan's heirs, its owner, Mme. André, was a comfortably successful merchant from the southern region of Anse-à-Veau who had married a local man.

Consolidation of Peasant Lands

Only one generation passed before the small and middle-sized estates of Croix des Pères endured a devastating attack. Mme. André's descendants lost one-quarter of their estate; Tonton Ogoun's heirs lost two-thirds of their modest property; Tonton Ogoun's father-in-law's family lost 40% of their lands. A single individual initiated this assault using strategies deployed by elite Haitians to recoup the means of production lost to the peasant heirs of the slaves. He was a cosmopolitan coffee-sugar magnate whose business patronized a major German financial and coffee and cacao empire. His life and career exemplified the Creole proverb "Powerful men don't sport their money in Haiti" (*Gran nèg pa jwi kòb yo Ayiti*). He was born in Léogane and acculturated and educated in France. He returned to Léogane to pursue his fortune and retired in the Pyrenees to a chateau he nostalgically called "Ville à Léogane." Just before retiring to his chateau in the Pyrenees, he leased the vast, undivided territories, accumulated from countless small plots, to the new American-owned sugar company. Thus Léogane was incorporated into an expanding American sugar empire, an empire that designated and structured Haitian labor generally as a cheap, mobile work force in the Caribbean region.

His name was Joseph Lacombe. Joseph Lacombe had already amassed vast stretches of hillside coffee plantations before turning his attention to the Plain. By the beginning of the American occupation li 1915, he had consolidated more than half of Croix des Pères, which he could view from any one of four second-story verandas of the elegant mansion he built in the neighboring estate of Brache, whose 300 carreaux were also his dominion. In 1917, when the Haytian American Sugar Company negotiated contracts to lease land in Léogane (as well as in the Cul-de-Sac), they had only to approach the 67-year-old entrepreneur. According to Mozart Desmesmin, Joseph Lacombe's secretary and *l'homme de confiance*, his property extended "from the tip of the mountains to the sea, and across from Petite Rivière to Grande Rivière. He also had land in Mathieu, Tiapon and Bainet." His properties in the plain exceeded those of any other party with the exception of the state, from which he also leased territories, and they produced about 20% cent of the cane (West India Management and Consultation Company 1916:17).

For descendants of the "first testaments" of Croix des Pères, Joseph Lacombe had no equal. One Ti Rivyè resident reflected on Lacombe's omnipotent power. He said, "They would have made him president. He refused. He said, 'Poor people take that job.' He was the state himself. He had a prison at his house. He was greater than the president. No one could say to him [when he seized our land], 'What do you think you are doing there?' (*Yo ta ba li plas prezidan. Li refize. Li di se mounn pòv ki pran sa a. Leta ki tèt li. Li te gen prizon lakay li. Li te depasan prezidan. Nan pwen mounn ki pou mande li, "ki sa ou fè la a?"*)

Another elder recounted, "Lacombe said that the president could be his overseer" (*Lacombe te di se prezidan pou jeran ni*). (Overseers are expected to signal their inferiority to the owners of the properties they manage with marked deference [Woodson 1990:537–564].) Yet another senior characterized Lacombe's power using a play on the Creole adage, "After God, it's the state" (*Apre Bondye, se leta*). This peasant proverb "invokes divinity as a metaphor for the power and charisma of high office and the measure of social hierarchy" (Smucker 1982:66). (The Creole term for state quite aptly confounds the governmental structure with officials.) "Lacombe was worse than the government," he said. "After Lacombe, it's the state [government]" (*Lacombe te pi mal pase leta. Apre Lacombe, se leta.*)

Joseph Lacombe owned about 1,275 acres (400 carreaux) in the Plain, all but 30 planted in sugarcane. Piece by piece he annexed between 70 and 80 carreaux, about half of Croix des Pères, 13 carreaux in neighboring Merger, and 300 carreaux in the nearby *bitasyon* of Brache.

Among his holdings in Croix des Pères were the remains of the Dominican mission, the chapel, the irrigation system, fields, and water-powered mill. Brache, which President Boyer (1818–43) had allegedly granted to his mistress, became the center of Lacombe's sugar operations and a modern, steam-powered mill.

Lacombe designed and built for his wife a magnificent gingerbread-style palace in the middle of the Brache plantation, where they retreated during weekends. Joseph Lacombe's grandson, a French citizen and architect, told me that an article about this *perle de chateau* appeared in a French journal, *Rusticat*. The carved moldings on parlor ceilings were painted in gold; silk damask wallpaper covered the walls. While Joseph and his family relaxed in the splendor of the house above, hapless prisoners were, according to legend, confined to the dark cells of the prison below. (Several local residents made this claim; I failed to have Joseph Lacombe's heir deny or confirm it.) The guardian of the estate, which today lies in ruin, showed me two cells, one for women and one for men. After Lacombe, comes the state.

Lacombe's consumption practices epitomized the late-19th- and early-20th-century Haitian elite's faculty for "bovarysme collectif." Jean Price-Mars ([1928] 1983:8), founder of the ethnological and noiriste movements, adapted Gaultier's use of the term to critique the elite's "nostalgia for the lost mother country" and their antipathy toward "all that is authentically indigenous—language, customs, sentiments, beliefs." The impact of the elite's indulgences were not, however, frivolous. Their appetite for French and European luxuries skewed an already unbalanced trade, a legacy of a colonial economy oriented to monocrop export agriculture and imported staples. French and German commercial firms benefited tremendously from the tiny elite's enormous appetite for imported luxury goods, which the corrupt state helped to offset by taxing gasoline and flour more than perfume, wine, and lace (Trouillot 1990b:66–67). These asymmetrical commercial relations between the cosmopolitan elite and the metropolitan powers provoked and abetted the increasing domination of foreign interest in all sectors of Haitian commerce, the eventual eclipsing of the local entrepreneurs by power-

4.2. Joseph Lacombe's house, Brache, December 1983.

fully connected foreigners, and the ultimate loss of sovereignty to the United States (Plummer 1988:41–66).

These European creditors funded the coups d'etat that put the generals into the presidential palace (Plummer 1988; Schmidt 1971). Simmonds Brothers, the German banking and commercial firm, was the "collection agent" in 1915 for President Vilbrun Guillaume Sam (Plummer 1988:216). Simmonds connected Léogane, Petit Goâve, Jacmel, Dame Marie, Port-au-Prince, and Paris in its huge financial, coffee, and cacao orbit (Gould 1916:24). Simmonds was Lacombe's patron.[1] Camolien said, "Simmonds said Lacombe could be his overseer" (*Simmonds di se Lacombe pou se jeran ni*). If the president could aspire to be only Lacombe's plantation overseer, and Lacombe could hope to rise only to the station of Simmonds' manager, then the president was truly second class!

In 1984, I interviewed Joseph Lacombe's youngest daughter and only surviving child, Clotilde, and her son, who was visiting from France. Clotilde was 90 years old. Grateful for my interest in her father and the opportunity to speak about his achievements, she proudly talked of her family, aided by a lucid memory for names, dates, and details. Clotilde assisted her father in his business affairs. Hardly a native of "the mountains" (a pejorative for "outsider"), as Camolien described him, Joseph Lacombe was in fact a native of Léogane who grew up in France. His paternal grandfather, Charles, was the son of French colonists who owned a plantation in the Cul-de-Sac Plain. Clotilde described Charles as a kind of beneficent and benign rebel, who preferred the newly independent Haitian state and its population of ex-slaves to life in France, but suppressed his desire until after he satisfied his filial obligations.

> His parents were colonists. They left after the revolution. But then President Pétion, yes, I think it was Pétion who liked them very much.... They shouldn't have had to leave because they never had slaves and were always very good. Well my [great] grandfather, Charles Lacombe, who was 14 at the time, didn't want to leave. All of the peasants said, "Leave Mr. Charles with us." But his family didn't want to. And then they told Pétion to send him back to them. President Pétion wrote to him. My nephew has the letter....

> Ses parents étaient des colons. Ils sont partis apres la révolution. Mais alors le Président Pétion, oui, je crois que c'était Pétion qui les aimait beaucoup.... Ils n'auraient pas du partir parce qu'ils n'ont jamais eu des esclaves et ils ont toujours été tres bons. Alors, mon (arrière-) grand-père, Charles Lacombe, il avait 14 ans à ce moment la. Il n'a pas voulu partir. Tous les paysans ont dit, "Laissez Monsieur Charles avec nous." Mais les parents n'ont pas voulu. Et alors ils ont dit à Pétion de le leur renvoyer. Président Pétion lui a écrit. Mon neveu a la lettre....

While he was living in exile, Charles tended "un bon souvenir" of the island and once he achieved independence from his parents, he returned to Haiti. He founded a hat business in the capital and also repurchased his parents' property. A report of 1820 cites his plantation as one of only three producing sugar in the former colony's richest plain (Lebigre 1974:44). Charles apparently failed to perpetuate his love for this estate among his four children, two of whom stayed permanently in France. His great-granddaughter said that "He had so much property that he got buried there so his children wouldn't sell the property. But they sold it anyway." She also said that the heirs sold the property to the northern general and later president Tancrède Auguste, the most important producer of refined sugar, known as *sik Trankrèd* (Tancrède's sugar), in the Cul-de-Sac Plain.

One of Charles's sons settled in the capital, while the other, Démosthène, went to live with his affines in the town of Léogane. Démosthène married a daughter of Louis Kernizan, who until the middle of the century was *un grand spéculateur* of coffee. The Crimean War of 1853–56 paralyzed his commerce; during the conflict, one of his vessels, which was loaded with coffee, was seized. Démosthène assumed control of his father-in-law's failing business and eventually restored it to a thriving trade. The remains of the grand coffee house still stand, including a large residence (rebuilt after a 1918 fire), several smaller buildings, servants' quarters, a warehouse with an overhang above two large scales, and a cement slab used for drying the coffee. Behind are the ruins of the compound used as barracks by peasants who each Friday came down from the mountain between Léogane and Jacmel to deliver their product and "make provisions" (*fè provizyon*) the next morning at the town market.

Like many of the cosmopolitan Haitian bourgeois of the mid-19th century, Démosthène sent his children to France for their acculturation and education under the guardianship of their women (who were immigrants). After completing his secondary education, Joseph intended to remain in France, but his father, Démosthène, prevailed upon him to return to Haiti and succeed him in the coffee house. According to Joseph's daughter, he at first tried to decline. He had wanted to be a notary. But Démosthène issued him an ultimatum, saying "I'm not asking you if you want to. I am ordering you. I'm giving you an order to continue the family business." In 1868, at the age of 18, he returned to Léogane. His father died suddenly the same year, at age 42.

Under his father's management, the coffee operation had involved mainly speculation, that is, the purchase of coffee, or *kafe acha*, from the peasants. Joseph transformed the business into one based on the control of coffee-producing land itself; the peasants who leased his properties compensated him with their *kafe obligasyon*, "debt coffee," and to acquit themselves of the coffee debts, they paid with their land. Joseph Lacombe amassed vast holdings in the mountains, including such sections as Petit Harpon, Fond Droit, Orangers, and Citronniers. He soon applied a similar strategy in the plain, patiently acquiring piece after piece, in modest parcels of less than ten carreaux, and thereby concentrated a sugar plantation large enough to support two mills.

Lacombe manipulated to his advantage the contradictions between the meanings of ownership in the official legal code and in the customary system of law. According to the latter, the estates purchased by the "first testaments" belonged equally and indivisibly (unless all consented to division) to all members of the lineage descended from that ancestor. Private property, owned by autonomous individuals, was the rule of the formal legal system. The persons who borrowed money from Lacombe "gave him a land title to hold" which did not belong to them as single entities, but rather to the entire "inheritance group" (*eritaj*). When he called in his debts, however, Lacombe applied the categories of the official code, treating these persons as individual owners of private property. Whole descent groups lost their inherited lands, including shrines and graves, when one of their members fell in debt to Lacombe.

Lacombe, it is said, took farm after farm as collateral for loans of a few cents, seed, livestock, a turkey, even a plate of food. The stories describe someone obsessively collecting titles to the land holdings of the poor. Lacombe's *homme de confiance* told me that he maintained a tall cabinet in his town office that was "filled from bottom to top with peasants' land titles." The inheritors of Mme. André and Tonton Ogoun's father-in-law lost land, ten and nine carreaux respectively, to Lacombe through this very process. A man named Maurice, a direct heir of both founders, secretly offered both titles as collateral to Lacombe. When Lacombe seized a piece of Mme. André's testament, he "accidentally" annexed portions of property belonging to Tonton Ogoun and a neighbor that were adjacent to hers. "Lacombe took the whole thing. He found a bargain." Asked why Tonton Ogoun's descendants failed to reclaim their land, an heir answered, "He did what he wanted. There wasn't anything we could do." After Lacombe, it's the state.

Eliphat St. Fort, a man born around 1909, was old enough to remember when Lacombe spent weekends at his gingerbread palace at Brache. He alleged that Lacombe had an entirely legal racket to defraud residents of their lands.

> There was a lot of the land he grabbed that didn't belong to him. He was a con man; he swindled the land. He ripped it off—a slick man he was. You come and ask to borrow a little money, 10 piastres [2 dollars], 30 piastres [6 dollars]. For every piastre [20 cents], each day he would add one centime [0.2 cents] to it. The money increased. When you couldn't pay—you gave him your land title to hold. After the person died—he took a lot of land. He would never ask you. He knew that you wouldn't have enough money to pay him back. There were things that sold without title.

> Gen anpil tè li pran ki pa t pou li. Li pran n nan konbinezon, li pran n nan espri l. Li pran ni a kout daso-youn mèt danm. Li voye ou youn bagay prete. Li fè ou abi. Ou vin mande li youn ti kòb prete, 10 pias, 30 pias. Chak piaslap mete youn santim sou li chak jou. Kòb la monte. Lè ou pa ka peye, ou bay li pyès tè a kenbe. Lè mounn nan mouri—li pran anpil tè. Li pa janm mande ou; li konnen ou pa gen kòb valè pou ou peye a. Gen bagay ki vann san pyès.

"Attorneys, Surveyors, Notaries: All Practice Land Thievery"

Joseph Lacombe targeted peasants who were vulnerable because of their lack of familiarity with the official code. Moreover, because of the high costs of surveying and certifying legal title to land, many peasants avoided the process altogether and transferred parcels according to the customary system. Because so few had access to legal knowledge/power and so few could afford the cost of surveying and titling, notaries, lawyers, and surveyors commanded (and still command) inordinate power. A rhyming proverb satirizes their proclivity to abuse this power: "Attorneys, surveyors, notaries, all practice land thievery" (*Avoka, notè, apantè: tout se vòlè tè*). In Léogane, at least, lawyers, surveyors, and notaries are among the largest landowners. Yet the illiterate freeholders were not Lacombe's only victims. Lacombe allegedly took advantage of an upper-class neighbor's death to encroach upon his land. His widow tried in vain to fight him through the legal system but lost nevertheless, according to information given me by her granddaughter.

As for politics, it was Joseph's brother, Victor, who led a distinguished political career, acting as mayor (*magistrat*) of Léogane and governor (*préfet*) of the district (*arrondissement*) of Léogane, Grand Goâve, and Petit Goâve. The owner of a large sugar plantation in Léogane, who went to school in France in the 1920s and visited Joseph Lacombe at his chateau, said of Joseph's involvement in government: "Joseph was in politics in the sense that he told people, if you want a political position, give me one carreau of your land."

Joseph's mastery of usury, the land market, and the judicial system was a realization of his youthful desire to become a warranter of titles and transferor of property. He systematically registered with the town commissioner land transactions involving parcels as small as one carreau, allegations of coffee producers' usufruct agreements and outstanding debts, and his own leasing of state lands. Thanks to this documentation, which has been preserved in the registers of the local Bureau de Contributions, and to which I had access, I traced his manipulation of usury and the formal legal system to expand his dominion in Léogane. The Bureau of Contributions' books of Actes Civiles dates to 1875, the Actes Judiciaux goes back to 1904.

"*Joseph Lacombe, spéculateur en denrées, demeurant à Léogane*," or variations thereof, appear frequently in the registers from 1875 until 1917, the year that Lacombe "brought HASCO into" the plain. (At various times during this period Port-au-Prince is listed as his permanent address.) Indeed, in 1904 and 1905, his name dominates all others. These records corroborate the little peoples' perception that debts were the means by which he appropriated small peasants' lands. He seems indeed to have targeted as borrowers smallholders who would prove unable to pay him back, in order to acquire their property.

Four entries in the record of 1875, for example, document how the 25-year-old Lacombe manipulated credit owed him to appropriate an entire estate in the hills of Nérette. First, an M. N. sold five carreaux of the bitasyon Nannon, section of

Orangers, to Lacombe for 350 piastres (1 piastre, or 1 gourde, equals 20 cents), installments of which Lacombe had been paying since 1871. One finds an entry for later the same week titled, "debt," indicating M. N.'s obligation to Lacombe of 150 p., for which he mortgages eight carreaux of the same *habitation*. Again during that same week, M. N. sells the rest of the habitation—the amount is not indicated—to Lacombe for 7,532 p. Given the difference in price between land he purchased from this man and land he took as collateral, Lacombe appears to have mastered how legally to acquire land at very little cost to himself. Comparison with contemporary prices of land noted in the same register further corroborate the accusation that Lacombe "found bargains." A carreau of land in the same section sold for 60 p.; in this instance, Lacombe got eight carreaux for only 150 p.

These civil registers document contracts whereby persons leased Lacombe's lands in the mountains in exchange for annual payments in coffee. Rental of Lacombe's properties apparently yielded not only coffee, but coffee debts and through them, more lands. The following four excerpts from 1905 document his pursuit of one such coffee obligation:

1. On August 16, an M. A. is ordered to pay "without conditions or delay the quantity of 695 pounds of coffee at the price of 20 g. for 100 pounds; for a total of 139 g.

2. One month later the court issues a second order to the defendant.

3. In November, M. A. is ordered to pay fines of interest as well for "the sum total of 152 g., 81 c."

4. Two months later, two men deemed to be neutral parties, accompanied by police officer, seize M. A.'s property and land.

An item inserted in the record of 1915 collapses these separate phases into one:

On the part of Mr. Joseph Lacombe. . . to the citizen L. P. C. residing and domiciled on the Desiser Plantation, Citronniers Section. . . . The amount of 4100 pounds of coffee equivalent to a rate of $30. for 100 pounds guarantying this loan obligation. . . all of the real property that were left to heirs by his late father, P. C.

Through lawful racketeering of the judicial system and manipulation of the discrepancies between the formal and the legal codes, Joseph Lacombe transformed the property map of Léogane's mountain and plain. Ti Rivyè smallholders' 19th-century victory against latifundia agriculture proved even more fleeting than those of some of their counterparts in other regions of Haiti. By the end of the first decade, 1910, their myriad small estates of three, five, or a dozen carreaux had once again been consolidated into vast, undivided plantations. Ti Rivyè's topographical map now consisted of large tracts of the best lands —all Lacombe's—and, scattered and squeezed among them and crowded especially into the marginal lands by the shore, peasant habitations with their adjacent minuscule gardens. The land distribution today is the same. The aerial photograph taken in 1983 for the national sugar factory illuminates the contrast between the checkerboard of tiny plots and little shaded residential compounds and the spacious plantations. Each of these large, undivided plantations is a present or former Lacombe property. The latter parcels were sold during the 1960s to wealthy residents of Léogane and Port-au-Prince.

Ti Rivyè's peasants responded to the encroachment by becoming sharecroppers on Lacombe's vast holdings. Oral traditions give the impression of unlimited land to work and a Joseph Lacombe so desperate to recruit farm labor that he personally visited the peasant homesteads offering money to residents to help meet their planting requirements for sharecropping his lands. According to Eliphat,

> He needed to sharecrop his land so bad that he would come to your house and ask, "how much money do you have?" He loaned you money to plant his gardens. If you needed [to compensate] a work group, he would loan you money. [The cooperative labor group was typically compensated with a good meal and an exchange of labor.]

> *Tant li te bèzwen tè travay demwatye, li vin lakay ou. Li mande, "konbyen kòb ou genyen la a?" Li prete ou kòb pou plante jaden an. Si ou bezwen kòvé, li prete ou kòb.*

The local residents also responded to the encroachment by leaving for Port-au-Prince. They pursued opportunities in servicing the bourgeoisie (as cooks, maids, house boys, gardeners, dock workers), learning trades like tailoring, trading in the internal marketing of food and wares (a mainly female occupation), and, at the same time, schooling their children. There were few schools in the rural areas. Worse-off Ti Rivyè parents, feeling pressured to feed their children, sent them to serve as domestic servants with slightly better-off relatives in the city in exchange for room and board and, sometimes, schooling. Many of the elders I interviewed had spent part of their harsh childhoods in Port-au-Prince as domestic *rèstavèk*. Mika Jean-Jacques' parents, for example, consigned him to a better-off paternal aunt in the capital who beat him so badly that his parents consented to his pleas to take him back to Léogane.

Port-au-Prince's population grew from 26,000 in 1861 to 101,000 in 1906; one-third of the residents came from Jacmel and Léogane (Saint-Louis 1988:117;

Moral 1959:39). The growth of the capital epitomized the broad processes of centralization and corresponding provincial decline that had been fostered by the increasing foreign mercantilist domination. German- and French-owned businesses, which dominated as much as 80% of Haitian commerce, undertook to build centralizing infrastructure, which hastened the decline of the independent ports (Plummer 1988:57; Schmidt 1971:34–35). Most important was the German-built (and American financed) railroad connecting the plains of Cul-de-Sac and Léogane to the newly modernized Port-au-Prince wharf (Plummer 1988: 150).

Sharecropping in the Plain

To cultivate his cane, Lacombe employed the land tenure mode universally used on large plantations: *demwatye*, or "sharecropping." Accounts from this period describe the sharecroppers in the western plains in the most pathetic terms. Moral (1961:54–55), who synthesizes this literature, poses a contrast between the sordid fate of the sharecropper in the plains and the happy, independent small farmers in the mountains. The following description of the wretched sharecroppers in the Cul-de-Sac and Léogane plains was given by a New York management consulting firm in a 1916 report to the prospective financiers of an American agribusiness venture in sugarcane production and refining:

> The "de moitie" system, which is a system of half-and-half . . . is a most ingenious and wonderful arrangement. The laborer is supposed to plant, irrigate, cultivate and harvest the crops. The proprietor furnishes the land. When the crop is harvested and sold by the proprietor the laborer is supposed to get half of the proceeds. It is a mighty small half that he generally gets and more often than not he gets nothing, as "expenses" often eat up all the profit. The laborer has no way of getting "behind the returns" and has to take his medicine, although the landlord usually gives him a present to keep him happy . . . [He] has been exploited for so long by his own race that he has no ambition whatever left, if he ever had any (West India Management and Consultation Company 1916:26).

This arrogant report served to support a recommendation (on the same page) for shifting to wage labor—at one-third the rate paid to migrant workers (including Haitians and Jamaicans) at American-owned plantations in Cuba. The picture I gleaned from elder Ti Rivyè residents of "life during Lacombe" contradicts this pathetic picture but it, too, is biased. The contemporary legend invites idealization because it was relatively long ago, relatively brief (about two decades), and relatively benign compared to the ensuing consequences of Lacombe and his elite counterparts' compromises with North American capital. Mika, who was born the same year Lacombe retired to France, romanticized the life his parents and grandparents led under the patronage of Lacombe. He was himself sent to the capital to work as a domestic servant for a cruel aunt.

> Haitians were comfortable then. They built houses, had children. We lived on the land as if it were a grant. The sharecroppers took 3/4, and gave the owner 1/4. Except for the cane—he separated that equally. He had a mill. If Lacombe were still here, every Haitian would be rich. He made you live; he gave you the benefit. He had a lot of money, he gave charity.

> *Ayisyen te alèz lè a. Yo bati kay, fè pitit. Yo viv sou tè a kòm youn don. Demwatye pran twa ka, bay mèt youn ka. Men kann nan, li te separe egal. Li te gen moulen. Si Lacombe te la, denye Ayisyen tap rich. Li fè ou viv, li ba ou avantay. Li gen lajan anpil, lap fè charit.*

Mika's account corrects the consultant's misconstruction of the land tenure term *demwatye*. Although demwatye literally means "two halves," the sharecropper typically received and still receives between three-fifths and three-quarters of the harvest and, as Woodson (1990:514–516) points out, gets to eat from the harvest and pre-harvest as well. Sharecropping connotes the owner's beneficence, for instead of exploiting the more profitable labor of hired wage workers, an owner chooses "to make a poor person live" (*fè malere a viv*). (An owner lacking the cash to pay day labor and the wherewithal to work him or herself may also "give" land to sharecroppers.) Thus both owner and sharecropper get a profit (*avantay, benefis, garan*). "Making a garden" (*fè jaden*) even on someone else's land, gives the farmer "something to hope for in your future" (*youn bagay pou espwa pou demen*) —specifically, reaching the next status in the mixed tenure system, leasing and ultimately ownership.

Lacombe and his sharecroppers divided the sugar syrup equally between them —that is, after Lacombe subtracted the value of processing in *his* mill. Lacombe "got the profit" from the cane, then, in virtue of his control over the means of processing and distribution. The farmers, on the other hand, got the "benefit" (*avantay*) of three-quarters of the harvest of the interplanted food crops. These crops required more "care" (*swen*) than sugarcane, for once the ground was weeded and beaten and as long as it got enough water, cane was and is still thought to "grow by itself, like grass." The sweet potatoes, plantains, peas, corn, peanuts, manioc, melons, and cucumbers planted between the cane furrows furthermore confined the growth of weeds and reduced the labor needed to remove them. The sharecroppers controlled the distribution of the staple crops,

4.3. Tenten in his intercropped field. Ti Rivyè, 1983.

which yielded income and food throughout the year (unlike annual cane rattoons).

This "uneconomic" demwatye/intercrop arrangement baffled the West India Management and Consultion Company team who came in 1916 to study sugarcane production in the western plains on behalf of prospective American investors of the Haytian American Sugar Company. Despite the "great fertility" of the soil, the consultant firm reportedly saw only "wild" sugarcane in Léogane with the low estimated return of five tons per acre growing among vigorous peasant staples. This level of "inefficiency" satisfied Lacombe's mercantilist purposes but it scarcely met the productivity requirements of the agrocapital venture under consideration. The firm complained that:

> With very few exceptions all of the cane inspected was most inferior. . . . This very poor condition is entirely due to neglect, as right alongside of some of the poorest cane seen, we noticed peas, beans and corn growing luxuriantly. . . . These other crops of course, absorb a great quantity of plant food from the soil and give nothing back to it, for as soon as the different vegetables, etc., mature, the whole plant is pulled up and carried away, the vines, stalks, etc. being fed to the animals. If the cane survives after this treatment it is because of its natural hardiness and in spite of neglect by the farmer. He lives on the vegetables, fruits, etc., and if any cane grows on his land after he gets through, he considers what he can make out of it clear profit (West India Management and Consultation Company 1916:10).

HASCO's Coming to Léogane

Only four years after Greif submitted this report, "cultivated" monocrop sugar-cane had indeed replaced the undernourished "wild" cane and robust food crops on all of Lacombe's plantations. Cane was even pushing up on top of bulldozed graves of "first owners of the estates"; Lacombe had already appropriated the cemeteries, but left them intact for worship by heirs. Twenty-cents-a-day wage-laborers had succeeded the too-independent sharecroppers even though they were (correctly) suspected of cultivating personal legume and vegetable inter-cropped gardens inside vast fields of cane (cf. Moral 1961:146). The Haytian American Sugar Company (HASCO) had opened its operations in the Cul-de-Sac and Léogane Plains under the direction of none other than A. J. Greif. HASCO bought out the German-built (and New York Bank financed) railroad connecting the plains of Cul-de-Sac and Léogane to the Port-au-Prince wharf and completed construction of a modern mill on the north side of the capital with easy access to the wharf. (HASCO also added a two-and-a-half kilometer extension to the railroad running along the perimeter of Lacombe's property.)

Although the American administrators imposed changes in the constitution in 1918 and 1922, allowing foreigners to purchase land and to gain rights to puta-tively vacant areas of the national domain, HASCO purchased only 2,600 car-reaux in the Cul-de-Sac and none in Léogane, with the exception of sites for the railway and depots (Lebigre 1974:90). HASCO gained direct access to sugar plantations mainly through long-term leases from the landholding elite. Two-thirds of the land HASCO leased in Léogane belonged to Lacombe. HASCO leased all of Lacombe's lands with the exception of the 13 carreaux surrounding the gingerbread palace and the courtyard of the 17th-century St. Dominique chapel. Joseph Lacombe's daughter (and her father's accountant) recalled that HASCO paid him $6,000 to lease his lands for 40 years, beginning in 1920.

Eliphat St. Fort recalled the sweeping feeling of shock and betrayal when, all of a sudden, Lacombe expelled the sharecroppers. "Lacombe signed the con-tract that brought the foreigners here. No one knew it." (*Lacombe sinyen kontra a ki menen blan isit. Nan pwen mounn ki konnen.*) When Joseph Lacombe "put HASCO inside Léogane" (*antre HASCO Léogane*), he was 70 years of age and retired at Ville à Léogane in France, where several of his children permanently remained. HASCO's immediate offers of employment to dig irrigation canals, cut trees, and plant and cut cane initially drew many of the evicted sharecroppers. At first, Eliphat said, "Everyone was making money. The money was fresh." (*Denye mounn yo t ap pran kòb. Kòb la te frèsh.*) Mika said, "They had never seen so much money. When I heard someone had $20, I thought, 'that's too much money!' They carried it around in their hats." (*Yo pat gen lajan menm. Lè m tande youn mounn* *gen $20, "twòp lajan!" Yo te konn mete l nan chapo.*) Their enthusiasm waned, however, as they began to realize that HASCO's day work did not pay enough to "make them live." HASCO, not the laborers, got the "benefit." The laborers said they felt trapped in a syndrome where they earned only enough to eat that day and, to be able to eat tomorrow, had to go back to work. Mika, whose father was an overseer for HASCO, misplaced the blame for the wage laborers' entrapment on the Haitian salaried employees who managed the Léogane operation.

> In the beginning, when HASCO just came, it was better. Then later it was less good. At first, HASCO really paid out. They hired people to dig canals, plow, plant, cut down trees. They dug a lot of canals—The peasants used to steal some of the canals to water their own gardens. . . . It was good, when they first came here, the thing was sweet. But later it was us Haitians who ruined it. The foreigners gave the positions of director, controller, and manager to Haitians. . . . They did whatever they wanted. They wanted it all for themselves. . . . [The Haitian manager] didn't pay the people right. When you went to get paid, he came with the money bag. You earned ten piastres [$2.00], he gave you eight [$1.60]. Those people who built [small, private sugar] mills did it off the wages of the poor.

> *Okonmansman, lè HASCO fèk rantre, li te pi bon. Pit ta, li vin mwen bon. Lè li te nivo, yo mèt lajan deyò. HASCO peye mounn fouye kanal, bite, plante, braze bwa. Yo fè anpil kanal-peizan te konn vole kanal pou rouze jaden yo. . . . Li te bon, lè yo fèk antre, bay la te dous. Men pi ta se nou menm Ayisyen ki gate li. Blan bay Ayisyen pozisyon direktè, kontrolè, jeran. . . . Yo fè sa yo vle. Nèg renmen tout pou kò yo. Pradon mal peye mounn. Lè pou ou touche, li vini ak sak lajan an. Ou te travay pou 10 pias, yo ba ou 8. Ou tande mounn monte moulen, yo fè sa sou lajan malere.*

For the increasingly desperate wage workers, accumulation of property in Ti Rivyè itself by a corrupt, every-man-for-himself Haitian lower-level management was a cruelly tangible symbol of exploitation. At the root of their immiseration, though, were the occupation administration's labor policies in favor of capitalized companies, however unstable, like HASCO.

Mika hinted at one means by which peasants resisted HASCO's wage labor program: "stealing" water from the irrigation ditches. Mika's father certainly set an example. Titè used his low-level job as a field overseer to put land into food production. Because Titè shared with others the opportunity to subvert HASCO's piddling wages, he became a local hero. Any land under his management unsuited to cane production or inaccessible to HASCO's plows became a sharecropped garden. In addition, Titè hid gardens in the middle of vast cane fields.

Mika said his father's formula was one carreau of bean garden for every seven carreaux of cane. With smooth access to HASCO's irrigation, they were able to cultivate the most profitable and thirstiest food crop, red and black beans.

Richelieu Darius, who worked for HASCO as a young man, said that the "little money" (*kòb piti*) HASCO paid him was not enough to "make him live." In 1924, Richelieu left by foot for the Dominican Republic with one of Eliphat's uncles. He migrated seasonally until 1939. On his first voyage he was arrested; virtually all of the migration to Dominican Republic was and remains illegal. He was in "Balaon" (Barahona) in 1937 when 15,000 to 25,000 ill-starred Haitian migrants became Trujillo's nationalistic sacrifices for a slump in the sugar trade. A warning from a Haitian consular officer helped him elude death when other workers were rounded up and slaughtered.

> I cut cane there, whatever work the company demanded, any kind of hard work. They didn't pay well. It was for the company, an American company, the same as HASCO. In those days it was awful! After six months cutting cane you come back, people look down on you. You come back with nothing. . . . Over there they treat you worse, I mean, the company managers [who were] Dominicans and Puerto Ricans, too. They used to harass people. They would swear at you. They put us in barracks of 30 rooms apiece. Where I stayed wasn't so bad. What was bad was that they didn't pay you.

> *M te koupe kann. Depi sa travay konpani-tout vye travay. Yo pat peye byen. Travay konpani—Ameriken-menm a HASCO. Lè sa a, li pa t bon menm! Ou fè si mwa koupe kann; ou vin isit; yo mal regade ou. Nan pwen kòb pou ou vini. . . . Se lòt bò yo mal gade ou. Chèf konpani, Dominican, Puerto Rican, tou. Yo konn fè dezòd a mounn. Yo joure ou. Yo bati kay ral ak 30 chanm. Kote m te rete a li pa t mal. Se lajan yo pa t bay.*

Richelieu did not need prompting from the anthropologist to articulate connections between the desperation of former farmers in Ti Rivyè, the coming of HASCO, migration to the Dominican Republic, the migrants' insecurity as undocumented persons, and the vehement exploitation that continues unabated today (Lemoine 1983; Martinez 1991).

The Haytian American Sugar Company operated in Cul-de-Sac and Léogane for 60 years. Léogane's farmers supplied 25% of HASCO's cane, and three-fourths of the Léogane supply came from independent farmers of all strata who weighed and sold their cane at the many depots along the railroad (Lebigre 1974:89). HASCO competed for supply with the small mills and rum distilleries, who gave cane planters a better return. To bolster the new American firm during the occupation, the administration imposed a heavy tax on the rum producers, forcing many into bankruptcy (Moral 1961:65). HASCO nonetheless faced a chronic shortage, and in its sixth decade of operation functioned at only 40% of capacity.

During the late 1970s, despite dwindling cane production, the Haitian state launched into sugar refining. The Duvalier regime nationalized—or personalized among their clique—all sugar processing operations. After seizing control of the private mill in the Northern Plain and, temporarily, HASCO, as well, the state embarked upon the construction of a modern, Italian-built sugar factory. The site was the Darbonne village of Léogane, paradoxically close to the relics of the colony's first sugar mill (Debien 1947:19). The project drew criticism in unprecedented unity from all three bilateral lending institutions. Their scorn only deepened with subsequent revelations of the diversion of millions of unaccounted dollars earmarked for factory construction (Péan 1985:27).

The team of engineers and agronomists hired to run the Usine Sucrière Nationale de Darbonne typified the "technocrats" who repatriated to Haiti during the Jean-Claude Duvalier regime to promote business and industry.[2] Determined to defy critics and turn the USND into a successful development project, the energetic team initiated a comprehensive program of road building, canal digging, and agrotechnical support. This rural infrastructural improvement of course bypassed the town, which by 1984 had some of the worst streets in the county! A fleet of gleaming new John Deere tractors regularly crisscrossed the new rural dirt and stone roads, plowing large and small farmers' fields and hauling the cane to the factory on credits to be deducted from the selling price of the cane—virtually the only form of agricultural credit ever formally extended to Léogane's small farmers.

The residents' high expectations of the USND were even expressed in the setting of worship. In August 1984, during a ritual dance sponsored by an (absent) emigrant for the purpose of propitiating certain inherited spirits, Marie-Louise Clairant, a locally renowned singer, introduced two song verses thanking President Jean-Claude personally for building this factory. The songs were enthusiastically received by the chorus, who quickly learned the words to the antiphonal refrains. During Marie-Louise's recitative-styled solos, she articulated her expectations of further infrastructural improvements, including potable water and electricity.[3]

President Jean-Claude,
What you do for us here,
What you do for us here,
We send you our thanks.

You give us our livelihood.
You gave us the beautiful factory.
You built the palace.
You gave us the beautiful factory.
Yes, President Jean-Claude,
What you do for us here,
What you do for us here,
We send you our thanks.

Prezidan Jan-Klod,
Sa ou fè pou nou la;
Sa ou fè pou nou la;
Nou voye di ou, "mèsi."
Ou ba nou lavi.
Ou ba nou bèl izin nan.
Ou monte pale a.
Ou ba nou bèl izin nan.
Oui, Prezidan Jan-Klod,
Sa ou fè pou nou la,
Sa ou fè pou nou la,
Nou voye di ou, "mèsi."

Sit, sit,
Sit comfortably, Jean-Claude.
Jean-Claude,
You gave us the factory.
Jean-Claude,
You give us roads, after all.
Sit, sit,
Sit comfortably, Jean-Claude.

Chita, chita,
Chita kè poze Jan-Klod.
Jan-Klod,
Ou ba nou izin nan.
Jan-Klod,
Ou ba nou chemen, atò.
Chita, chita
Chita kè poze Jan-Klod.

While the Darbonne factory aggressively pursued its program to improve cane quality and increase production, the state imposed a scale of compensation destined to undermine these very incentives. The state refused to increase the price per ton (which had not been elevated since the mid-1970s) despite repeated pleas from the management of the Usine. Between 1970 and 1984, the price paid to the cane producer relative to the ex-factory sugar price declined from 51:49 to 29:71 in 1984, the lowest ratio in the world, according to an international sugar expert who visited Léogane (World Bank 1985:21). Yet the Duvalier state resold sugar for the internal market at several times the going world rate.

Despite the initial willingness of many planters to sell cane to the source of the first positive infrastructural development they had encountered, they sold more cane to some of Léogane's 38 "little mills." One "middle peasant" farmer, who was also the overseer of a large plantation in (former) Croix des Pères and the father of two sons living in New York, crystallized the cane farmers' poor choices between the factory and the little mills:

> The state wants to make us slaves. I sold my cane to the factory to set an example but I lost money. The [landlord] sold his cane to the little mill. Why should a small planter sell to the factory? If the government would raise the price of cane, even a little, the people would desert the little mills. The government has to decide.

> *Leta vle fè nou esklav. Mwen te vann pa m nan nan izin pou m te fè ègzanp, men m te fè pèd. [Mèt tè a] te vann pal la nan ti moulen. Pou ki sa pou youn ti kiltivatè vann izin? Depi leta monte pri kann nan, menm si se pa anpil, mounn yo ta kite ti moulen. Se pou leta deside.*

The "little mills" are owned by "big men" (*gran nèg*) of the town and the capital. Most of the syrup produced by little mills is transported to local distilleries, typically owned by little mill proprietors as well, to be made into raw rum. (Bakeries also purchase some of the sugar syrup.) State depression of the buying price of cane at the factories has also driven down the supply costs of the "little mills," which can still make a profit by offering farmers a 30% better return than the factory. Since HASCO's reign, the state has levied unfair taxes on the little mills in order to redirect the cane to the big factory.

The Darbonne management told me they considered strategies of buying out the little mills or undercutting them by producing their own syrup for the distilleries. Deficient supply thus continued to frustrate the USND and, by siphoning HASCO's already dwindling Léogane supply, the USND also crippled the latter enterprise. The Darbonne factory closed in 1987 by order of Leslie Delatour, the World Bank consultant who became the post-Duvalier junta's finance minister.

4.4. Just-harvested sugarcane field in Ti Rivyè, December 1983.

Delatour had criticized the Darbonne project in a 1983 report commissioned by USAID. The factory left a debt of $46 million (World Bank 1987:45).

Given the poor return for their cane crop, the farmers' decisions to keep planting it testifies to the dearth of agricultural alternatives in this increasingly arid zone. Small farmers turn to cane production because of marginalization to inferior lands, as well as the late-19th- and early-20th-century obliteration of the forests for exportation of dye and hardwoods and ongoing production of charcoal. Without access to good land and irrigation, the farmers are left with few alternatives to sugarcane. Cane requires lower rainfall and labor input than alternative food crops. Planting more lucrative food crops would, of course, require access to capital (or credit), irrigation, and labor, and, to justify these investments and improvements, greater security of land tenure. These microstructural changes could be effective only if the macrostructuring of the region as a source of production and reproduction of cheap labor were to change as well.

Hiding the Rural Proletariat

Sidney Mintz (1973:101) has described how proletarian adaptations are "embedded within . . . peasant communities, particularly where kin ties between the landed and the landless . . . affect the quality of economic relations." He suggests that the peasant society preserves its "peasant quality" by "concealing" the contributions of its landless, rural proletarians. This cloak benefits both capital, which exploits the "peasant difference" to extract more surplus labor, and elements of the peasantry, who stand to benefit most from the preservation of traditional peasant social and economic relations:

Peasant . . . communities almost always include some or many landless workers—Lenin's "agricultural proletariat" or "semi-proletarians"—whose sustenance depends at least in part upon the sale (or less commonly, on the barter) of their labor. It is far from clear how the presence of such persons, sometimes in large numbers, affects the specification of a "peasant" community; and, in certain cases, the difficulty may be compounded if the thoroughgoing "peasant" quality of the community is dependent precisely upon the presence (that is, the labor power) of these landless individuals. *Such persons may hardly be visible, figuratively and literally, in local affairs; in fact, the greater their alienation from the "typically peasant" pattern, the less visible they may be.* . . . In many situations, the landless laborers may be concealed, so to speak, by the nature of their ties to others and to the means of production, and by the particular character of life in these small agricultural settlements, where some self-sustaining peasant landholders live. This "concealment" . . . originates in several different factors. First of all, the landless may be the kinsmen of the landholders, and may even occupy the same household or compound. Secondly, such kin relationships, if they do exist, will probably color other ties between landholders and the landless. Thirdly, the exchange of goods and services between landed and landless (perhaps particularly if they are kinsmen) may not involve cash payment. This, like the kinship upon which it may be predicated, makes less simple and obvious the economic ties, since they are embedded in many-sided relationships of other kinds. Fourthly, the agricultural services rendered by the landless may differ according to whether the object of their labor on the land of others is to produce goods for consumption or for outside sale. Finally, where land is held in units by kin collectivities, households, nuclear families, etc., rather than in large estates, one would not normally expect to find a wholly uniform landholding group or class, in terms of the quantity or quality of land, or of the purposes for which such land is worked (Mintz 1974b:305) (emphases mine).

Cultural constructions of wage labor reinforced the structuring of Haitian labor as a low-wage mobile work force. Wage labor is degrading and, to avoid its extreme stigma, members go outside their communities (Smucker 1982:316–324). They work for wages where no one from their community can see it. Their wage labor is invisible. Thus, as Mintz (1973:94) has argued, "poor peasants permit themselves to be exploited so that they can remain peasants; and in so doing, they provide viability to the economic adaptations of those peasants richer and more secure than they."

Most of the men I interviewed in Ti Rivyè defined their occupations as independent farmer (*kiltivatè*) or fisherman (*pechè*). When I elicited their occupation histories, I found that many had performed some wage labor in their youths. Virtually all pursued this stigmatized labor outside, in the capital city or in other rural areas. "Outsiders" and "mountain people" come to Ti Rivyè to do the agricultural day labor. They are said to *fè djòb* (do jobs), "sell the morning" (*vann maten*), and "sell the day" (*vann jounen*). They are derisively called "jobbers" (*djobè*) and "zombies" (*zonbi*). Edouard was one of the "mountain people" doing waged farm work in Ti Rivyè in 1983 and 1984. He had also cut cane in the Dominican Republic. Edouard told me that "Where I came from, people criticize me [for doing wage labor]. That's why I came to [do wage] work here. People who go away will do any old job. People back home don't know what they're doing." (*Kote m sòti, mounn ap kritike mwen. Se pou sa m vin travay isit. Mounn ki pati yo fè nenpòt ki dyòb. Mounn lakay pa kon sa yap fè.*) The stigma of wage labor reinforces its substandard remuneration. Employers "do not give you a return" (*yo pa ba ou garan*) so that you can live and they are not expected to do so. The disgrace of working for a superior is profound. Recall that the condescending remark, "you can be my overseer," was used by peasants to show that even the rich and powerful can be cut down a notch with the dishonor of working for someone else.

Because selling your manual labor to another puts you in the most disadvantageous position possible, peasants go to great lengths to create occasions to "do personal favors" (*rann sèvis*; literally, render services) for one another. Taking in a poor relative as an unpaid domestic is one example. Sharecropping is another. Sharecropping is widely practiced in Ti Rivyè—53% of all plots I surveyed in the three contiguous estates involved demwatye. (These plots were equally divided between owned and rented gardens.) Sharecroppers along with owners and renters of plots also employed the extremely stigmatized wage labor of "jobbers." (Wage labor was used to varying degrees on 22% of all the plots I surveyed, including sharecropped plots.) As I noted above, despite the marked status difference between the "master of the land/garden" (*mèt tè/jaden*, less frequently a woman owner, hence *mètrès tè/jaden*) and tenant, the concept demwatye connotes some mutual respect as well. Instead of exploiting the more profitable labor of subaltern hired workers, a benevolent "master of the garden" chooses "to make a poor person live" (*fè malere a viv*). (A lesser owner lacking the cash to pay day labor and the wherewithal to work the land him or herself may have no choice but to "give" the land to sharecroppers.) Malgre Sa, who was a farmer before immigrating to Florida, explained the contrast between sharecropping and paid labor:

As long as you [do paid] work for another person, s/he will not respect you. A country person wouldn't respect you. Sharecropping is different. [Answers my question, does the master of the land respect you?] Is there respect? Yes, in a way because you work the land, you divide the harvest, you give him/her two [fifths], you take three [fifths]. Sometimes the master of the land doesn't respect you. He might not regard you as a person; he might make you feel inferior because you don't own your own land. He would say that behind your back. But there is definitely more respect than with paid labor. There are people—you work someone's land, he makes the person live. Paying people doesn't make them live. The thing [relationship] will never get to the point where the [owner] will respect you. When I was young, I worked [i.e., sharecropped] people's land, old people who couldn't work anymore.

Depi ou travay pou yon mounn li pa respete ou. Abitan pa respete l. Demwatye se yon lòt bagay. Gen respe? Wi, youn bò. Paske ou travay tè. Ou separe, ou ba l 2, ou pran 3. Pafwa mèt tè pa respete ou. Li pa gade ou pou mounn, fè ou konen ou pa gen tè. La di sa dèyè ou. Li gen plis respe ke anpeyan. Gen mounn, ou travay tè li, li fè mounn viv. Peye mounn pa fè mounn viv. Bay yo pa rive pou mounn respete ou. Lè m te jenn, m te travay tè mounn, gran mounn ki pa ka travay ankò.

In the mid-1980s, many of Léogane's sharecroppers suddenly lost their tenure arrangements and faced the humiliating prospect of rural wage labor. Small landowners no longer needed sharecroppers because the Darbonne mill was offering to satisfy their most formidable labor need: preparing the field for planting. Before the plowing-on-credit initiative, an owner too poor to supply and compensate the requisite labor for this most labor-intensive phase of cultivation would have "given [the garden] to a sharecropper" (*bay demwatye*). The sharecropper would provide all of the labor and often hire itinerant day laborers to cut the cane. (Indeed cane production, whose annual rattoons obviated the need for yearly replanting, flourished partly because of the farmers' lack of access to capital to pay agricultural labor.) In light of the monopsonistic state's repression of cane suppliers, large and small alike, the few landowners who continued to "give to" sharecroppers rather than the factory's tractors were lauded as particularly big-hearted for *fè malere yo viv*, "making the poor live."

In conversations with the Darbonne staff, I raised the issue that the plowing program had indirectly resulted in denying the young men access to sharecropped land to launch their independent farming careers. The director revealed that while the factory had not designed the plowing credit program with this particular outcome in mind, he regarded it positively. Sharecroppers meant inter-cropping and intercropping meant undernourished cane. Any obstruction to the parasitic food crops was a welcome blessing. The director's solution was to offer local labor a high enough rate to entice them to do it without shame. He said he faced opposition to raising wages from both the state and the planters, who, while receiving the lowest milling price in the world, were hardly receptive to reducing their profit even further with higher farm wages.

In 1984, Bo lost the two sharecropping arrangements that had been barely sustaining his family of seven. The owner took back the land after Darbonne offered the plowing-on-credit program. Bo analyzed his miserable situation in broad terms:

> As soon as they see that there could be a return (*garan*) from it, that there could be a profit (*benefis*), they don't want you to be the one to realize it. They don't want you to pull yourself up. They take everything that has a return in it for themselves. That's why the [big planters] plant cane and give you the sweet potatoes to sharecrop [a strategy also to confine the growth of weeds and the need to pay labor to do weeding]. If they saw there were some return in the sweet potatoes they would take that too.

Bo clarified that doing wage labor was hardly an acceptable alternative. "If you work for these planters," Bo said, "you earn 5 gourdes [$1.00] a day. You know what they call that, don't you? They call it 'selling the morning (*vann maten*).'" He used a repulsive tone. "I wouldn't do that here (*M pa tap fè sa isit*)."

I offered, "you would be ashamed to do it," to which he responded with an affirmatively French "voilà!" and extended his hand for me to shake.

Bo's reference to the degradation of doing "selling the day" inspired me to explain that it was just this type of work that his brother and cousins were doing in the United States. I described the corrupt system of migrant labor, underscoring the poor conditions of labor camps, the constant rip-off of wages, the violent crew leaders. Bo was interested and believing. I said that there were things—rights—that he would lose if he went to "Miami," rights that he had in Haiti. "People won't respect you. Americans treat Haitians like, like . . ."

"Animals," he filled in the word for me. "I agree with you, Kèl [a nickname he created for me after learning the English pronunciation of my name], but I wouldn't be miserable there. I would be doing something for my children. Here, I'm not doing anything. If you are doing 'selling the day' elsewhere, so be it. Because it is outside, you don't lose your self-respect."

Bo was desperate to immigrate to Florida but not yet desperate enough to enlist for the sugar plantations in the Dominican Republic. His three attempts to emigrate by boat failed. The first time he "missed the boat." The second time he and the other voyagers were arrested and held without charge for two months until a well-connected patron obtained (and purchased) his release. He waited several years before trying to leave again. He was the organizer of the kanntè of 13 people, including 12 men and 1 woman. The futile voyage ended tragically and weighs heavily on Bo's conscience.

They had gotten lost at sea, spending 11 desperate days trying to find their way. The woman was seasick and could not eat or drink. They turned back when she died. Anticipating arrest, he hid out for three months in the capital in the home of a man from Ti Rivyè, eating only bread and water. He returned in the middle of the night. The state did not prosecute him.

Bo's repeated attempts to escape in order to become a wage laborer outside were to help his family inside avoid proletarianization and remain peasant. Both capitalists and different strata of the peasantry have exploited migration to preserve the peasantry. The "greater" the pressures toward alienation, the more disguised the wage laborers and the more peasant the community appears (Mintz 1973:94). As will become clear in our discussion of the moral and ritual imagery and practice, pwen are spirits who do alienated Magical work for wages. Their vitalizing labor is also concealed so that they may yield the benefit of that labor to the traditional "African" system.

Summary

At the turn of this century, Petite Rivière's emergent peasants found themselves squarely in conflict with the processes transforming the Haitian peasantry generally into a supplier of a regional mobile labor force. Not long after winning their land revolution and their economic autonomy, however, the peasants' gains were recouped by a member of the cosmopolitan elite. In response to this encroachment and marginalization, they became his sharecroppers and they also searched for livelihood outside, especially in the capital. Foreign capital penetration had been advancing the centralization of commerce in Port-au-Prince at the expense of regional centers. German-American construction of the railway linking Cul-de-Sac and Léogane with the Port-au-Prince wharf during the first decade coincided, therefore, with the first important labor displacement to Port-au-Prince. The subsequent arrival of American sugar capital returned capitalized monocrop sugar production to the plain. Exploitation of local labor's comparative advantage induced more profound rural upheaval: monetization of labor, removal of land from food production, and, of course, internal and international migration. As "life" became increasingly estranged from "livelihood" for Léogane's residents, the area meanwhile became a magnet for poor young men from the other areas—the south, primarily—who came to be "jobbers" in the sugar economy.

In the wake of these displacements, a transformed kinship/ritual unit emerged: the "family" (*fanmi*) or "inheritance [group]" (*eritaj*). While Lacombe and HASCO were sitting on portions of the inherited lands and offering wage labor at artificially depressed rates to the very people who were its rightful owners, the descendants of the 19th-century freeholders Tonton Ogoun, Mme. André, Michèl Pè, and their affines were discovering their "authentic African" (*fran Ginen*) character. The claim to African authenticity veiled and compensated for the increasing monetization of labor, social stratification, and dislocation. The following chapter takes up the emergence and effects of these invented traditions on Ti Rivyè religion and society.

5

Discovering the African Traditions

Vèvè-lò it is the ounsi who makes the gangan.
The ounsi falls down, the gangan gets up.
Vèvè-lò it is the ounsi who makes the gangan.

—*A lwa song cited by Alfred Métraux in* Voodoo in Haiti.

Ritual and Social Change in Lowland Haiti

Despite continued academic interest in the rich and vital religious life of Haiti, with the important exceptions of Gerald Murray (1977, 1980) and Serge Larose (1975a), relatively little attention has been devoted to complex interrelationships between local level religious and social change. This chapter documents and analyzes ritual change in twentieth-century Léogane, demonstrating how practices attributed to ancient traditions were actually reinvented in response to the assault on the peasant economy and penetration of wage labor described in the previous chapters. These shifts, which were echoed elsewhere in the densely settled plains surrounding the capital city, involved the monetization of ritual including adaptation of practices in urban, temple Vodou congregations, professionalization of male ritual leadership (which old timers derisively referred to as "buying the *ason*"), and new rites of passage. These "invented traditions" were represented as traditional peasant practices, imbued with the timeless authority of the ancestors who came from Guinea, Africa. In actuality, the new practices were concomitant with the consolidation of peasant lands in the hands of outsiders, the increasing exodus of labor to escape internal wage slavery, and the growing conflict between a communal, family ethic of sharing and a modern or capitalist ethic of individual accumulation.

The literature on Haitian religion has used Alfred Métraux's ([1959] 1972: 60–61) distinction between "domestic Voodoo" and "public Voodoo." Elaborating Métraux's vocabulary, Glenn Smucker (1984:38) writes that domestic Voodoo, found mainly in rural areas, is "linked to inheritance rights and is economically significant in terms of the cost of ceremonies and the traffic in land. There are ceremonials with a public character but these are . . . traditional family rites of the *lakou* and have no connection to a temple." Public or "temple Voodoo" (Smucker's term) is characterized by a congregational structure based on fictive kinship ties to the priest (*gangan ason* or [*h*]*oungan ason*), elaborate and expensive rituals carried out by female initiates (*ousi, ounsi,* or *hounsi*), and a separation between the roles of performer and spectator. Métraux conducted his famous research on public Voodoo during the 1940s in Port-au-Prince and, at least on one occasion, in Ti Rivyè ([1959] 1972:236–243). The ethnographer ([1959] 1972:60–61) suggested that public Voodoo was fast displacing domestic Voodoo, not only in Port-au-Prince and the densely settled lowlands around the capital but in more remote areas of Haiti as well. As I trace the processes of ritual transformation in Ti Rivyè over the past half century, however, I will demonstrate that the motivating dynamic of religious change was not the obliteration of the domestic cult but rather the "domestication" of urban, temple practices.

Ritual and the Transformation of Descent

In areas of rural Haiti where peasants still control some of their means of production, the key social and ritual corporate unit is a nonresidential descent group. In Ti Rivyè, this unit is called either *lafanmi* (the family), *fanmi,* or *eritaj.* (Fanmi also has a more general meaning, as Larose (1975b: 498) notes, of "unrestricted ego-oriented [relative or] set of relatives"; eritaj literally means "inheritance" and can also apply to the inherited land, *tè eritaj.*) With the exceptions of Serge Larose (1975b) and, more importantly, Ira Lowenthal (1987), ethnographic research has ignored both descent groups—the only corporate group of any type in peasant Haiti—and the rich symbolic constructions of the idea of descent. While Larose (1975b:498) defines the unit as a "cognatic descent group," Lowenthal (1987:192) defines it as an "ambilineal descent group." He argues for the use of the term ambilineal, rather than cognatic or non-unilineal, in order to emphasize the conceptual differentiation of distinct family "lines"—for example, the difference between my great grandfather's line and my great grandmother's line (1987: 192–193). While one person's potential eritaj affiliations are multiple, in practice, persons maintain active membership in only four or fewer eritaj.

The fanmi/eritaj name typically commemorates the "first owner of the plantation" (*prenmye mèt bitasyon*). Members of the eritaj not only share rights in the family land, but, according to the same principles of ambilineality and partible inheritance, they also inherit through their blood all of the anthropomorphic spirits, or lwa, served by the founder. These spirits are "specific" and "exclusive" to particular eritaj (Lowenthal 1987: 216). The lwa's powerful sway over the heirs derives from their inclination to afflict or "hold" (*kenbe*) them. Careful reckoning of genealogy is critical to any diagnosis and cure of a lwa-caused illness. When a member falls sick, the medium typically divines that the offender is a lwa from a particular line of descent, e.g., "my mother's father's descent group" (Lowenthal 1987:224; Murray 1984:198).[1]

When eritaj members assemble it is only for the purpose of collectively propitiating their indivisible lwa. Feeding is the primary mode of placating, and exerting symbolic control over, the spirits. The portion of inherited family land where they gather to "feed" their lwa is called *demanbre*. This sacred, reserved property usually consists of a homestead (*lakou*), often contiguous with the original homestead of the founder, a shrine housing the vessels containing the spirits of the founder and the ancestors, and various other landmarks personifying eritaj identity—the ruins of the foundation of the founder's house or well, certain trees favored by various inherited lwa, or a cemetery. The inalienable character of the inherited land pivots around the need for the lwa to have a permanent place to consume, and, as Lowenthal has pointed out, the spiritual complement of the eritaj can ultimately be enticed—through the offering of food—into moving to a new, permanent abode. The spirits' acceptance and ingestion of food gifts on the new demanbre, in other words, personifies and substantiates the ties between the heirs and the new parcel of land.

Little is known about the beginnings of the eritaj during the nineteenth century. What I have been able to reconstruct reaches back to the second and third decades of the 20th century in the wake of a period of extreme social and economic disruption that culminated in the incorporation of Haiti as a periphery of the United States and the structuring of the peasantry as a producer of cheap regional labor. Joseph Lacombe encroached upon plot after plot in Ti Rivyè and finally amassed vast holdings. In 1920, he leased the plantations to the American-owned sugar company, HASCO. Consequently, legally situated on and among peasants' lands, HASCO offered wage labor at rates that "did not make people live." Residents were increasingly compelled "to pursue livelihoods outside" as disenfranchised peasants from other regions of Haiti migrated in to perform the wretched "work."

The continuity of the descent group depended on the international circulation of its members who remained tethered to their "first testaments" in Ti Rivyè. These collective connections were ritual feeding obligations at the site (*demanbre*) believed once to have been the founder's residence. A new cadre of professional ritual intermediaries, or *gangan ason*, became managers of these shrines. They introduced new rites of passage to establish (and control communication with) the "first testament" inside the shrine and, following them, the rest of the "dead" members (ancestors) of the descent group. They formalized a body of temple-voodoo-like liturgy, specialized roles for women, and core rituals epitomizing the identity and charter of the descent groups. They redefined the channels of communication between dispersing members of the descent groups and their gods. Having become indispensable to the relations between the lwa and members of the descent groups, no matter how far afield, the professional gangan ason were well situated to prosper from the waves of outmigration that had occurred over the preceding two decades.

The Gangan Ason Trade in Ti Rivyè

Gerald Murray's (1977, 1980) ethnographic study of the connections between economic and religious change in Kinanbwa (the fictive name of the Cul-de-Sac community where he studied during the early 1970s) sets the stage for our present inquiry. Murray's research aimed to substantiate residents' interlinked perceptions of greater use of paid ritual intermediaries, heavier ritual expenditures, and increasing incidence of serious spirit-caused afflictions.[2]

The first key shift concerned the role of the ritual specialist from charismatic, clairvoyant shaman to professional priest. Although the temporal frame is unclear, at some point a new cadre of professional gangan rose to prominence. Their source of power derived from a lengthy and expensive initiation ritual under the guidance of a well-established gangan. The novice was (and is) said to "take the ason" (*pran ason*), the sacred gourd rattle and bell used to "call the lwa" (*rele lwa*). ("Taking the ason" is actually the culminating stage in the initiation rite.) Through the use of the ason, the professional gangan created a monopoly on new forms of communication with the *inherited* gods, which, as Murray points out, obviated the pre-existing channels of access to the lwa, dreams and possession, that were open, at least in principle, to everyone:

> Possession . . . lost its oracular function. When instructions are sought from the [lwa], rather, a specialist trained in the use of a sacred gourd-rattle [ason] must now be called in. Working behind a closed door, the officiant summons the [lwa] and has them talk directly from a clay jug [*govi*] (1980:300).

Harold Courlander, who conducted his research between 1937 and 1955, quoted one aged man from Belladère who was quite cynical of the rise of the gangan ason in Port-au-Prince and the adjacent Cul-de-Sac Plain. Courlander had solicited this man's opinion of the new ritual of "mystical marriage" (described later in this chapter). The man's analysis of what had changed was that people could no longer *talk* to their inherited lwa (except by means of the professional priest).

> It [marriage to a lwa] is impossible. People serve [lwa], they do not marry them . . . Some of the things that are going on down there in the Plain are not right. They are not the old way. In the old days we did things differently. We did not always run to the houngan. *The grand famille knew how to talk to the [lwa].* Up here we don't do things the way they do them down below in the city (Courlander 1960:71–72) (emphasis mine).

Significantly, the man did not locate the rupture in communication between person and god; he dealt rather with the so-called grand famille and their lwa. The descent group could no longer talk to their gods. Neither could gods retain the faculty of speech.

Turning from the ritual history of the Cul-de-Sac Plain to Ti Rivyè in the adjacent Léogane Plain, I consulted Camolien AlexAndré, who had helped me reconstruct the early-twentieth-century local land tenure picture reported in the previous chapter. In his ninth decade, Camolien had a cynical view of the evolution of religious leadership in Ti Rivyè over the course of the century. He recalled when people like his father, rather than an elite few, "knew everything" (*papa-m te konn tout bagay*) to protect and nurture themselves and their families. Increasingly alienated from what he called "the gangan's trade" (*komès gangan an*), Camolien continued to rely on what his inherited lwa told him in his dreams:

> What I know, the gangan [ason] do not know. As soon as the lwa speak to me—you won't find me at dances or anybody's prayers. I don't go to the gangan. I didn't grow up seeing my father involved in it. . . . I am my own gangan. If I should do this, if it's that "root" [lwa], I see it all in my sleep. After that, I have nothing to do with the lwa.

> *Sa m konnen an, gangan pa sa konnen. Depi lwa pal avè m, m pa nan dans, prie pèsann. M pa al kay gangan. M pa leve jwenn papa m ladan n. Mwen se gangan tèt mwen. Si se fè sa, si se rasin sa a, m wè sa tout nan dòmi. Apre sa a m pa konn afè lwa.*

As for the ason, the rattle and bell apparatus used by the gangan to summon the lwa, Camolien clarified that the language of "giving" and "taking" the ason obscures what is, in fact, an act of selling and buying. He said that before, gangan absorbed their knowledge directly from Guinea. Some were thought to travel there (in their dreams and in trance) to the far-off homeland "across" or "under the water." Some of their Guinea ancestors were said to be gangan who brought their magical objects with them in a sack. (Contemporary shaman who are not initiated and do not run templelike congregations are sometimes called *gangan makout* or *houngan makout*, literally "gangan with a sack.") Camo's African ancestor, Christophe, for example, supposedly carried in his sack a sapling of the magically potent silk cotton tree (*Ceiba pentandra*) which he planted in a rural section of Léogane:

> Christophe himself came from Africa. He was a gangan. He came with a little *mapou* tree in his sack. He planted it and it became large. The *mapou* is still there but it is far from us, in the Gran Rivyè rural section.

> *Christophe sòt nan Afrik li menm. Li te gangan. Li vin avèk youn ti pie bwa mapou nan makout li. Li plante li epi li vin gwo. Mapou-a la toujou men li lwen nou . . . nan seksyon Gran Rivyè.*

Today the priests "buy" their credentials. Camolien called their qualifying ason "a purchased thing" (*bagay achte*). He dismissed the gangan ason's secrets as "a bunch of lies."

> The gangan of the old days had real knowledge but the gangan here have a lot of lies. Those gangan, they didn't give the ason. The lwa was the one who gave it to you. You went to get it under the water. That was called the Guinea ason. The ason these gangan give today is something you buy.

> *Gangan lontan te gen bon rezon men gangan isit gen anpil manti. Gangan sa yo, yo pa bay ason. Se lwa ki ba ou. Ou al pran ni anba dlo. Sa rele ason ginen. Ason gangan bay—se bagay achte.*

Although the gangan ason's power was something purchased, it came to be substantialized by kinship ties to the descent group, the inherited land, and the lwa. An (inherited) lwa is said to be the one who asks the gangan to "take the ason," while Loko, another ancient African Guinea lwa, presides over the initiation. Moreover, "calling the lwa (and the dead) with the ason," came to be deemed necessary for the most important and "traditional" rituals involving the descent group, the ancestors and their lwa. Through the formalization of new rites of passage, the gangan ason group guided the transformation of the descent group and positioned themselves as managers of the shrines on all of the large estates.

In the case of Ti Rivyè, the catalyst for these profound shifts in the ritual management of the descent group was an extremely charismatic and powerful gangan ason named Misdor. Misdor succeeded his father and grandfather in the role of gangan. But he was the first in his line, to use Camolien's words, to "buy" his secrets and then "sell" them to others. One of Misdor's younger sons, who played the lead drum at their rituals until he immigrated to Florida in 1986, estimated that his father "gave the ason" to more than 150 "students" (*elèv*) but that he had initiated far too many servitors (*ounsi*) to even approximate. This man eventually "took the ason," following in the steps of three of his elder brothers. Moreover, several of Misdor's grandchildren, including one woman, have since become professional ritual leaders in the locality, heading their own temples.

Misdor's house mediated new practices coming from urban shrines, and he apparently encouraged his son, who went to school in the city, in the appropriation of ritual practices he encountered in Port-au-Prince. Aiscar proudly told me, for example, that at the local celebration on All Souls Day, a raucous dance honoring the Gede lwa, "I was the one who brought the Banda here. I was at school in Port-au-Prince. I saw how they danced the Banda. I came here, and I did it here." (*Se mwen ki mennen Banda isit. M te lekòl Port-au-Prince. M te wè jan yo tap danse Banda la-a. M vin isit, me fè-l isit.*)

After Misdor's death in 1967 at the age of about 75, he was succeeded by two sons (of different mothers). The elder, Victor, was widely regarded as the most powerful gangan ason in Ti Rivyè, despite his declining health (he suffered from diabetes and died in 1989 at the age of 72). Victor succeeded his father at the shrine on their paternally inherited estate and he also managed two other shrines on maternally inherited land. Aiscar, a younger son by a different mother, managed a shrine about five kilometers away after replacing his maternal uncle in the role of gangan ason. As Victor declined, Aiscar asserted his authority to ensure that other local gangan ason, most of whom were his father's, brother's, or his own disciples, remained faithful to the traditions (however recently introduced) of his father's "house." Pointing to the temple where his father presided, Aiscar told me, "Misdor gave the ason to everyone [every gangan ason] here. Everything they know comes from this house."

Misdor had a keen facility for mediating relationships across class by playing simultaneously the humble peasant and the enlightened leader.[3] A tall man with a commanding presence, his charisma attracted the patronage of elite practitioners of "Voodoo" and foreign ethnologists. A key contact was Odette Mennesson-Rigaud, who conducted much of her rich research for the Haitian Bureau of Ethnology during a period of fervent nationalistic and *noiriste* interest in peasant folklore and religion. She was the guide of the foreign ethnographers who came to study Haitian religion, including Harold Courlander, whom I interviewed in 1993. "She was an insider, the outstanding non-Haitian. She knew everybody. She was the best informed of all researchers and scholars." Maya Deren (1953:13), author of *Divine Horsemen*, Alfred Métraux ([1959] 1972:17–18), author of *Voodoo in Haiti*, and Erika Bourgignon (pers. comm.) also acknowledge their debts to Mennesson-Rigaud.

In a 1951 article, Mennesson-Rigaud describes the charming Misdor welcoming his guests:

> Friendly and conscientious, he put us at ease right away. He is a peasant with an open mind who is happy to welcome you to his house and make you feel at home. Immediately, we had the same feeling as relatives who, on a happy occasion, would come to spend a few hours in a familiar place. (Mennesson-Rigaud 1951:38)

Misdor's son remembered Mennesson-Rigaud's presence along with other foreigners at a December 24th *maji* ritual that became so "hot," the foreigners fell into trance:

> Mme. Milo Rigaud used to take foreigners here during Magloire's term [1950–56]. Magic was jamming at Misdor's shrine—the 24th of December. Everyone lost it. Mme. Milo had escorted 15 foreigners. All of them lost it. . . . The Magic [music] overtook them, entered them. The Magic took over everybody.

> *Mme. Milo Rigaud te konn mennen blan isit sou Magloire. Maji tap tonbe Kay Misdor youn 24 Desanb . . . Se pa moun nan kay-la ki gen konesans. Mme. Milo mennen kenz blan. Tout te tonbe. . . . Se maji ki pran yo, ki rantre nan kò-yo. Maji te dominen tout moun.*

Indeed both Mennesson-Rigaud (1951) and Métraux (1954–55, [1959] 1972) wrote about a maji service celebrated in December 1947 at Misdor's shrine. Mennesson-Rigaud's (1951) article, "Noël Vaudou en Haïti," is a detailed description of the maji ritual, in which she praises his elder son, Victor, for his lead singing and Aiscar for his virtuosity on the lead drum (Mennesson-Rigaud 1951:46–47). Métraux ([1959] 1972:236–243) provides a lively description of the same ceremony.[4]

The foreign, academic audience may have contributed to shaping the ritual traditions emerging from Misdor's "laboratory." The elite's appetite for ritual, or Misdor's perceptions of their expectations, reinforced the trends toward codification of elaborate ritual performance. Misdor encouraged his foreign visitors to participate in the spectacle, even to the extent of "experiencing" trance. His successors have perpetuated his style. Outsiders from the capital and beyond come to view the spectacle in Ti Rivyè, and the Ti Rivyè gangan ason have gone with their drummers, singers, and other kin to stage "peasant" ritual performances in the capital.

Misdor's most profound influence on ritual practice in Ti Rivyè may have been his introduction of two rites of passage from temple voodoo: post-funereal mortuary rites and the initiation of women (*kanzo*). These practices were incorporated into the charters of local descent groups, transforming the representation and enactment of their corporate identity. Next is a detailed analysis of the emergence of these decisive ritual innovations.

The New Mortuary Rites of Passage

Death rites practiced throughout Haiti generally include wake, funeral (in a chapel, if possible), procession to the cemetery, and burial, if the "dead" (*mò*) wishes to avoid eternal disgrace, in an aboveground tomb. Thanks to the recent, massive labor migrations of Ti Rivyè's young, few of those at Home any longer worry about repose under the ground. After a church funeral and burial the nine-day mourning period begins, in which relatives and neighbors of the deceased gather nightly to mourn, chant Catholic texts, socialize, recreate, and cajole the dead (with food) to take leave of the living for the world of the ancestors. The culminating "final prayer" (*denye priyè*) may precede or coincide with an elaborate and generous banquet for the guest of honor—the dead him or herself—and for scores of discriminating relatives and neighbors equally presuming to be received with generosity and grace. Because this reception requires a huge capital outlay, it may be postponed until survivors muster the funds and assemble the key participants, who may be working outside the country.

To this ritual funerary structure practiced throughout rural Haiti, the gangan ason annexed the temple customs of "sending" and "retrieving the dead from the water" (*voyel wete mò nan dlo*).[5] Thus in Ti Rivyè, after "the final prayer," as part of a relatively modest ritual, the gangan ason today performs the ceremony known as *dragozen* that "sends" the spirit of the deceased "under the water" (*anba dlo*) far below the earth's surface. Before departing, the spirit of the deceased typically attempts to speak to the family but his/her fragile voice, sounded through that of the gangan ason, fades out before he/she can communicate anything substantive. The family is resigned to wait until the ancestor emerges to "speak" at the far more elaborate and expensive "retrieval from the waters" ceremony to learn more fully the circumstances of his/her death.

No sooner than a year and a day, but sometimes as long as several years later, the gangan ason, assisted by a corps of initiated female servitors (*ounsi*), performs the "retrieval." Because of the high expense, kinsmen often collaborate to retrieve several of their dead relatives at the same time. Although each family must purchase their own ritual objects and a new set of white garments and shoes for the dead, they may share the burden of fees for the gangan ason, offerings, and food and drink for guests. This collaboration lowers the cost for each unit. The voice of the ancestor is heard from inside a white tent, where at least two gangan ason—I have seen as many as four—are sitting. The main Guinea spirit authorizing the rite is Loko, the same spirit who confers Guinea authority to the gangan ason. Loko responds to the rhythmic language of the ason beseeching him to go and fetch the dead under the water. Speaking through a gangan ason, Loko narrates his journey to a faraway body of water where he encounters the ancestor, who only reluctantly agrees to move from the liquid oblivion into a basin of water that has been placed inside the tent (the dead's element is fluid; they cannot locomote on the earth).

The retrieval of the dead provides the frame for a "social drama" (Turner 1957). Everyone expects the ancestor to settle personal accounts as his or her spirit individually addresses each relative and close friend he or she left behind. The ancestor is thought to have been in a kind of time warp and to have no knowledge of what has transpired since being sent into oblivion. Neither is the ancestor able to see who is present. Hence the ancestor typically addresses persons who have since died or emigrated or who chose not to attend. The assembled answer in their stead, bringing the ancestor up to date on their fates or excusable absences. An unexcused absence may be interpreted as an admission of guilt.

In the case of Bréton, whose excruciating demise (in 1983) gossip blamed on the malevolence of his trading partner, the testimony of the ancestor during the reclamation rite a year later publically absolved the accused. The anxiety had mounted in anticipation of Bréton's disclosure. The ancestor was in no hurry to relieve the tension. He individually addressed 40 or so relatives, including the accused (the 18th to be greeted): "So-and-So!" (*Entèl!*) "Yes, sir?" (*Plètil?*) "What's new with you?" (*Ban mwen nouvèl ou?*) Suddenly the ancestor paused to explain the cause of his death: "a bad 'gas' curdled my insides [under my heart]" (*Yon move gaz andan vin kaye anba kè m*). The accused now had an opportunity publically to excoriate her slanderers in an indirect way, without mentioning anyone's name. "The whole country, everybody said it was me. It's not true." (*Tout peyi a, denye mounn ki di se mwen. Se pa vre.*)

The gangan ason through whom the dead spoke was Bréton's brother-in-law, Victor, the son of Misdor. Victor deftly managed the "social drama" regarding what caused Bréton's untimely death—manipulating the relatives' anxiety by delaying talking about the cause of death and then removing the albatross from the woman who was "falsely" accused. Victor also used this performative frame to question his own integrity in public and, thereby, diffuse doubts as to the veracity of his "secrets." From inside the tent or the altar room, where gangan ason alone have access to the spirits, the ancestor and/or lwa voice cynicisms that people assembled outside may be thinking privately. Thus Bréton's ancestor cautioned the surviving family members just before he departed, "A person didn't kill me. Don't let the gangan lie to you." (*Se pa mounn ki touye m. Pa kite gangan ba ou manti.*) Maya Deren cites a related example where an ancestor questions the financial motivations of the ritual specialist, to which the gangan ason retorts with convincing anger: "'Business must be pretty good,' [the ancestor] says to the [gangan], 'if the family can manage to pay your fees.' The crowd bursts out laughing, and the [gangan's] angry retort is lost in the noise" (1953:52).

The reclamation rite progresses with the gangan ason mediating the conversation between the bereaved and the ancestor until the lwa, Loko, barges in to terminate the dialogue. The departure of the dead leaves the microphone available, as it were, to certain key lwa with whom the deceased was known to have shared a special relationship. These lwa take turns addressing both individual members of the descent group and the group as a whole. At least one lwa can be expected to remind the assembled of the dead's outstanding ritual "debts." The threats by the lwa to harm the descent group if they fail to collaborate to "pay up" typically elicit repeated, earnest pledges on the parts of the assembled. The same gangan ason is likely to be the one to consult when the heirs begin to fall sick, to divine the lwa's continued displeasure as the source of the afflictions, and to direct the ceremonies required to acquit the heirs of the debt.

Once the lwa finish settling their scores with the family, the gangan ason and the ounsi perform a ceremony that uses fire to consecrate objects or people. Known as "burning pots" (*brule wazen*), this frequently required Guinea transformation ritual can only be carried out by specialists who have "taken the ason." At the close of the "burning pots," a vessel consecrated for the ancestor is set on the altar of the shrine next to those of the other ancestors. Henceforth, whenever a descendant needs to communicate with the ancestor, he or she may go to the shrine and employ the gangan ason to summon the ancestor to speak in the jar.[6]

Tenten was Bréton's half-brother (and also Victor's brother-in-law). Many regarded Tenten as the de facto historian of the community, and that is how I was first referred to the closest collaborator in my research. I inadvertently learned about Misdor's introduction of rites for reclaiming the dead during a conversation with Tenten about Bréton's reclaiming ritual. Tenten mentioned that he had witnessed the first "reclaiming of the dead" in the village, a fact of which he was genuinely proud. I asked him to explain. With great enthusiasm, he proceeded to recount the story of how Misdor removed his paternal great-grandfather, the founder of a descent group, from the waters below the earth. It was around 1937; Tenten said that he must have been about 15 years old at the time. Tenten recalled that

> they pitched the tent in front of the mouth of the well. Misdor and his assistant went inside—there weren't a lot of gangan [ason in those days who might accompany him inside as they would today]. He went inside with the ason in his hand. He called the lwa with his ason. Papa Legwa, Papa Loko —they have to come first. Papa Loko . . . went to fetch him. Papa Loko said, "The man doesn't want to come out!" He preferred to stay and make trouble.

> *Yo fè kad-la devan bouch pi a. Misdor e laplas li te rantre andan—pat gen anpil gangan lè a. Li te rantre nan kad la ak ason n nan men an. Li rele lwa ak ason n: Papa Legwa, Papa Loko—fò yo parèt avan. Papa Loko . . . l al chache li. Papa Loko di, "Misye pa vle sòti, non!" Li pito rete fè dezòd.*

Suddenly there was a loud splash that wet the people standing nearby, yet no one observed anything falling into the well. Because the ancestors are thought to need water—recall the basin of water inside the tent—the splash was a tangible sign of the ancestor's presence. The spray of water from the well convinced Tenten that what the skeptics said about the gangan ason was untrue:

> That's why, when people say they don't believe in what the gangan do, I say, "it's because you don't understand." It's the real thing. There is no science— they say they [the gangan] lie. They do real things. They really do take people out of the water.

> *Se pou sa-a—moun di yo pa kwe sa oungan fè-a. Se paske ou pa konprann. Se bon bagay, wi. Nan pwen syans-yo di se manti yo bay. E bon bay yo fè. Yo retire moun nan dlo vre.*

Although in contemporary practice the period of the "dead's" submersion in the abysmal waters rarely lasts more than a few years, approximately 60 years passed before Misdor advised his heirs that it was time to retrieve Tonton Ogoun from the water. I asked Tenten why his family had waited so long to retrieve Tonton Ogoun's spirit from the abysmal waters. According to Tenten, until Misdor's introduction of the reclamation of the dead, his family had not practiced the custom of retrieving the dead from the waters: "Long, long ago, they didn't take dead out of the waters. When someone died you left them there." (*Lontan, lontan, yo pat retire mò nan dlo. Mounn nan mouri, ou kite l la a*).

Tenten explained that his grandparents "did not understand the African Guinea ways back then" (*yo pat konprann afè Lafrik lè a*). Even though Tenten had frequently professed to serve "authentic Guinea" (*fran Ginen*) in the way of his ancestors (who were direct descendants of Africans), he was now asserting that those very ancestors were not familiar with the genuine Guinea practices! During the mortuary ritual, he heard the ancestor, Tonton Ogoun, imparting new ritual instructions to the assembled family, even though he now seemed to be asserting that Tonton Ogoun himself was not enlightened about these same ritual practices. Tenten's apparent innocence of the contradictions posed by that statement suggests just how convincingly the professional gangan ason had laundered the changes in ritual practice.

The emergence of the custom of performing the two-phased mortuary rite signaled a shift in the ritual "function" of the dead. Instead of being "out there," the ancestor could now be ritually transformed through the flames of the "burning pots" ceremony, contained in a vessel, and managed through the language of the ason. When the dead spoke through the clay vessels inside their shrine, it was to give ritual instructions. The ancestors now functioned, in other words, to solicit the fidelity of descendants to their (the ancestors') newly discovered authentic Guinea legacy.

The introduction of rites for retrieving the founding first testament may well have been the single most pivotal social innovation during the first half of the century. The mortuary rites of passage facilitated transformations of "the eritaj," the incorporation of a formal charter, and the annexation of a pseudoprofessional temple voodoo hierarchy. These changes in the minimal definition of "the eritaj" in Ti Rivyè account for the ascendance of a few "families" and the disappearance of many more who lacked the organization necessary to fulfill the "Guinean" spiritual legacies of their founders.

The Kanzo: Initiation Rites for Women

Misdor's influence on ritual practice in Ti Rivyè is also felt in the incorporation of temple voodoo's formalized ritual roles for women into the African traditions of the eritaj (descent) groups. At the end of the ten-day initiation the novices achieve the rank of ounsi, qualifying them to perform a specialized role in the lineage's core rituals under the direction of (male) gangan ason.[7] When I interviewed Camolien about the ritual innovations introduced by the gangan ason over the last half-century, the topic of kanzo seemed to exasperate him more than any other. In his view, the practice of kanzo was a racket for the gangan ason, who benefited not only from fees collected from the initiates, but also from their unlimited supply of "free" labor whenever the gangan ason was hired to direct a descent group's rites. Camolien said that

> Long ago there weren't a lot of ounsi. My mother wasn't an ounsi. We didn't have people who were ounsi. My mother—they inherited the lwa, they served the lwa. Now, there is no lack of ounsi. It's so the gangan can make money, beat the drums, pay—Long ago we didn't have this—all this nonsense. Now there is all this business. That's why I don't pay attention to them.

> *Lontan pat genyen anpil ounsi. Manman m pat ounsi. Nou pat gen mounn ounsi. Manman m—yo leve jwenn lwa, yo sèvant lwa. Kouniyè a pa manke ounsi. Se pou gangan fè lajan, bat tanbou, peye-Lontan pat gen bagay sa yo— bann tenten sa yo. Kouniyè a gen tout komès sa. Konsa tou m pa okipe yo.*

The formalization of the woman's role of ounsi had to do with the gangan ason's consolidation of communication with the inherited lwa and the countervailing decline of the oracular function of possession. There appears also to have been a shift in the usage of metaphors for possession: from possession as a means of speech to a mode of dance. The oracular sense of possession, conveyed by the image of "to speak in the head of someone" (*pale nan tèt*)—for example, "Ezili Dantò speaks in the head of Sirina"—has been replaced by a metaphor of display; that is, "to dance in the head of someone," e.g., Ezili Dantò dances in the head of Sirina.

Thus when I asked a gangan ason (who "took the ason" from Misdor) why there were no women in the community who had become full-fledged ritual leaders (*manbo ason*), he responded, "Men take the ason here and lwa dance in the heads of women." (*Isit gason pran ason; lwa danse nan tèt fi*). (In fact women came from elsewhere to take the ason from Misdor and his son but they did not "practice" locally.) It was less acceptable for men to become vessels for the lwa at public rituals, as Ravenscroft (1965:178) found during his fieldwork with Misdor and his family. Occasionally a gangan ason's body would quiver momentarily or appear to totter off balance. I was told that these involuntary motions meant that a lwa was attempting (in vain) to "mount" the gangan ason.

When the lwa manifested themselves through ounsi, it was not primarily to *talk* to the descent group, but rather to *dance* to the drums and songs. Put to silence, the lwa became virtuoso performers. However profound the truths that can be communicated through dance, possession-performance has been transformed into the least congenial setting for the lwa to speak directly to the heirs.

The lwa dance and gesture rather than speak. When they do converse it is through pantomime. The male gangan ason supplies the words to interpret the "charades" for everyone else.

Access to the lwa was now restricted to two channels controlled by the gangan ason: the language of the ason (more often heard from across the wall of a tent or shrine) and initiated ounsi women. Ounsi had become the appropriately mute "horses" for the lwa at increasingly spectacular and costly "services for the gods" (*sèvis lwa*), replete with drumming, singing, flag bearing, parades, etc. It was rare for a lwa to overtake the body of an heir who was not either an ounsi or preparing to become one. But it was not uncommon to see a lwa overtake a guest of the gangan ason, that is, someone who was not a member of the descent group and whose lwa was not specifically invited to the ceremony.

Kanzo and Affliction

The kanzo initiation today is a ten-day rite of passage during which novices "lie down" (*kouche*) in the altar room of the shrine in utter submission to the old, venerated, African, male spirit named Danbala Wedo. "Lying down for Danbala" (*kouche pou* Danbala) does not symbolize sexuality as much as symbolic death in preparation for rebirth into a new identity. The novices are dressed in white cloth and are treated as though they were delicate, vulnerable newborns.

The social expectation that every woman go through kanzo notwithstanding, it is assumed that a lwa "claims" (*reklame*) a woman to go through the rite of passage. The spirit Danbala Wedo typically communicates this request by "holding" (*kenbe*) her, that is, by making her sick. He temporarily releases her once she makes the commitment to get initiated.

In contrast to the severe, life-threatening afflictions caused by gods of the "hot" or "bitter" pantheons, illnesses sent by Danbala and other members of his relatively "cooler" and "sweeter" pantheon tend to be non-acute and chronic, and affect any part of the body. These afflictions are diffuse enough to accommodate a broad constellation of symptoms that nevertheless respond to one, and only one, remedy: kanzo. (The term is used as a noun, adjective, and verb). Our census of all of the households in the community included questions about ritual affiliation. The senior woman in each house was asked whether she was an ounsi, where she got initiated, her age at the time, the name of the gangan ason leading the rite of passage, and his relationship to her. (The same series of questions was asked about any other ounsi in her immediate family; i.e., mother, sister, child.) The next question posed to her was, "why did you get initiated?" The uniform response was, "I was sick." The 71 respondents identified headache as the most

Symptoms of Affliction Leading to Initiation

Symptom (English)	Symptom (Creole)	Frequency (%)
headache	*tèt fè mal*	41
respiratory ailment	*maladi lèstomak*	11
asthma	*oprèsyon*	
chest pain	*lèstomak fè mal*	
tuberculosis	*maladi pwatrin*	
virus	*gripe*	
spit up blood	*jete san nan bouch*	
fever	*lafièv*	10
digestive problem	*maladi vant*	10
eating up stomach	*manjezon vant*	
can't eat	*pa ka manje*	
stomachache	*vant fè mal*	
blindness	*pa ka wè*	5
sudden weight loss	*sèch debout*	4
toothache	*dan fè mal*	4
screaming, crying, madness	*rele, kriye, foli*	4
deafness	*soud*	3
other ailments	*lòt maladi*	8 (1.4 each)
leg ache	*doulè nan piye*	
breast pain	*tete fè mal*	
stiffness	*kò rèd*	
trembling	*kò tranble*	
fainting	*endispoze*	
rash	*gratèl*	

common ailment leading to the decision to kanzo (41%), followed by respiratory problems (11%), fever (10%), digestive ailments (10%), sudden blindness (9%), sudden weight loss (4%), and other suffering (15%) including toothache, hearing loss, emotional crises, and pain in body and limbs.

The afflictions cited as causal factors in a woman's decision to kanzo are not specifically women's illnesses. With the possible exception of breast pain, men suffer from these same ailments. And although most of the respondents were initiated between the ages of 15 and 44, a phase when fertility is of primary concern, not a single respondent mentioned infertility as a reason for kanzo.[8] No one mentioned "perdition" (*pedisyon*), the state of arrested pregnancy caused by spirits who shrink and "hold" a fetus in the womb until ritual resolves the condition (Murray 1976; Richman 2002). Neither did anyone link their reasons for kanzo with "bad blood" (*move san*) or "spoiled milk" (*lèt gate*), the diseases of sadness or shock suffered especially by women (Farmer 1988b). Hence the types of affliction and healing linked to Danbala's demand for kanzo do not explicitly mediate either a woman's reproductive processes or the embodiment of her interpersonal pain.

Yet the social aspects of a diagnosis and cure associated with kanzo have much in common with those accompanying the determination and treatment of "perdition" and/or "bad blood." Just as a diagnosis of emotions embodied in "bad blood" gives public meaning to a woman's suffering and spurs a critique of the actions of the individual causing her pain, so is kanzo a catalyst for bringing a woman's discomfort into realms of collective discourse and action. Kin get involved in (and feel empowered by) finding a diagnosis whose cause turns out to be an inherited spirit belonging not just to her, but to the family as a whole. A sister, daughter, wife, or mother who perhaps has been overlooked through benign neglect or whose personal crisis remains unstated may find comfort in becoming the object of others' special concern. For the whole period of kanzo she will be excused from providing for her kin and spouse, and from cooking and cleaning for them as well. She can also look forward to enjoying the respect accorded a woman who endures the demanding rite of passage and achieves the status of ounsi. These affirmative personal experiences enhance the effectiveness of the kanzo remedy at the same time as they reinforce the patriarchal authority of ritual leaders and the incorporation of temple voodoo practices into the charters of local descent groups.

Between the months of June and October in 1983 and 1984, most local gangan ason sponsored an annual kanzo for an average of six to eight novices. Until the early 1980s, Misdor's elder son, Victor, held *three* kanzo a year in order to accept all of the ailing women needing to be "cured." (No wonder Victor's younger brother said that Victor had initiated too many ounsi to count!) The public ceremonies and dances accompanying the retreat of the novices, and their emergence as ounsi at the end of the rite of passage, were the most important and festive social events of the summer season. They were attended by hundreds of white-clad ounsi and their relatives. Initiation rites were also competitive occasions for the gangan ason and their ounsi. People ranked the kanzo according to the "heat" of the music and dancing, the refinement of the ritual, how many attended, the generosity and etiquette of the hosts and hostesses, etc. (cf. Deren 1953:161).

The conspicuous expenditure of financial resources by the novices is a significant social achievement. Everyone is keenly aware that such-and-such woman has succeeded in amassing the considerable funds associated with the kanzo initiation: fees to the gangan ason, drummers, a lay Catholic priest, and the novice's

5.1. Ti Madanm and her niece, Michou, wear their clothes of initiation (kanzo). Ti Rivyè, September 1984.

5.2. Ti Madanm shows her beads of initiation, Ti Rivyè, September 1984.

5.3. Michou dressed her doll for initiation. Ti Rivyè, September 1984.

5.4. A chamber in a shrine where the novices are secluded for ten days, Ti Rivyè, August 1984.

5.5. Novices' limbs are passed over the flames of the burning pots, Ti Rivyè, August 1984.

5.6. Novices emerge from the chamber in public for the "feeding the head" ceremony. They form a procession, carrying their head pots, Ti Rivyè, August 1984.

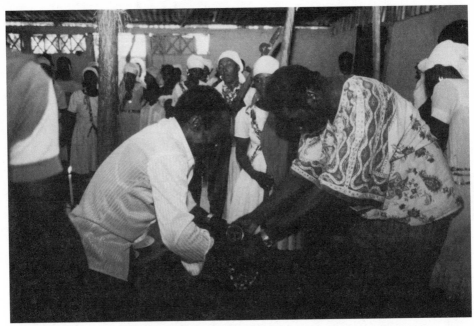

5.7. Gangan ason (male ritual leaders) salute one another with their ason in hand, Ti Rivyè, 1984.

5.8. Novices kneel as they are consecrated during the flag procession. *Veve* of Danbala Wedo, patron of the rite, are drawn on the ground in front of the novices, Ti Rivyè, August 1984.

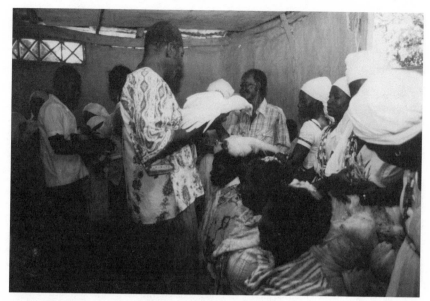

5.9. Sacrificial white chickens eat food placed on the heads of the novices, Ti Rivyè, August 1984.

5.10. Novices kneel before the sacrifices of the white chickens,
Ti Rivyè, September 1983.

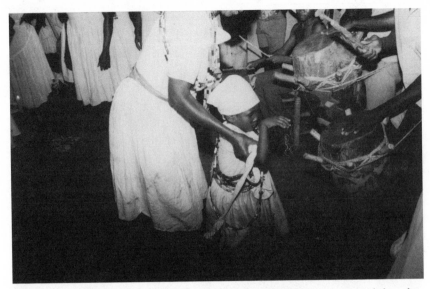

5.11. The dance at the ceremony. A girl who is being initiated with her mother is guided to salute the drums, Ti Rivyè, August 1984.

5.12. The dance at the ceremony, Ti Rivyè, August 1984.

5.13. The procession headed by the La Place, *gangan ason*, flag bearers, and *ounsi* on the beach toward the freshwater stream, Ti Rivyè, August 1984.

5.14. Spirit mounts ounsi and proclaims, "This is my first testament!" Ti Rivyè, August 1984.

5.15. Procession reaches freshwater source, Danbala Wedo's haunt, Ti Rivyè, August 1984.

5.16. Danbala Wedo arrives in the body of an *ounsi*, Ti Rivyè, September 1983.

5.17. Danbala Wedo welcomes the new *ounsi*, Ti Rivyè, September 1983.

ritual "mother" as well as purchases of ritual objects, three sets of new garments, sacrificial victims, various offerings to the gods, and food and beverages to be served to scores of guests on four separate public occasions. Not to be ignored as a cost is the loss of the novice's labor for almost two months, which means, of course, forgoing income and/or compensating someone else to take her place. Today, these funds come primarily from wages remitted by the ounsi's emigrant children, brothers, and sisters. In case the ounsi herself decides to emigrate, "she leaves," as Pepe, a gangan ason, put in, "on a contract" (*li pati sou kontra*). Should she neglect her lwa by failing to send money home for ritual purposes, the lwa, who can instantly traverse international borders, may show their displeasure by afflicting her with chronic illness, provoking her employer to fire her, or causing her savings to vanish.

Even by local standards (elsewhere in Léogane), this particular Ti Rivyè community had a reputation of being especially disposed toward the kanzo. One individual's perception that "every woman was initiated" (*denye fi kanzo*) was supported by my calculations that fully half of the adult women had gone through this expensive rite of passage and the majority had done so within the past decade. Some ounsi novices were young girls who had not yet been "claimed" to get initiated but rather accompanied their mothers into the altar room. Among the eight novices getting initiated at Tonton Ogoun's shrine in 1983, for instance, were four adult women and four girls ranging in age from 9 months to 15 years. The mother of the three-year-old told me that she had decided to take advantage of the reduced rate to initiate her daughter. She fully expected that the girl would eventually need to kanzo. Ironically, it was becoming increasingly common for ounsi to submit to the kanzo ordeal a second time, it having been divined that immunization conferred by the first initiation had lost its effectiveness.

The extent of kanzo initiations in this community provides evidence of profound success by Misdor and his sons in disciplining people to be good and loyal producers and consumers of new ritual "products." Women fulfilled their duty to "the family" by becoming ounsi and then expending enormous amounts of labor in the performance of ritual duties. But they also learned—as did their spouses, children, and siblings—the "good" habits of contributing lavishly to ever more codified and spectacular rituals. More than other "children of the lwa," ounsi and their close kin can be expected to contribute regularly and generously to the lwa.

The novices' confinement ends on a Sunday morning with a cheerful and festive rite of incorporation. The novices emerge from the altar room dressed in crisp, new dresses of sky blue but still under cover of large straw hats and towels. (Because of their heated condition, they are susceptible to exposure to cold.) The novices have not only recuperated; they are more beautiful than before. While standing among relatives and friends attending their emergence, I heard flattering comments as to how healthy the various fattened-up individuals looked.

After the lay priest baptizes the new ounsi, they fall into rank behind the gangan ason, his assistant (*laplas*), and the two flag bearers in an enormous processional of white-clad ounsi and their families. When the descendants of Tonton Ogoun and his neighbor, Mme. André, carried out this parade, their destination was a freshwater spring at the edge of the sea, the haunt of their respective Danbala Wedo(s). At the spring they would perform a ceremony invoking the divine water serpent. Two or more Danbala would appear in the persons of already initiated ounsi to welcome the new ounsi into the fold. The "serpents" would fall into the water with a great splash and wriggle around until ready to creep onto land, where they would be helped to standing by the gangan ason. The Danbala would perform the devotional greeting to the gangan ason, an acknowledgment of the authority of the latter, and then each new ounsi would greet the spirit(s).

On their way to the spring, the procession paused to perform ceremonies at certain sacred places (*demanbre*) that symbolized the history and charter of "the family": various trees that were "depots" (*depo*) for the ancestral lwa and the remains of the homestead of the apical ancestor—a piece of the foundation of his/ her house, the ruins of a well, or the stump of a tree (cf. Lowenthal 1987:275–283). The ceremonies included tracing flour blazons (*vèvè*) identified with individual lwa, libations, chants, flag waving, and often possession. As they knelt to kiss the flour blazons of the lwa identified with each of these sites, the novices were initiated into the spiritual legacy of "the family," united in a single web of connection with the lwa, the founder, the ancestors, and the family land.

At the climax of a kanzo initiation rite in August 1984, a lwa served by Mme. André, the founder of a descent group, mounted one of the heirs. Just as the participants arrived at the site by the beach where Mme. André's house once stood, an elderly ounsi named Yanpwin was overcome by Mèt Olokan. The lwa paraded back and forth over a narrow space loftily proclaiming "this is my first testament! This is my first testament!" (*Se prenmye tèstaman m! Se prenmye tèstaman m!*) Mèt Olokan/Yanpwin's declarations could have been heard as a proud and forceful affirmation of collective identity, a stirring testimony of the unity of the lwa, the descent group, and their land. The great lwa failed, however, to announce that only about a third of that testament stayed intact "for all the heirs" (*pou tout eritye*). Neither did Mèt Olokan/Yanpwin mention the unequal distribution of the land that remained, nor the relatively disadvantaged position of Yanpwin herself. Although Yanpwin was a descendant of Mme. André, she did not have access to her rightful share of the estate land. She controlled only her homesite in the maternal homestead she shared with her sister and nieces and their children.

Yanpwin's first (cross) cousin, Yvon, was the gangan ason of the fanmi. Yanpwin ritually addressed him as "papa" even though he was 18 years her junior. He could count on this ounsi to re-enact the "history" of Mme. André's estate. Significantly, Yanpwin underwent a "second" kanzo initiation by Yvon the following year. Misdor had initiated her along with her mother when she was a young child. At age 68 she again "laid down for the lwa" at the shrine established during the 1960s by Yvon's father, who had been a "student" of Misdor.

The grand processional of new ounsi during the final rite of incorporation culminates in a metaphoric sacrifice. The only other occasion when the whole "family" files in procession to the places on the inherited land that epitomize the descent group's spiritual charter is the ceremony preceding animal sacrifice at the annual feeding of the lwa. Just before its blood and testicles are to be "fed" to the lwa, a majestic bull, having been consecrated, cleansed, and adorned, is led among scores of ounsi and members of the descent group to these same sacred spots where the victim is physically identified with the land itself, the ancestors who worshiped there, and their spiritual legacy.

Considering the "positional meanings" (Turner 1967:51) of these two parades leads to the conclusion that the kanzo is also a sacrificial rite. Like the half-starved bull who has been symbolically turned into a splendid offering to the gods, cold, frail, "dried out" (*shèsh*) women are ritually transformed into "hot," "healthy," and "plump" ounsi. If, at the annual rite, the descent group sacrifices the life of the bull to the "hungry" lwa, at the kanzo they offer the fidelity of ounsi to Danbala and the rest of the "foreign" (*blan*) or "vodou" lwa. (Blan means foreigner and, because of the experience of domination by European and North American powers, implies light complexion.) These "alien" lwa paradoxically validate "the family's" rights (and use of discipline) over their future offspring.

The role of the "sacrificer" in the kanzo relates to C. A. Gregory's (1980) insights on the role of intermediaries in a system of "traditional" ritual gift exchange. Elaborating Mauss's (1967) distinction between "gifts-to-men" and "gifts-to-gods," Gregory (1980:645–647) suggests that the latter entail the "alienation of the inalienable" and, therefore, also imply the potential for accumulation. Intermediaries with the means of removal (of sacrifices and other wealth set aside for the gods) accumulate assets but no debts. The gangan ason are likewise intermediaries who can "remove" the ounsi's surplus labor offered to the spirits of the entire descent group. "Vèvè-lò it is the ounsi who makes the gangan / ounsi falls down, the gangan then gets up / Vèvè-lò it is the ounsi who makes the gangan," goes a song cited by Métraux ([1959] 1972:165).

The Guinea Prayer

The eritaj appropriated newly invented temple voodoo occupations into its authentic African charter. This charter is solemnly recited during the Guinea Prayer (Lapriè Ginen) at the beginning of virtually every ritual conducted on the estate. The exceedingly somber and reverent style of the Guinea Prayer proceeds in marked contrast to the exuberant drumming, singing, and dance that immediately follow. Accompanied only by the percussion of his ason, the gangan leads the group in dronelike antiphonal chanting of invocatory formula.

The Guinea Prayer is rendered by repeating a strophe in the esoteric ritual idiom called *langaj*, spoken only by lwa and gangan ason, into which a genealogy of names is sequentially inserted. The gangan ason solicits the assistance of the participants to complete the genealogy, who duly display their "genealogical erudition" (Lowenthal 1987:251). During the performance described below, for example, the gangan ason twice asked the assembled, "who else is there?" (The young gangan ason's need to ask this question can also be taken as a mark of his inexperience.)

Listening to the descent group's "genealogical myth" gives one the impression of an uninterrupted continuum of descent from the time of Guinea and the lwa to the moment of purchase by the First Owner of the Estate (Prenmye Mèt Bitasyon), the generations of his or her descendants, and, last but not least, the temple staff mediating the descent group's connection with its Guinea legacy. Thus the formalized temple roles have been completely integrated into the substance and identity of "the family" in Ti Rivyè.[9]

Let us take an example of the Guinea Prayer as it was performed during a ritual whose purpose was the establishment of a "spirit house" (*kay lwa*). The litany began by invoking the names of 36 of their lwa "nations" followed without a break by the title, Owner of the Estate. The gangan ason routinely chanted the title, Mèt Bitasyon (Owner of the Estate) by itself, without reference to any particular individual. Then, in the next strophe, he invoked the actual name of the apical ancestor who was the first owner of their estate; in this case, Mme. André. After Mme. André and four of her kin came the name of Mika, the founder of this descent group, who had purchased the land from Mme. André's heirs. Mika's spouse (mother of his children) and certain of his children and grandchildren were chosen to be honored apparently because of the greater involvement of their offspring in the particular service at hand as key sponsors. The Guinea Prayer next cited founders of affines of the ancestors. The litany ended with a listing of the temple hierarchy and the customary expression of pardon to any whose names may have been overlooked. The following is a list of the names inserted in the strophes:

Marasa (twins)
Marasa Dosu (offspring succeeding twins)
Legba Atibon
Loko Atisou (patron of gangan ason)
Danbala Wedo (patron of ounsi kanzo)
Aida Wedo (Danbala's partner)
Mètrès (Mistress) Ezili
Agwe Taroyo
Mètrès Lasirenn (Mistress Mermaid)
Mèt (Master) Olokan
Kaptenn (Captain) Charles
Kaptenn Balendyo
Oshenago Oshenagi
Ogoun Shango
Ogoun Balenza
Ogoun Batagri
Klèmezinn
Zaka Medi (a peasant)

Zakasiya (his wife)

Agaou Badè

Gede Nibo (patron of the homestead, cemetery)

Gede Ontou

Gede Denibo

Gede Majawè (the hot Gede, serves Magic)

Mèt Gran Chemen (Master of the Highway)

Mèt Kalfou (Master of the Crossroads)

Mèt Simityè (Master of the Cemetery)

Mèt Granbwa (Master of the Woods)

Larenn Simityè (partner of Simityè)

Simbi Dezo (Simbi of two waters)

Dan Petwo (Zandò escorts)

Ezili Dantò

Onman

Anmin Sinigal

Kongo Wangòl

Kaplaou Petwo

Mèt bitasyon (Founder of the estate)

1. Mme. André (first owner, who sold to Mika)
2. Joseph André (husband of 1)
3. Charles (??)
4. Ti André (son of 2)
5. Mika (founder of eritaj)
6. Agouda (founder's father)
7. Tonton Michèl (father-in-law of 8)
8. Tonton Ogoun (founder's father-in-law)
9. Titè (founder's son)
10. Prophète (founder's paternal grandson and father of sponsor)
11. Yaya (founder's sister)
12. Zina (founder's niece)
13. Lejena (founder's paternal granddaughter, mother of a victim)
14. Ti Bòl (maternal grandfather of 13)
15. Alenscar (founder's paternal grandson, grandfather of victim)
16. Dieu Grace (founder's daughter)
17. Grann Rosiette (founder's mother-in-law)
18. Grann Mina (founder's wife, mother of his children)

Manbo-houngan (shaman-priest)

Tout houngan (all of the oungan)

Laplas (houngan's assistant)
Hounsi kanzo (initiated female servitors)
Pòt drapo (flag carriers)
Houngantiè (first drummer)
Segondyè (second drummer)
Hountòman (third drummer)
Tout sa m konnen, tout sa m pa konnen a yo
(All of those I know, and all of those I do not know)

Ritual Change in Context

Although little is known about the social and ritual structures of late-nineteenth-century Haiti, generally, and Léogane, specifically, it appears that the first half of the nineteenth century was a fertile period for inventing traditions affecting ritual leadership and practice. The compelling Misdor appears to have been the primary agent of ritual change in Ti Rivyè. Under the guidance of this charismatic, well-connected leader, certain descent groups "discovered" their ancient and authentic Guinea traditions. Temple rituals and roles were incorporated into the substance and charters of these "great families" and henceforth mediated the enactment of descent. Those descent groups that were not so transformed eventually disappeared. After Misdor's death, his charismatic sons, Victor and Aiscar, worked to insure that everyone else remained faithful to the traditions of his "house."

The perception of Misdor's ritual innovations as authentic Guinea traditions handed down by the "first owners of the estate" concealed the fact that they were *bagay achte*, "things you buy," born out of money. Ritual practices had been thoroughly monetized, elaborate and spectacular. Professionals mediated access to the ancestors and the lwa; a member of "the family" had to employ the gangan ason to "talk" to the ancestors and inherited lwa because possession and dreaming had lost their oracular functions. The concept of "claiming" was redefined such that an inherited lwa "held" a person to buy power, that is, to get initiated. Loko, the refined, priestly, inherited lwa who legitimizes the gangan ason's authority and rescues the "dead" from the abyss, is said to "claim" his "godchild" (*fiyèl*) to *purchase* his privileged access to the Guinea cosmos. The metaphor of the Catholic ritual godparent-godchild relationship is apt. In a godparent-godchild relationship, a contractual relationship (which may overlap with kinship since godparents are often close relatives) becomes substantialized. The children of ritual co-parents refer to one another as "brother" and "sister" and they and their children are prohibited from marrying one another.

In the wake of the turbulent incorporation of peasant land and labor into the expanding American empire, the descent group was being redefined as a traditionally African Guinea ritual unit. By the time Tonton Ogoun's heirs retrieved him from the abysmal waters, for example, the Haytian American Sugar Company was sitting on half of the estate (which they had leased from Joseph Lacombe) and offering wage labor to the very people who were its rightful owners (at artificially depressed rates insuring the corporation's comparative advantage). Even as outsiders violated the founders' estates, "the family" accorded their founders the status of deities (but not lwa). The shrine, which became a constitutive symbol for the descent group, housed the spirit of the "first testament" in a clay jar surrounded by vessels containing the spirits of all other ancestors whose spirits had been reclaimed from the waters below the earth. Places where the first "testament" (*tèstaman*) once dwelled or fetched water or served lwa became sacred sites (*demanbre*) worshiped during "the family's" core rituals.

These transformations can be understood in terms of a tension between substance and contract. The nineteenth-century lawyer and ethnologist Sir Henry Maine viewed modernity as a "movement from status to contract" (Maine [1884] 1970:165). David Schneider (1968) and Steve Barnett and Martin Silverman (1979) have invoked Maine's model of substance and contract in their ethnographies of kinship and other social relations in alienated and nonalienated contexts. Substance has to do with things internal and inseparable from persons. In the Ti Rivyè case, substance is blood, feeding, and descent. Contractualized relations, on the other hand, are established between putatively independent, free, autonomous actors; they refer to things that are separable from persons, and they are realized by the exchange of money for something else. The alienation of people from their means of production and the sale of their labor power to capital is the quintessence of contract. Ritual transformation in Ti Rivyè involved both the contractualization of substance and the substantialization of contract. The expectation that full-fledged female heirs should pay to become initiated ounsi in order to "feed" their supposedly indivisible and inseparable spirits is an example of the commodification of an inherent or substantial relation. The discovery of the substantializing discourses of Guinea and "the family" to authenticate—and disguise—the new monetized ritual relations is an instance of the personalization of an impersonal, commodified practice. The domestication of temple voodoo was not a movement from status to contract, but rather a dialectic between substance (status) and contract.

This dialectic was a cultural and religious reformulation of the *equivocal* incorporation of peasants as both producers of exportable, alienated wage labor (contract) and producers of traditional peasants and traditional peasant culture (substance). Cloaking or concealing the vital essence (or pwen) of this incorporation was a "moral" imperative for all parties concerned: capitalists, local mercantile elites, authentically Guinea peasants, and rural proletarians, who acquiesced to exporting their alienation *so that those at home could remain peasants.* All parties collaborated in preserving the nonalienated, peasant character of their society. The dialectical ritual processes that simultaneously resolved and perpetuated this emerging ethical contradiction are explored in chapters 6 and 7.

6

The Dialectic of Guinea and Magic

Tie the bale, tie the bale,
The children don't know what I did.
Tie the bale, tie the bale,
The children don't know what's in the homestead.
Tie the bale, tie the bale,
The children don't know what their father served.
Tie the bale, tie the bale,
The children don't know what he celebrated.
Tie the bale, tie the bale,
The children don't know how the lwa was served.
Tie the bale, tie the bale,
The children don't know what the lwa eats.

—*Petwo/Zandò Lwa Song led by Pepe Michel at a ceremony in Ti Rivyè, April 1988*

The difference between lwa and pwen is like the difference between Regular
and Diet Pepsi. Regular Pepsi and Diet Pepsi are not the same.

—*Mercina D'Haïti, November 1989*

The more weakened and compromised a peasantry, the more traditionally peasant its invented customs may be made to appear. Guinea ritual discourse expanded while the local agricultural producers were being disrupted, undermined, and annexed as producers and feeders of mobile wage labor. The discourse privileged peasant morality so that the peasants' increasing acclimation to alienated (wage) labor could be concealed. The peasants'—and the dominant classes'—

ambivalence to proletarians was reformulated in Guinea's ambivalence toward Magic's pwen. This "bad" pwen represented "work" and "making money." The labor was sold and purchased by corrupt, ambitious individuals. It was alienated outside. I argue that although Guinea repudiated "pursuit," it depended on the incorporation of Magic's hot, life-giving contagion, just as the peasant system required the labor of proletarians in order to remain peasant. To maintain its authority, Guinea concealed this dependency. I will demonstrate how ritual processes incorporated pwen's vitality into Guinea and, at the same time, upheld Guinea's moral superiority.

Guinea and Magic

While investigating the Guinea-Magic dialectic in relation to broader social and economic changes will require charting a new course of inquiry, it will also entail assimilating the contributions of three ethnographers in particular. Maya Deren (1953), first of all, broke new ground in her elegant and meditative *Divine Horsemen* by viewing the dichotomy between the two main categories of spirit, Rada and Petwo (roughly analogous to Guinea and Magic in Léogane), as a contrast of complementary ideologies rather than as a simple opposition of two distinct pantheons. Karen McCarthy Brown (1987, 1989, 1991), Deren's successor in both style and approach, writes of the Rada and Petwo symbols as "existential options" or "ways-of-being-in-the-world." Brown's insights derive from her work with temple congregations in Port-au-Prince and New York. Third, and most important to this discussion, is "The Meaning of Africa in Haitian Vodu," the brilliant and subtle essay on the Guinea-Magic dialectic by Serge Larose (1975a), whose research site was also in Léogane, only a few miles from my own.

Larose (1975a:86, 89) has defined Guinea as "tradition, unswerving loyalty to the ancestors and the old ways and ritual they brought from overseas ... a particular form of social authority ... through which power is legitimated." "Authentic Guinea" exists only insofar as it can eclipse—and exploit—another way-of-being-in-the-world. Larose identifies this alternative existential option as Maji or "Magic."

Maji is often used in a narrow sense to mean sorcery and the class of powers known as pwen. As the dominant symbol of an existential, moral option, Magic connotes transience, contract, and individualism. As Larose argues, Guinea uses Magic as a "ground figure," to define what it is not. Guinea constructs its moral discourse of authority, authenticity, substance, and hierarchy *against* Magic's images of abstract, contract relationships with strangers, living money, and illegitimate power.

Mercina, an emigrant from Ti Rivyè, summed up the constructed, or false, opposition between Guinea and Magic by analogy to the soft drinks, Regular Pepsi versus Diet Pepsi. Regular Pepsi exists only in virtue of the Diet alternative. "It's like Regular Pepsi and Diet Pepsi," she said. "Regular Pepsi and Diet Pepsi are not the same" (*Se tankou Regular Pepsi ak Diet Pepsi. Regular Pepsi e Diet Pepsi pa menm.*) Since immigrating to this country 11 years ago, Mercina has become an avid consumer of commercial television and carbonated beverages (which she drank in Haiti). She quite accurately perceived the Pepsi advertisers' message; namely, Regular and Diet Pepsi are not mere beverages: they represent distinct views of the world. Moreover, they exist only in relation, or in opposition, to one another.

Larose (1975a:106) suggests that precedence, on the one hand, and pursuit, on the other, epitomize the dichotomy between Guinea's morality and Magic's corruption. People frequently defend their integrity (and their poverty) by asserting, "I serve what I grew up with; I don't seek" (*M sèvi sa m leve jwenn; m pa chache*). They typically defend the morality of a specific ritual practice by pronouncing, "That's how I grew up seeing my parents do it, it's not something I sought." (*Se kon sa mwen leve jwenn papa m e manman m ap sèvi, se pa yon bagay mwen chache.*) To characterize a practice as Magic, Larose (1975a:89) points out, is to consign it to the present and to question its integrity. (Recall Camolien's depreciation of the gangan ason's newfangled ritual commerce in the preceding chapter.)

The opposition between tradition and pursuit informs a wide range of vivid metaphor and metonym. Brown's (1976) exploration of the cosmological geometry of ground paintings, for example, emphasizes the contrast between down and up, below and above. Guinea's long, steady and authoritative past is associated with the ground and bodies of water while powers that ascend and dissipate—fire or dew, for example—epitomize the illegitimacy and transience of Magic. Larose (1975a:110–111) alludes to the opposition between below and above in his elegant description of the downward and upward growing root systems of the sacred arbors associated respectively with Guinea and Magic. (Virtually every species of tree is identified with a particular category of spirit.) Guinea's calabash tree (*Crescentia cujete*), he writes, "is like an iceberg whose larger part lies underground, invisible to the eye." Its huge, ancient roots provide a steadfast anchor against destructive cyclones; even when all the branches are sheared off it regenerates itself. Its "well-defined trunk . . . stands for the legitimate power that originates from Guinea." The first people presumably served and ate their meals in bowls fashioned from the calabash fruit (s. *kwi*). These simple vessels, like the anthropomorphic lwa of Guinea and the traditions practiced by the first ancestors, constitute the venerable class of "root things" (*bagay rasin*).

Discussion of Guinea's eternal arbor inevitably leads to the origins of humanity. The story of God's (Bondye's) creation of the first Guinea "people" (*nasyon*) assimilates an important theme in the Guinea-Magic dialectic: God gave Guinea precedence at the expense of power. Guinea has authenticity but no productive force. The discovery of the African traditions and the incorporation of temple voodoo structures entailed a reshuffling of the pantheons of lwa. The lwa lending legitimacy to the temple hierarchy were elevated in stature, imbued with authenticity, symbolized by extreme old age, and reified as the quintessence of Guinea. I learned about the cost of Guinea's authority during a conversation with Little Caterpillar. I asked him why Guinea did not embrace an inside power, why it did not have a pwen.

K:　Guinea does not have a pwen?
　　Ginen pa gen pwen?
L:　[Guinea] wasn't made for that purpose.
　　Non. Li pa fèt pou sa-a.
K:　If it doesn't have pwen, what does it have?
　　Si l pa gen pwen, ki sa li genyen?
L:　Guinea is the first nation [people] God created.
　　Sa se prenmye nasyon Bondye te kree.
K:　Without pwen?
　　San pwen?
L:　Yes. [God] didn't create it with pwen.
　　Ya. Li pat kree l a pwen.
K:　Why?
　　Pou ki sa?
L:　God says to you, "You'll all live [survive]."
　　Bondye di ou. Nou tout ap viv.

Despite God's intentions, however, Guinea cannot live on precedence and authority alone. To perpetuate Guinea, to support the root things they grew up with, loyal servants of authentic Guinea periodically must stray from their grounded calabash in "pursuit" of the immoral potency descending from the banyan tree.

Magic's distinctive arbor, the banyan or fig tree (*Ficus benghalensis*), presents a powerfully direct ground-figure to the venerable calabash tree. The calabash grows inside the homestead (*lakou*), offering protection to the family members. The fig germinates in the open and supposedly harbors malevolent winged spirits of the air. Compared to the ancient, deep and invisible root system of the Guinea tree, the aerially descending roots of the fig are plainly "illegitimate." Even a description of the tree from a seemingly impartial encyclopedia carries an impassioned tone of moral indignation:

> Some fig-trees commonly start life from seeds deposited by birds, squirrels, monkeys or fruit-eating bats, high up on a palm or other native tree. The roots grow downward attached to the trunk of the supporting plant. . . . they pass their early life on the trunks of trees but subsequently become connected with the ground by their own root-system. The name of "strangler" has become attached to fig-trees which grow in this way since their descending and encircling roots become largely or entirely confluent, forming a pseudo-trunk, hollow at the center through which the dead or dying host plant passes. These fig-trees are roots and not stems. (*Encyclopædia Britannica*, cited in Larose 1975a:110–111)

Magic, like the fig tree, is imaged as "never-ending roots" whose illicit powers descend from the above and the outside. A fig tree regenerates by transforming its parent into an empty, lifeless, pseudotrunk. Magical production similarly reverses the normal processes of procreation and descent. Magical agents breed independently, and out of this abstracted independence turning in on itself spring multiple litters of malevolent air-borne creatures which lodge in the boughs of the fig tree and feed on innocent people (i.e., heirs of Guinea families).

The Foreign Lwa

A paradox of authentic Guinea's authority is its representation as foreign at the same time as it embodies precedence and authenticity. The most authoritative, venerated Guinea spirits are referred to as lwa blan, from the French *blanc* (white). Blan means "foreigner," and connotes white skin. (The word for "white" is *blanch*. A nonwhite foreigner may be identified as a *blan nwa* [black foreigner], for example, or a *blan wouj* [reddish foreigner].) Indeed in pigmentation, ethnicity, and appetite, the lwa blan resemble the cosmopolitan outsiders who, step by step, dominated Ti Rivyè during the early 20th century. From Joseph Lacombe to HASCO, these blan (foreigners) annexed peasant lands, devalued peasant labor, and so coerced their incorporation into agrocapitalist production. As Malgre Sa told me, "the lwa blan are bourgeois" (*lwa blan se boujwa*).

These venerable, foreign spirits are also the ones who rose to confer authority upon the mediators of temple voodoo that transformed ritual practice in Ti Rivyè during the early to mid-20th century. Loko was and remains the source of the gangan ason's legitimacy. Danbala Wedo directs initiations of ounsi. References to modern state power reinforce the authority of the foreign lwa. Aiscar, a gangan ason, compared Loko to the president and Danbala to a cabinet-ranked minister. His brother Victor said, though, perhaps thinking of the lyrics of a song praising Danbala, that he is "the one who commands all the lwa" (*se li ki konmande tout lwa*). Significantly, among a list of spirits informally recited by a man from a community that was not (yet) oriented toward the ranking of spirits associated with temple practices, Danbala's name was at the very bottom.

Virtually every student of Haitian religion has pursued the insight, articulated by Herskovits (1937:314), that ritual songs (*chante lwa*) comprise "the holy word of vodun theology and [are] an important device in stabilizing the details of belief."[1] Sacred song texts thus reproduce the authority of these "authentic African" spirits and the professional ritual leaders and servitors whose initiations they are believed to supervise. The songs honoring Loko, Danbala, and other members of the foreign pantheon portray a class of pale personalities who are not only authoritative but also aged and effete.

When we listen to the songs in ritual sequence, we invariably first encounter Legba, the preeminent lwa who mediates "the gate" (*bayè a*) between Guinea and this world. Legba is crippled with arthritis; songs allude to his "old bones" and his need for a cane (Deren 1953:100). Proceeding to the other cabinet-level lwa, there is Grandfather Danbala. One honorific song repeats, simply, "Danbala Wedo is an old man" (*Danbala Wedo gran mounn*).

Old age, though, is like a second infancy and the lwa vodou frequently exhibit the erratic and childish behavior characteristic of persons in their declining years. I have often heard it said that "the lwa are children" (*lwa se ti mounn*). They are impulsive, mischievous, and prone to extremes of emotion. "One minute they love you, the next minute they hold you [i.e., make you sick]" (*yon moman yo renmen ou; yon lòt moman yo kenbe ou*). The ever-dependent lwa vodou need attention and when they feel slighted or neglected (i.e., when they are left to go hungry), they take revenge and play childish pranks on you (*fè ou malfezan*).

The sacred texts, which typically present the lwa singing in the first person or engaged in negotiation with people who serve him/her, are in balance a whiny and anguished repertoire. As the invocations progress through the ranks of the spirits, each lwa receives an opportunity to vent his or her anxiety about being consigned to oblivion and forced to starve. To take only two examples from an immense repertoire, in the first, the lwa Ogoun complains that his "children" dutifully invoke him to traverse the vast ocean separating Guinea from the ritual space in Haiti because they think they should, rather than because they genuinely want to commune with him. He pleads with the heirs to pay attention to him once he arrives and to accept him for what he is. In the second song, the lwa, Danbala Wedo, protests being used, addressed by such obsequious titles as Grandfather or Divine Serpent, and then discarded.

> Ogoun oh,
> You are the one
> Who led me here;
> Care about me.
> Accept me the way I am,
> Care about me, Ogoun o.
> Accept me the way I am,
> Care about me, Ogoun o.
> You are the one
> who took me here;
> Care about me . . .

> *Ogoun o,*
> *Se ou menm*
> *Ki mennen m isit;*
> *Pran ka mwen.*
> *Pran lè mwen,*
> *Pran ka mwen, Ogoun o.*
> *Pran lè mwen,*
> *Pran ka mwen, Ogoun o.*
> *Se ou menm*
> *ki menen m isit;*
> *Pran ka mwen . . .*

> I say, Wedo, Grandfather
> I say, Wedo
> They don't need me anymore.
> When they need me
> They address me as Grandfather.
> When I go past,
> They say, "you're a serpent."
> I say, Wedo, Grandfather
> I say, Wedo
> They don't need me anymore . . .[2]

> *M di Wedo, Papa,*
> *Mwen di Wedo sa a*

Yo pa bezwen m ankò.
Lè yo bezwen m,
Yo rele mwen papa vre.
Lè ke mwen pase,
Yo di, "se koulèv nou ye."
M di Wedo, Papa,
Mwen di Wedo sa a
Nou pa bezwen m ankò . . .

Semantics of Lwa Blan Food Offerings

Feeding is the epitomizing symbol of the production process—creating persons and personal relationships—so it is not surprising that feeding would encompass ritual relationships as well. Nurturing the lwa is the constitutive activity of the eritaj descent group. "The family" assembles only to "feed" (worship) their spiritual counterparts on the inalienable segment of the eritaj land known as demanbre. We may recall that when a member says, therefore, "I serve my spirits" (*mwen konn sèvi lwa m yo*), s/he means hosting them with food. (Haitian peasants never say "I am a voodooist" or "I practice voodoo.") Although rituals also involve spirit possession, prayers (many of which are from the Catholic liturgy), song, drumming, dance, and processionals, feeding is the encompassing metaphor. Ritual songs get "cooked;" the dance gets "stirred up." Rituals are often called simply "feedings of the gods" (*manje lwa*). The lwa's appetite is also a metaphorical measure of their mood. Neglected lwa are said to be "hungry" (*grangou*) and their need for energy drives them to "hold" (*kenbe*) the heirs; that is, to make them sick. A well-fed lwa can feel disposed to do them good.

Given the preeminence of feeding in worship, we would expect to find an abundance of esoteric meaning articulated in the selection and arrangement of foods given to the lwa. Images of the foreign lwa's tradition, authority, restraint, and impotence are conveyed through subtle analogies to conventions of nutrition, diet, taste, and etiquettes of serving and eating. Most "foreign lwa" feedings suggest containment by taking place inside (a shrine, a tent, a boat) and by being oriented downward, toward the earth. Since the foreign lwa are said to be of "cool" (*frèt*) temperaments and to inhabit cool waters (Danbala lives in streams, Agwe resides in the ocean), they demand libations of cool, clear, and bland liquids. Clothes worn by their devotees reiterate this composure; they are either monochromatic white or pale blue. Sacrificial victims are white fowl or sheep. Other food offerings tend toward pale, "cool" colors and are often highly processed or transformed, resembling easily digested preparations served to infants and toothless old people.

The symbolism of food and drink offered to spirits reveals a complex under-standing of the political, transnational structuring of production and consump-tion. Meals served to the supreme pantheon of "foreign lwa" eschew all ingre-dients and vessels identified with the peasants and with (less expensive and devalued) domestic food production. The lwa blan eat dessert, a course foreign to the peasant diet, served in fine porcelain, china, and glass (Métraux 1951:35). They enjoy imported finger foods that define the *heure de l'apéritif*: cured meats (sausage, ham, salami) in miniature, Camembert, and other cheeses while sipping gin and vermouth. They like sweets whose processing requires baking in ovens or refrigeration rarely seen in the countryside. The authentic African spirits drink sweetened coffee, cocoa, and sodas, all made from sugarcane, the archetypal product of harsh plantation slavery. They have a marked preference for Barban-court rum, produced since the colonial era for export abroad. Rhum Barban-court is the quintessential sign of the Haitian tourist industry, as anyone passing through the national airport can attest. Though Haiti's golden age of tourism had ended by the 1960s (Plummer 1990), a must on any determined tourist's itinerary is still the Barbancourt stone castle in Boutiliers where guests are invited to sample the many flavored rums and feel the power of colonial splendor while overlooking the bayside capital below.

In addition to imbibing Haiti's only exported liquor, the foreign lwa savor the

6.1. Feeding Agwe and other foreign *lwa*, Ti Rivyè, August 1984.

6.2. A table set for Ezili Freda and other foreign *lwa*, Ti Rivyè, February 1984.

tropical "fruits" of so many ephemeral production-for-export ventures imposed on Haitian peasants after (or as punishment for) freeing themselves from French colonialism. Though several varieties of bananas and mangoes are cultivated in Haiti, "foreign lwa" offerings select only the exported strains (*fig gwo michel* and *mango fransis*) (Moral 1961:310; Pierre-Noel 1971:185–186).[3] Cultivated both to suit the palates of foreigners and to capture the exotic essence of the tropics, the fruits straddle the same hidden paradox as tourist-oriented "folk" art.

The allure of Haiti's exotic fruits beckons in *A Puritan in Voodoo-Land*, a memoir by Edna Taft (1938), an early tourist to an industry launched by using the return voyages of Standard Fruit ships to carry people to the islands. The Puritan tried vainly to sublimate her desires for the Other (the allure of mulatto women nearly drove her over the edge). *A Puritan in Voodoo-Land* divulges how the tastes and smells seduced her: "One's palate never forgets the fiery, yet smooth, Haitian rum; nor the smoky black Haitian coffee. Nor the aromatic, flower-fragrant *mangot, gouyave, corossol, quéneppe.* . . . One soon learns to call them all by their Creole names." (Taft 1938:377).[4]

Offerings to the foreign spirits thus present abundant gastronomical symbolism about the foreign spirits. Consider one particular ceremony, a "coffee for Master Agwe" that took place in April 1984 on the Ti Rivyè beach. Its sponsor, though unable to attend, was a migrant man nicknamed Ti Son (Little Sound). A white half-dome tent was erected in the sand. Under it stood an elaborately laid, white-clothed table decorated with vases of colorful tissue paper, a candle, and three vases of plastic flowers. The centerpiece was a pastel pink iced layer cake, purchased from a Port-au-Prince bakery. There were plates holding four pieces of bread spread with margarine, French toast, various biscuits, and four meat-filled pastries. There were sausages from Puerto Rico, a wrapped piece of La Vache Qui Rit cheese, a scrambled egg and a whole hard-boiled egg, and breaded and fried eggplant sprinkled with white sugar and fried fish. Fruits comprised two red delicious apples, red grapes, five bananas (in their skins), one fried banana, one sliced mango fransik, a yellow melon cut into five slices, four oranges, and two grapefruit. Beverages included two cups of coffee (one salty and one sweet), two glasses of white milk, two glasses of chocolate milk, bottles of Cinzano (an Italian sweet vermouth), Night Train, Rhum Barbancourt, imported and artisanal brandies, Coca-Cola, and Haitian carbonated cola brands. There were two cigars, a tube of Colgate toothpaste, and a bottle of French perfume for the lwa to use after taking the refreshment.

Agwe's "dessert" does not qualify as "food." "Food" is something that, according to Malgre Sa, "holds" (*kenbe*), "sustains" (*fòtifye*) and "gives strength" (*bay fòs*). Agwe's feast consisted mainly of "mouth passers" (s. *pase bouch*). A mouth passer, Malgre Sa told me, "is something that doesn't do anything for you, that doesn't fill your stomach. It is not a food that fortifies you" (*Se yon bay ki pa fè anyen pou ou, ki pa plen vant ou. Li pa yon manje ki fòtifye ou*). Throughout Haiti and much of the Caribbean, "food" is epitomized by starches. As Alvarez and Murray (1981) explain in their meticulous description of food classification and behavior in a Cul-de-Sac village, "food" connotes high carbohydrate root, vine, grain, and tree crops known as *viv*. (Viv derives from the French word *vivre*, "to live" or "living.") Only when one's serving is based on a high carbohydrate can a person consider her or himself to have "eaten" (*manje*). Consumption of a meal based on "life-sustaining" viv qualifies one to claim afterward, "I have eaten" (Alvarez and Murray 1981:153).[5] Ritual offerings to the foreign lwa imply, therefore, that they do not need to fill up on "food," the class of local starches that constitutes the backbone of the peasant economy and meal. Rather, they nibble lightly on nonnutritious, imported snacks.

Analysis of the etiquette of ritual offerings to this pantheon reveals further symbolism of their imagined character. Their "mouth-passers" are conjugated with a symbolic grammar of utmost differentiation. A typical banquet table contains myriad cut glass, porcelain, and enameled dinner and dessert plates, fruit, cereal, and rimmed soup bowls, goblets, tumblers, and coffee cups. "Separating" (from the French verb *separer*, meaning to divide and distribute) prepared food is the decisive convention regarding the service and consuming of food. In their insightful commentary on separation etiquette, Alvarez and Murray (1981:178–180) observe that Creole lacks a term for "meal," in the sense of a social event. (The Creole term manje, as we have seen, can mean the verb "to eat" or the noun "food," which is typified by the category viv or the gerund "feeding," as in *manje lwa*, "a feeding of the gods.")[6]

Unlike the cosmopolitan elite, Haitian peasants classify and treat the *consumption* of food as a biological function; they have constructed few social norms to govern eating etiquette. People tend to consume their food rapidly and somewhat apart, seeing no reason either to prolong the process or to involve others in it. They are not familiar with the practice of the family dinner at which a father, mother, and their children assemble around a table with identical place settings, serve themselves from common platters, eat together, and converse as equals (Visser 1991). Intensive social mediation and cultural valuation instead converge upon the *separation* of food. Separation articulates the bonds and structure of the peasant domestic unit, just as consuming an evening meal together at the dinner table stipulates the equality and cohesion of the upper- or middle-class nuclear family. The status of the person who allots the portions is crucial; the preparation of the food has little governing etiquette. Whereas the woman who prepares the food is usually of junior rank or a quasi servant, the *separator* is a senior woman of unquestioned authority.

In all but the poorest peasant households, a female of relatively low status—a young and/or unmarried daughter, junior daughter-in-law, or poor female relative who acts as an unpaid domestic—typically spends the better part of the day cooking the food in the kitchen, a one- or two-room structure located near the house. When the food is ready, she notifies the senior adult woman, who enters the kitchen to dispense the individual servings of food. If people were standing around during the cooking, they leave. This woman's judgments as to the order in which food is parceled out and the relative amounts to be placed in each bowl are deemed beyond reproach. The senior separator may be responsible for exact separation of many servings. Miri, the woman with whom I exchanged meals, daily apportioned at least 15 servings to members of the household, other households with whom she regularly exchanged plates of food, and the ever present "guest(s)." Her high status in her community was made most tangible to me during one of the most important and elaborate of ritual food presentations, which is performed only every generation or so. (A description of the spectacular rite, known as Agwe's Barge [Bak D'Agwe], was provided in the preceding chapter.) Among the scores of initiated women (ounsi) attending, the lead gangan ason selected Min to separate the food.

The more differentiated the serving, the higher the rank. Food served to the husband/father and any high-ranking guest is dispensed into at least two dishes. A serving involving a viv (starch), a bean puree, and a high protein (*vyann*) in sauce, for example, will be so divided onto three plates (two flat plates and one soup bowl) for the man. As Alvarez and Murray (1981:178) point out, the custom of serving the senior male or guest in more than one vessel presupposes that he will sit down at a table inside the house, alone, to a *kouvè*, or place setting of utensils used by no one else in the household. When he finishes eating, he is served a glass of water or other beverage, carried to him on a tray. All the others receive their food mixed up in single bowls. They find relatively private spots in a corner, on a chair, or on the ground or the floor, and consume it with their hands or a spoon.

To be a "person" (*mounn*), a member of a household, then, is to have one's portion *separated in relation to* those belonging to members of the same unit. And through daily exchanges of bowls across households, each "person" relates to those units of "persons" as well. The relative degree of single portion differentiation, the size and shape of the vessel, and the order of serving formulate metaphoric images of the person's rank in the age- and gender-coded domestic hierarchy.

Exaggerated separations of lwa vodou/blan feasts identify the recipients as "persons" of superior rank in the descent group (the kinship unit of reference). Symbolic manipulations of form, color, and texture construct these "persons" as restrained, cool, and refined. The nutritional semantics of what they consume connote an incapacity "to sustain" or "to give strength." These overly differentiated, "mouth passer" banquets signify an opposition to the utter chaos of redundant combinations of nourishing viv shoved at the illegitimately liminal lwa descended from Magic. At these latter rituals, hoards of "non-persons" (manifesting themselves in possession-performance) jostle their way to grab whatever they can of the undifferentiated offerings. By contrast, when a lwa vodou appears to accept an offering "in person," s/he typically tastes a portion and then reseparates it into portions for the assembled.

A moving example of the responsibility of the senior mother who separates food among the family was provided for us when an Ezili Dantò mounted Andreli, an elder woman, during a rite in February 1984. Dantò/Andreli tasted several of the elaborately differentiated items and then redivided portions among the assembled heirs. With tenderness, she then proceeded to feed them one by one from a glassful of cake soaked in water (prepared for the lwa Ibo) by placing a spoonful in each person's mouth. She also carefully "fed" their heads—the head is the point of physical contact between a person and a lwa. While the heir knelt in front of her, she poured her favorite beverage onto the top of the person's head and then, with her hand, firmly but gently massaged it into the hair and scalp.

The Need for Vitalization

The cool and effete lwa vodou are at the top of the pantheon. Exemplars of "authentic Guinea" monopolize "separation" and restraint at the expense of fertility and strength. The resources to nourish and revitalize Guinea come from elsewhere, from behind. Magic—unrestrained, undifferentiated, hot—produces the "food" (viv) to sustain the dependent, temper-prone grandparents who had become the authentic representatives of Guinea. If to survive, however, Guinea feeds vicariously on the life-giving powers or pwen ("point") of its Other, to maintain its moral hegemony Guinea has to conceal its exploitation of Magic.

Pepe, a gangan ason in Ti Rivyè, used a metaphor of a ship to explain the Guinea-pwen dependency to me. The lwa Ginen stand at the bow, the hot pwen are at the stern. They are the motor or the "big wrist" that propels Guinea's appearance of authority. He asserted, "[The pwen] is the one who has more power, the bigger wrist. The lwa Ginen is in front, the hot pwen is behind." (*Se li k gen pi gwo fòs, ponyèt. Lwa Ginen an devan, pwen cho a dèyè.*)

I introduced the concept of pwen in the opening chapter. To review, a pwen is the hidden, vital pith of a relationship or a thing. Mimesis is central to the Creole concept of pwen. In a provocative book inspired by Benjamin's (1968) commentary on the mimetic faculty, Michael Taussig (1993) states that mimesis is a double process involving imitative action and embodiment, copying and contact, miming and bodily perception. There is no analogous term in English. Karen McCarthy Brown has provided the best translation. Indeed getting hold of the meaning of pwen has been a continued focus of her work (1976, 1987, 1989, 1991, 1995, 1997), and the starting point for this discussion. Brown (1987:151–152) defines *pwen* as "anything that captures the essence or pith of a complex situation" and reformulates it so it can be easily grasped and remembered. A pwen is "an elegantly simple image."

Pwen are mimetic ways, then, to use Benjamin's terms, to "get hold of an object at very close range by way of its likeness, its reproduction." A pwen seizes or stops the power inside the other by reproducing it. Moreover, a pwen only exists as a relation; that is, insofar as someone *other than the one who created it* can perceive it. Pwen exist, therefore, to be exchanged, "sent," or "thrown." Thus it is said that every pwen has an "owner" (*mèt*) to "gather it" or "pick it up" (*ranmase li*). The owner of the pwen, not its sender nor its creator, subjectively determines what the pwen is, what it means, and what it can do.

In the context of Magic, pwen symbolize alienable labor power. They are a peasant society's representation of the immorality of wage labor and an inhumane capitalist system that exploits it. Like the proletarians marginalized within the peasant society, the pwen must be concealed, or exported. And like migrants, they sell their labor outside in order to preserve the "integrity" of the peasant system. In a peasant moral economy of "the limited good" (Foster 1967), anyone who acquires new wealth can be presumed to have "sought" or "purchased" (chache, achte) a pwen (in contrast to those who serve only what preceded them). Indeed "progress" (pwogrè), a paramount ethic of capitalist culture, is a negative metaphor for the illicit work of a pwen.[7]

Since these instruments of wanton greed putatively cannot be bought and sold within the borders of Guinea's moral community, anyone suspected of buying the illicit power is thought to have pursued it elsewhere. An ambitious Léogane resident voyages to "the Artibonite valley," "the North" or "the South" (just as his/her corrupt counterpart from, say, the Artibonite travels to the wasteland of Léogane in pursuit of a pwen.) Inside a kay lwa (Guinea shrine), while acting as "right-handed" priests of authentic Africa, local gangan ason do not sell pwen. In the dark of a separate dwelling dedicated to Simbi Makaya or another "purchased lwa" (a type of pwen), they practice with the "left hand." They manufacture pwen (for clients from the Artibonite, North or South).

Magical pwen exaggerate the essence of alienated production or "work" (travay). The following song, which Se Byen led in call and response at a Maji rite, celebrates the working pwen.

The pwen
I bought a pwen
So I could work
To make the magic move.
I say the pwen
I bought a pwen.
Its so I could work my pwen
To make my work move.

Pwen an
M achte youn pwen
Pou mwen travay o
Pou m fè maji a mache.
Mwen di pwen an
M achte youn pwen o
Se pou m travay pwen mwen
Pou m fè travay mwen mache.

Pwen are construed as faceless, contagious, and prolific. Pwen "work fast" (*travay vit*) for their masters, efficiently carrying out assignments without questioning their morality (Larose 1975a:115). Pwen get the job done; they "attack" (*atake*) and "execute" (*egzekite*). They "break down" (*distile*) obstacles that might retard their work, while fickle lwa Ginen may take their sweet time deciding whether to support—but never to "work" for—their servants. Pwen "make you gain big money" (*fè ou genyen gwo lajan*), "make you sell" (*fè ou vann*), and "make your business hot [successful]" (*fè afè/ komès ou mache pi cho*).

The Transformation of Pwen

Anyone who professes to serve "what they were raised with," and who denies the desire "to seek," will nonetheless admit that pwen are part of their Guinea heritage. The ancestors had pwen, but their pwen were different. The ancient Guinea ancestors carried out their Magic in a moral, Guinea way. When located in the distant past, pwen absorb the morality of Guinea. When projected into the present, on the other hand, these same powers sponge up the corruption of Magic.

Representations of former uses of pwen in fact emphasize bodily protection. Pwen defended soldiers, watched over children, safeguarded livestock and prevented accidents.[8] According to Misdor's son Aiscar, for example, the venerable African-born ancestors had a God-given gift or talent to make certain "drugs" (*dròg*) which they remembered when they emigrated from the homeland. Notably missing from this image were allusions to pursuit, purchase, or working for individual gain. "Long ago our ancestors were immune to bullets. They had a type of drug. . . . That's what became pwen. People came from Guinea with these drugs. They were like a natural gift." (*Nan tan lontan gran paran nou yo pat pran bal. Yo gen yon seri dròg. . . . Se sa ki tounen pwen. Mounn sòt nan Ginen ak dròg sa yo kòm don.*)

The process of creating a living pwen simulates the conception of human or animal life. To create a fetus, three elements interact: God's will, male fluid, and female blood. As Larose describes (1975a:107), when a gangan manufactures a pwen, another (pre-existing) pwen, or a soul symbolically stolen from a corpse (*zonbi*), takes the place of God to breathe life into the mixture. Into a bottle, the gangan pours ingredients of (male) water and (female) blood (among other "ingredients" [*medikaman*] sold in specialized "pharmacies"). In contrast to Guinea's obsession with separating pale, pure colors from more vibrant or darker ones, the life-giving colors of red and white flow into one another. Larose recorded these words used in the manufacture of a garden pwen: "now you have water and you have blood: you are a living one. I want you to be the soul of that garden and to kill any intruder" (1975a:107). The vessel, itself a means of containment, is further restrained by "tying" (*mare*) the outside with a cord, which Larose (1975a:107) likens to the chains of the enslaved spirit.

The gangan then sets the conditions of the contract with the buyer. Once the new owner takes possession of the bottle, he or she proceeds symbolically to contain and restrain its volatile, productive contents. First, the owner buries it in the floor or doorway of the house. The pwen must then be regularly propitiated; in other words, its capacity for production must be controlled with regular prayers, candle-lighting, and offerings of certain specified foods and drinks and such other objects as toiletry items (perfume, towels, soap), according to the conditions specified in the "contract."

Although the client has to pay the pwen (i.e., the gangan who manufactured it) only if it "works" for him or her, as Zo Guerrier explained, persons greedy enough to buy a pwen are hardly inclined to pay the pwen its rightful wages when it completes its task.

> A pwen can work for you. You could go to a gangan and buy a pwen because you want to have a car. The pwen could make you have two or three cars. You owe the pwen only if it works for you. If the pwen made you win three thousand dollars, to give the pwen a thousand of it is nothing.

> *Lwa yo la pou pwoteje ou. Men yon pwen ka travay pou ou. Ou gen dwa al kay gangan paske ou te vle genyen youn machin. Pwen an ka fè ou genyen de ou twa machin. Ou dwe pwen an sèlman si li travay pou ou. Men si, pa egzanp, pwen an fè ou genyen twa mil dola, bay pwen an mil ladan ni se pa anyen.*

It is commonly assumed that anyone who buys a pwen will be hard pressed ever to settle with it. Once a loyal servant, the pwen becomes, as Pepe, the gangan ason, said, "your master": "When you buy a pwen, you don't settle with it easily. It can—pow!—kill you in a second. The lwa Ginen are not like that. S/he can hold you, make you sick. You bought the pwen, it's your master." (*Lè ou achte pwen an, ou pa regle avè l fasilman, li gen dwa—pop!—tou, li touye ou nan menm enstan. Lwa Ginen an pa nan sa. Li gen dwa kenbe ou, fè ou malad. Se achte ou achte pwen an mèt ou.*)

Ti Yòyòt Bought a Pwen

Ti Yòyòt had been a rice trader of modest means. Her abrupt achievement of prosperity, manifested by a new business of loaning people money to emigrate, aroused suspicion that she had pursued a pwen. The post-mortem diagnosis of her sudden, acute illness and agonizing death convinced them. Ti Yòyòt bought a pwen; the pwen made her a lot of instant money; the pwen devoured her. After her death, her family discovered a cache of money hidden inside her house.

Narratives of Ti Yòyòt's retribution were told to me independently by two of her distant cousins, Tenten and his sister Filoza. They brought up Ti Yòyòt's case in the context of conversations about the current crisis, described later in this chapter, involving a pwen who was "eating" its deceased owner's daughter. Filoza asserted that Ti Yòyòt died as just punishment for her excessive greed; she refused to redistribute some of her new-found wealth to local beggars, as stated in the "purchase contract." Dispensing alms on the steps of a church is a ritual require-ment associated with Guinea rites of healing and passage. Filoza implied that Ti Yòyòt had been too corrupted by Magic to yield to her Guinea duty to help the poor. Filoza evidently resented Ti Yòyòt's older sister (who happened also to be her sister-in-law), for she seemed to accuse Sirina of hoarding the unearthed for-tune rather than dispersing the money among more deserving and/or more needy relatives.

> Ti Yòyòt bought a pwen that ate her . . . They found a lot, a lot of money under the mattress. Sirina collected it [for herself]. And all she had was a little rice trade. The pwen told her to kill a cow every year to feed to the beggars at [the church of] St. Michèl. She couldn't bear to part with the money. That's why the pwen killed her.

> *Ti Yòyòt te achte yon pwen ki te manje li . . . Yo jwenn anpil, anpil lajan anba matla. Sirina te ranmase li. Epi se yon ti komès diri li te genyen. Pwen an te di pou li touye yon bèf chak ane bay pòv devan St. Michèl. Se regret li te regret lajan. Se pou tèt sa pwen an te manje li.*

According to Tenten's version, Ti Yòyòt went down South to buy a pwen. The pwen failed to produce results. Ti Yòyòt forsook it and traveled to the North to pursue a second pwen. When she realized great success, she incorrectly attributed her profit to the second one. The first pwen, slighted by her error, took her life.

> Ti Yòyòt bought a pwen that made her a lot of money—she used to loan people money [at 100% interest] to emigrate. Did she have money! When she died, that suitcase [pointing to my foot locker] couldn't have held all of her money. She had a pwen working for her. The pwen ate her up. She didn't pay it. A gangan in the South did that for her. She bought the pwen in the South. It didn't do anything. She went to make another one in the North. After two or three days she found the fortune. She thought it was the one from the North that gave it to her.

Ti Yòyòt te achte yon pwen ki fè l gen anpil lajan—li te konn eskonte mounn lajan pou yo pati. Li te gen kòb! Lè li mouri, valiz sa a (lap montre m gwo valiz mwen an) pat ka kenbe lajan n. Li te gen yon pwen ki tap travay pou li. Se pwen an ki te manje li. Li pa tal peye l. Youn gangan nan Sid fè sa pou li. Li pran yon pwen nan Sid. Li pat fè anyen. La l fè youn lòt nan Nò. Apre de, twa jou li jwenn byen an. Li panse se sak onò ki ba li l.

Ti Yòyòt was an ounsi, a servant of Guinea who "laid down for Danbala." But she bought a pwen. Her situation provoked contempt or envy, depending on the interpersonal relations and partisan interests of the judges. To defend their mask of moral probity, "children of authentic Guinea" who compromise themselves in secretive pursuits of pwen may well level the most unforgiving censure of others suspected of doing the same. Guinea's tendency to deflect its illicit essence to Magic may partly explain Filoza's desire to blame Ti Yòyòt.

Filoza was herself a successful trader. Tenten, on the other hand, was a poor man obviously limited "to what he was raised to serve." Having nothing personal to conceal (and deflect), he could afford to portray Ti Yòyòt's mistake in a more charitable light and even go so far as to muse owning a pwen. Tenten was described (by himself to me, by others to me alone, and by others in front of both of us) as someone afflicted by persistent bad luck of the kind perpetrated by lwa Ginen. Indeed both private and public rituals I attended with Tenten produced diagnoses of his chronic ill fortune as retribution from a neglected inherited lwa named Ezili. Tenten once said to me, "I don't have enough good luck to buy a pwen. I don't have good luck. It would kill me. I make do with lwa Guinea. I don't buy pwen." (*M pa gen chans pou achte pwen. M pa gen chans. L ap touye mwen. M sèvi avèk lwa Ginen. M pa achte pwen.*)

Rites of Incorporation

Pwen owners' tendency to conceal their illicit pursuit victimizes their descendants. When an owner dies (of another cause), s/he takes the secret of the pwen to the grave, leaving children and grandchildren vulnerable to being "eaten" (*manje*) by the ravenous pwen. A pwen will devour its masters' heirs, beginning with the youngest and then consuming descendants one by one until it devours the owner her or himself. Ti Yòyòt was her pwen's first (and sole) victim only because she did not have any descendants.

According to Little Caterpillar, "I don't tell anybody, I die, there is nobody to serve the pwen. The pwen needs to eat people. . . . It finds me and kills me. It can eat up the entire family." (*M vin mouri, pa gen mounn pou sèvi pwen an. Pwen an bezwen manje mounn. . . . Li jwenn mwen li touye m. Li gen dwa manje kò fanmi a nèt.*)

The following song was intoned in 1988 at Little Caterpillar's family's shrine during a ritual for "picking up" a pwen:

Tie the bale, tie the bale,

The children don't know what I did.
Tie the bale, tie the bale,

The children don't know what's in the yard.
Tie the bale, tie the bale,

The children don't know what their father served.
Tie the bale, tie the bale,

The children don't know what he celebrated.
Tie the bale, tie the bale,

The children don't know what the lwa used.
Tie the bale, tie the bale,

The children don't know what the lwa eats.

Mare bal la e mare bal la,

Ti mounn pa konnen sa m fè.
Mare bal la e mare bal la,

Ti mounn pa konnen sa k nan lakou a.
Mare bal la e mare bal la,

Ti mounn pa konnen sa papa yo sèvi.
Mare bal la e mare bal la,

Ti mounn pa konnen sa l fete.
Mare bal la e mare bal la,

Ti mounn pa konnen ki jan lwa sèvi.
Mare bal la e mare bal la,

Ti mounn pa konnen sa lwa manje.

When a plague of "hot," violent illness and death overtakes several younger members of an eritaj, both the constellation of symptoms and the pattern of affliction suggest the revenge of a pwen. (They have probably already sought intervention from "biomedical" doctors [*dòktè*] and/or "leaf doctors" [*mèdsen/ dòktè fey*]). The doctors' inability to offer a cure will lead them to a gangan. The ritual specialist's lwa Ginen may help him "discover" that one of their lineal ancestors bought a pwen. The lwa cannot, however, reveal additional, crucial information about the pwen—its identity, location, or conditions of the contract. Only the deceased spirit or "dead" (*mò*) can disclose the facts indispensable to arresting the plague. This condition inevitably prompts the family to perform the rite of passage known as "taking the dead out of the water" (*retire mò nan dlo*). Once the "dead" is transferred to a basin of water and then into a clay *govi* jar to be set upon the altar of the shrine, the gangan ason can "summon the dead" and cajole the spirit to divulge the information needed to arrest the persecutions and contain the pwen.

In the last chapter, I described the retrieval of one founder's spirit, which was said to be the first performance of this rite in the village. The rationale for lifting him out of the abyss, as is now apparent, was to contain Tonton Ogoun's pwen. When I visited Tonton Ogoun's grave with his great-grandson, Tenten, I learned that Tonton Ogoun had been captured during a war, no doubt one of the civil wars that periodically raged throughout the 19th century, and his personal power saved him. "When they came and took him—he had gone to war. He was going to die. When they hung him—they hung him, what he served saved him. When the war was over they sent him home." (*Lè yo vin pran ni—li tal nan gè. Li ta mouri. Lè yo pann ni—yo pann ni, se sa l te konn sèvi ki sove l. Lè gè a fini yo voye l vini.*) Tenten added with some pride that at the rite of retrieval, the old soldier's spirit requested a military gun salute. Shots were duly fired.

According to this narrative, Tonton Ogoun's pwen had been content to remain in its underground den for 70 years or so before an abrupt surge in its appetite for third- and fourth-generation heirs. Then the pwen suddenly started "bothering people, giving them festering sores on their legs, eating people." As with the formalization of the kanzo rite of passage, it appears that illness etiology provided a rationale for ritual innovation. Neglected pwen were all of a sudden persecuting heirs and their containment necessitated "taking the dead out of the water." How better to naturalize this new affliction and to deflect skepticism regarding its timing than to presume that the founding ancestors themselves had served pwen and failed to divulge their secrets to their heirs.

Periodic disclosures that such steady exemplars of authentic Guinea as a First Owner of the Land, like Tonton Ogoun, or an ounsi, like Ti Yòyòt, had sought pwen insured the perpetual reproduction of the Guinea-Magic co-dependency process. Every generation or so, another heir or heirs will fall victim to an errant pwen, the agent of some ambitious relative who was too ashamed to admit the ambitious deed before she or he died. Such was the case with a Ti Rivyè man who died in 1983 and took the secret of the illicit source of his wealth with him to the grave.

Abandoned by its owner, the hungry pwen had attacked one of his daughters, a robust young woman of 18 years, with a ghastly, inexorable paralysis. Reaching a diagnosis had eluded her uncle, a gangan ason, and the family consulted the more experienced Aiscar, who finally divined that she was being eaten up by her deceased father's pwen. Her collapse was likely the eruption of her mounting disease with her personal situation (the details of which I do not know), a cry for help that she could not otherwise voice.[9] Her deceased father's alleged practices provided a credible context for her affliction, and elicited thereby support and recognition she needed at that time. He had died just 12 months before—a serendipitous correspondence with the minimum acceptable term between the funeral and the rite of removing the dead from the water. His affines (his daughter's maternal kin) quickly prepared for the removal. Four gangan ason officiating from inside the white tent apparently could not coerce the dead spirit to confess to his "little thing." But when the time came to make a clean breast of his pursuit, the deceased, speaking through the gangan ason leading the rite, denied any knowledge of the pwen.

This incomplete finale inspired considerable discussion. In my subsequent conversation with Filoza, she said, "Pay no attention to him! He buried it alive in front of the door of the shrine. . . . there was [a] progress there! (*Pa okipe li! Li te antere l tou vivan devan pòt kay la. . . . te gen yon pwogrè la a!*) Later, in a more forgiving tone, Filoza opined that the reason the deceased backed out of his promise, made during the earlier, private divination, to divulge his little thing in public, was that his daughter had shamed him. When the deceased greeted her, she retorted defiantly, "I'm fine!" (*Mwen byen*), implying in addition, "no thanks to you." A polite response would have been, "I'm no worse." Feeling ashamed, he refused to cooperate. Yet another private seance was needed, therefore, to uncover the details of his pwen. He admitted then to having buried a live pig under the portal of his shrine.

Containing the "dead" and giving him/her a voice opened the conduit for a new and crucial series of rites. Tenten was present when Misdor retrieved his great-grandfather's spirit and the spirit, speaking through Misdor, revealed formulae for these new rites. Tenten said:

Tonton Ogoun spoke. He told his children what they should take care of for him. They should take care of that problem, to "do the zandò" for him. They [later] collected that zandò in front of me! He said after they collected the zandò, they should tie the bundles. And after tying the bundles they should "beat gè on them" and put them in the shrine.

Tonton Ogoun te pale. Li di sa li genyen pou pitit li okipe. Genyen pwoblèm sa pou yo okipe, pou yo fè zandò pou li. Yo ranmase zandò sa a devan m! Li di lè yo fin ranmase zandò, pou yo mare pake. Lè yo fin mare pake, pou yo bat gè sou li, mete yo nan kay lwa.

Thanks to the rigorous control exerted over the "liturgy" by Misdor and his sons, the triadic rites of picking up the zandò have become African traditions of the descent groups. To my knowledge, the ritual process of *ranmase*, or gathering, has not yet been described in the literature. (Larose [1975a:111–112] does mention that some of the zandò imported from the mountains may have started out as "points," but he does not identify the ritual processes that accomplish this transformation.) The key to the "picking up" rites was to vitalize Guinea with Magic's illicit heat while at the same time preserving Guinea's morality. The rites symbolically transformed pwen into a class of lwa known as zandò. Once their association with Magic—or alienable labor power—was concealed, they could be incorporated into the descent group's Guinea legacy. I will examine each of the three ritual stages involved in collecting the pwen to vitalize Guinea.

The first is *ranmase*, or "picking up." Ranmase, from the French word *ramasser*, means to collect, to gather, to scoop up, or to muster. Ranmase implies the imposition of ownership, order, and containment upon forces or things that were separated, disarrayed, and dispersed. The ranmase ceremony, conducted by a gangan ason, thus exercises Guinea authority to possess, order, and contain a pwen. *Resevwa*, or "to receive," accomplishes the ritual of ranmase. Just as one "receives" guests at a formal social occasion involving the exchange of food, so the heirs of the deceased owner, aided by the gangan ason, receive the pwen by feeding it according to the conditions specified in the purchase contract (and revealed by the "dead"). Little Caterpillar recounted:

If [the gangan ason] takes the "dead" out of the water, the dead will say there was this thing your father had. He has to tell you how to receive it. That means you collect the lwa. You put out all of the things the pwen eats. He tells you how to serve the pwen and how not to serve the pwen, if with a basin, perfume, a meal, towel, whatever. When you finish collecting it you put it in the house and leave it there.

Ou al kay gangan. Si li dekouvri sa la sove mounn. Si li rete mò nan dlo, mò a ap di men tèl bagay papa ou te genyen. Fò l di ou ki jan pou resevwa li. Sa di ou,

*ou ranmase lwa. Ou a mete tout bagay pwen an manje. Li ba ou men ki jan
pou sèvi, ki jan pou pa sèvi, si se kivèt, odè, yon manje, sèvièt, tout bagay. Lè ou
fin ranmase li, ou mete l andan kay, ou bandonen l.*

The ritual of gathering and receiving constitutes only the first stage of a triadic
ritual process of domestication. The second ceremony, known as "tie the bundles"
(*mare pake*), entails the preparation of brightly colored cloth talismans that hold
powerful leaves, powders, remnants of animal sacrifices, money, and other items.
The bundles can be used to treat victims of malevolent magic, and we will return
to this usage.

According to Little Caterpillar, at least 7 and at most 21 bundles must be prepared. These ritual numbers epitomize Guinea; twenty-one lwa "nations" comprise the Guinea pantheons. Several of the songs I recorded during a *bat gè* ceremony involved counting. For example,

If you have enough for one,
You must have enough for two.
If you have enough for two,
You must have enough for three.
If there are bundles to be tied,
Give them to us, we'll tie them.
If you have enough for three,
You must have enough for four.

*Si ou genyen pou youn,
Fò ou genyen pou de.
Si ou genyen pou de,
Fò ou genyen pou twa.
Si ou gen pake pou mare,
Ba nou, na mare yo.
Si ou genyen pou twa,
Fò ou genyen pou kat.*

The third phase in the taming process is called "beat gè" (*bat gè*).[10] A sack
containing the bundles is placed on the floor of a shrine. Four persons wearing
red scarves across their chests and holding machetes kneel over it, the two pairs
facing one another. Then they proceed, using the flats of their blades, to "beat gè"
on the sack. All night long they thwack in rhythm without rest—substitutes replace the weary without missing a beat—accompanied by singing, drumming,
and dancing. Someone else scrupulously counts the cycles of strikes and tallies

them with chalk on a board. Later, the gangan ason who oversees the rite places the bundles inside the shrine.

Domesticating a pwen requires nothing less than this strenuous and concerted effort. The four persons literally beat the bundles, which have already been "tied up," into submission to their new roles. The painstaking accounting of the night-long beating reminds one of the "performance" of corporal discipline. A child transgresses; the parent threatens a specified number of strikes; as the child kneels to receive the punishment, he or she literally counts the blows out loud lest the angry parent exceed the aforesaid limit.

The ritual metamorphosis of pwen into lwa explains why, in his description of the gathering, Little Caterpillar said, "you collect the lwa" rather than "you collect the pwen." The verse of the following song, which was intoned following a gathering ritual held at the family shrine of Little Caterpillar's father, similarly refers to "collecting lwa" rather than collecting pwen. They gathered a lwa zandò, not a pwen.

Collect,
I'm going to collect the lwa.
Collect,
I'm going to collect my lwa.
Collect,
I'm going to collect the lwa.
It's their problem, the stupid ones
Who don't collect their lwa.

Ranmase,
M pral ranmase lwa yo.
Ranmase,
M pral ranmase lwa m yo.
Ranmase,
M pral ranmase lwa yo.
Zafè sa ki sòt o
Ki pa ranmase pa yo.

Collecting and receiving generate the metaphoric processes of containment, domestication, and incorporation that symbolically transform the pwen of Magic into a category of Guinea known as lwa zandò.[11] To reiterate, the heirs do not collect a Magical spirit owned by one of their more ambitious members. Instead, they gather a group of lwa zandò and incorporate them into the spiritual charter of "the family."

The Zandò

Because gathering is a concealment process, it is difficult to situate the zandò. Where do zandò come from? There was a consistent gap in the explanations I elicited. Notice, for instance, how Grann (Grandmother) Dada described the origins of zandò. She shifted from talking about pwen (pursued for protection in a moral, Guinea way), hatching malevolent litters, to the generation of zandò. "You go to the gangan's 'house' to get something to protect your children. He gives you a bottle, you plant it in the ground. The next day it hatches and bears a litter. That's how, you see, everybody got these zandò. Soon they demand a goat or a pig. . . ." (*Ou al kay gangan pou pran yon bagay pou pwoteje pitit ou. Li ba ou yon boutey, ou plante l nan latè. Demen li kale, fè pitit. Se kon sa ou wè tout mounn vin gen zandò sa yo. Demen yo mande yon kabrit, yon kochon. . . .*) Her explanation of the origins of zandò paralleled Aiscar's. "The pwen," he said, "hatches like a plant under the earth. After a few generations, it creates a zandò" (*Pwen an kale tankou plan anba tè. Ras an ras li vin fè zandò*).

I assumed from these statements that pwen sire zandò. When I articulated this assumption during a conversation with Little Caterpillar, he strenuously objected to the postulation of any connection between pwen and zandò. He insisted that zandò was "true Ginen," so ancient as to hail directly from the Creator while pwen are made by humans for illicit purposes. They could not be more opposed to one another.

L: The true essence (pwen) of the zandò is something ancient that comes from God. A child grows up seeing it done that way, generation after generation grows up seeing it done like that. It is ancient, ancient, ancient. Zandò is the very work of God.

Vreman pwen zandò a se yon bagay danti ki sòti pa Dye. Pitit leve jwenn ni la; pitit an pitit leve jwenn ni. Se yon danti, danti, danti. Zandò se travay Bondye menm.

K: But aren't zandò the offspring of pwen?

Men zandò pa pitit pwen?

L: No! [If anything] pwen are the issue of [i.e., come after] zandò. A pwen is something you make. A zandò is a spirit from God who was created for that very reason.

Non! Pwen se pitit zandò. Pwen se bagay ou fè. Zandò se yon nanm pa Dye ki sòti menm pou sa.

Although zandò are inherited as Guinea, they retain the violent and unruly attributes of their Magical origins (which in turn justifies the need for Guinea's discipline). Zandò are aggressive, dark, and burning hot. Thorns are conjured up in images of zandò. They roost in mapou (silk cotton, Bombacaceae) trees studded with stout, sharp thorns. Unlike the cooler lwa who typically "hold" heirs with nonacute ailments, zandò "pierce" them with frightening epileptic seizure, madness, and hemorrhage. Zandò prefer the bush, the night, and the air, as opposed to the lwa vodou's penchant for the inside of shrines or homes, the day, water, and the earth. Recorded during a bat gè ceremony in Ti Rivyè in 1988, this song comments on the linkage between the affliction of a member of "the house" (shrine of the descent group) and the spirits roosting in the silk cotton tree:

Mondong, they don't come to see me.
Mondong, they don't come to see me.
There is a sick person in the house.
The mapou is dangerous.

Mondong, yo pa vini wè mwen.
Mondong, yo pa vini wè mwen.
Gen maladi nan kay la.
Mapou a danjere.

The etiology of pwen afflictions and "authentic Guinea" rituals to gather, domesticate, and discipline them were "discovered" during a period of decisive ritual and social transformation. "The family" was being redefined as an African ritual unit directed by a professional gangan ason and a corps of initiated ounsi women dedicated to the service of African traditions. The consolidating moment for the family was apparently the introduction of rites of passage to "reclaim" the spirits (or "dead") of their founding testaments from the water, and to give them a voice to disclose the authentic Guinea traditions (in the clay vessel or govi) to tame the bad powers and incorporate their bad essence into the traditions of the family. Inevitable outbreaks of the burning hot afflictions and divinations of yet another member's pursuit inside the fig tree ensured the perpetuation of this process and, of course, the continual incorporation of pwen as lwa zandò, or Magic, into Guinea.

The dialectic of Guinea and Magic pivots on the transformative process of gathering pwen as lwa zandò. Authentic Africa, hallmark of morality and precedence, vilifies the immoral pursuit of pwen. At the same time, an effete Guinea needs to harness the vitalizing contagion of pwen to rejuvenate itself. Under the pretense that Guinea has to contain the pwen before its ravenous litter consumes Guinea's children, Guinea appropriates their life-giving productivity. Instead of gathering a "bad" pwen, the "essence" of Magical production, Guinea gathers ritually sanitized zandò. Gathering is also, therefore, a method of obfuscation. Ritual gathering protects the standing of the superior by maintaining the illusion of its independence. The complex of rites described here—gathering, tying the bundles, beating gè—accomplish the domestication of pwen, the absorption of their vitalizing heat into cool Guinea and the incorporation of new lwa zandò into the charter of "the family." Larose (1975a:112) provides an elegant description of this dynamic (even though he does not identify the ritual "gathering" processes that maintain it):

> Like the fig-tree, which in time, becomes connected to the ground with its root-system, so "points," even if they always retain something of their evil origin, become for the inheriting generations, part of the so called "Guinea heritage." Born out of the private ambition of one man, they come to define, in the subsequent generations, the collective interests of family groups and are thus incorporated into society along traditional lines.

The dialectic of Guinea and Magic allows Guinea to redraw the moral boundary of the asymmetrical relationship between cool and hot, sterile and vital, depending upon its shifting interests (Larose 1975a:96). In some contexts the relationship is construed as a hierarchical interdependency, in others as independent systems. The highest ranking lwa vodou/blan are thought to have originated in the sacred homeland of Afrik Ginen but the lower-classed "zandò," as Aiscar, the gangan ason, explained to me, "have documents from Guinea but they were born in Haiti" (*zandò yo gen dokiman ki sòt nan Ginen men yo fèt an Ayiti*). He likened the zandò to the lowly militia who accompany the cabinet-level bureaucrats of Guinea. Every recitation of the Africa Prayer, the lwa by lwa and ancestor by ancestor litany of the spiritual charter of the descent group, re-creates this hierarchy beginning with the lwa vodou and descending to the inferior zandò. The sequencing of ceremonies at the annual "feeding" further reinforces the difference between the foreign lwa and the incorporated zandò.

The scheduling of events at the kanzo initiation can be seen as a particularly discreet attempt to define and control the interdependence between these opposing domains. Forty-one days after their emergence from seclusion and the final rite of reincorporation, the ounsi return to the shrine to participate in a low-key ritual that, to my knowledge, has not been reported in descriptions of the rite of passage. They go back into the chamber where they previously "laid down" for the cool patriarch, Danbala Wedo, and remove the white garments signifying initiation. They put on new bright red and blue dresses. Costumed in honor of the hot spirit, Ezili Dantò, the new ounsi are made to come into contact with a ritual fire and then join in the "final dance for Dantò" (*denye dans Dantò*). Ezili Dantò is the quintessential domesticated pwen, the ground-figure to her cool counterpart, Ezili Freda. The ounsi's temporary embodiment of Dantò's heat makes tangible cool Guinea's implicit and covert need for Magic's "bad" heat.

The separation between the cool and the hot spirits is further reiterated in longer ritual cycles. Today the "authentic Guinea" lwa eat at least every year; zandò feast only once or twice a generation (hence the representation that they are perpetually starving). The cool lwa are fed during the hot months of summer and the hottest lwa feast during the cool season.

A scheduling conflict threatened to blur these separations during the summer of 1984 and a significant ritual dispute ensued. An imminent zandò feeding overlapped with a kanzo initiation (which was nearing completion) on the adjacent estate (bitasyon). The gangan ason leading the kanzo spread word of his dissatisfaction with his colleague for creating a conflict since many ounsi and a few gangan ason were expected to participate in both rites. "Hot and cold do not mix" (*cho e frèt pa melanje*), he charged. (He of course ignored that 41 days after their kanzo consecrating them to the cool Danbala, the novices would exchange their white garments for red and blue to dance in worship of the hot Ezili Dantò.) The leader of the zandò rite, however, defended his position. His descent group had not carried out a zandò feeding for more than two decades and ravenous zandò had "pierced" two younger members, the seriousness of whose conditions would not permit further delay. Another gangan ason, who was committed to participate in both events, mediated a unidirectional compromise that affirmed the hegemony of the lwa blan. Servitors would be allowed to pass from the cool kanzo rite to the hot zandò, the direction of dominance and the "gathering." But they would not be permitted to move in the direction of vitalization because of its implication of Guinea's dependency. The impropriety was instead represented as polluting the cool with contaminating heat.

Semantics of Zandò Food Offerings

The semantics of ritual food offerings further distinguish between these classes of lwa. While the lwa vodou dine indoors and at table, the zandò eat outdoors. Zandò are not worthy of being received inside. Zandò are fed away from authentic Guinea shrines and sites, in the wooded perimeters of residential compounds where the apical ancestors are believed to have buried their (moral, Guinea) pwen. As Ilavert, a gangan ason "student" of Misdor's, explained, "they are served in the woods. They cannot be inside. . . . they are not people" (*Yo sèvi nan bwa. Yo pa fèt pou kay. Yo pa mounn*). The quintessential Guinea lwa feast upon foods that have been so thoroughly "separated" as to render their high-ranked, personified "diners" impotent. The etiquette of zandò feasts, on the other hand, symbolically transforms the diners into overfertilized savages. They are treated to undifferentiated mixtures of food thrown into an assemblage of baskets, basins, half-calabashes, and tubs that are used to transport raw produce, water, and other materials. While sterile, cool elders one by one taste easily gummed but nutritionally worthless "mouth passers"; wild, hot zandò "eat" life-giving viv, the symbolic quintessence of "food."

Zandò feedings do not happen more often than once a generation or so in Ti Rivyè. (I was fortunate to attend two such rites during my year-and-a-half residence there.) Although the common perception is that zandò do need to feed more frequently, the heirs callously delay feeding them. Crazed with hunger, they start afflicting the youngest generation, just as pwen and lwa do, as a way of retaliating against parents. When the latter finally assent to hosting the zandò, the spirits, appearing in possession-performance, grab and hoard the offerings. Take Tenten's explanation of the zandò's behavior.

> They [the zandò] are stingy. [It's because] they only eat every 15, 20, or 30 years. The others [lwa] eat every year or year-and-a-half. It has been at least 30 years since Lerose's [zandò] last ate. [Lerose is the founder of a nearby eritaj.] The heirs don't want to [feed them]. The [zandò] have to resort to holding [afflicting] people to get them to feed them.

> *Yo chich. Yo manje tou le kenz an, vent an, trant an. Lòt yo manje chak ane, chak ane e demi. Pa Lerose yo gen menm 30 an depi yo manje. Eritye yo pat vle. Se kenbe yo kenbe moun ki fè yo ba yo manje.*

The feast for the zandò of the Michel Pè descent group took place in October 1984. (Michel Pè was Tonton Ogoun's father-in-law.) During the feeding of Michel Pè's zandò, the zandò couple, Marinèt and Ti Jean, "dancing in the heads" of two female heirs, swept up baskets of starches and darted frenetically among the assembled participants, stopping only to stuff another yam or plantain into their mouths, hair, or bodices. The agitated lwa climbed a tree and "hid" sacks and baskets of the mixed offerings in the branches. At intervals, Marinèt and Ti Jean approached certain heirs, defensively protecting their booty. Participants occasionally pretended to cajole the zandò to share a morsel of food to the great amusement of others.

At least since the 1940s, recorded descriptions of rituals for the zandò describe offerings that epitomize peasant agriculture and eschew the tastes of the outside world.[12] The prestations have included staples produced only locally and distributed through the internal marketing system. The serving pieces consist of assorted containers used to transport food in its raw state: large, undecorated (Haitian-made) baskets of varying shapes, unpainted half-calabashes, plastic tubs, and enameled basins. The peasants' black pigs were the main animal sacrifice until 1983, when the breed ceased to exist. Goat substituted for pork for several years until pigs were available again.

Offerings to the zandò consist mainly of bulky hunks and lumps of dry, simply boiled or roasted yams, plantains, taro, millet, sweet potatoes, cornmeal, beans, and breadfruit. Virtually the whole panorama of the viv (starch) class is represented, except for imported starches: white rice and bulgur. (The viv category excludes nutritionally less valuable breads and pastas made from imported wheat, favorites of the sophisticated "foreign lwa.") White rice is identified either as an import or as an internal (Artibonite Valley) product of large-scale capitalized agriculture. The most expensive viv, white rice is also the most highly esteemed, the only appropriate grain to serve a high-status guest. White rice pudding is an appropriate food gift to the lwa blan. Bulgur is the prototypical "disaster relief food" (*manje sinistre*). While most of the foods presently offered to the zandò are less expensive than those tendered to the superior "bourgeois lwa," the avoidance of bulgur, the cheapest cereal available in the local market, underscores the fact that price is not the evaluative criterion in this classificatory system. Instead, food

6.3. Feeding the *zandò* on Michel Pè's land, Ti Rivyè, September 1984.

6.4. Feeding the *zandò* on Michel Pè's land, Ti Rivyè, September 1984.

products have meaning by virtue of their nutritional classification and their relations of production, circulation, and consumption.

Zandò meals are oppressively "dry" (*shèsh*). "Dry" is an inauspicious condition. It implies not only absence of moisture, but also lack of highly valued fat. "Dry" can describe a precarious physical state, in contrast to a round, healthy appearance; for example, someone who looks emaciated and drawn is said to be "dry." Dry food is analogously neither appealing nor nourishing. Fondness for generous amounts of grease is thus reinforced by the presumed nutritional role of fat in digestion. As Malgre Sa put it to me, when you consume a "dry" plateful, "your stomach doesn't get enough grease to absorb the strength of the food" (*pou vant ou ka grese kont pou pran fòs manje a*).

Accordingly, a "very good" (*vreman bon*) meal consists of a combination of cooked foods: a viv (high carbohydrate, the meal base) and a "protein" (*vyann*) which has been cooked in, or is fried and accompanied by, a generously fat, vegetable-based "sauce" or *sos* (Alvarez and Murray 1981:166). In the homestead where I lived, only on Sundays and holidays, therefore, did "households" (meaning people who eat from the same cooking pot) regularly consume and circulate three-pronged meals with a viv of white rice.[13] During the rest of the week, the better off kitchens prepared lesser, but nonetheless acceptable, primarily meatless meals. These meals consisted of a viv served with a (greasy) sauce with a bit of fresh or dried fish in it. The poorer households typically consumed and circulated platefuls containing only "dry" viv. A household head "sending" platefuls of the dry viv to the other household is therefore obliged to apologize before presenting it by saying, in effect, "it's dry, you know" (*Li shèsh, wi*). The lumps of dry starches offered to the zandò, then, constitute a dry meal barely nutritious enough to "support" those too poor or shameless to reject it. As Pierre said to me (in English) while looking at my photographs of the Michel Pè zandò feeding, "It's like saying to them, here's your food, just—just—take it! At least they could say they ate and filled their stomachs."

Feeding and the Dialectic of Guinea and Magic

The semantics of ritual food offerings suggest an approach to the dialectic of Guinea and Magic. The exemplars of authentic Guinea personify not peasants, but the forces encompassing them: the cosmopolitan elite, transnational agro-industrial corporations, and the neocolonial power. They look white. They eat only imported foods, or the exotic fruits of capitalist export "speculation." These forces, the rituals seem to be saying, have the authority to dominate. But they are only authority. *They have no pwen of their own.* They feed off the vitality of others whom they can dominate. This Guinea "gathers" the vitality of the peasants, the producers of zandò foods and redundant peasants for export. The gifts exchanged between parents, spouses, and siblings residing at home with migrants abroad symbolize their place in a transnational feeding process. The peasants send packages of viv to their migrants laboring abroad.

Authentic Guinea lwa do not *need* to "eat" or "drink" because they can gather the vitality of pwen who get incorporated as zandò. The zandò's willingness to barely sustain themselves on dry, high-carbohydrate viv, particularly in the wake of the elimination of the black pigs, their preferred sacrificial victims, and the resultant scarcity of palatable, sustaining fat, keeps the high-class lwa dining more often, in fine cosmopolitan style. Their acquiescence allows Guinea to remain Guinea. The beneficiaries are transnational corporations, the merchant elite, and those who gain more by appearing more peasant.

Feeding the zandò sums up this process. The rite takes place by the tree where the apical ancestor buried her or his own pwen. Members collaborate in a collective regathering of all of the pwen ever purchased by members of the descent group, for new bundles are prepared, tied, and beaten for all of the pwen/zandò. The timing of the zandò feedings further suggests that these rites are a mode of reproduction or "re-feeding." Zandò feedings occur about once a generation, in order that the higher ranked lwa can dine at least once a year. These events, which are documented by marks carved into the bark of the founder's tree, symbolically define the beginnings of the long-term ritual feeding cycle.

Conducting a zandò feeding depends on equal contributions by the entire membership of the descent group. Unlike rites for the higher ranked spirits, which necessitate the participation of the professional staff and the sponsor, the zandò rites cannot take place unless every member who can participate does so. Illnesses dispersed across different lines of descent escalate until the eritaj as a whole reacts. One branch of the family may want to release their daughter or son from a zandò's hold, but they cannot fully or properly appease the zandò until the entire descent group collaborates in the worship. Each branch of the eritaj takes responsibility for a relatively modest share of the economical feeding burden. This collective feeding of the original pwen, and all those who, over the generations, alienate themselves for the sake of Guinea, starts the cycle anew.

When, for instance, Komè fell ill in Martinique, she sent a cassette letter to her parents in Ti Rivyè. They immediately went to the shrine of one of their eritaj to "summon the lwa." Divination revealed that Komè was being "held" by a hungry zandò inherited through her mother. In addition, there were other victims belonging to the same eritaj descended from the early-19th-century ancestor Michel Pè. The success of her mother's efforts to liberate her migrant daughter from the jaws of the zandò depended on the willingness and ability of the Michel Pè descent group collectively to pacify their zandò. Filoza visited cousins from each of the 11 branches of the family to solicit their commitment to the ritual endeavor.

The following year, fourth-, fifth-, and sixth-generation descendants of Michel Pè's 11 children gathered in a clearing on the land he had bought for them a century and a half before. The zandò of the Michel Pè eritaj satiated their hunger with heaps of dry starches. They did release the migrant, Komè, working in far-off Martinique from their grip. But it was neither the first nor the last time the spirits worshipped by Komè's peasant ancestors would interfere with her body and her life and threaten her well-being.

The next chapter explores in more depth how beliefs in the mobility of affliction keep human pwen-migrants tethered to the home. Spirits and sorcerers, whose powers migrate anywhere, can interfere with migrants' ability to alienate their labor power abroad. Migrants can guaranty their productivity by remitting funds to their families to feed their lwa. These public acts of ritual generosity help diffuse suspicions that the migrants have become arrogant and greedy individuals, suspicions that bring punishment through sorcery. Such unearned chastisement is the onus of human pwen working out of sight on behalf of ambivalent Guinea patrons.

7

Guarantying Migrants in the Core

Here is the difference between lwa and pwen. A lwa is a member of your family. A pwen is a stranger from far away. The lwa Sobo has children, Ogoun has children, Loko has children. A lwa is like your mother. Whenever she feels like it she can make you kneel and give you a spanking. The root lwa can hold you at any time—if you don't take care of them. The lwa are there to protect you. But a pwen can work for you. You could go to a gangan and buy a pwen because you want to have a car. The lwa could make you have two or three cars. You owe the pwen only if it works for you. If the pwen made you win three thousand dollars, to give the pwen a thousand of it is nothing. If you don't pay the pwen, it can eat you.

—*Zo Guerrier, January 1984*

I have my protection here. My protection won't abandon me in anything I could achieve, in anything I could get, it is there with me.

—*Little Caterpillar, November 1986*

Guinea and Magic are the representations of a peasant society whose African ancestors rose in violent struggle against plantation slavery of colonial Saint Domingue. Joseph Lacombe exemplified the late-19th-century cosmopolitan elite who, with support from their European patrons, moved to repossess the peasants' land. Their encroachment on the peasants' principal weapon in their struggle to stay free made it easier for the new, 20th-century colonial regime to commandeer the peasants' labor power. In Léogane, Lacombe's greed for land paved the way for Americans to dominate the labor force, exploiting most on local (formerly peasant) sugar plantations and sending others to the Dominican

Republic and Cuba. Today the vestigial peasants "freely" export their children to be exploited by capital abroad.

The beliefs and practices described in the previous chapter make sense out of this woeful history. The structures encompassing the peasants and the peasants responses to these forces lurk in representations of Guinea and Magic and in the songs, offerings, sacrifices, and rites for lwa, pwen and zandò. Some truths are telescoped, others redefined, still others consigned to oblivion. The descent group's recitation of the Africa Prayer defiantly remembers the homeland their slave ancestors were supposed to forget and valorizes the first testament's heroic seizure of freedom by means of purchasing land. But the litany also naturalizes the descendants' acquiescence to professional ritual intermediaries and their standards. Offerings to the spirits parody habits of the cosmopolitan elite and peasantry alike. The sacred songs make meaning out of a 400-year experience with the pain of displacement as well as the recent indignity of living off the remittances of loved ones who dared to take their canoes all the way to Mayami.

The dialectic of Guinea and Magic is a symbolic reformulation of this community's history as peasants who freed themselves from slavery and, more recently, as producers of migrants and consumers of remittances. How do these representations inform relations between persons and between persons and their lwa? If, in addition, three out of every four families in Ti Rivyè have at least one immediate kinsman Over There, how does this ideology influence the triadic relations among people in Ti Rivyè, migrants, and lwa? Home kin stand to their migrants as Guinea to its pwen. Given the exodus of pwenified persons to distant lands, ensuring the flow of remittances is an important preoccupation of families and ritual specialists back home. The lwa can affect the migrant pwen's productivity abroad by holding the person and making him or her sick. The threat of spiritual affliction is an indirect means of disciplining the peripatetic agents of their home families' livelihood (and of Guinea's vitality) to keep the wages flowing home. At another level, narratives of migrants' spirit-caused afflictions provide appropriate explanations for the disappointments they encounter in the promised land. Their home kin are meanwhile affirmed in their respective efforts to find and carry out the ritual healing that will restore their migrant's health.

Feeding and Interdependence

The interdependence between close kin and the reciprocal dependence between kin and their spirits (to whom they are also related) are mirrors, or "models of and for" one another (Geertz 1973). On both sides of this mirror, feeding is so valorized that it not only stands for this mutuality but also constitutes it. Heirs sustain their inherited lwa through an elaborately encoded system of feeding.

Two oft-repeated words characterize the relationship between the kin and their lwa: *sèvi* and *okipe*. Sèvi, as I described earlier, means hosting with food. Okipe means "to take care of" by providing material support for domestic consumption: food, clothing, shelter. Okipe defines, for example, a husband's reciprocal responsibilities to his wife, for which she exchanges her "respect" (*respè*) (Lowenthal 1987:125). (Women do not "okipe" their husbands and lwa do not "okipe" people.)

The construct of Guinea Africa, the dominant cosmographic metaphor, conditions the reciprocal exchange of feeding for protection. The lwa reside in the far-off mythical homeland of Ginen, or "Africa" (despite the equally salient assertion of metonymic connection between the lwa and portions of the land set aside for their feedings and worship). The lwa complain of being forgotten by their "heirs" and left to starve in Guinea. They have a credible fear of abandonment from the alienation of the land and the lwa installed in shrines there, migration, and heirs converting to Protestantism or otherwise choosing not to serve their lwa. They extort attention to their deplorable fate by threatening to "hinder" or "thwart" (*anpeche*) the heirs. They afflict them with illness, accident, or misfortune. The heirs, in turn, struggle to satisfy the lwa's appetites for spectacular ritual entertainment and exorbitantly costly ritual feasts in order to avoid having to kneel down for the lwa's punishment.

These burdens are both imposed and subtly contested in ritual performance "frames" conducive to exaggerated, stylized, competitive expression. Meetings between the heirs and their lwa entail pragmatic maneuvering and stroking on both sides to sustain this difficult mutuality, behaviors that arouse both humor and tension at performances. The lwa whine, protest, and intimidate; the heirs vow, procrastinate, and cajole. While the lwa take to the moral high ground of Guinea Africa, the heirs tread a thin line between genuine exaltation and obsequious mockery.

The chief performance settings for these meetings, apart from dreams, include

1. Family members go to a shrine and pay the gangan ason to "summon the lwa in the govi jar." The gangan ason, who sits alone inside the altar room, uses his ason (rattle and bell) knowledge to "make the lwa speak." The lwa, speaking through the medium, converse with the heirs sitting on the other side of the wall. (A govi seance with Danbala, Ezili, and Gede will be described in this chapter.)
2. Members of the family sponsor a rite to "retrieve the dead from the waters" (*retire/wete mò nan dlo*). The gangan, ason in hand, enters a white tent alone or with other professional priests. He summons the lwa vodou who will fetch the ancestor out of the waters in order to place it in a jar in the shrine

whence it, too, will communicate with the descendants. The lwa and the ancestor, speaking through the gangan ason inside the tent, converse with the ancestor and the family members assembled outside.

3. A lwa "mounts" a member's "head" and interacts with the heirs in possession-performance. Ironically, the lwa is least likely to talk to the heirs in this frame. The oracular function of possession has been replaced by professional use of the ason. The lwa now "dance" and gesture rather than "speak" in their "horses'" heads. When they do converse it is through pantomime. The gangan ason supplies the words to interpret the "charades" for everyone else.

4. Ritual song texts, intoned in solo-chorus antiphony at all rituals, represent the spirited discussions that take place in the above-mentioned settings. Song texts capture these strained interactions either intratextually, in a series of mutually contradictory song texts, or within a single song text. During a ritual performance, a praise song might well be followed by a song featuring an enfeebled lwa warning of his or her imminent demise and then another featuring excerpts from a tense conversation between an indignant lwa threatening revenge and an overly contrite heir vowing to settle the "debt" with the requisite ritual offering. For example, in the following ritual song, the god Agaou uncovers an outstanding "debt" (a ritual offering or sacrifice). He demands a response: "What does the family have to say to me about it?" The members—his pwen—appeal to him to be patient, entreating, "don't you see we'll settle it?"

Agaou, oh, Agaou, oh
Look at a debt, oh!
I say, look at a debt
That the family owes.
Oh, don't you see we'll pay up?
Friends, what do you say for it?
Friends, what do you say for it?
Call out, *ago!*
Look at a debt, oh.
My friends, look at a debt
That the family owes.
Oh, don't you see we'll pay up?

Agaou o Agaou o
Gade youn dèt, o.
M di, gade youn dèt
Ke lafanmi yo dwe.

Ou pa wè nou pral akite, o vre?
Mezanmi sa nap di pou sa?
Mezanmi sa nou di pou sa?
Kriye ago!
Gade youn dèt o.
Mezanmi gade youn dèt
Ke lafanmi yo dwe.
Ou pa wè nou pral akite o vre?

This song quite accurately captures the tenor of negotiations between demanding, intimidating lwa and heirs with their backs to the wall. Indeed I heard these very phrases during a "reclaiming the dead from the waters" ritual in July 1984, described in chapter 5. At the ritual, the patron lwa who had "loved" and "claimed" Bréton appeared to extort "payment" from "his son's" surviving relatives. From inside the tent, we heard the distant voice of someone weak from desertion and famine: it was Bréton's Ogoun Balendyo.

The likeness between the two texts suggests that the song text, in turn, may have structured the lwa/gangan ason's discourse. Ogoun addressed the whole "family" (*fanmi*). He referred to himself in both the first and third person, which is also typical of song "grammar." In stylized speech paralleling that of verses, he reminded Bréton's family of the unpaid "debt"; he demanded, "what does the family have to say to me about it?" He warned the family "to cooperate to feed him" and to restore his "energy"; otherwise he would "play dirty tricks on them."

Good evening. How are you, my friends? My son Bréton owes Ogoun. Who will pay up for him? Mister Bréton didn't give me anything. Everything he did—selling plantains, selling breadfruit—I am the one who helped [literally, made] him sell. What does the family have to say about it? You had better cooperate together because Bréton owes me. If you don't cooperate together to feed me I'll play dirty tricks on the family. You have to give Ogoun energy.

Bonswa. Ban mwen nouvèl ou, mezanmi. Gason m Bréton dwe Ogoun, ki sa kap peye pou li? Ogoun travay li pa manje. Misye Bréton pa ban anyen. Tout sa l fè, vann banann, vann veritab, se mwen k fè l vann. Sa la fanmi sa ou ap di avè m? Se pou nou kole tèt nou ansanm paske Bréton dwe m. Si nou pa kole tèt nou ansanm, ban mwen manje map fè la fanmi malfezan. Se pou nou bay Ogoun kouray.

Bréton then started singling out individuals. First he named Tenten, Bréton's paternal half-brother; the two were especially close. Tenten retorted, "I have my own responsibilities." The lwa was not in fact in Tenten's line; Bréton inherited the lwa through his mother. (The gangan ason's/Bréton's genealogical acumen must have been flawed that night.) Ogoun then fixed his demands upon Bréton's full sister and her daughter, who had returned from Guadeloupe for the event (Bréton had no direct heirs.) After an instant the two were promising, "yes, we'll do it, we'll do it."

Ogoun went on to identify the substance of Bréton's debt: Bréton owned Ogoun for defending his livelihood. Bréton, who died shortly before I arrived in the village, was described to me as a successful plantain trader, a generous brother and uncle (he had no heirs of his own) and a fervent, devoted "lwa fanatic" (*fanatik lwa*). So when Ogoun asserted that he (Ogoun) made Bréton's trade prosper, no one doubted the lwa's claim. Ogoun warned Bréton's relatives that if they did not acquit themselves of their brother's/uncle's ritual debt, he might "play dirty tricks on them"—antics that would interfere with their respective abilities to succeed. If they fed Ogoun, on the other hand, he might accede to safeguard their earnings as well.

The Pwenification of People

When Ogoun claimed credit for overseeing his "son's" trade, he clarified how the Guinea-Magic dialectic encompasses relations between lwa and the people who struggle to "serve" them. The lwa "pwenify" people. Just as Magic's illegitimately productive pwen provide the vitality to produce ever-moral Guinea, so are heirs made to work on behalf of their lwa. Every heir is not, however, equally "pwenified." Only some perform the "bad work" that vitalizes the Guinea system. They labor Outside so that Guinea can hide their proletarianization—and their absolute exploitation. Pwenification is nevertheless veiled by a discourse of "do for," as opposed to "work." "Doing for" (*fè pou*) is a category of authentic, or moral, Guinea discourse. "Working" (*travay*) is associated with illicit Magic. People-who-are-pwen are said to "do for the lwa." This euphemism obscures their alienation so as not to tarnish Guinea's character. Guinea indirectly bullies their pwen into "doing" on their behalf by offering to "protect" (*pwoteje*) their pwen's ability to "work."

Given Guinea's self-interested need to "gather" the productive vitality of pwen, it is not surprising that the lwa's counter-gift amounts to labor insurance. Neither is it surprising that Guinea's ambiguous production program yields a contradictory and arbitrary return gift. "Protection" is a *negatively* construed concept. That is, the lwa protect the people who "serve" and "feast" them by consenting *not* to chastise them (cf. Murray 1984).

Protection is an appropriate function for concerned, loving grandparents, a prevailing representation of the dominant pantheon. Grandparents command absolute respect from their grandchildren, for whom they frequently act as caretakers—and stern disciplinarians. Bastien (1961:488) comments in this regard that "the grandparents exercise authority equal to the parents' over the grandchildren in matters of socialization and behavior, and commonly children fear the sternness of their grandfathers more than that of their parents." Speakers in fact use the same term of address, *papa*, for father and grandfather. (They use different terms for mother and grandmother). When people refer, in song lyrics and in spoken word, to Papa Danbala or Papa Loko, they pay respect to a familiar but feared grandfather.

Zo emphasized the theme of discipline when I asked him to explain the contrast between Guinea's lwa and Magic's pwen. He began with the contrast between family and strangers and then shifted to the theme of parental authority. He emphasized that a lwa, like a parent, can mete out harsh discipline arbitrarily, punishments whose sting derives more from the humiliation and inconvenience they cause than physical discomfort.

> A lwa is a member of your family. A pwen is a stranger from far away. The lwa Sobo has children, Ogoun has children, Loko has children. A lwa is [like] your mother. Your mother can make you kneel and give you a spanking any time. The lwa are there to protect you.

> *Lwa se fanmi ou men lwa achte [pwen] se etranje. Se tankou lwa Sobo gen pitit, Ogoun gen pitit, Loko gen pitit. Lwa a se manman ou. Manman ou gen dwa mete ou a jenou. Li gen dwa kale ou nenpòt lè. Lwa lafanmi yo la pou pwoteje ou.*

When Zo said that the lwa "protect," then, he meant that the lwa temporarily consent not to discipline their "grandchildren" too severely. Sickness is the epitomizing metaphor of this antiprotection, even though the affliction is typically a polysymptomatic onslaught including illness, accident, and bad luck. As we saw in the embodiment of Danbala Wedo's demand that women get initiated in the kanzo rite of passage, the illnesses associated with this pantheon are chronic, debilitating, and nonacute, in contrast to the "hot" seizures, hemorrhaging, paralysis, and acute afflictions sent by forces associated with Magic.

The lwa's ambiguous "protection" amounts to "obstructing" or "thwarting" (*anpeche*) people-who-are-pwen's power to labor Outside. Little Caterpillar conceptualized his patron's promise of protection as insurance on his "achievements." He praised his patron lwa, Baron la Croix, for chaperoning his migration. He told me, "I have my protection here. My protection won't abandon me in anything I could achieve, in anything I could get, it is there with me" (*M gen pwotèj mwen la. Pwotèj mwen pa sa kite m menm nan tout sa m te kapab realize, nan tout sa m te kapab genyen, yo la a avè m*).

Little Caterpillar's cousin, Pepe, elucidated the lwa's offer of protection. Pepe is a charismatic, successful professional gangan ason in Ti Rivyè. His ritual successes evince his masterful appropriation of old and new forms. Though he is illiterate, he has enlisted the assistance of his literate offspring to modernize his practice. A hand-painted mural on one side of his "worksite" lists the professional services he offers. Inside, he sits at a chair behind a desk. His patients sit facing him across the desk. Nonliterate healers/sorcerers like Pepe have long used the aura of writing in their magical "work." While preparing charms, they inscribe signs on a paper in order to appropriate the inside, or pwen, of capitalism's perceived means of accounting gains.[1] In 2003 Pepe was selling his clients a photocopied, handwritten inventory of the petitions used in the session, which will continue to be effective when they carry the paper on their person.

7.1. Pepe Michel, gangan ason, Ti Rivyè, June 2003.

Pepe's engaging speech is a charming blend of "with it" idioms and traditional imagery. Using this discursive *bricolage*, he offered me insight into the experience of migration and the lwa's lever in it. Pepe explained to me how the lwa intervene in the lives of their emigrant "servitors." He stressed the term "guaranty" (*garanti*), meaning both to "ensure" and "to yield a return" (*garan* means return or profit). Haitian migrants, including Little Caterpillar, frequently use this concept to articulate the goal of their migration.

In addition to "guaranty," Pepe improvised its antithesis: *degaranti* ("to deguaranty"). Degaranti is the same as anpeche. It means to thwart or to undermine your return. To illustrate, he referred to the case of Lamerci, a resident immigrant of the United States and an initiated ounsi who contributed to the annual "work of the house" with presents of the lwa's favorite beverage or toiletry for the annual feast. When possible, she returned to attend the rites. He said,

> There are people like Lamerci. She always returns to see how the [annual] festival is going. She sees how the work is going. It guaranties her. It supports her. It satisfies her. She knows that if she doesn't find anything today, tomorrow she'll find. She knows too that if she is employed, she won't be fired for any old reason. Instead of de-guarantying her, it always guaranties her little bonus even higher.

> *Gen mounn tankou Lamerci. Li toujou vini pou l wè kouman fèt la ap pase. Li wè jan travay la ap mache, li garanti li. Li apiye li. Li satisfè l. Li konnen jodi li pa jwenn, demen lap jwenn. Li konnen tou, si li nan yon travay li pa ka revoke pou nenpòt kondisyon. Angiz li degaranti li, li toujou garanti ti bonis li pi ro.*

As long as Lamerci continues to nurture her lwa back Home in *Haiti*, they may reciprocate by guarantying her "little bonus" in *the United States*. The alternative, in Pepe's words, is the option of de-guaranty. Pepe described how an emigrant might be de-guarantied by a lwa:

> If the person is in a job that pays $200 or $300 [a week], the lwa can make you lose your job. The lwa can make you sick so you'll never find work and you'll spend everything you saved. The lwa can also make you get into a car accident, lose your job, and make you an alcoholic so that you can never guaranty anything in that country.

> *Si mounn nan yon travay lap touche $200., $300., lwa a gen dwa fè ou pedi travay la. Li gen dwa fè ou malad pou ou pa janm jwenn travay e ou depanse tout sa ou te genyen. Lwa a tou gen dwa fè machin fè aksidan avèk ou, pedi djòb ou, li gen dwa fè ou bwè rom, kleren pou ou pa garanti oken anyen nan peyi a.*

Summarizing the lwa's reciprocity with migrants, then, the lwa expect diligent feeding or demonstrations of remembrance from people who "leave to search for livelihood." In return, the lwa protect the migrants' capacity to produce in "Miami." Guinea, in other words, guaranties its workers' labor power Outside. The lwa take revenge for migrants' neglect by interfering with or "de-guarantying" the same.

The lwa's leveraging of "protection" over migrants' power to labor makes them indispensable to the whole experience of labor migration. The lwa are said to be busier than ever chaperoning the work of their mobile pwen. I met one of these divine, peripatetic escorts inside a tiny, thatch-roofed shrine in Ti Rivyè in November 1984. Speaking through a gangan, Ezili Dantò boasted of her familiarity with the most remote corners of the Haitian diaspora, rattling off names of host countries and cities in North America and the Caribbean. She then announced that tomorrow she was off for Miami again. She added, "every three days I am in Miami. . . . I have to keep watch over everything that goes on. Miami is where the core is" (*Tou le twa jou m Mayami. . . . Fò m veye tout sa k pase. Se Mayami noyo a ye*). Ezili Dantò thus distinguished Miami (anywhere in Florida) as the "core." At that time (1984), "Miami" hosted two-thirds of all the migrants from Ti Rivyè.

Affliction in the Core

Descent structures the transference of feeding obligations and the passage of affliction. Everyone is believed to inherit their lwa substantially, through his or her blood. The "protection" of putatively every member of the descent group hangs upon careful reckoning and fulfillment of these inherited obligations. As Murray (1980) and Lowenthal (1987) have suggested, the construction of etiologies of affliction for outstanding ritual obligations is the eminent symbolic impetus for reaffirming descent. The members re-create this genealogy (from the lwa, through the "first owner" of the estate, to the "dead") during the "African Prayer" (*Lapriyè Ginen*), at the beginning of each ritual on the inherited land—the only occasions where the fanmi gathers as a corporate unit (Lowenthal 1987).

Typically, when a member falls sick with a suspected *maladi lwa*, it is eventually divined that the offending spiritual agent is a "hungry" lwa who is *inherited* through such and such line of descent. When Komè fell ill in Martinique in 1983, as I described previously, she sent word home. A gangan ason there divined that a lwa zandò on her mother's father's "side" (read: fanmi) was "holding" (*kenbe*) her. This zandò was attributed to Michel Pè, the founder of six ascending generations. After hearing the gangan ason's divination of the cause of her daughter's illness, Komè's mother, Filoza, recorded a cassette-letter to her, including this excerpt:

I hear that you are sick, my child, I don't know what's ailing you. Your father went to Ilavert's shrine. He found out that it's my lwa that's holding you, a lwa belonging to the Ka Pè [descent group]. The lwa played a dirty trick on you. You have a blood [disorder]. Don't you go and make bad blood [hypertension] too, do you hear, my child? Don't worry about the lwa at all. Ilavert told us that the lwa played a dirty trick on you; a lwa zandò from Ka Pè that played the dirty trick on you. I ask you now, how are you?

Ilavert gave me a candle. I lit it to ask for mercy for you, so that your body could return to normal. And when they call me [I will] give money so that I can get out of the lwa's business. Well my child, don't worry about what Roland [who offered a contradictory diagnosis in Martinique] said to you—the lwa from Ka Pè is holding you. So I made the promise. Send a message about how you are feeling so I can know if it's this or that, if what Ilavert said is right.

M tande ou malad, pitit mwen an, m pa konen nan ki kondisyon ou malad. Papa ou tal fè yon vizit kay Ilavert. Li jwenn se lwa m ki kenbe ou, lwa Ka Pè. Li f'ou malfezan tou. Ou gen youn san nan kò ou. Pa fè move san, tande pitit mwen, pa okipe li di tou. Ilavert te di nou se lwa ki fè ou malfezan; lwa zandò Ka Pè ki fè ou malfezan. Mwen voye di ou, ki jan ou santi ou?

Ilavert te ban mwen yon balenn. Mwen te limine li pou mande gras pou ou, pou ou vin nan nòmal nan kò ou. Avèk lè pou yo rele mwen pou m bay kòb pa m nan pou m pa konn afè lwa di tou. Alò pitit mwen, pa okipe lè Roland di ou-lwa Ka Pè ki kenbe ou. Alèkile mwen te fè pwomès la, pou ou voye di mwen ki jan ou santi ou. Pou m konen si se te sa, si se te pat sa, si sa Ilavert te di mwen se sa.

Filoza informed her daughter that she had made a promise to contribute to a "feeding" for the zandò on her father's mother's "side." When a lwa accepts a promise, he or she is expected to reciprocate with a qualified but immediate release of the victim. Filoza thus asked Komè to respond at once with a report of her condition. If Komè sent news of recuperation, Filoza would know that the gangan ason's diagnosis and advice were on the mark. Accustomed to seeking second and third opinions, Filoza was prepared to go to elsewhere for help. Komè did recuperate. Ten months later, Filoza's father's mother's descent group held a "feeding of the zandò" (*manje zandò*) in a clearing on the Michel Pè estate (described in chapter 6). Komè was not the only member who had been "held" by the zandò. Two of her cousins on her "mother's father's side" were sick as well.

It was no accident that Komè rather than her mother was the victim. Gods control parents (their pwen) by afflicting their children. When a parent neglects to feed a hungry lwa, the latter typically retaliates by "holding" a child or children while leaving the parent unharmed. In her cassette-letter to her daughter, Filoza articulated her disquiet with a system that persecutes innocent children. She would offer to endure the lwa's punishment if they would spare her children but the lwa are selfish "children" unwilling to heed reason.

> Komè, my child, the lwa make me feel so bad. You remember, a lwa held you, a lwa of Grandmother Rose [fanmi of Filoza's maternal grandfather] held you. Your father swore [because it was his child the lwa chose to persecute rather than any of another hundred or so heirs]. Since then I have told the lwa on my mother's side and on my father's side if they have to, "hold" me instead. The lwa is childish; that's why s/he holds you. So I went ahead and promised the lwa [so s/he would release you].

> Komè, pitit mwen, lwa ban m santi santiman. Ou sonje, yon lwa te kenbe ou, yon lwa kay Grann Rose ki te kenbe ou. Papa ou te jire. Depi lè-a m te di lwa bò manman m, bò papa m, si yo bezwen, kenbe mwen pito, men pa kenbe pitit mwen-an, paske lwa-se ti-mounn li ki fè l kap rive kenbe ou. Ki fè mwen fè pwomès la.

While the lwa's choice to persecute innocent members of the younger generation may seem childish and unreasonable, their conduct makes practical sense. A father or mother might take risks with his or her own health, endlessly delaying payment of a "debt" (dèt). But, as Filoza and the father of six of her seven children continually demonstrated during the 18 months I shared with them, a parent will go to all lengths to save the life of a child—and the source of his or her own guaranty. He or she will lose no time in performing the offerings required to release the child from the grip of a lwa.

Diagnosis and Intervention

The series of events leading to Komè's affliction, her parents' intervention, and the gangan ason's mediation of the resolution illustrate a typical scenario. The episode often begins when the migrant sends a letter (or cassette tape) with news of illness, loss of a job or failure to find employment, accident, or troublesome dream—the crisis is routinely polysymptomatic. By the time the family receives the message, the migrant has probably already ruled out that s/he suffers from a *maladi Bondye,* or "Creator-God/natural illness." A maladi Bondye is independent of one's social relations with either spirits or people. Because they are impersonal or unmotivated, maladi Bondye can be treated by biomedical and lay doctors and cured with medicine from pills, syringes, leaves, or roots. Most illnesses are attributed to this diffuse source.

Visits to doctors and experiments with different remedies having failed to relieve the person's suffering, the migrant suspects she or he is suffering from a different category of illness. If the family suspects a lwa is the cause of their child's affliction, they will go to the shrine where the gangan ason "calls the lwa" (*rele lwa*). The lwa, speaking through the gangan ason from behind the closed door of the altar room, usually confirms the already alleged etiology: the victim has a *maladi lwa* (lwa affliction) and is under the "hold" of a lwa. (Gangan ason often control their clients by, as Komè's mother remarked, avoiding "opening the whole thing at once" [*debouche bay la nèt*]. The family may have to go back to the shrine for another seance to find out what they must do to release their child from the grip of the lwa.) The lwa who claims responsibility for "holding" the child tells the parents (or siblings) what they have to do to get him/her to release their child. The parents (or surrogate) return home and light a candle, make a promise to meet the ritual obligation, and petition the lwa to release their child until payment of the "debt." They send word to the migrant and, after however long it takes for the person to raise the funds, months or even years, they sponsor a public ritual feeding on the family land.

If the migrant cannot return for the ceremonies, he or she can still participate in the rites. Audio and increasingly video recorders have been integrated into healing rituals so that the rites now take place across a vast performance space. The person holding the recorder typically narrates the flow of events for the absent sponsor. Others may approach the device to speak to the far-off listener. Even spirits, who appear "in person" at the ceremonies, will approach the recorder to speak or sing to the migrant sponsor, and others expected to hear the tape.

The gangan ason may surprise the family by divining that the distress has nothing to do with the lwa. Gangan ason occasionally attribute cause to something beyond their control, temporarily forfeiting revenue, while promoting their long-term credibility among clients. At the same time, they exploit unpredictability as a strategy of control. On one occasion, for example, Komè sent word to her parents that her sister and her sister's husband of one week had been injured in a car accident. The timing of the accident suggested interference of "exigent" forces, so without waiting even to listen to the entire taped message, Loremi and Filoza decided to go to Yvon's shrine to "call the lwa." Four of their relatives and I accompanied him.

Yvon went inside the altar room. From the other side of the wall, we heard the rhythmic shaking of the rattle and bell of the ason, then chants of invocation, and, after a while, the faint sound of far-off whistling. It was Legba, the old man, who "opens the gate to let the other lwa in." From the gangan ason's rhetorical questions and answers, we could decipher the lwa's "language." Four lwa followed Legba: Danbala, Ezili Freda, Ezili Dantò, and Gede Madyawe. Through the gangan ason, each lwa conversed with everyone present in the room. Gods and persons engaged in dramatic repartee of complaint, petition, joking, and demand.

The lwa, by the way, demanded to know who that "red-skinned" woman and "stranger" was. I had arrived two months before and each of the lwa wanted to know who the "stranger" was, sitting among their children. The gangan ason explained a version of the following: I knew members of the family "over there"; I was the godmother of so-and-so's child in the United States; I was living with so-and-so in the village. Then each lwa addressed me directly (through the gangan ason). Danbala asked me when I was going to kanzo (get initiated). The request had already been put to me. At a rite two weeks before, an Ezili Freda, dancing in the head of an ounsi, approached me and caressed my head, the part of the body that is the focus of relations with the spirits and of the initiation rite in particular. A conversation among Filoza, her husband, and Danbala (speaking through Yvon) was about whether the recently arrived foreigner could tolerate the heat inside the closed-off altar room, drink the water, or eat the food. Danbala seemed satisfied with the idea of a shortened rite of passage lasting only three days. Next Ezili Freda spoke to me, living up to her reputation for promiscuity by challenging me to admit whether I, like she, desired to keep four lovers. Not to be outdone, the male Gede Madyawe asked when he would have the opportunity to savor the "red cocoon" (*koko wouj*).

When Ezili Dantò arrived, she tormented Loremi. She excoriated him for the scrawny bull they had offered at last year's service. What was *he* prepared to offer as a sacrifice for the upcoming rite? Feigning the humble servant, he responded to her pressing interrogation: "yes, Grandmother, I remembered . . . yes, Grandmother, I will get a bull . . . yes, Grandmother, it will be bigger than the one we gave last year." As we walked to our homes after leaving the shrine, Loremi told me that Komè would buy the bull.

Ezili Freda "spoke" about their other daughter. She told Loremi and Filoza that their daughter and her groom's car accident was "nothing"; i.e., not caused by a lwa or a sorcerer. Their daughter and son-in-law would enjoy rapid and full recovery. Loremi was relieved that "nothing" would interfere with their daughter's recuperation. Filoza, on the other hand, was not entirely convinced and wanted a second opinion. She "consulted" (*konsilte*) another gangan ason the following day to solicit his reading of the significance of the accident, which did confirm the first non-diagnosis. Filoza explained why she both continues to consult several gangan and why she remains skeptical of every diagnosis:

For every 40 lies gangan have, Karen, there is only one truth. When they divine, if they don't see the thing clearly, they tell you any old lie. Ilavert might give you one thing; you go to Aiscar's place, he tells you another thing; you go to Yvon's place, he'll tell you still another thing. You follow the remedy Ilavert gave you and after [it fails] you go far away [to find another gangan]. If the [gangan] there tells you the same thing as Ilavert, he's the one who told you the truth.

Once I was very sick. I was in bed. I went to Victor's place. He had me light two candles. The next day I couldn't get up at all; I was worse. He told me [I was being held by] a Grandmother [Ezili Dantò]. Ilavert [Filoza's brother-in-law] came the next day and saw that I was sick. He divined for me. He said that it wasn't a lwa; it was a persecution; that means, an evildoer who hated me for my success. [Ilavert] had me buy things [for the treatment]. The next day I sat up. You see that Ilavert was good?

Pou chak 40 manti gangan genyen, Karin, gen yon sèl verite. Lè yo divinen, si yo pa wè bay la byen, yap ba ou nenpòt manti. Ilavert mèt ba ou yon bagay;, ou al kay Aiscar, lap di ou yon lòt bagay; ou al kay Yvon, lap di ou yon lòt bagay toujou. Ou ap swiv remèd Ilavert ba ou e apre ou pral lwen. Si gangan di ou menm bagay ak sa Ilavert di ou a, se li ke te di la verite.

Yon lè m te malad byen mal. M te kouche. M tal kay Victor. Li fè m fè iliminasyon ak 2 balenn. Demen m pa ka leve menm; m te pi mal. Li te di mwen se te yon Grann. Ilavert te vini nan demen-an li wè m malad. Li fè leson pou mwen. Li di se pa lwa, se yon pèsikisyon, sa vle di malveyan ki pa t vle wè tout sa m te genyen. Li fè m achte bagay. Demen m leve chita. Ou wè Ilavert te bon?

Filoza was thus both a skeptic and a faithful client of the professionals. In order to keep her lwa from deguarantying her children, she needed to be able to communicate with them. In chapter 4 I describe how ritual innovations introduced by Misdor and his successors have changed the forms and access to this communication. As speech communication with the lwa during possession declined in inverse proportion to the expanding role of pantomime and dance performance, calling the lwa with the ason came to be deemed necessary for any interaction between members of the fanmi and their inherited lwa. Having become indispensable to the relations between the lwa and members of the descent group no matter how far afield, the gangan ason were well-situated to prosper from the intensified out-migrations.

The spirits' control over migrants' productivity immerses families and ritual intermediaries back home in the diagnosis of affliction and the quest for a cure. Affliction episodes are the key means whereby the lwa deguaranty migrants' productivity: the lwa express their hunger and displeasure somatically upon the pwen, rendering him/her unable to "do for" anyone, including him- or herself. When parents perform a "ritual feeding of the gods" on behalf of an absent child, they release the pwen to be productive again. The symptoms of having tampered with protection cover the range of ailments and disappointments commonly experienced by mobile, low-wage workers living and working in unsanitary, overcrowded, insecure conditions. Often perceived as streaks of bad luck, these afflictions are typically multistranded: chronic ailments, failure to find and keep employment, accidents, and ominous dreams. Narratives of afflictions Outside circumvent the Home family's scorn and instead solicit their help and their concern. Diagnoses of spiritually caused interference in the migrants' productivity reconstruct an oppressive, dehumanizing experience. The episodes transform externally imposed conditions into something the migrants and their families back home *can* control.

The Cases of Gérard and Toro

The cases of two migrant brothers, Gérard and Toro, will illustrate how the lwa intervene in mobile workers' abilities to alienate their labor Outside and to build the guaranty Inside. Because they were susceptible to the activities of the spirits, they depended on their families back home (as well as on the gangan ason) to carry out ritual obligations required to maintain their continued productivity. By acting as the Guinea managers, in effect, of their emigrant pwen's well-being, their family in Ti Rivyè simultaneously ensured their own social and economic reproduction.

Toro sailed to Florida in 1978, in one of the first kanntè to sail from Ti Rivière to Miami. Toro was a successful migrant, profoundly devoted to his family. He constructed a house for two sisters and their children and filled the salon with wood and formica furniture, a black velvet wall hanging of a forest scene, an electric wall clock that never ticked (because there was no electricity), and glass-beaded door hangings. Behind the glass of the breakfront were photos of Toro and his boss at the porcelain statue factory where he worked.

Two years after Toro left, Gérard attempted to "take the kanntè." He tried on three separate occasions; each time he was arrested and put in prison. In 1981, Toro purchased a visa for Gérard, who then joined his brother in Delray Beach. Among their immediate family left behind in Haiti were their father, Gérard's wife and three children, and five sisters. Two of their sisters (and their sisters' children) lived in "Toro's house," which was built in 1980. Until 1982, when one of the sisters accused Gérard's wife of infidelity, she and their three children had also lived in the *lakou* (compound). After Gérard's wife moved out, two of the children remained in the yard under the care of Gérard's sister. In 1984, Gérard sent back money to finance the building of a cinder-block house next to Toro's.

Toro and Gérard were working in Delray Beach, Florida, when Gérard fell off a second floor at a construction site. When the family got news of his accident, they went to the shrine on their mother's paternal estate. Ilavert, the resident gangan ason, and their maternal aunt's husband, summoned the lwa. Speaking through Ilavert from behind the door of the altar room, a lwa, Gede Nibo or Guardian of the Yard (Jeran Lakou), claimed that he had protected Gérard from more serious injury. Gérard's father and sisters promised Grandfather Gede/The Guardian then that they would feed him. According to Gérard's older sister, "they had been anticipating the funds to take care of the lwa for him" (*nou tap tann kòb la rantre pou nou kapab okipe lwa pou li*) when they received an urgent message from Gérard. The family and I assembled in the yard to listen to the cassette tape. Gérard was anxious. He complained that the spot where he had bruised himself in the fall last year was eating him up inside (*manje l andan*). He wanted his family to proceed with fulfillment of his obligation to The Guardian. He told his aunt Filoza to take the funds necessary for a ritual feeding from the money he had sent her for the construction of his house.

That evening, Gérard's father and two sisters returned to the shrine. Ilavert "called the lwa." Grandfather Gede/The Guardian of the Lakou and their mother's "dead" spirit gave instructions for the ritual offerings. The Guardian told them that he desired only a modest feast without drumming or dancing and that he expected only their branch of the descent group to be present (that is, Gérard's mother's full siblings and his mother's and father's descendants). (The Guardian was being pragmatic; Gérard could not afford a more spectacular "feeding of the gods," nor the costs of receiving many more guests with food and beverages.) Grandmother (Grann) Ezili, a lwa inherited through his *father's mother*, also spoke. She requested that Toro present her with her own "dessert" upon her altar place inside Toro's house. At about 8:00 one morning the next week, the family gathered inside and around Gérard's partially finished house. Gérard's sisters and their children and spouses, his father, and two of his maternal aunts and uncles and some of the latter's children and I were present. A tape recorder (in addition to my own) was also present. In a few days, Gérard would listen to the recording of the rite he sponsored.

While we were waiting for Ilavert to begin the ritual, I talked to Tenten, Gérard's maternal uncle, about The Guardian. The Guardian's wooden cross was planted at the boundary of his great-grandfather's estate. He described The Guardian as an "enormous protective force" (*gwo pwotèj*), "a good lwa" (*yon bon lwa*) who "stands up for us" (*kanpe pou nou*). Tenten went on in this tender tone to describe how The Guardian manifested himself to family members through trance, at once affirming the person's unique qualities and linking the individual to the "generation to generation" (*pitit an pitit*, literally "child to child") continuity of the whole descent group. He described how when he was young, this "good lwa" used to "mount" his cousin Caridad and, after she died, The Guardian "chose" Lina, Gérard's mother (who was also an ounsi). (Lina died when Gérard and Toro were children.)

An inherited lwa can "love" only one member of the descent group at a time— each unit has enough lwa to furnish everyone with plenty of "love." Until the chosen heir dies, the lwa cannot "love" another. (Emigration also separates lwa from their descent group; as long as the migrant "horse" is Outside, the lwa cannot attend his/her own "party." This dilemma is continuously reworked, as opposed to resolved, in globalist ritual performance.) Some of those chosen by the lwa also become "horses" for their patrons to "personify" themselves in possession and create virtuoso performances as dancers, singers, counselors, and comedians. A generation or more may pass before the lwa communicates her or his "love" (*renmen*) for another heir through media of dreams, divination, or possession, often in the context of affliction. Until the lwa claims a new heir, the entire kin group loses touch with this source of support, connection with the past, and, not to be understated, means of entertainment.

Thus the lwa had visited the family only once since Lina's death 25 years before, and Tenten regretted not having been there. He had heard that a sorcerer had also stolen the lwa out of Filoza's head during the possession and had kept it away from the descent group. Tenten wondered if The Guardian would come to the service to accept Gérard's offering that morning, or, if he did appear, who the lwa would mount. So when, during the ritual bathing of The Guardian's goat, the spirit all of a sudden mounted Filoza, Tenten and everyone else were profoundly moved and satisfied. Seeing the lwa proclaim his "love" for this worthy new horse in possession-performance dramatized the continuity of substance from one generation to the next, even as it evoked memories of The Guardian's performances in Caridad and Lina, horses who were no longer living. The rare manifestations of these beloved, long departed members make possession a full and rewarding experience for any member of the descent group who witnesses it. Writers obsessed with the spectacular features of possession in Haitian "voodoo" inevitably fail to perceive this point.

7.2. Father of the sponsor of the rite for Guardian of the Yard, Ti Rivyè, November 1984.

7.3. Sponsor's father holds the sacrificial goat for Guardian of the Yard, Ti Rivyè, November 1984.

7.4. Tenten has sacrificed the goat, Ti Rivyè, November 1984.

7.5. Guardian of the Yard arrives in the head of the sponsor's aunt. Tenten supports "him," Ti Rivyè, November 1984.

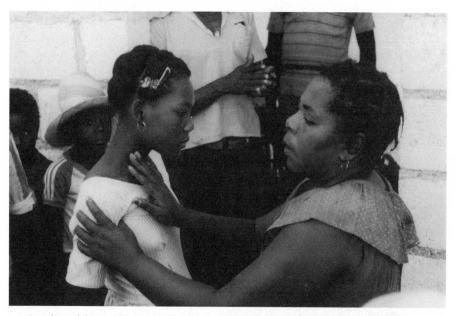

7.6. Guardian of the Yard blesses family members, Ti Rivyè, November 1984.

7.7. Guardian of the Yard greeting a family member, Ti Rivyè, November 1984.

7.8. Guardian of the Yard chastises the member using pantomime,
Ti Rivyè, November 1984.

I was the first to notice the onset of Filoza's possession and grabbed her arm
to keep her from falling hard to the ground. The lwa swung the horse around
and we supported "them" until "he" gained enough composure to stand by himself. His eyes finally focused straight forward after having been rolled hideously
up and backward into his horse's head. The Guardian was a somber, gentle old
man. He lovingly greeted and blessed each member one by one, drawing them
close, taking their hands in his and then extending their arms straight out to the
side as he pressed his forehead solidly to theirs. Their adjoined foreheads became an axis fixing the slow rotation of two moving as one, side to side, side to
side. The Guardian also treated Fifi, Filoza's daughter-in-law, who was about six
months pregnant, to a tender massage of her round belly and full breasts.

The lwa was mute; he signed messages by pointing his fingers, patting his fists and thrusting his whole body in one direction or another. Ilavert, the gangan ason, interpreted the mime for the others. He indicated his satisfaction with the offering and chose Filoza's brother to immolate it. He told Filoza's other brother to drop out of a sorcerer's society in Archaie and join the local one.

The lwa went away after the sacrifice, meaning he crossed the yard and dropped into a chair on Filoza's porch. Filoza awoke a few minutes later. The goat and chickens were killed above a hole in the ground between the two emigrant brothers' houses into which their blood was allowed to drip. Gérard's sisters and their daughters then started cooking the ritual meal. To meet Toro's obligation to their Ezili, they laid a "dessert" table with a pink frosted cake and sweet drinks in the altar room (ogatwa) inside Toro's house. A plateful of cooked food was also placed on the shrine. The goat's skull was later hung from a rafter in Gérard's house. That afternoon and evening everyone ate extremely well. The next morning, Gérard's 15-year-old niece, who had never before eaten so much meat, complained that she had suffered all night with a stomachache. Her mother and sister were already off serving bread and coffee to beggars at the local church, as the lwa had instructed them to do.

It is often said of the lwa that they are "like children" and that displays of favoritism, however naive or innocent on the part of parents, can provoke a jealous rage or a vengeful spate of "dirty tricks." Toro, Gérard's younger brother, fell victim to just such a petty reprisal only three weeks after the feast for The Guardian and Grann Ezili. His relatives at home were caught entirely off guard when they received Toro's exigent message; he was ill with fever, weakness, and digestive dysfunction. Toro's sisters and father returned to the shrine where they had summoned The Guardian of the Yard. Ilavert divined that Toro was being held by two lwa from his paternal grandfather's descent group, Grandmother (Grann) Dantò and Simbi. Simbi had "claimed" Toro long before and used to "dance in Toro's head" in possession-performance. (Until his "horse" returned, Simbi of course could not manifest himself to the heirs.) Toro's sister told me:

> We called the lwa at Ilavert's shrine. It's a lwa on my father's father's side. The lwa is jealous because we bought a goat for Grandfather Gede and we made a dessert for Grandmother. Grandmother Dantò is holding him. Simbi is an escort. He needs his own food. They're both hard. Both are holding him . . . Grandmother requested that he buy a pair of speckled white chickens, rice, plantains, yams, dessert, rice cooked in milk, porridge. Simbi will eat a pair of chickens. We will do it in Merger, on [our father's father's] inherited land. We will send him a candle to light while he speaks to the lwa and asks the lwa to give him strength to work.

Nou rele lwa kay Ilavert. Se yon lwa bò papa papa m. Li fè jalouzi pou tèt nou
achte kabrit pou Papa Gede avèk nou fè desè pou Grann-nan. Se Grann Dantò
ki kenbe l. Simbi se yon eskòt. Li bèzwen manje pa l. Tou de rèd. Tou de kenbe
l. . . Yo mande pou l achte menay poul pent blan jonn, diri, banann, yanm,
desè, diri ole, laboui. Simbi ap manje yon menay poul. Nap fè l Merger, nan tè
eritaj-la. Nou pral voye balenn pou l limen pou l pal a lwa pou di li, ba li fòs
pou l travay.

Toro's sister's final comment summed up the impetus of the reciprocal dependency between lwa and heirs whose laboring capacity is *at stake* for one and *the*
stake for the other: "Give him strength so he can work again."

Toro got better temporarily. He returned in 1986, before getting his green card,
to recover from a hernia. But having "done for" his family by building the first
migrant-financed house in the yard and supporting his sisters, nieces, and nephews placed him in the direct path of a sorcerer. Toro died after a long and painful
decline in early 1991. The loss of this devoted kinsman devastated the extended
family. They blamed an envious paternal uncle who putatively "preferred not to
see him [alive] because of what he had" (*pa t vle wè li pou sa li genyen*) rather than
accept what he had achieved through his migration. This phrasing is standard in
the explanation of sorcery deaths. Envious persons would rather see someone
dead than abide his or her achievements.

Sorcery is called *maladi mounn*, affliction caused by people. It is distinguished
from the two other categories of affliction: *maladi lwa* and *maladi Bondye*, illnesses sent by the High God. Sorcery is a peasant social weapon to wield against
individual ambition and greed (which are the pwen of capital). People who accumulate wealth must have done something immoral to gain it such as using sorcery to steal wealth from someone else, or buying a pwen. Because people-who-
are-pwen are the means by which families can advance themselves socially and
economically, successful migrants are preferred targets of sorcerers. Migrants believe that they can be "hit" with a sorcerer's poisonous powders anywhere in the
world, and some Ti Rivyè natives are believed to have been "hit" in Florida. The
likelihood of getting hit is believed to be far greater, though, back home. Indeed
some migrants avoid returning for fear that they will be magically poisoned.

A sudden sensation of a weight on the back of the neck, an ominous dream and
loss of eyesight are some of the symptoms suggesting the spell of a sorcerer. Sus-
pecting sorcery, a migrants' parents will privately approach a gangan who practices counter-sorcery and sorcery too, since revenge is usually linked to the remedy. If they engage a gangan who has taken the ason, the latter reinforce the gulf
between Guinea and sorcery by meeting them in a different location from the
Guinea shrine—in a separate room inside the House or in a detached dwelling.

A migrant's prestations to Guinea, which redistribute resources, serve to demonstrate generosity and preempt accusations of greed. Feeding the lwa "cooks" the illicit money, transforming it into a moral gift. In return, a grateful Guinea lwa will not only guaranty the migrant's productive capacity but also protect the migrant against sorcery. Tenten asserted that The Guardian, the family spirit who held Toro's brother Gérard, "stands up" for the heirs when malefactors approach to harm them. Neglected lwa won't defend their children. A person abandoned by his or her lwa is vulnerable to sudden attack by sorcerers. Pepe told me (while discussing the migrant's guaranty), "If you [the migrant] abandon them, you are abandoned too. Then you will—pow!" (*Si ou bandonen yo, ou bandonen tou. Epi ou gen dwa plop tou!*)

Nonetheless some migrants decline to trust their well-being entirely to fickle and vindictive Guinea. Since success as a migrant emissary stirs up envy, they seek out gangan to purchase more protection, or "guards" (*gad*). Pepe admitted to me that "the money comes in more clearly" (*lajan-an rantre pi klè*) when he performs magical "work" for migrants. The latter occasionally share their guaranty with the gangan who help them by bringing foreign clients who pay foreign rates for their services. During my stays in Ti Rivyè, I have encountered native-born citizens of the United States, Martinique and Guadeloupe patronizing local gangan.

The migrant's solicitation of extra protection would seem to suggest that Guinea's power is only artifice, commanding from the bow of the ship, as Pepe would say, with no motor or pwen of its own. Further recognition of the limits of Guinea's power appears in the familiar representation of lwa as stern grandparents. However real a child's fear of its grandfather's discipline, the latter cannot defend his heirs against those who wield real political and economic power. The peasants' powerlessness is reconfigured in realms they can control through representations of their power to help or hurt one another.

Toro's family had to make sense of the loss of their beloved and dutiful migrant. They found an answer in sorcery. They blamed an accessible neighbor instead of the remote system that turns Haitian peasants into pwen for transnational capital. A narrative of sorcery provides another way for Guinea to displace its responsibility for turning migrants into pwen. Guinea sets up its migrants to be targets of sorcerers and then fails to protect them. Censure falls on the competitive neighbor who can't stand to see someone else's migrant thrive. Because of the positive value of retribution, the neighbor's life may be next.

Pwenification, Migration, and the Transnational Tenth State

The equivocal interdependence between Guinea and Magic, or foreign lwa and pwen, is a symbolic model of and for relations within mobile, peasant families.

Heirs must alienate themselves to feed and energize the effete, dependent but authoritative spirits in Ti Rivyè in exchange for protection of their capacity to sell their labor power Outside. Parents stand to their migrants as Guinea to pwen: the older (and more dependent) the parent, the more like Guinea; the greater the migrant's "wrists" (a metaphor for laboring capacity), the more he or she symbolically becomes a pwen in need of Guinea's discipline and restraint.

The consciousness of this transnational, domestic pwening order is pervasive. A measure of its potency was its recognition in national political discourse. The setting was the inauguration of the president, whose fleeting electoral victory embodied the emerging consciousness of transnational migration. President Aristide's sympathy for the breeding of these transnational antagonisms strengthened his support among migrants. When Aristide was elected, he established Haiti's "Tenth Province" (Dizyèm Depatman) and at his inaugural celebration he hosted a special reception for the migrants of the "Tenth" in the white house garden. In the midst of his address, which was delivered without notes, the new president moved to defuse feelings of hostility and shame generated by the pwening order, but he stopped short of reconstructing the pwen's vitalizing role. Instead he encouraged the "bank of the diaspora" to continue following and abetting the remigration of capital, all the while regarding "Home" as a loving parent, a secure depository for investments and a tourist's vacation land.

The president stated his hope for migrants to lead the revival of the moribund tourist economy, dubbing them "good homegrown Creole tourists" (*bonjan pitit kay tourist kreyòl*). He launched into a lyrical description of imaginary Creole tourists on voyages of "discovery of the countryside," painting a bucolic scene of a migrant returning to visit his/her grandparents in a remote hilltop village. Abruptly he shifted focus from the cheerful Creole tourist to the cynical hosts. "What will they see?" he rhetorically asked the audience of "the Tenth." He answered the question:

> They won't see a child who came home dressed to the hilt to show off and to make them ashamed that they couldn't go away to return all dressed up like that too. No. No. They will feel that [touching his earlobe while encouraging the audience to join in with the well-known proverb] "for every ear there is one earring in a pawn shop." If every family didn't have one member in the Tenth Province—oh oh! You know how it would be. You know how it would be. You did it; you want to continue doing it, regardless (Wilèk Film 1991).

> *Yo p ap wè youn pitit k ap vin taye banda, vin chèlbè, pou fè lòt yo santi krenn paske yo pa t kapab ale pou yo tounen bwodè konsa. Non. Non. Y ap santi ke "chak zòrèy [l ap fè jès pou moun yo pale tout ansanm avèk li] gen youn grènn*

zanno kay ofèv." Si chak fanmi pa t genyen youn grènn manm nan fanmi nan
dizyèm depatman an-Hmm! Hmm! Ou konnen konman sa ta ye. Ou konnen
konman sa ta ye. Ou fè l, ou vle kontinye fè l, kan menm (Wilèk Film 1991).

The elder peasants, President Aristide asserted, will suppress the inference that
the arrogant migrant is intentionally trying to humiliate them. They will drop
their symbolic weapon of sorcery, used to discipline violators of their peasant
moral economy. The subsequent earring proverb conveyed simple imagery in
nonthreatening, familiar language. The (female) ear is naked without its (typically gold hooped) earring. A severed pair of earrings makes each one useless
without the other. Perhaps people at home would pick up its message and confront a difficult truth about their unjustifiable behavior toward migrants without
whom they would be exposed and disabled. President Aristide related the proverb
to every family at home dependent on a migrant by saying, "if every family didn't
have [at least] one family member in the Tenth Province, you know how [desper-
ate] it would be, oh, oh! You know how it would be!"

Next the president directed his message to the assembled audience of the
Tenth Province to praise them for their perseverance. Despite myriad obstacles in
the host society and the ambivalence of the very people who consume their repatriated wages, they continue abiding their onerous domestic, transnational contracts.

Yet another truth was embedded in the portrayal of migrants' opulent attire as
well as the continued reference to personal adornment through the earring proverb. Migrants, in particular, fall victim to the contradictory politics of personal
style or consumption. People at home expect a returning migrant emissary to
wear the sartorial signs of his or her—and also their—success abroad. One who
dresses modestly for the long-awaited reunion back home might cast his reputation and judgment in doubt. Yet the "child who comes home dressed to the hilt"
can also be accused of trying "to show off and to make [those at home] ashamed
that they couldn't go away to return all dressed up like that too," inviting sorcery
from envious others. Outfitting oneself to meet these ambiguous standards is
another cross borne by the migrant who yearns to produce for and still be accepted by the society symbolized by Guinea.

The logic of this aesthetic finally became intelligible to me while I was living in
the Ti Rivyè village, participating in a welcoming scene not unlike the one President Aristide described. Yvon, the first of his siblings to go abroad to "do for" his
family, was returning home for the first time. It was a sweltering afternoon in July.
Having traveled from the airport in the back of a converted pick-up truck, and
walked the rest of the way to the family yard, he was drenched in sweat, covered in
dust, and dressed in a tuxedo.

Summary

Because Guinea has authority but not power, it needs to be vitalized by the contagion of Magic. The ability of Magic to vitalize effete, authentic Guinea is the pwen of the Guinea-Magic dialectic. Guinea conceals its exploitation of pwen by exporting them, but migration also creates conditions for the worker to forsake the home. Guinea is anxious about emissaries who might exploit their exploitation for their own ends. The activities of the peripatetic lwa, "protecting" migrants in the core and threatening to punish them with "deguaranty," are means of controlling faraway pwen and ensuring the homeward flow of remitttances. Yet Guinea also sets up its most dutiful emissaries to be the targets of sorcery, as punishment for being capitalistic pwen.

8

They Will Remember Me in the House

Aesthetics of Contest and Persuasion on Cassette Letters

When it's one of your own
My friend, look across from you;
They don't know your worth.
When you are away, yes,
They look at how much you weigh.
I say, the day is here,
The day is here.
There is a time, brother,
They will pick me up
When they are in need.

—*Little Caterpillar, August 1983*

Separation is a huge ocean. It mixes everything up, shakes it all up
like a dice box. You see with your ears, you hear with your eyes . . .

—*Simone Schwarz-Bart, Ton Beau Capitaine*

The ability to use song as an interpersonal weapon is a valued skill in many Haitian communities. Where social norms emphasize the avoidance of direct confrontation, singing, typically under the transparent veil of nondirected, objectified discourse, serves as a vehicle for persuasive maneuvering, venting hostilities and exercising personal power. The singer can deny any specific aggressive or partisan intent because responsibility for assigning "meaning" to the message belongs to the unnamed target hearer, or overhearer, rather than to the sender. Haitians call this genre of performance "throwing points songs" (*voye pwen chante*) or "singing the point" (*chante pwen*).

The widespread and protracted, transnational dispersal of kin during the last two-and-a-half decades has provided ample cause for sending and singing pwen. Mutual ambivalence of long-separated home kin and their migrant emissaries is one of the untoward costs this mobile society pays for its harsh incorporation into the regional economic system. Suppressed by cultural norms limiting direct confrontation, these latent hostilities become ideal fodder for indirect critique through the authorized and aesthetically esteemed frame of sending point songs.

Out of the experience of transnational migration came a new medium for sending oblique musical messages: cassette-tape correspondence. Cassette tapes, rather than written letters, are the universal mode of correspondence across this transnational community. In their cassette letters, "writers" perform point songs to advance and to contest the conflicting interests of kin who leave and kin who stay at home. A single vocal repertoire predominates in their musical missives: spirit songs. They implicitly deem these ritual verses, which capture aspects of the Guinea-Magic dialectic, especially suited for capturing uncomfortable truths about their experience as producer of migrant workers for export and consumer of low-wage remittances. This chapter explores the aesthetics of "audio writing" and the logic of sending ritual verses as point songs in the cassette correspondence of the far-flung, yet unitary, Ti Rivyè community.

Cassette Correspondence

The portable radio-cassette player is a prominent, "multivocal" symbol—a model of and for—this transnational, mobile society. The apparatus is likely to be prominently displayed in the migrants' Florida apartments. A "boom box" is likewise an appropriate gift to send home, especially with the price tag still conspicuously attached. The device radiates the vitality of the dispersed family's ties to one another. As a symbol of conspicuous consumption—like any art object—the apparatus at the same time connotes the migrant's success abroad.

Guadeloupian playwright Simone Schwarz-Bart (1987) keenly appreciated the extent to which the portable cassette recorder has, since the late 1970s, symbolized and mediated the Haitians' interpersonal relationships across national boundaries. *Ton Beau Capitaine* is set in the crude interior of a small cabin on a Guadeloupian plantation; the dramatis personae: Wilnor, a Haitian immigrant agricultural worker and his battery-operated "radio-cassette"; the action: Wilnor listens to a cassette letter from his wife and he "writes" a response. This vital appli-

8.1. Jean with radio-cassette player at a ritual dance,
Ti Rivyè, September 1983.

ance structures the audience's experience, as it does the protracted separation of the couple, obliging all, as Wilnor comments, to "see with your ears and hear with your eyes." Corresponding on cassette has become so normalized that the term "to write [a letter]" (*ekri*) signifies recording a cassette rather than the epistolary form. Audiocassettes offered poor Haitians a creative way of seizing control of their nonliteracy in the colonial language of French. On tape, they correspond in their own beloved tongue, Creole.

Before the advent of the cassettes, poor, unlettered Haitians wanting to correspond had to solicit scribes to translate their Creole words into French. The alienation of the authors from their own words was mirrored at the receiving end, as someone other than the recipient read the letters out loud in French or retranslated them into Creole. Furthermore, these translated letters had a distinctly maladroit style, a product of the stilted and unequal, diglossic relation of the vernacular to French (Ferguson 1959). The letter was composed in the authoritative code, despite the scribe's uncertain command over it. Although the scribe had attended school, the antiquated education system demanded that the student master mimetic production of French orthography and rhetoric, more so than its comprehension. He (for it was typically a man) learned, as the satiric Creole expression suggests, to *pale Franse* (speak French)—and to write the vapid speech with a lovely hand.

Such appropriations of French's epistolary conventions fit Bakhtin's (1971: 181) definition of "semi-stylized" expression. "The weaker the original seriousness of a style becomes in the hands of its epigone-imitators, the more nearly its devices become conventionalized-imitation thus becoming semi-stylization." Indeed the letters exchanged across Haitian transnational communities seem to freeze in time the beginnings of popular letter writing in early-modern France, where conditions of literacy anticipated those of contemporary rural Haiti: namely, a rough transition from an oral culture to a "scriptural economy" and the instability of the written form over the "patois" (De Certeau 1984). Like the correspondence across Haitian transnational communities, the letters were conspicuously intended for the ears of a community rather than the eyes of a private individual (Chartier 1997a:15).

The sources of these stultified conventions were *secrétaires*, or collections of model letters. Although they were long accessible to the aristocracy, the first secrétaires for popular consumption date back to late-16th-century France. The etymology of the term is instructive. Secrétaire initially meant one who inscribed the dictations of others. According to a dictionary published in 1690, which Roger Chartier (1997b:62) cites, there was a hierarchy of secrétaires, from the officers of the king, to clerks, to "those wretched scribes who write letters for servants and for such people as who know not how to write." Reference to the lowest class of secretarial practice was insinuated in the slide in meaning from scribe to book. Chartier argues that the compilations of model letters were paradoxically designed to ensure the ignorance and inferiority of those who imitated them. The secrétaires were "devoted to disseminating a form of know-how whose allure depended on its exclusivity, the status of *ancien régime secrétaires* was inevitably ambiguous and unstable, like that of a secret that was bruited abroad" (Chartier 1997a:7–8). As Chartier explains, the new secrétaires taught the forms of politesse, but not their meanings and rules. The texts were intended, in other words, to deprive the consumers of knowledge of how properly to practice the etiquette they were imitating.

When members of this transnational community do in fact resort to the epistolary form, the new conventions of cassette correspondence intrude upon the "semi-stylized" French formulae. The free-flowing orality of colloquial Kreyòl threatens to overtake the discipline of the scriptural French. As the letter continues, unpretentious sounds of Kreyòl career onto the paper, juxtaposed with parodies of *ancien régime politesse*. Pieces of face-to-face conversation appear. Moreover, the oral aesthetic of cassette correspondence intervenes and the distinct syntax and formulaic greetings of cassette writing resound. (The missive nonetheless manages to reassert French control at the closing.)

These occasional epistolary letters offer further evidence that a distinct genre of cassette discourse has evolved with distinct etiquette for greetings and salutations, and its own "grammar" for conjugating "indirection." Cassette writing accommodates a medium that is perceived to be indirect, as opposed to the telephone, which is direct. Thus "writers" employ the double-verb constructions meaning communication by a messenger, with *voye* (send or throw) before a second verb, as in *voye di* (say/tell) and *voye mande* (ask). (Rendering this syntax in English produces a cumbersome translation, and an even more inappropriate tone. I thus translate the terms using the single verbs: say, ask, give, etc.)

The first and last words a "writer" utters on a cassette letter are the same as those universally delivered at the beginning and end of a telephone conversation: "hello" (*alo*) and "good-bye" (*babay*). Then, after identifying himself or herself and saying the date, the "writer" launches into a variant of a distinctive greeting that is repeated at the close of the cassette letter as well. The singularity of this greeting is its requirement to praise the receiver in the specific, concrete time when she or he actually hears it. And since the "writer" cannot predict that moment, his or her greeting should respectably accommodate any possible time the cassette will be heard.

But there is no all-inclusive term of greeting in Kreyòl. The language does not tolerate speculative assertions (or the passive voice). (The pithy and oblique discourse of proverbs does provide an escape from the burdens of concreteness.) Every assertion seems to call for its negation in order to cover all possibilities. For instance, Caterpillar has said to me on tapes, "I can't tell you what to do, I can't tell you what not to do." (*M pa ka di ou fè sa, m pa ka di ou pa fè sa.*) Another example of his use of these thorough, balanced couplets is, "God knows what s/he will do with me, God knows what he will not do with me." (*Bondye konen sa l ap fè avè m; Bondye konen sa li pap fè avè m.*)[1]

Hence the appropriate model for the greeting, which covers all possibilities, is "If the cassette arrives in the morning, I bid you 'good morning.' If the cassette arrives in the afternoon, I bid you 'good evening [*ou*].'" (*Si kasèt la rive maten, m voye bonjou pou ou. Si kasèt la rive aswè, m voye bonswa pou ou.*)

Few competent cassette-tape correspondents would utter this greeting in such unadorned style. Only children, who are still mastering cassette discourse, or an adult speaker in a rush to get through with the message, would fail to embellish it. Most adults improvise upon on this pattern to fashion ever more earnest-sounding greetings. Some variations include "I bid you a great good day and I bid you a great good evening" (*M voye youn gwo bonjou pou ou; M voye yon gwo bonswa pou ou*) or "I bid you a very, very good day and I bid you a very, very good evening" (*M voye youn gwo bon jou pou ou anpil, anpil, M voye youn gwo bonswa pou ou anpil, anpil*). Little Caterpillar frequently liked to quantify the enthusiasm of his greeting, invoking absurdly precise amounts of salutation. For example,

> If you see the cassette arrives in the morning, I send 2,000 kisses and 2,000 good mornings to you and your husband. If you see the tape getting there in the afternoon, I send 3,000 kisses and 3,000 good evenings to you.

> *Si ou wè kasèt la rive maten, mwen voye 2,000 beze, 2,000 bonjou pou ou a tout misye ou. Si ou wè kasèt la rive apre midi, mwen voye 3,000 beze, 3,000 bonswa pou ou a tout misye ou, a tout pitit ou.*

Propriety in the new cassette aesthetics also demands that the recipient's community receives a formal greeting as well, an indication of the value of constituting personhood within a thick social web. The speaker typically names all of the members at the end of the greeting, and then adds categories into which anyone

8.2. Little Caterpillar with his radio-cassette player in his tenement room in Fort Pierce, Florida, November 1986.

whose name was omitted might fit. Thus Little Caterpillar continued on the tape by sending his best to "everyone where you are, your friends, all of your people" (*tout moun kote ou, zanmi ou, tout moun ou yo*). On a taped letter from my friend Filoza, she asked me to extend greetings to "everyone in general without distinction" (*tout moun an jeneralman san distenk*).

Listening to a cassette recording is likewise a performance event (Bauman [1977] 1984). As Little Caterpillar told his family on one letter, "You see, when I'm going to replay the tape, I don't replay it inside my house. When I replay it, I turn up the cassette player so everyone can hear it." Family members and neighbors gather round to hear a faraway relative personally greet them individually. They may interact antiphonally with the voice, interjecting "yes," "no," "oh my," etc., as if the speaker were present.

Cassette-tape correspondence is thus far more than a means of circumventing illiteracy. Nor is it a mere way of protecting ties that distance threatens to break. The tapes have an aesthetic all their own. They are venues for extending an oral culture that prizes proverbs, figurative, indirect language (epitomized by the art of sending pwen) antiphony, and fluid shifting between speech and song, especially verses drawn from the sacred song repertoire. As means of competitive, public, personal performance, then, the tapes differentiate distant kin as much as they unite them. "Persons of words" exploit the medium to maintain and advance their vocal reputations across the vast distances separating their community.

Throwing Pwen

The concept of pwen is complex. It involves the symbolic power of imitation. Our discussion has focused on the pwen of Magic. Pwen are the peasants' symbolic imitations of alienated labor power, the inside essence of capitalism. Through representatives of pwen, the peasants symbolically control and make sense of their incorporation as producers of alienated wage laborers for export to capital abroad. Here we focus on sending pwen on cassette letters as a genre of indirect, contentious, interpersonal discourse. To understand how this discourse genre operates it is useful to review Karen McCarthy Brown's broad definition of pwen as "anything that captures the essence or pith of a complex situation" and reformulates it so it can be easily grasped and remembered (Brown 1987:151). Using abstraction, intensification, and exaggeration, a pwen crystallizes "an elegantly simple image," simple enough to be instructive. A personal name, a proverb, a song, a cross drawn on the ground, a Magical power—each fixates worlds of social and cultural meanings.

Haitians are extremely fond of conferring personal names—so fond that an individual's close kin may never know the person's formal name (*bon non*). There are two types of informal appellation: "nickname" (*non jwèt*) and "pwen name" (*non pwen*). Nicknames may be based on the "real name," with the addition of such endearments as "little" (*ti*). I, for example, am usually addressed as either Ka (for Karin) or Ti Ka (Little Karin). Nicknames may also represent a description or caricature, for example, Little Spider (Ti Krab) or Little Lady (Ti Madanm).

A pwen name, on the other hand, summarizes an interpersonal situation to inform others. Joseph Météllus received his pwen name, Malgre Sa, in infancy. His siblings' deaths were attributed to sorcery. When baby Joseph fell ill, his parents summoned a gangan to exorcize the affliction. When it appeared that he would survive, the gangan pronounced, "*Malgre sa, li pa mouri*," meaning, "In spite of it, he didn't die." After hearing the shaman's statement, Joseph's mother called her baby Malgre Sa. The name Malgre Sa was an indirect message sent to the suspected malefactor(s): the family persevered "in spite of it." The pwen name, then, "captured the essence" of a hostile, interpersonal situation.

The Haitian practice of "throwing," "sending," or "shooting" (*voye, tire*) pwen has counterparts throughout the African diaspora, including the "passed remark" in Antigua (Reisman 1970), the "thrown word" in Jamaica (Fisher 1976), and "signifying" and/or "loud-talking" in the United States (Mitchell-Kernan 1972). Each of these styles engages the "triangular form" of discourse, described by Lawrence Fisher (1976:229) in his insightful analysis of the comparable Barbadian speech practice of "dropping remarks." The triangle involves sender, sham receiver, and target overhearer.[2] Malgre Sa gave an example: "You are passing by a place where you stole a cow. Two people see you and one says to the other loudly enough for you to hear, 'man, this place doesn't lack for thieves!'" (*zòn sa a pa manke vòlè, papa!*)

A pwen name also involves a triangle. Malgre Sa's naming included his parents (the senders), the child who bore it (and any other sham hearer), and the unnamed sorcerer (the target). Shooting a pwen does not require the target to be within earshot of the utterance of the message. A person may throw a pwen with the expectation that the target will overhear others gossiping about the situation or, in the case of appellation, simply uttering the pwen name.

According to Fisher, sham hearers will recognize the onset of a "ritualized" —but indirect—confrontation and assume the role of passive audience. The targets may perceive, probably correctly, that they are aligning themselves with the sender merely by "maintaining the fiction of non-aggressive discourse" (Fisher 1976:235). As will become clear forthwith, cassette recordings present a remarkable opportunity for exploiting an enormous, dispersed, passive-and-partisan sham audience.

"Social accountability," Thomas Kochman's (1986) term for assigning responsibility for interpretation of a message, rests with the target receiver, or "perceiver," not with the sender. Malgre Sa identified the target as the "owner" (*mèt*) of the pwen, a usage that apparently derives from the Magical context, in which pwen are the quintessence of alienable, or private, property. I asked him to explain. He said that "you throw the pwen through the air. It turns true when it falls. If the pwen resembles you, you collect it. You are its owner." (*Ou voye pwen an lè. Lè l vin verite se lè li tonbe. Si pwen an sanble ou, ou ranmase li. Se ou ki mèt pwen an.*) Malgre Sa cited two proverbs that communicate "if the pwen resembles you, you collect it; if not, you don't collect it": "Hang your hat where your hand can reach" (*Kroke chapo ou kote men ou ka rive*), and "If the shoe fits, wear it. If it doesn't fit, don't put it on." (*Si souliye a bon pou ou, mete l. Si'l pa bon pou ou, pa mete l.*)

Ranmase, meaning "collect" or "pick up," is crucial to understanding pwen. Ranmase, as we saw in our earlier discussion of Guinea and Magic, is a process of perceptual transformation. It means crystallizing indeterminate, scattered forces into accessible, intensified, meaningful images. Until someone scoops up a pwen, it lacks meaning.

I have been told that people communicate by means of pwen to make others "understand" (*konprann*) and "reflect" (*kalkile*). Instead of imposing a particular "meaning" on the target, which would only alienate him or her, Brown (1987:153) suggests, a pwen gets the listener to "understand" by leaving it to her or him to decide what the message means. A direct accusation would force the sender to commit to a particular "line" and the target to throw up impenetrable defenses, while indirect pwen discourse keeps the channels of interpretation open.[3] If the target does not collect this pwen, perhaps she or he will choose to gather another.

Indeed, when I suggested to Malgre Sa an analogy between shooting a pwen and shooting an arrow, he rejected the comparison. Volition made the two incomparable. The overhearer of a pwen actively chooses how to perceive the message (and transform it thereby). The target of an arrow is a passive victim (who cannot alter the *form* of the transmission):

KR: Is shooting pwen like shooting an arrow?
     Tire youn pwen se tankou tire youn flèsh?

MS: It's not like an arrow because it's your own will that makes you gather it.
     Non, se pa kankou flèsh paseke se volonte pa ou ki fè ou ranmase li.

The arrow metaphor captures the difference between a speaker-based system of social accountability, which holds that the shooter "assume(s) full responsibility for all the targets that are hit," and a receiver-based one where "the person shooting the arrow is responsible only for its general direction, not for the target the arrow hits, since it is the target that actually guides the arrow home" (Kochman 1981:900).

According to Malgre Sa, when you gather a pwen, "it hurts you in your heart. It feels like a pain. You think about it" (*Li fè ou mal nan kè. Li santi kòm youn penn. Ou kalkile l*). He continued to explain that the "owner" can respond in one of three ways, a choice mediated by the context of the message and consideration of the status of the parties involved. First, one may admit guilt in a socially acceptable way by reacting passively. Someone of inferior age or status might have no choice other than to "lower his/her head and walk away." Second, one can get angry and start a quarrel, which only marks the target for teasing and ridicule by the community. This inappropriately direct response is tantamount to an admission of guilt.

The third option is returning the pwen, the only good alternative. Returning the pwen turns a defensive tactic into an offensive advantage and perpetuates the frame of nonprovocative discourse. The target strategically removes him- or herself from a position of social accountability and challenges the new target to take ownership of his or her message.

Throwing Pwen on Cassettes

The cassette letter is a congenial setting for throwing pwen because of its potential for exploiting a multitude of sham hearers. Although pwen may be spoken, the message is more effective when it is sung, and most effective in public antiphonal exchange between leader and chorus. Any song text can become a pwen when its nondirected language is used to capture a second, hidden message about an interpersonal situation. The gifted singer, while speaking into the recorder, may interrupt speech addressed to the second person and will intone a pwen directed at a third party. Bystanders may not only listen to the triangular routine, but "innocently" sing along, subtly aligning themselves against the target.

To show off his or her vocal skills and simultaneously to intensify the embarrassment and "painful reflection" of the target, the singer uses a public occasion involving antiphonal singing to throw a pwen (on his/her own or someone else's behalf) toward the far-off recipient of the cassette. In ritual events involving call-and-response singing, the lead singer may mark a target by selecting song texts identified with a lwa known to be that emigrant's special patron. Even the gods who "come to party" (*vin banboche*) in person, i.e., through possession, may address the temporarily absent participants.

The unfolding of performance across a vast transnational space has shifted the frame of pwen songs, resulting in more direct and more openly aggressive texts. A

8.3. Ti Zanzin leads the call-and-response singing of songs for the *lwa* at a *vodou* rite, February 1984.

tape is perceived as an indirect medium, owing to the temporal discontinuity between the speaker and the listener, as opposed to the telephone, which is viewed as a temporally direct means of communication. The tape's inherent circularity allows the singer to take more license than would be socially acceptable in the audient presence of the target. On cassette, as the examples below indicate, the sender can *name* her or his prey.

Harold Courlander's (1939, 1960) comprehensive studies of Haitian "folk" music describe a rich diversity of song genres, all of which seem congenial to throwing pwen. Among them are songs honoring inherited spirits, which are intoned at rituals, Mardi Gras, and Lenten (*rara*) parades and cooperative labor groups. Gage Averill's (1997) book on Haitian popular music as social and political commentary and Jenny Smith's (2001) recent study of peasant organizations, including their use of song pwen, are two important contemporary studies of how otherwise powerless Haitians wield songs as vital social and political weapons.

In the context of cassette correspondence, however, pwen songs are almost invariably drawn from the vast, well-known ritual repertoire, which Herskovits (1937:314) called "the holy word of vodun theology and . . . an important device in stabilizing the details of belief." Family members corresponding by cassette improvise verses from the main ritual repertoires (*rit*, or "rites") associated with inherited Guinea lwa (*rit vodou*, *nago*, etc.), the category of incorporated spirits (lwa zandò, rit petwo), and with Bizango, the symbolic protectors of Guinea. The choice of musical repertoire, whose distinct rhythmic and melodic patterns can be discerned immediately, sends the first pwen. This message compares some aspect of their long-distance relationship to that of Guinea and Magic. The subsequent flow of the pithy, sententious poetry of the song further clarifies and intensifies this "truth."

The appeal of ritual song texts lies in the perception of an affinity between their content and the experience of this transnational society. The ritual repertoire seemingly offers ideal spatial-symbolic imagery for perceiving migration. The reciprocal dependence between people and their inherited, anthropomorphic spirits, or lwa, the subject of most ritual songs, clarifies the difficult and cumbersome interdependence between those who leave and those who stay at home. Moreover "lwa songs" (*chante lwa*) concern parties of vastly different status who are symbolically separated by a vast territorial distance: the lwa are said to live in the far-off homeland of "Africa," or Ginen. The songs can be "thrown" to "capture" aspects of the long-distance relationships between kin of differing age ranks in the domestic hierarchy, who are separated from one another by protracted international migration.

The lwa Ginen are simultaneously construed as venerable authority figures and needy, temper-prone children. They depend on people to "feed" (*ba yo manje*) and "take care of" them (*okipe yo*). People, on the other hand, need the lwa to "protect" them or, more precisely, to agree not to punish them with illness or misfortune. The ritual song texts portray (and poke self-conscious fun at) the pragmatic maneuvering and stroking by each side to sustain this difficult "international" separation. Many lwa songs narrate pairings of tense conversations. Agaou's song, described in the last chapter, "Look, a debt! Look, the family owes [me] a debt," is a one example. The lwa whine, protest, and intimidate to persuade their "children" to remember them; the heirs cajole, praise, and promise, hoping to postpone a retaliatory "de-guaranty" while preparing the onerous ritual offering. To voice feelings of neglect to a wayward emigrant, a parent may improvise a Guinea text about an anguished, enfeebled spirit begging to be "remembered." These verses usually recapitulate or anticipate the whining prose in the parent's spoken section of the letter.

Some songs grasp the pith of pwenification—vulnerability, repudiation, and exploitation—conjuring up agonizing images of orphaned beings starving in the periphery. The texts may be used to crystallize the lamentable prospect of complete rupture and the torment of persevering, despite unrelenting ambivalence and misunderstanding. The images perceive the comfort, however partial, of "picking up" and return.

Variations on this aesthetically and ritually esteemed repertoire are recorded on cassette letters circulating between the home and the emigrant communities. To throw a pwen song, a skillful singer can vary the objectified discourse of a spirit song to confound the voice of the god with the voice of someone who left. A needy parent at home improvises a ritual song to an undisciplined emigrant child, for example, implying an analogy between his or her willful estrangement and an abandoned pwen starving for a new master to pick it up. An emigrant improvises a song portraying the tearful gathering of a long-scorned pwen as a vehicle to protest being exploited. Or, a parent, indignant about increased dependence on an emissary, sends a pwen song message that he or she (representing Guinea) perseveres despite the neglect of an insubordinate pwen. Each improvisation on a sacred song text holds still one unforgettable image against the panorama of this distorted Guinea-Magic dependency.

Four Pwen Songs in Cassette Correspondence

In the following section, I explore how the Guinea-Magic dialectic, implied in ritual song texts, is used to promote and to contest the relations between migrants who seek a livelihood Outside and of those who remain Inside. The interpretation is, and must be, an intersubjective process involving the triangular complicity of sender, target, and sham audience. International migration and the "indirect" medium of the cassette recorder have transformed this triangle into a square; throwing pwen via tape exploits two sham audiences—one each in the home and host community. This discussion endeavors to maintain the dynamics of this four-way communication. I present the compositions and commentaries of senders, targets, and audience, of which I am one, though I have yet to attempt to throw a pwen song on a cassette letter.

Pwen Song One: "Do for Me. I'm Going."

"Do" (*fè*) is a category of moral Guinea discourse. It is opposed to "work" (*travay*). Guinea uses "doing" as a means of obscuring the alienated conditions of its vitalization. Residents of Ti Rivyè, standing as Guinea to pwen, candidly rank emigrants by their degree of "doing," distinguishing those who "already sent to do" (*deja voye fè*) from those who have "not yet sent to do" (*poko voye fè*). "Sending to do" means remitting money to invest or *fè ekonomi*—literally, "to make economy" exclusive of remittances for family members' immediate consumption, namely, purchases of food, clothing, medicine, etc. They expect their pwen in the goldsmith shops Outside "to do" by financing the construction of a new home out of such high-status materials as cinder block, cement, mosaic tile, and corrugated zinc, ideally on a newly purchased plot of land. Other symbols of "doing" include buying or renting cultivable land, purchasing livestock, buying a fishing boat, investing in a trade, financing children's school fees, or sponsoring a relative's emigration. Emigrants also should "do" by shouldering their families' ritual obligations and being "responsible" (*reskonsab*) for the funerary rites and burials of close kin.

The zandò song with the "do for me" phrase in the refrain has enjoyed considerable play on cassette letters circulating between Ti Rivyè and "Miami." The rudimentary lyrics of the choral refrain, typically intoned in response to the soloist's improvisations, are:

Do for me; I'm going, oh God.
Do for me; I'm going.
So-and-so left;
And didn't leave behind.
So-and-so left;
And didn't leave behind.
Whoever remembers God
Will do for me. I'm going.

Fè pou mwen, m prale.
Fè pou mwen, m prale.
Entèl ale,
Li pa kite dèyè.
Entèl ale,
Li pa kite dèyè.
Sa k sonje Bondye
Ap fè pou mwen, m prale.

One subtle marker identifying this song with the existential option of Magic, as opposed to Guinea, is its reference to an alienated compact between two individual units, one a pwen, the other an owner, as opposed to a substantialized bond between a descent group and their lwa. The song interprets the anxiety of a pwen whose "owner" has died "and didn't leave behind." "Leaving behind" may refer to either persons or things, or both. In other words, the master failed to specify either anyone and/or any means to assume his/her contractual obligations to the pwen. The orphaned pwen teeters on fading into oblivion. The voice calls out to an anonymous public ("whoever remembers God"), hoping to find one sympathetic listener who will consent to pick it up.

Malgre Sa and I have been bystanders when cassette recordings of this song were replayed before "Miami audiences." Malgre Sa explained that the "do for me" song—when thrown to clarify a migration relationship—invokes an unsavory image of someone who departed and failed to "do" back home. (This formulation poses overlapping analogies between the emigrant and both the deceased owner and the abandoned pwen.) On hearing the song, the target will realize that "someone who left and didn't leave behind is worse off than someone who never went away." An unproductive pwen is more pathetic than a poor but obedient member of Guinea. Malgre Sa said that

> You become like a person with no family, someone who didn't leave anyone behind. If you are here working, you have to have something saved. You can be ill for who knows how long. . . . If you don't have behind, if you don't leave behind, if you are deported, what will you live on? . . . And as long as you don't send to do, you are nothing.

> *Ou se yon san ras. Yon mounn ki pa kite dèyè. Si ou isit ou travay, fò ou gen youn bagay sere. Ou ka fè konbyen lè malad. . . . Si ou pa gen dèyè, si ou pa kite dèyè, si ou depòte, sou ki sa ou pral viv?. . . . E tout o tan ke ou pa voye fè, ou pa anyen.*

The Case of Sergo

Menmenn (Germaine's nickname) and Zo (Joseph's nickname) are a poor couple who have resided virtually all of their lives in Ti Rivyè. Menmenn gardens with Zo and occasionally manages a very modest trade in charcoal. Menmenn is as tiny and delicate looking as Zo is imposing. A disarmingly gentle man, Zo enjoys a wide reputation as a self-effacing wit and a virtuoso musician who is a lead singer, drummer, and conductor or "operator," as he calls himself, of the local kongo and rara bands. Menmenn blends into the background; the charismatic Zo orchestrates the action in front.

Menmenn and Zo have been bitterly disappointed by their late son and only child, Sergo, an affable but utterly irresponsible man whom I first met in 1981. A cassette letter they "wrote" to Sergo in 1987 responded to a disturbing message indicating the prospect of his deportation. (Sergo was then 33 years old.) Zo intoned 12 pwen songs (10 zandò and 2 Guinea); Menmenn sang only one verse of the "do for me" zandò song, a preview of the scorn this drifter pwen would reap upon himself (and upon his exposed Guinea masters) should he return with nothing more than the clothes on his back to show for his migration (CD, track 3).

8.4. Zo Guerrier, Ti Rivyè, June 2003.

8.5. Sergo Guerrier and Mercina D'Haïti at Farmex farm in Tasley, Virginia, July 1985.

Just before singing the "do for me" song, Menmenn raved about the grand two-story dwellings that emigrant members of Sergo's cohort were busily constructing in the higher-status location of the town—*after* having completed homes for their "mothers" in the village. Then she depicted the humiliating symbols of Sergo's utter failure as a migrant and a son: a crude, wattle and daub, one-room hut—his parent's home—and beside it, a decaying, hollow wood frame and dwindling piles of building materials, ravaged by weather and thieves, which they had purchased in vain anticipation of Sergo's continued remittances. Menmenn's increasingly frantic speech culminated with a tirade comparing Sergo to a few of his fellow emigrants who had been involuntarily repatriated for drug trafficking and had disgraced themselves and their families (for their failure to discipline them) by coming back before they had "done."

> This makes me so sick inside I can't take it! When night falls I lie down and I don't know if I'll ever get up. This thing is killing me! People here criticize people who return from over there who didn't do anything. They are saying, "there is so-and-so, so-and-so who didn't do." I'm praying, I'm pacing, I'm in prayer.

> *Sa ban m youn lògey nan lestomak mwen, pitit! Sole kouche m kouche m pa konn si map leve. Bagay sa ap touye m. Mounn isit ap kritike sou mounn ki sòt lòt bò ki vini ki pa fè anyen. Yap pale, "men entèl, entèl ki pa fè." Map priye, m ap mache, m lapriyè.*

Menmenn abruptly stopped speaking and began singing in a frail, mournful voice the "do for me" pwen song.

> Do for me; I'm leaving.
> Do for me; I'm leaving.
> Sergo left; he didn't leave behind.
> Sergo left; he didn't leave behind...

Sadly, Menmenn and Zo's messages failed to persuade Sergo to "send to do" at home. Sergo eventually stopped communicating with them at all. More than a decade later they finished construction of the modest, tin-roofed house, which has yet to be painted. Neither did they succeed in influencing their son's pursuits Over There. They already knew of Sergo's arrest, the year before they "wrote" this letter, for unlawful possession of a very small amount of drugs. (I helped him in the case.) They knew that deportation was likely to follow, though Sergo did manage to elude deportation. He never returned to Little River. He was killed during a drug deal in Florida in 1995. His parents do not know where he is buried.

Pwen Song Two: "I'll Buy a Winnow to Gather a Life for My Children"

At the same time they "wrote" to Sergo, Menmenn and Zo apparently anticipated the possibility of Sergo's continued rejection, which they sought to counterbalance by throwing pwen songs to elicit the emotional and material support of members of the Miami audience expected to hear and overhear the cassette letter. The pwen songs provided an appropriately elegant medium for indirectly expressing sentiments they could or would not have spoken directly. Indeed, they sent the cassette letter to their cousin and age-peer, Little Caterpillar, who invited me to listen to the cassette letter inside his cabin on a labor camp in Virginia during the summer of 1988.

One of Zo's 12 pwen songs—Menmenn threw only the "do for me" song— invoked Caterpillar's name along with his son's. The lyrics were based on a ritual text simulating an anxious interaction between an incensed lwa and a distraught parent. Their relationship turns on pwenification: the lwa, standing to the parent as Guinea to a pwen, rebukes the parent for failing "to do." The lwa threatens revenge, which, because of the pwening order, means harming not the parent but the latter's most precious products: progeny. Desperate for the spirit to respond, the parent calls out, "where are you?" Fearing that the ravenous spirit will devour the children, the parent pledges to perform the rites of "gathering" and "receiving," symbolized in the text by the winnowing tray upon which ritual food offerings are placed.

> Chini, Godfather of my son
> I send a message
> How is Sergo doing?
> Sergo, my son
> I send a message
> How are you doing?
> Sergo, where are you?
> Sergo, where are you?
> I am going to buy a winnow
> To gather life for my children.

> *Chini, o, m di konpè mwen,*
> *M voye di*
> *Koman afè Sergo a ye?*
> *Sergo, pitit gason m nan,*
> *M voye di ou*
> *Koman afè ou ye?*

Sergo, kote ou ye?
Sergo, kote ou ye?
M pral achte youn laye
Pou m ranmase lavi zanfan m yo.

It seems Zo improvised on this song in order to arouse Little Caterpillar's intense regret for failing (as Zo's Guinea accomplice) to influence Sergo to be a better son to his parents so that they, in turn, could meet their ritual obligations. Before Sergo and Little Caterpillar set sail together for the United States, Little Caterpillar (who is Zo's peer), promised Zo that he would look after Sergo. Although Little Caterpillar represented a pwen to his own family, in his relationship to Sergo he was a surrogate Guinea, managing the conduct of migratory pwen. Indeed Little Caterpillar vented his exasperation with the incorrigible Sergo directly to Zo and Menmenn, as he indicated in this cassette letter. I have also been an audience for Little Caterpillar's grievances with Sergo. In virtually every cassette letter he sent me from Florida, he complained bitterly of Sergo's irresponsible behavior and his unwillingness to heed Little Caterpillar's advice.

Manipulating Caterpillar's frustration, the singer confronts his Guinea accomplice with a question both parties know has no favorable answer: "Little Caterpillar, I ask you. How is my son doing?" The subsequent lines, the parent's frantic beckoning to his son, would likely intensify this target's disquiet. Having failed in his capacity as a representative of Guinea to discipline Zo and Menmenn's pwen, Little Caterpillar began in 1987 "to take responsibility" for them.

When Caterpillar added Zo and Menmenn to the list of relatives he regularly "does for" back home, he also capitalized on a subtle advantage. Their "gratitude" could serve to buttress the conditions of working as a pwen on behalf of his own Guinea owners. He shifted control over his "doings" back home out of the hands of a dominating, hostile Guinea master into the certain hands of a sympathetic partner in Guinea. (An irony of the Guinea-Magic compact is that Caterpillar had to wrestle control of the funds away from his parent in order to help the same.)

Se Byen and Little Caterpillar

Every year after Little Caterpillar sailed to Florida in 1980, he labored in the lowest rung of American agribusiness, primarily in Florida and on the Eastern Shore of Virginia. Little Caterpillar's (and Sergo's) experiences in agricultural labor were unfortunately all too typical of illiterate, unskilled Haitian immigrants: squalid temporary quarters, worksite accidents, crooked bosses, chronic illness, theft, and violent crime. On his first job, as I related in the introductory chapter, he was beaten and stabbed by a group of white men. When he was convalescing in a hospital, a government official appeared and asked him, through an interpreter who happened to be from a wealthy Léogane family, if he wanted to be sent back home to Haiti. He declined, he said, because he hadn't yet "sent to do" anything in the United States. Guinea, in other words, will not pick up pwen who have not yet done for them. Unlike Sergo, though, Little Caterpillar never shirked from carrying the burden of "doing" back home, as he reminded his older brother, Se Byen (It's Fine), on a cassette letter:

I know I left you in Haiti and leaving you means that if I were to come to Miami and get ten dollars, I should eat five and save five. Why is that? The other five I have to put in a letter and send to you.

M konnen m kite nou Ayiti, nan kite m kite nou an, si pou m ta rive nan Mayami, pou m ta genyen di dola, pou m manje senk, pou msere senk. Sak fè sa? Lòt senk la fò m mete l nan youn lèt, voye l ba nou.

Little Caterpillar willingly limited spending of his paltry migrant farm worker earnings to "eating," or basic consumption, so that he could remit to his dependents back home. Even after Caterpillar's index finger was amputated in an orange grove accident, leaving him with a chronic neurological condition, he sent a quarter of his workman's compensation checks to those "he left behind." Unlike Sergo, he chose to refrain from pursuing conjugal unions that might compete with his Haitian wife's and siblings' claims to his earnings.

Se Byen is the eldest of Little Caterpillar's siblings. He is a farmer (who "gives land to sharecroppers"), the owner of a cock-fight stadium and the ritual healer and gangan of his paternal (father's father's) kin group. Little Caterpillar had long been expected to succeed Se Byen in this position, just as Se Byen replaced their father, and in early 1991 Se Byen formally offered and Little Caterpillar formally accepted to "keep the shrine" (*kenbe Kay la*, literally, keep the House). His succession seemed to be a source of subtle tension between them because Se Byen was threatened by the idea of being exceeded by his successor.[4] (Little Caterpillar occasionally applied his "knowledge" [*konesans*] to serve Haitian immigrants by divining and healing. He had a reputation for influencing the outcomes of soccer matches between teams representing various immigrant enclaves of South Florida. Some of his English-speaking acquaintances refer to him as "the voodoo man.")

While Sergo rejected playing the part of pwen in the Guinea-Magic production, Se Byen and Little Caterpillar were equally entangled in its drama. Se Byen, caught closer to the moral and reproductive center, bore the ultimate responsibility to keep the Guinea system afloat. Signs of his resentment toward the weight of this lonely responsibility were evident in his correspondence with Little Caterpillar. The Guinea-Magic covenant manipulated Se Byen, then, as much as he used it to manipulate others.

As gangan and surrogate father, this Guinea representative was obliged to discipline his pwen in the wage-laboring periphery of "Miami" in order to maintain the homeward flow of remittances. (As Zo's surrogate, Little Caterpillar tried in vain to exert similar Guinea authority over Sergo.) Se Byen's ambivalent behavior toward Little Caterpillar was typical: he deliberately ignored his mercenary, disavowing thereby his consumption of the latter's tainted wages. At the same time Se Byen accused Little Caterpillar of assuming a callous arrogance, of frivolously squandering his money in the foreign country while his family in Haiti went hungry.

Little Caterpillar's improvisations of zandò song texts imply an analogy between his migration and the role of pwen. He felt that he broke his back laboring in hostile territories "to do for" someone who repudiated him for ever having left. Even more onerous, he felt obliged to delegate control over his remittances to this same kinsman who wasted his hard-earned wages on selfish frivolities. He knew that his "guaranty" at home—symbolized by his reputation for "doing" there—did not ride on his good intentions for his wages, but rather on how his latently indignant trustee ultimately decided to dispense them. In addition to bearing the humiliation of "not yet having done" in Haiti, he worried about how he would manage should he suddenly have to return to Haiti because of illness, accident, or deportation.

Little Caterpillar once related to me, "I told Se Byen, I'll guaranty you in Haiti; you guaranty me, too. Because I can be here in this country and they can take me and send me back to Haiti." (*M voye di Se Byen, map garanti yo Ayiti; garanti pou tèt mwen tou. Sa k fè sa, m kapab la nan peyi a, yo kapab pran m yo voye m Ayiti.*) Se Byen, however, played his triple roles of surrogate parent, dependent, and trustee against one another in order that he, rather than Little Caterpillar, accumulate the limited "guaranty."

Se Byen preempted Little Caterpillar's challenging his use of remittances by laundering the funds through a consummate Guinea symbol: "the House" (*Kay la*). The House is the descent group's zandò/petwo shrine, the repository for inherited lwa zandò and the center for "gathering" spirits purchased, worked, and abandoned by deceased "children of the House."[5] In 1982, Caterpillar sent $1,800 to Se Byen earmarked to construct a personal residence for his wife and himself. Se Byen used the funds to finance the renovation and enlargement of the House, which included enclosing the bower (*tònèl*) to serve as a public ritual performance space, or *peristil*, and converting the former peristyle into his residence. In addition to gaining personally by securing this (or another) place to reside, Se Byen stood to benefit professionally from the face lift of his place of work. Little Caterpillar said Se Byen used the money to "guaranty" the House instead of Little

Caterpillar. Se Byen "guarantied" himself, too, since he furnished the professional services necessary to its functioning.

Se Byen never publicly acknowledged Little Caterpillar's contribution. After having consumed Little Caterpillar's remittances in the lwa's House, Se Byen then chided Little Caterpillar (on the publicly performed cassette letter described below) for "not having done anything in Haiti," including, of course, not contributing to renovating the House.

Se Byen correctly anticipated that once Caterpillar learned about this diversion, he could hardly protest against its laudable end. As Caterpillar later commented to me about Se Byen's action (using the second person):

> You do for the lwa; I am not angry about the lwa. I wasn't the one who sent a message saying, "you weren't supposed to do it." Even the lwa have already seen (the truth). But I haven't spoken any crooked words about that.

> *Ou fè pou lwa a, m pa fache pou lwa. Se pa mwen ki voye di ou, "ou pat pou te fè l." Menm lwa menm gen tan wè. M pa pale okenn mo kwochi nan sa.*

While Caterpillar's leverage improved somewhat in 1987, after he asked Zo to manage his remittances, it improved even more after 1988, when he procured permanent residence in the United States. Now that he can return home regularly without jeopardizing his immigration status, he can better control the allocation of his personal savings, which are managed by his wife and Zo rather than by Se Byen. Little Caterpillar did build the house for his wife. Caterpillar, of course, continues to support Se Byen and the other siblings left behind.

Se Byen responded flexibly in defense of Guinea's interests. For example, Caterpillar went home in 1990. Almost immediately after he re-entered Florida, Se Byen fell acutely sick. Caterpillar received word and returned to Haiti right away. The diagnosis: Se Byen was being "held" by his vindictive patron lwa (Ti Jean) for failing to meet his ritual obligations. Caterpillar pledged to "take responsibility" for these duties. Se Byen recuperated. (I will take up Ti Jean's maneuvering on Se Byen's behalf below.)

For Caterpillar, the asymmetries of correspondence protocol are a sore emblem of the double standard applied to those who leave (pwen) and those who stay behind (Guinea). Emigrants must constantly demonstrate their productivity and devotion, while home residents can neglect their pwen with impunity. Se Byen, for example, expected Little Caterpillar to "write" him every month— "write" can also be a euphemism for "send money." Little Caterpillar willingly accepted this responsibility. Paradoxically, in Little Caterpillar's view, Se Byen felt no obligation to reciprocate. Caterpillar said,

Those people, Karen, if they have someone in a foreign country, if a month goes by and you don't write them, they don't need to know about your problems, if you have any [money] or if you don't have any [before they start criticizing you]. It's only when you have and you write [i.e., send money] to them that you will hear their good news. When they should be writing to you, they won't write to you. They don't need to know if you're sick or if you're not sick, they don't need to know it.

Mounn sa yo, Karin, nenpòt mounn ou genyen nan peyi etranje, depi ou fè youn mwa, ou pa ekri yo, yo pa bezwen konnen pwoblèm ou—si ou genyen, si ou pa genyen. Se kan ou genyen ou voye ekri yo, lè a alèkilè ou ap tande bon nouvèl nan men yo. Tout tan yo gen pou ekri ou yo pap ekri ou, non? Yo pa bezwen konnen si ou malad, si ou pa malad, yo pa bezwen konn sa.

Eli (short for Joseph-Elie), another emigrant from Léogane, was equally primed to rant over this double standard. He summarized the injustice with the well-known proverb about the lowly donkey who toils without rest for the benefit of the dominant horse. The reference for this proverb, the poet Jean-Claude Martineau explained to me, was the military convoy of the 18th century. Donkeys hauled heavy loads of provisions and weapons; horses carried high-ranking officers decorated with metals and galloons. According to the proverb, "the donkey toils so the horse can get promoted" (*Bourik travay pou chwal galonen*).[6] Eli said:

You know what they think? They think that I'm their donkey. I break my back working here so they can advance in Haiti. When they need money they write to me. When you send money to them they don't even take the time to write to you to say, "yes, thank you, we received the money."

Ki sa yo konprann? Yo konprann m se bourik yo. M ap bourike isit pou yo menm yo ka galonen an Ayiti. Lè yo bezwen lajan yo ekri m. Depi ou voye lajan ba yo, yo pa menm pedi tan pou yo ekri ou pou di ou, "wi, mèsi, nou jwenn kòb la."

Frustrated and disappointed at being ignored, Little Caterpillar decided to retaliate by withholding remittances during the spring of 1989, just before I arrived to begin research in his village. I had meanwhile understood that Little Caterpillar, who corresponded regularly, had sent a message to Se Byen to expect me. I had no clue that I was the message and the messenger. *I was the pwen!* When I presented myself to Little Caterpillar's family, Se Byen smelled his younger brother's mischief in my sunny, unexpected arrival. In his taped letter to Caterpillar, Se Byen declared that while he was pleased to get Little Caterpillar's news, he was displeased with its form of transmission.

Well my friend, I'm very happy I got your news, but I don't see your voice. . . . Now that I've heard your news, I'm content. But the way I got your news, it's not as if you sent it to me yourself; the way I got your news, it's not as if you gave it to me yourself. You should make a cassette letter and send it to me so I can hear your voice.

The imperial Guinea horse retaliated against the mule by commandeering me to assist in recording this same vitriolic cassette letter repudiating the "bad" pwen. Se Byen feigned that he was too poor to own a portable radio-cassette player, too ostracized to be able to borrow someone else's appliance, and definitely too ignorant to know how to operate one. In my enthusiasm to start off well with him, I was only too delighted to return with my cassette recorder and a tape. (A few months later Se Byen allowed me see his swanky beige affair with a price ticket of $180 still conspicuously attached to it—a gift from Little Caterpillar.) To clinch his coup, moreover, Se Byen used my network, rather than one of the local "messenger services," to transfer the tape.

At least, in Little Caterpillar's view, he—or we—succeeded in provoking some response from Se Byen. For like Eli, Caterpillar viewed receiving mail from home as an affirmation of "the guaranty" at home. Aside from rare packages of home-grown starches (*viv*), there are few other symbols of their commitment. Because this guaranty produces personal status in the migrant community as well, he felt doubly humiliated by Se Byen's indifference. (He assumed that his fellow migrants received mail from home more often.) When he received Se Byen's long-awaited correspondence, he replayed the letter in public. As he reported to Se Byen in his reply letter, he wanted fellow Haitian immigrants to know that he was "a person" (*youn mounn*), that is, "a member of a family," and "someone who left [concerned kin] behind." He did not want them to think of him, he said, as a "cow without a herdsman" (*youn bèf san gadò*). (People keep and tend individual cows. A cow's main social "relationship" is with its "guardian" [*gadò*], typically a youth.)

You see, when I'm going to replay the tape, I don't replay it inside my house. When I replay it, I turn up the cassette player so everyone can hear it, so they don't think of me as a cow without a herdsman, you understand? When they see me with them, they should know that I am a person, that I have relatives in Haiti like every other person.

Lè ou wè m vinn pase kasèt la, ou wè se pa andan kay m pase l. M pase l; m ouvè radyo a pou tout piblik tande l, pou yo pa gen konprann ke m se youn bèf san gadò, ou konprann? Lè yo wè m nan mitan yo, pou yo gen konprann ke m se yon mounn ki gen paran Ayiti tankou tout mounn.

To show his friends his shepherd had not abandoned him, he was willing to risk that when they heard the hostile messages they might align themselves with Se Byen against him. After publicly airing Se Byen's spurious accusations, Little Caterpillar moved to limit the damage. Caterpillar could not defend himself with documentation of his "doings"—a photograph, for instance, of the fine cinder block home he would have built had Se Byen invested the funds as he had requested rather than diverting them to expand the House. Se Byen in fact excoriated Little Caterpillar on the tape for neglecting his duty to help rebuild the House. But Little Caterpillar could show receipts of moneys he had sent home in the three years since arriving in the United States. Immediately after airing Se Byen's cassette letter, Caterpillar obliged his cabin mate to sort through the contents of his suitcase to locate the evidence, as he recounted to Se Byen in his reply letter:

> You know Julien from Darbonne? His son shares a cabin with me at the [farm labor camp]. Last night, after I got your cassette, I had to empty out my suitcase for him. I made him look at the check receipts of the money I sent you in Haiti. I did it so people wouldn't think it was true that I have never sent five cents to you.

> *Men m gen youn-li menm-pitit Julien, Darbonne, li nan kay la nan kontra a avèk mwen. Lè m vinn resevwa kasèt la, me sètoblije deboure malèt mwen, iyèswa, ba li. M fè l gade resi chèk yo, kòb mwen voye ba nou an Ayiti. Pou piblik la pa gen konprann vre m pa janm voye senk kòb ba nou.*

Two-and-a-half years after helping Se Byen record the cassette letter, I went to Fort Pierce, Florida, and spent several days talking with Little Caterpillar. I had seen him three times since returning from his home, but this was our first opportunity to speak at length about such "research" questions as his relationship to Se Byen and my relationship to Se Byen. Although I did not think I needed to convince Little Caterpillar that I doubted him and that I had sided with Se Byen, he still made me rummage through the heap of letters, receipts, envelopes, sales vouchers, and pay stubs in his suitcase until we had satisfactorily registered his remittances for 1980, 1981, 1982, and 1983. Because he could not read well enough to sort the papers, he saved them all; that is, every document he had collected since the last suitcase was stolen. I was recording our conversation while examining the sundry pieces of paper. Little Caterpillar said,

> When I was in Virginia [on the farm labor contract], I sent $1,000 to Haiti, $200 for Se Byen, $200 for Adan [his brother], $200 for Eve [his sister], and $400 for Maxia [his wife]. That's one.

Then when I came back from the contract, I sent $1,800 home to Se Byen for him to buy wood, sand, zinc roofing—for Se Byen to build a house for me. Se Byen took the money. [Laughing at my surprised expression] Look at you, Ka! [my nickname] I'll show you the receipts of checks from '80, '81, '82, '83.

Now you see this [other] money here I made from picking oranges in Palatka, I made this money before the big frost killed the oranges. And all of this money was completely wasted by the people in Haiti. When I left Palatka, I went to pick the trees in Fort Pierce. I hadn't been in Fort Pierce for even three weeks of work before my finger got cut off.

Lè m te Virginia [an 1982] m te voye $1,000 an Ayiti, $200. pou Se Byen, $200 pou [sè m], $200 pou [lòt frè m], $400 pou [madanm mwen]. Sa di ou younn. Lè m vinn sòt nan kontra, m voye $1,800 lakay pou Se Byen achte bwa, achte sab, achte tòl, pou Se Byen monte youn kay pou mwen. Se Byen pran kòb la. [Li ri m.] Gade Ka! Map montre ou resi chèk '80, '81, '82, '83.

Lajan ou wè m fè Palatka ap keyi zoranj—tout lajan sa a m mete avan gwo fredi touye zoranj Palatka. Tout lajan sa gaspiye nan men mounn Ayiti yo nèt. Lè m vin kite Palatka, m vinn keyi bwa Fort Pierce, m antre Fort Pierce, m poko gen twa semenn travay menm, dwèt mwen koupe.

Pwen Song Three: "Little Caterpillar Falls; Se Byen Does Not Fall/ The House Falls; Ti Jean Remains"

I wish to present just two of the many pwen songs exchanged by Se Byen and Little Caterpillar on the occasion of my arrival at their home. Se Byen chose a loaded setting for beginning this round of the competition: the House. To visualize the House, imagine a large, windowless rectangular structure with a corrugated zinc roof standing out among half-a-dozen homes in a residential yard (*lakou*). Coarse outlines of human figures are traced in white on its tangerine colored exterior. A thatched arbor extends the entire length of one side. The bulk of the interior is a large open area, the site for creative, multimedia events involving prayer, drumming, singing, dancing, ground paintings, food offerings, animal sacrifice, blessings, and the making and dispensation of protective medicines. Here Se Byen, Zo, Menmenn, Pepe, Little Caterpillar, and others displayed their virtuoso musical, ritual, dance, theatrical, and verbal talents.

A door on the right side of the performance space opens into the shaman's cramped and musty "office." There is a low altar dedicated to Ti Jean, the shaman's patron spirit, and other inherited lwa who are said to "go with him" (*mache avè l*).

Among them is a lwa who has "claimed" Little Caterpillar, Baron la Croix. On the left is a passageway leading to another dark, closet-sized sanctum, which is allotted to the secret Bizango society, whose membership roughly corresponds to that of the descent group.

Se Byen led me into the eerie Ti Jean office, and then indicated that I follow him into the far more unnerving Bizango cavern. His cousin and ritual assistant, Frankel, followed. We sat in near darkness on three rickety wooden chairs. Frankel lit a tiny oil lamp, leaving us in shadow. I placed the tape recorder on a cement altar and nervously waited for Se Byen to indicate his readiness to start recording. Se Byen opened his letter to Caterpillar with the conventional cassette greeting. He continued speaking and then suddenly interrupted his artful monologue to intone a sacred song, and then another. Frankel accompanied on the rattle and sang the choral refrains to the antiphonal verses.

Zo appeared with a drum and started beating the clipped petwo (zandò) rhythm. Soon Menmenn and other "bystanders" crowded into and around the portal, and we moved to a larger room in the shrine. Two more drummers arrived holding the smaller of the two zandò drums and the iron striker, completing the zandò orchestra. Several rival lead singers and persons-of-words, including Zo, Pepe, and Miracia, took turns displaying their virtuoso vocal talents on this extraordinary two-cassette message. And, as if Little Caterpillar needed to be reminded of my conspicuous participation in the 35-strong sham chorus, Se Byen shouted into the microphone over the chorus's refrain to one of the zandò songs, "the woman is sitting here listening to this. She is ashamed to find out that her friend doesn't write to his family." (*Men sè a chita la a. Li wont pou li wè zanmi ni pa ekri fanmi ni.*)

Se Byen's letter opened with a poignant allegory of a lwa left to languish in Guinea. Adroitly manipulating proverb, rhyme, and rhythm, this master orator designed a pathetic portrait of his devastation since his "child" abandoned him.

Hello, Pierre Dioguy. Se Byen Dioguy is speaking to you, your big brother. I haven't heard from you at all. We started out communicating just fine. But it's been three years since I got any news from you and because of it, I am not managing at all. Our mother had seven children; my man, you were the one here with me. You looked out for me; I looked out for you. But I never thought you would do this to me. After all, you left merely to pursue a livelihood.

Well, man, I'm letting you know that I haven't heard from you and I'm wasting away. The way you remember me is not how I look today. I haven't seen you; I can't live, I can't drink. When I think about you, I don't know how I am. I'm hungry; I don't see you. I'm bare naked; I don't see you. You are hungry; I don't see you. You are bare naked; I don't see you. Man, I'm letting you know that I'm dirty; I'm torn; the work doesn't go the way you remember it—in Haiti. But when you're down, you take what comes, if nothing comes your way, you accept it.

Alo Piè Dioguy, se Se Byen Dioguy k ap pale avèk ou, gran frè ou. Mon chè, m pa pran nouvèl ou di tou. Nan bon kondisyon nou t ap pale tre byen, nou te konmanse. Men gen twa zan, m pa pran nouvèl ou di tou. Ou fè m pa ka viv di tou. Manman nou te gen sèt pitit, monchè, se te ou menm ki te la ansanm avèk mwen. Ou te pwotèy mwen; m te pwotèy ou tou. Men, m pat kwaye ke se ta ou menm ki ta fè m sa. Se lavi ou tal chache.

Men, monchè, m voye fè ou konnen m pa pran nouvèl ou; kò m ap desann kouniyè a. Jan ou te konnen m nan, se pa kon sa mwen ye. M pa wè ou; m pa viv, m pa bwè. Lè m kalkile ou, m pa konn ki jan mwen ye. M grangou; m pa wè ou. M touni; m pa wè ou. Ou menm ou grangou, m pa wè ou. Ou touni tou, mwen pa wè ou. . . Mon chè, mwen voye di ou mwen sal, mwen chire. Travay pa mache menm jan ou te konnen an—an Ayiti. Men kòm jou ou piti ou pran, jou ou pa jwenn nan tou, ou rezinye ou.

A perfunctory closing drew Se Byen's extended harangue to an end. Suddenly, Se Byen reversed himself, adding a postscript: "there is one more thing I wanted to let you know. You will get the message of what it means." (*Gen yon sèl bagay map voye di ou. Depi m voye di ou sa, ou a gen konprann ki sa m voye di ou.*) Se Byen's "afterthought" conveyed a subtly poised admission. The masterfully scored overture was a ruse; he would air his serious message next. This earnest message was a pwen song.

Se Byen chose as his first pwen song a verse based on a text from the Makanda ritual repertoire. This repertoire belongs to the Bizango club. Although such clubs have been classified in the literature as secret societies, they are hardly secret. The band organization is an inversion of the temple structure: the gangan is the leader and the ounsi and their relatives are the members. Like the ranks, the band's discourse inverts Guinea morality and signifies in relation to Guinea's impotency. Whereas Guinea concerns the delicate reciprocal dependence of heirs to their lineal spirits, Makanda is a brazen, offensive discourse of power. Many of the songs boast of wielding vast cosmic powers to protect the members against un-named slanderers and other enemies.[7] The Makanda genre was a fitting vehicle for Se Byen's aggressive message. He used the metamessage of the genre to reclaim the upper hand and silence the gossip that his younger brother had surpassed him. A whiney "lwa song" would have hardly been effective here. Once he had established his command through the Makanda text, Se Byen did throw pwen based on lwa songs.

Se Byen's song conjured up the image of a crumbling, abandoned House (where we recorded the tape). Despite persecution and/or neglect, the House, including the patron spirit, Ti Jean, perseveres:

The House falls down;
Ti Jean doesn't fall down.
The House falls down;
Ti Jean doesn't fall down.
Brother Chini, my friend,
It's for their big mouths, true.

Little Caterpillar falls down;
Se Byen doesn't fall down.
Little Caterpillar falls down;
Se Byen doesn't fall down.
Brother Caterpillar, my friend,
It's for their big mouths, true.

The House stumbles;
The House is mad;
Ti Jean sits there.
The House goes on;
Ti Jean sits there.
Little Caterpillar, my friend,
It's for their big mouths, true.

First verse repeats

Kay la tonbe;
Ti Jean pa tonbe.
Kay la tonbe;
Ti Jean pa tonbe.
Frè Chini, monchè,
Se pou dyòl yo, vre.

Ti Chini tonbe;
Se Byen pa tonbe.
Little Caterpillar tonbe;
Se Byen pa tonbe.

Frè Chini monchè,
Se pou dyòl yo, vre.

Kay la bite;
Kay la fache;
Ti Jean chita la.
Kay la ap mache;
Ti Jean chita la.
Little Caterpillar, monchè,
Se pou dyòl yo, vre.

Two-and-a-half years later I listened to the tape again with Caterpillar. I asked him to explain how he "collected" the pwen song. Se Byen, he said, felt indignant about their divergent destinies: Se Byen remained tethered to the deepening grind at home and to Caterpillar's remittances while Caterpillar apparently found success abroad (a false impression Caterpillar was hardly inclined to correct). Se Byen improvised the song to proclaim defiantly, in effect, "I don't need your money anyway."

What does it mean when he sends a message to me, "the House falls down and Se Byen himself doesn't fall down"? It means just because I'm in a foreign country don't assume that Se Byen is worse off when I don't send money to him.

[As for the message that] I forget him: He is in Haiti; I am in a foreign country. He's bad off. That's the first message. It's my good luck; it's his bad luck. My life and his life did not turn out the same. And so [he thinks] I forgot about him.

Lè li voye di m kon sa, "kay la tonbe, li menm Se Byen pa tonbe a," sa vle di la a? Mwen menm m gen tan nan peyi etranje, pa panse gen konprann li pa mal si m pa voye ba li.

[Li voye di] m bilye l. Li menm, li an Ayiti; mwen menm, m nan peyi etranje. Li mal. Sa se mo devan an. Sa se chans pan m, se devenn pa l. Vi pan m a vi pa l se pa menm. La, m bilye l.

Little Caterpillar continued to explain the song. Suddenly he figured out there was a pwen within the pwen!

"The House falls down, Ti Jean is still there." That means that when I return, I have to come into the House. The House endures. I'll be damned, it's a pwen!

"Kay la tonbe, Ti Jean la," sa vle di, lè m vini fòk se nan kay la pou m vini. Kay la toujou la. Se youn pwen, tonè kraze m!

Whenever Caterpillar returned, he would have to enter the House to face his judgment. There he will simultaneously confront Se Byen-Ti Jean, that is, both Se Byen and the ruthless spirit who rides him.

The confounding of Se Byen, the shaman, with Ti Jean evokes a means of communication with which we are already familiar. Karen McCarthy Brown's (1987: 152) insight is that possession-performance can be perceived in the same way as a pwen message. First is the confounding of the lwa's character with that of the "horse." This symbiosis derives from the concept of "claiming," the lwa's choice of an heir "to love." As Pepe, a gangan ason, explained to me, the union "depends upon your heart" (*se selon kè ou*). Possession-performance reveals this analogy to everyone who witnesses it and so, as Brown (1987:152, 162–167) writes, it becomes a way of "balancing" character. Grammatical use of the possessive form emphasizes this connection: one speaks of Se Byen's lwa (*lwa Se Byen an*) not only belonging to him, but being of him. Ti Jean crystallizes Se Byen's character in a unique and socially meaningful way and vice versa.

Se Byen's lwa can also serve as a socially appropriate and roundabout medium for communicating feelings or judgments that should not be stated directly. Since possession is seen to be involuntary and the "horse" unconscious of the lwa's actions in her or his body, the person cannot be held socially accountable for the lwa's message. Ti Jean could (putatively without Se Byen's knowledge and independent of his volition) voice feelings or perceptions Se Byen could not himself speak without losing face.

Ti Jean was the quintessential zandò, but in relation to Little Caterpillar, a pwen, Ti Jean was the exemplar of Guinea. Little Caterpillar could expect the lwa to use his Guinea authority to intimidate him into compliance with his—and Se Byen's—interests. Caterpillar could expect to be treated like a pwen, with haughty contempt, even as he relinquished the tainted fruit of his hard labor Outside. Indeed, the message Se Byen conveyed defining the "rules" for Little Caterpillar's restoration to the fold posed a conspicuous analogy to the symbolic process of gathering pwen. This rendezvous *in the House* is also the subject of Little Caterpillar's return pwen song, which we consider next.

Pwen Song Four: Caterpillar's Response: "The day is here.
There is a time you will gather me so you won't need."

Little Caterpillar recorded his reply to Se Byen at the labor camp in Virginia. He treated composing the letter in the presence of his friends as an opportunity to outclass Se Byen, Zo, Pepe, and the other lead singers. By throwing pwen, Little

Caterpillar put his antagonists on the defensive. He now dared them to take ownership of the hostile messages and to reflect on their "clarified" and "painful" meanings. At the beginning of his recorded letter, Caterpillar acknowledged having understood the messages: "I picked up all of the pwen songs you sent me. I understood them all." (*M ranmase tout pwen chante ou voye di m. M konprann yo tout.*) He then proceeded to improvise five poignant ballads that took up Se Byen's challenge in both style and content.

The text of Little Caterpillar's first zandò pwen song is cited here in full. The far-off voice of the "anonymous" narrator belongs to an exiled member or *pitit kay,* literally, "child of the house." Even before his departure—while he was living "in the middle of the army"—his kinsmen rebuked him. He had no name. He was poor and deemed unlikely to lift himself or his relatives out of misery. Now that he has emigrated, those who remain behind busy themselves calculating his "size" and "weight" as if estimating the profits to be gained from the labor of chattel— a cow, a burro or a pwen. The refrain, "The day is here/There is a time/You'll gather me so you won't need" foresees the end of the home residents' highhanded and selfish conduct when, humbled and contrite, they collect their neglected pwen.

The gathering takes place in the House. That is where Se Byen had said it would be. Se Byen had painted a musical portrait of the imperious Ti Jean sitting in the House waiting to adjudge the repatriated pwen. In interpwen dialogue, Little Caterpillar challenged Se Byen to collect a different message inside the imagery of the House. Little Caterpillar wove the very mechanics of pwen discourse into an unforgettable portrait of a target painfully discovering and gathering up his pwen.

Se Byen and his family search for Little Caterpillar in the House, but they cannot find him. They weep. Now that they are genuinely ready to care about their brother and to treat him with respect, he reappears. They learn his name—not his familiar nickname—but his full and formal title, Pierre Dioguy. Pierre Dioguy has become a *mounn,* a person, not a "cow without a herdsman" senselessly "doing for" his family back home:

They forget me.
There is a time
They will remember me.
You throw me out.
I say, neglect.
There is a time, brother Se Byen,
Look, you will need me.
I say, the day is here,

The day is here.
I say the day is here,
The day is here, my brother.
There is a time
You will gather me
So you won't need.

When it's one of your own
My friend, look across from you;
They don't know your worth.
When you are away, yes,
Look, the people will know.
You're in the middle of the army,
Look, they don't need you.
When you go away, boy,
Everyone will know,
Look at how much you weigh.
I say, the day is here,
The day is here.
There is a time, brother,
They will gather me
So they won't need.

They will remember me in the House.
Look, they are searching for me.
Look, they can't even see me.
You will look for me in that House.
Look, you can't see me.
When I was together with them
Look, they didn't know my name.
When I truly turn my back on them
You will know my name, brother.
I'm in this country;
Look, the day is here.

I'll turn my back and leave,
Look, when I turn around, brother,
Look, everyone is weeping.
When everyone is weeping

For whom are they asking?
It's Pierre Dioguy
They wanted to see him,
Look, they can't see him.
I say, the day is here, my son.
There is a time
When I appear before them
Everyone will be happy to see me.

Reprise of first verse

Yo bilye mwen.
O gen youn tan
Ya sonje mwen.
Adye, nou jete mwen.
M di, lamepriz o.
Gen youn tan, frè Se Byen,
Gade, ou a bezwen mwen.
Mwen di jou a la,
Jou a la o.
Mwen di, jou a la,
Jou a la frè mwen.
O gen youn tan
Ou a ranmase m
Pou ou pa bezwen.

Lè ou gen youn pitit kay ou
Monchè, gade anfas ou;
Yo pan konn valè ou.
Se kan nou deyò, vre,
Gade pèp la ap konnen.
Ou nan mitan lame a,
Gade, yo pa bezwen ou.
Kou ou sòti deyò, ti gason,
Tout mounn ap konnen,
Gade sa ou peze.
Mwen di, jou a la,
Jou a la, vre.
Genyen youn tan, frè

Ya ranmase m
Pou pa bezwen.

Yap sonje m nan Kay la.
Gade, yap chache mwen.
Gade, yo pap sa wè mwen.
Nap chache m nan Kay sa.
Gade nou pap sa wè mwen.
Lè m te ansanm avèk yo
Gade, yo pa konnen non mwen.
Kou m vire do m ba yo vre
Ou a konnen ki jan m rele, frè.
M nan peyi a,
Gade jou a la o.

Map vire do mwen pati,
Gade, kou m vire, frè
Gade tout mounn dlo nan je yo.
Lè tout mounn dlo nan je yo
Pou ki mounn yap mande?
Se Pierre Dioguy o
Yo te anvi wè li,
Gade yo pa sa wè li.
M di, jou a la, ti gason m.
Genyen youn tan
Lè m parèt sou yo
Tout mounn ap kontan wè mwen.

Caterpillar's pwen song reformulated the confrontation between Guinea and its pwen. Se Byen, as the imperious and ambivalent Guinea, goes to the House to gather up the chattel pwen. Instead he collects a pwen message compelling painful reflection. The humbled Guinea is ready finally to welcome home this long-forsaken child of the House.

Caterpillar and Baron La Croix Return

When Little Caterpillar and Se Byen taped their songs, they had already been separated for three years. Five more years passed before Caterpillar, like many Haitians who sailed to this country between 1979 and 1981, was permitted to leave the United States without forfeiting his immigration status. Almost immediately after receiving residency status, he returned to Ti Rivyè. As Se Byen had predicted, the House mediated his, and his spiritual patron's, reunifications with the family. Little Caterpillar spent $500 for a "feeding of the lwa" and a ritual dance that lasted two days. "All of the lwa appeared" (*tout lwa te parèt*), he reported to me when I saw him in Virginia six months later. It is inappropriate to ask someone, "did you get possessed?" For it implies that the horse was willfully conscious of the trance; in other words, that the person staged the possession.[8] So I inquired whether Baron la Croix "came to dance" as well. A wide, satisfied smile across Little Caterpillar's lips conveyed "yes."

Little Caterpillar gave me a copy of the cassette recording of the lwa's "party" (CD, track 4). Zo, who was both drumming and singing, recorded the tape for his migrant son, Sergo. At one point, the voice of Zo is heard, shouting with delight over the electrifying petwo rhythms (coming from his own hands at the drum), "Look, Little Caterpillar is in trouble! Baron just mounted him! Aaaaaaaaaaah! [laughs]. He'll never dismount him! Baron la Croix mounted him!" [laughing] (*Little Caterpillar angaje la! Men Baron ap sele l la! Aaaaaaaaaaah! Li pap janm desele l! Baron la Croix sele l!*)

The Relationships of Migration

Cassette-correspondence has provided a vital link between Haitian family members compelled to follow and reinforce the asymmetrical movements of capital. As illustrated in *Ton Beau Capitaine*, Simone Schwarz-Bart's (1987) drama about a Haitian couple separated by migration and connected by cassettes, circulating tapes keep members who are dispersed across oceans of contention intimately engaged in negotiating their churned-up relationships. The portable tape recorder has also both perpetuated and transformed the esteemed tradition of throwing pwen. Pwen crystallize difficult interpersonal situations; they bare truths through elegantly clear and simplified imagery. Each of the four pwen songs considered here captures a perception of the cumbersome and sometimes hostile interdependence between those who left and those who remain behind.

The growing literature on domestic relations across transnational communities suggests that mutual ambivalence between long-separated home kin and their migrant emissaries is very widespread (Basch, Glick-Schiller, Szanton Blanc 1994; Brown 1991; Gmelch 1992; Wolk 2000). These latent hostilities are among the social costs of being incorporated as producers of low-wage mobile labor. In the normative context of the Haitian transnational community described here, these hostilities can hardly be acknowledged or assuaged in an open discussion. As a result, they are ideal fodder for commentary, contest, and negotiation through sending pwen. The four songs presented here capture personal perceptions of truths that are common to transnational domestic relations in their own and many other communities.

Those at home worry that their migrant kin will assimilate to the host society and abandon them. Zo and Menmenn sent pwen songs concerning relations between a kin group and one of their estranged spirits to try to keep their migrant loyal and productive. They targeted their son with the words of the "Do For Me" song. They addressed the wider migrant audience with the "I'll Buy a Winnow for My Children" lyrics, hoping that other migrants would rein in their errant son. Migrants often interpret their home kin's behavior as unfair accusations that they have already abandoned them. Yet migrants who remain tethered to the home may also incite the latter's resentment. Se Byen's pwen song, The House Falls, bared truths about his resentment toward his devoted younger brother, Little Caterpillar. Those at home, including Se Byen, feel the migrants have used their experience abroad as a reason to condescend toward the folk who stayed behind. Se Byen thus accused Little Caterpillar of a newfound pretentiousness and he chose the defiant Makanda repertoire to squelch it.

The home kin's protracted dependence on the migrants' remittances symbolically elevates the migrants, who are typically younger, to a superior status. To preempt the migrant benefactor's opportunity to feel superior, the home kin often ignore migrants by not writing them to acknowledge receipt of remittances or by avoiding them when they return home for visits. Se Byen similarly disavowed a responsibility to thank his brother for his money gifts. By doing so, he also protected their egalitarian ethic of exchange. Their practices prohibiting praise, ignoring the benefactor, and/or disparaging the gift are meant to undermine the hierarchical potential of gift giving. Even though Little Caterpillar has internalized this gift-giving logic, and practices it in his exchanges with others, he cannot easily "see" its rationale from his side of their difficult long-distance relationship.

Migrants, meanwhile, feel that they slave away in hostile, foreign countries for the sake of people who resent them for ever having left. Those at home claim the moral high ground, simply because they remained in place. They arrogantly treat the migrants as if they are donkeys—beasts of burden. Migrants, furthermore, harbor unrealistically sanguine views of the economic conditions back home. Frustrated that their remittances have failed to lift the social status of their home families, some blame the latter for having frivolously squandered their hard-earned wages rather than investing them. They accuse their home families of expecting to live entirely off remittances, not having to work anymore (rather than scrutinizing their actual opportunities for earning income). The migrants' perception of insecurity in their home community, to which they expect to return one day, only intensifies their sense of vulnerability in the host society. Little

Caterpillar's long pwen song (from the same petwo genre used by Menmenn and Zo), "They Will Remember Me in the House," crystallized his understanding of the migrant's dilemma. His home family scorn their beast of burden, all the while calculating and profiting from his productivity. The final scene portrays the home kin, humbled and with changed hearts, tenderly gathering him into the fold.

The latent hostilities between Haitian kin struggling to keep one another afloat over the changing currents of transnational capital are ideal material for commentary and critique through the medium of pwen drawn from the vast and varied repertoires of ritual songs. Their creative appropriation of the tape recorder for their transnational correspondence is an ideal medium for it.

9

The Rebellion of the Pwen

Little Caterpillar's "guaranty" seemed to improve markedly after his joyful reunion in 1988 with his relatives and spirits back home. "Green card" in hand, he was finally free, after nearly a decade-long exile, to visit his home without compromising his right to return to work in the United States. Now he could more directly take charge of investments in his guaranty. He did eventually build the house for his wife, Maxia, fulfilling the conditions of marriage requiring the husband to build a house for his wife on her family land (in which he enjoys no actual legal right).

Both traditional and modern methods for investing migrants' wages appealed to Little Caterpillar. He bought a small plot of land for cultivation, to be farmed by a sharecropper. He purchased six cows to be tended by relatives. In addition, he started a business called "making a cinema" (*fè sinema*), screening videos to local patrons and turning a profit by charging admission. He bought videocassettes, a television, and videocassette player in Florida to ship to Haiti. For the theater itself, he rented a house in the nearby Léogane town center. He chose the town rather than the village because it had electrical service (however irregular).

But after he returned to Florida to work, his other (elder) brother appropriated his investments. Without Caterpillar's knowledge, his brother Adam, who was ill and needed money, approached the owner of the house he had rented for "making a cinema" and informed him that Caterpillar had changed his mind about the lease. Adam took back the $600. Next, Adam sold his cows, and their calves as well. According to him, Se Byen took Adam's side and forced their sister, Eve, who is Adam's twin, to relinquish the cow she was tending for her migrant brother. This time Little Caterpillar allowed himself to get angry and say "crooked words" about Adam. When Adam died, Caterpillar refused to attend the funeral, even though he was present in Léogane.

Then Caterpillar was injured again. He fell from a ladder while picking oranges in Fort Pierce. After the operation on his shoulder, the doctors in the hospital informed him of the onset of diabetes. He was unable to work for about a year, and he got by with gifts and loans from friends and the good patience of his landlord. Around the time his case finally settled (for $10,000), he called me on the telephone. His first words were, "I converted" (*M konvèti*). A stunned silence lingered on the phone line. Protestant conversion would have required absolute disavowal of relations with lwa and ancestors (as well as a break with Catholicism). It would have meant relinquishment of Caterpillar's vast ritual knowledge and talent, and of his expected accession to the position of gangan of the House. Trying to sound neutral, I asked, "You would have been gangan of the House?" He answered, "Se Byen had already given me the House last year, in January [i.e., during the annual feeding of their lwa]. I had already told him, 'yes.' But I'm not in it anymore. I am not involved with the lwa. After all I gave to the lwa, all they gave me was bad luck." He said to his conspicuously evangelical buddy, Lucien, "she's not talking," then to me, "Karen, I'm in a hurry. I have to go to church. I'll explain it to you in a letter."

Caterpillar's cassette letter arrived shortly by post (CD, track 5). His voice opened with the same courteous greeting I had come to expect from his correspondence (and he from mine). As is customary in cassette correspondence, he graciously saluted each person expected to be in proximity to the recipient, in this instance, my husband and son:

> Pierre Dioguy is talking to you. I ask you, how are you? I ask you, how are you feeling? I ask you, what are you up to? I ask you, how are your activities going, and Mark's and your child's? If the cassette arrives in the daytime, I say good day to you. If it arrives in the evening, I say good evening to you. If the cassette arrives in the daytime, tell Mister Mark I say good day to him. If it arrives in the evening, good evening to him. As for your child, if the cassette arrives in the daytime, give your child a great big good day for me. If it arrives in the evening, give him a great big good evening for me. Karen, I send a great big good day to you, truly, truly, truly, truly.

> *Se Pierre Dioguy k ap pal avèk ou. M voye mande ou, ki jan ou ye? M voye mande ou, ki jan lasante ou? M voye mande ou ki pwoblèm ou? M voye mande ou, ki jan mouvman ou ap mache? M voye mande ou, ki jan aktivite ou ap mache, ni Misye Marc, ni pitit la? Si kasèt la rive maten, m voye bonjou pou ou. Si l rive aswa, m voye bonswa pou ou. Si kasèt la rive maten, di Misye Marc*

m voye bonjou pou li. Si li rive aswa, m voye bonswa pou li. A menm enstan m voye pitit la, si kasèt la rive maten, di pitit la m voye bonjou pou li anpil, anpil. Si li rive aswa di l m voye bonswa bonswa anpil anpil pou li. Kalin m voye anpil bonjou pou ou, anpil, anpil, anpil, anpil.

Next Caterpillar launched into the promised defense of his conversion. His pleasant tone soured. The speech was a searing, extended narrative, framed antiphonally like the spirit songs he often improvised, returning after each verse development to a refrain. The bitter chorus consisted of a rhetorical question and its seething rejoinder: "And I have lwa? I heard I have lwa. There are no lwa." The agonizing letter demonstrated that Caterpillar never intended to abandon his family and their spirits. They had pushed him too far. He had to show them. He converted. He finally rejected the system that turned its migrants into pwen.

Well, Karen, here is the reason why I converted. Regardless, I would have converted anyway. How could I be serving lwa for all of these problems to keep on happening to me in both the land of Miami and in the land of Haiti? Why? When a lwa needs to eat, I provide for him/her. If I'm [sitting] over here working these lousy jobs, and Se Byen sends word that he's going to do such and such work in Haiti, like it or not, I have to send off $200 or $300. Why? For the lwa. And then, after I've done all that work, who should have the biggest problems but me. Look how long I've been in another country working. I could just tell you, someone would think I must have something wrong with me, because whenever I have money in my hands, I don't know what to do with it. I didn't know I bought a pwen. I didn't know I bought a lwa.

Well I found out that for my part, there are no lwa. No. There are no lwa. There is only nonsense. For my part, there are no lwa. I can't say that for everyone there are no lwa. I wouldn't say to somebody else, "you don't have lwa." It's just me, myself, for my part—I hear I have lwa. There are no lwa. If I have lwa, I have thieving lwa. I have cheating lwa. I don't have lwa. Why is that? When someone takes three or four hundred dollars out of his/her pocket, takes that money, and finds a steer to buy with it to feed to the lwa or finds a pig to buy to feed to the lwa, the lwa must see that when you spend that money, they should take you in. That's what lwa means. When I'm in poverty, should I light a candle and say, "look how the lwa help me?" No. You [lwa] see my problem, and then I am worse off. . . . As for lwa [spirits], the only place lwa [laws] exist is in court. For now, my lwa are in the hands of God. The lwa who are my companions—God is the one who is my companion. I am no longer involved with the lwa.

Why? I am standing here today. In one year alone, Karen, I sponsored a service at home. It cost me $1,500. I tell you up until the present I still owe Silien. I still haven't been able to pay off the money for that service. Does that mean you have lwa? For me to have done all those things for the lwa, for you to watch me borrowing to feed you, and slaving away at picking tree fruit to raise the money, well, as far as I'm concerned, there are no lwa anymore. My life is in God's hands. My life is in the hands of the Eternal. My life is not in the hands of the lwa. You understand? My life is in the hands of God. My life is not in the hands of the lwa. I remove myself from the lwa. I remove myself from Satan. Now I am in the hands of God. All of my being is in the hands of the Eternal.

And that's why I converted, Karen. It has given me a respite. For me to have to see someone who tomorrow, God willing, I would have been better off than they, and then I see that you are the one who is getting ahead. I'm not saying I converted so that God would make me rich. I am not saying s/he'll make me find money on the ground. I am not saying God will haul money in to me.[1] It's just that I have a fresh start in God, more than when I was outside. I have a strength in God, greater than when I was not yet converted. And I think that tomorrow, God willing, Karen, God can change me.

It's like if you have a shirt on your back, to change your shirt, you have to have another one to put on. Isn't that true? Well with me, after I fed—I heard I have lwa, after I fed those good-for-nothings—I mean no disrespect [literally, "out of respect for your face"]—after I spent every last penny I had in my pocket that I could have used, I took it, I fed the lwa, and then I became worse off than someone who begs for charity. So for the moment, in the name of God, if I have to beg for charity, I'll beg it from God. I'm not going to beg for charity for the sake of the lwa. The lwa are not going to make me beg for charity. You understand?

There are some people who left their country, they have some old lwa who are backing them up. Those lwa are truly useful to them, but what I see is that mine are a pile of shit. Excuse me, Karen. I mean no disrespect to you, Karen. I mean no disrespect to you. Excuse me. I'm swearing on the cassette. They are worthless. Well, that's why I converted. You understand? That's why I converted. I wouldn't have converted. . . .

As soon as a person is converted to a Protestant, you are a different kind of human being. You're not the same kind of human being. And, too, I would be pleased if one day, if God wills—I can't say to you, Karen, "go convert." I can't give you advice to get converted. If you were going to convert, you would have already converted. I can't say to you, "convert." Now is not the time, now that I am converted, to advise you to convert. No. You understand? You have to make your own decision. For myself, I converted.

And so, Karen, it was too much misery I suffered and too much hardship I endured from these people, and that's what made me convert. I'm taking a different road to see if God will help me. So s/he can see if s/he'll help me. I've endured too many hardships. I've endured too much tribulation. I've endured too much suffering. I've been doing for the lwa. But instead of being better off, I'm worse. I'm sitting over here and Se Byen sends word to me, "Little Caterpillar, I need 300 or 400 dollars for me to do the work for the lwa." I send it off. "Little Caterpillar, I need money to buy a steer for the new year to sacrifice for the lwa." I send off the money for the steer. For what good? After I did it, I went and paid for a ticket and I went to Haiti right away to do the work for the lwa. That money, if I had known, I would have taken it and put it aside, and now that I'm doing this lousy work, I would have found good use for it. And after I did that, look at how long it has been since I left Haiti. I left Haiti the 28th of January last year, the 28th of January that just passed makes it a year. They sent word that Maxia is sick. I haven't been able to find the money to buy even a ticket up until now. And then, I have lwa. I heard I have lwa.

Well Karen, all of this disappointment and all of this regret are the reasons I converted. I wouldn't have converted to leave Se Byen and the lwa. The lwa must see that when Se Byen sits there in Haiti and he doesn't have money to do the work, and sends out an appeal, I am the one who gives it to him. It's simply that the lwa have to see that I neither borrowed the little bit of money, nor got it dishonestly. I earned it and sent it off. You have to help me too. If you don't help me, I wouldn't help you either. There are no lwa.

Anben, Kalin, men pou tèt, rezon ki fè m konvèti. Nenpòt ki jan, fò m te konvèti kanmenm. M pa sa gen—m ap sèvi lwa pou tout pwoblem sa yo pede rive m nan peyi Mayami, kil peyi Dayiti. Sa k fè sa, lè lwa bèzwen manje, mwen bay li. Si kankou map chita la, m ap fè viye dyòb isi, Se Byen voye di m l ap fè tèl travay Ayiti, vle pa vle, fò m jwenn $200, $300 pou m voye ale. Pou ki sa? Pou lwa. Lè m fini, lè m fini fè travay sa yo, ki mounn pou ta genyen pi gwo pwoblem, se mwen menm. Gade dat m antre nan youn peyi m ap travay. M ta kòm di ou, ou a di s'on bagay mwen genyen, depi s'on kòb ki antre nan menm, pou m pa wè sa pou m fè ave l. M pa t konnen m te achte pwen. M pa t konnen m te achte lwa.

Anben mwen jwenn, nan pati pa m pa gen lwa. Non. Pa gen lwa. Gen tenten. Nan pati pa m pa gen lwa. M pa sa di pa gen lwa pou tout mounn. M pa sa di youn mounn, "ou pa gen lwa." Senpman mwen menm, pati pa m, m tande gen lwa. Pa gen lwa. Si m gen lwa, m gen lwa volè. M gen lwa visyè. Ou konprann? M pa gen lwa. Sak fè sa, lè yon mounn pran twa, kat san dola nan poch ou, ou pran lajan sa a, ou te jwenn bèf achte, ou bay lwa manje. Ou jwenn kochon, ou achte l, ou bay lwa manje. Fò lwa wè, lè ou depanse lajan sa a, se pou ba ou antre l. E sa k di ou lwa. Lè m nan mizè, m limen yon bout chandèl, pou m di koman lwa yo ede m? Non. Nou wè pwòblem mwen, lè a m vin pi mal. . . . Afè lwa, se tribinal lwa rete. Pou lè moman lwa m nan men Bondye. Lwa k kondisip mwen-se Bondye ki kondisip mwen. M pa nan afè lwa ankò.

Sa k fè sa, men mwen, men jodi a m kanpe la. Gen yon ane k ènsèl, Kalin, m fè yon sèvis lakay. Li koute m $1,500. Ma di ou Jiska mentnan m dwe Silien. Kòb sèvis Jiska mentnan m poko kapab fin peye l. Atò, ou gen lwa? Pou m fè tout bagay sa pou lwa, pou ou wè m prete, pou m ba ou manje, lè fini se redi an ba redi pou m ap keyi grenn bwa pou m sanble pou m peye lajan an. Anben, mwen, si se pou mwen, m pa nan lwa ankò. Lwa m nan menm Bondye. Vi m nan men Leternèl. Vi m pa nan men lwa. Ou konprann? Vi m nan men Bondye. Vi m pa nan men lwa. M retire m nan lwa. M retire m nan Satan. Kouliyèa m nan men Bondye.

Tout fòs mwen nan men Letènèl. Anben se sak fè, Kalin, mwen konvèti. Sa ban mwen yon reposite. Pou m wè moun, demen si Dye vle, m kapab miyò pase yo, m wè se ou menm kap pran devan. Mwen pa di m konvèti, Bondye ap fè m rich. M pa di la p fè m jwenn lajan a tè. M pa di l ap bwote lajan ban mwen. Senpman m gen yon lafrèsh nan li menm, pase lè m te deyò a. Mwen gen yon fòs nan li menm, pase lè m patko konvèti a. E m sanse ke demen, si Dye vle, Kalin, Bondye kapab chanje m.

Si tankou ou gen yon chemiz sou do ou, ou chanje chemiz la, fò ou gen yon lòt pou ou mete. N'est-ce pas vrai? Anben mwen mem, lè m fin bay—m te tande m te gen lwa, lè m te fin bay tenten sa yo manje, pa respe figi ou, lè m te fin depanse de pias m te gen nan poch mwen, ki ka itil mwen, mwen pran n, m bay lwa manje, lè sa m vin pi mal pase yon moun ki t ap mande charite. Anben pou lè moman, o non de Bondye, si pou m mande charite ma mande l pa Bondye. M pa pral mande charite pou lwa. Lwa pap fè m mande charite. Ou konprann?

Gen moun, yo kite peyi yo, yo gen viye lwa kap mache dèyè yo. Lwa yo itil yo vre, men m wè, pan m yo se yon bann kaka yo ye, o respe figi ou, Kalin. O respè figi ou, m mande eskiz, m ap joure nan kasèt la. Se yon tenten yo ye.

Anben se sa k fè m al konvèti. Ou konprann? Se sa k fè m konvèti. M pa ta konvèti. Ou konprannn? M pa ta konvèti, non?

Depi yon nanm ou konvèti se levanjil ou ye ou se yon lòt kretyen. Ou pa menm kretyen ankò. E tou, mwen ta renmen demen si dye vle-m pa sa di ou, "Kalin, al konvèti." M pa sa ba ou konsèy pou ou konvèti. Si ou tap konvèti, ou tap konvèti deja. M pa sa di ou pou ou konvèti, Se pa jodi a la m konvèti, pou m voye konsèy ba ou pou ou konvèti, non. Ou konprann, then, se ou menm kap fè lide ou. Mwen menm, m konvèti.

Anben, Kalin, se twòp mizè m pran, se twòp fado m pran nan lemoun, ki fè ke m konvèti. Mwen chanje chemen pou m wè si Bondye ta ede m. Pou l wè si l ta ede m. M pran twòp move fado. Mwen pran twòp tribilasyon. Mwen pran twòp tray. M ap fè pou lwa. Angiz pou m pi byen, m pi mal. Mwen chita isit, Se Byen voye di m "Ti Chini, m bezwen $300, $400 pou m fè travay pou lwa yo." Mwen voye l. "Ti Chini, m bezwen kòb pou m achte yon bèf pou ane a pou m touye pou lwa." M voye kòb bèf la ale. A quoi bon? Lè m fin fè l m pran m peye tike, m al Ayiti tout espre, m ap fè travay pou lwa. Lajan sa yo, si m te konnen, m te pran n, m te mèt yon kote, kouniyè a m gen viye travay map fè, m ta jwenn yo. Lè m fin fè yo—gade dat mwen sòt Ayiti, mwen sòt Ayiti pou le 28 Janvie ane pase, 28 Janvie la ki sòt pase a ap fè m en an. Yo voye di mwen Maxia malad. M pa sa jwenn kòb pou m achte menm tike a pou m ale pou jiska mentnan. Lè fini, m gen lwa. M tande m gen lwa.

Anben, Kalin, se dekourajman saa, se remòsite sa m genyen an ki fè ke mwen konvèti. M pa t ap konvèti, pou m ta kite Se Byen a lwa yo. Fò lwa yo wè, lè Se Byen chita nan Ayiti, Se Byen pa gen kòb pou l fè travay la, li voye mande m, se mwen k bay li. Senpman fò lwa wè, si e pa prete m prete, ni si e pa nan mal, mwen fè de pyès la m voye l ale, fò ou ede m tou, si ou pa ede m, m pa sa ede ou tou. Pa gen lwa.

"There are no lwa." The vindictive refrain decisively concluded Caterpillar's explanation of his conversion. He defended the charge in the first "verse" of his songlike narrative. The term lwa, he explained, refers to an entity that reciprocates your earnest offerings with material support. His present miserable status, despite diligent and continuous prestations to the lwa, demonstrates that "there are no lwa." He fashioned a pun to reinforce his denunciation. The pun played with the homonym relation of lwa, meaning "law," and lwa, meaning "spirit: As for lwa, the only place they exist is in court!" (The Creole term for law is the same as the French word, *loi*. The term for spirit is probably derived from Bantu [Courlander 1960:19, endnote 1].)

Caterpillar nonetheless clarified that he would not deign to extend his condemnation to others' inherited spirits: "I can't say that for everyone there are no lwa. I wouldn't say to somebody else, "you don't have lwa." It's just me, myself, for my part—I hear I have lwa. There are no lwa. If I have lwa, I have thieving lwa. I have cheating lwa. I don't have lwa." He later admitted that others do seem to have "some old lwa who are backing them up" and who "are truly useful to them." These valid and valuable lwa pose a stark contrast to his own "worthless" "pile of shit." For the first time in his decade-long correspondence with me, the ever-poised "writer" resorted to swearing, and he immediately apologized for doing so.

The predicament of the migrant who becomes a pwen "doing for" his family and their lwa back home was crystallized in Caterpillar's embittered narrative. The migrant toils away in a hostile, foreign country. He risks his life and dignity at lousy, dangerous farm labor jobs and squalid labor camps and seedy neighborhoods. Yet he is tarnished for ever having departed. His "easy" money is suspect. Throughout his painful narrative, he endeavored to defend the morality of his migrant wage labor and the source of his remittances. In the final verse he pleaded, "The lwa must see that when Se Byen sits there in Haiti and he doesn't have money to do the work, and sends out an appeal, I am the one who gives it to him. It's simply that the lwa have to see that I neither borrowed the little bit of money, nor got it dishonestly. I earned it and sent it off."

Caterpillar recited a history of the moneys he sent home to pay for ritual "work," meaning both the labor and the offerings. Caterpillar noted that whenever Se Byen owed this work, Little Caterpillar was the one who had to pay for it. Se Byen deflected his responsibilities—or pwenification—by the lwa onto his younger, migrant brother. To Se Byen's every request for money to do the "work" of the House, he had responded without hesitation. He parodied Se Byen's patterned requests and his instant monetary dispatches: "I'm sitting over here and Se Byen sends word to me, 'Ti Chini, I need 300 or 400 dollars for me to do the work for the lwa.' I send it off. 'Ti Chini, I need money to buy a steer for the new year to sacrifice for the lwa.' I send off the money for the steer." Yet, the spirits had not felt obligated to reciprocate the labor of their (pwen's) pwen, ignoring his plight when he needed them. After "spending every last penny" to feed those "good for nothings," he was "worse off than someone who begs for charity."

How else, he asked, would someone who didn't know about his considerable subsidy of his family's ritual obligations explain the case of a migrant who, despite having worked for years abroad, was nonetheless broke? The only possible explanation for such profligate spending would be the ambitious individual who bought a pwen. In other words, the magical power made so much money for its greedy master that the owner could not handle the wealth, irresponsibly losing or frivolously spending it all. This sort of irrational behavior could well be attributed to the treachery of the pwen itself. "I didn't know I bought a pwen," Caterpillar exclaimed angrily at the outset of his defense.

In Caterpillar's view, Se Byen (and other relatives) and the lwa were inextricably linked, doing one another's bidding to extract vitality from their pwen. Caterpillar treated Se Byen (standing for the family) and the lwa interchangeably in his critique; he confounded their names several times, and when using the second person, did not always distinguish whether the "you" was Se Byen or the lwa. To leave one was to leave the other. With deep disappointment and regret, he abandoned them both. More than once he confessed, "I wouldn't have converted to leave Se Byen and the lwa." Together, his kin and their lwa pushed their migrant pwen too far.

The Protestant Experiment

Caterpillar's cassette letter arrived with a small color photograph, a visible testament of his conversion. Little Caterpillar was austerely costumed in a white shirt, grey vest, and dark trousers, a marked shift from the stylish fashion he usually donned for photographic portraits. In the background were a small, decorated Christmas tree, a Santa Claus poster and a variety of other holiday adornments. Next to him stood his friend Lucien Bertrand, awkwardly attired in an ill-fitting beige jacket, white shirt, and dark tie, with large, thick glasses balanced on his nose and Bible in his left hand—the very stereotype of the *pastè* (pastor). The term pastè applies to any evangelical male regardless of rank, whether professional religious leader or church member, for the latter is nevertheless viewed as a future evangelical entrepreneur.

Caterpillar had known Lucien since childhood. They grew up in the same hamlet. But they did not become close friends until his first accident in the Indian River orange groves in 1983, which severed his finger. During that long and difficult period when Caterpillar was destitute and could not work, Lucien offered him support. Lucien, who is literate, helped Little Caterpillar in his struggle to receive compensation by deciphering and filling out the innumerable documents required of the nonliterate migrant and by accompanying him to appointments. (Caterpillar's lawyer, whom I assisted informally through the mail and by phone as he pursued Caterpillar's case, complained more than once about Lucien's brash ineptitude and ultimately asked me to tell his client that Lucien's interference was no longer welcomed.) If the "pastor" had taken his charge as a potential recruit for the church, Caterpillar had, for many years, rejected his overtures. He did not enlist in the Protestant "army" until conversion presented the ultimate personal weapon for resisting the ritual system that symbolically exploited him as a pwen.

9.1. Little Caterpillar sent me this photograph with the tape explaining his conversion. Fort Pierce, January 1992.

It seems plain from Caterpillar's commentary that resistance to ritual exploitation, rather than sudden, deep faith in a new, better religion, was the reason for his conversion. His periodic confirmations of confidence in the Protestant's God did not stand on their own; they were instead set against repudiations of his spirits. Neither did he seem committed to the evangelical stance, for he eschewed the convenient opportunity to try to proselytize me on the tape. (He never pressured me to convert during our subsequent visits in South Florida or in his cassette correspondence.) Nor was he persuaded by the evangelist's famed promise of eventual financial reward, which is routinely broadcast in hymns and sermons. "I'm not saying I converted so that God would make me rich," he professed. "I am not saying [God] will make me find money on the ground. I am not saying [God] will haul money in to me. It's just that I have a fresh start in [God], more than when I was outside." He was quite familiar, therefore, with the Protestant ideology of individualism, saving, and abstinence but he dismissed the idea that this ideology drew him to the religion.

Yet his words demonstrate that he had integrated at least some of the Protestant's discourse: its assertiveness. This challenging stance, Métraux ([1959] 1972:352) concludes, "convinces the peasants that this religion confers upon its adepts a sort of supernatural immunity." Gerlach and Hine (1968:35) similarly claim that "the certitude of Protestant ideology" is its missionaries' "greatest strength" in Latin America, a finding that has been repeated in numerous studies of the movement in the region (Sherman 1997; Chesnut 2003). The evangelicals teach this challenging ideology both in subtle, metalinguistic ways and through more obvious means. Military metaphors of armies, fortresses, forces, and strength proliferate. One well-known Haitian sect calls itself a "celestial army." A rhetoric of progress, change, and advance articulates with the militant tone, while simultaneously invoking an aggressiveness that is central to capitalist culture. In his letter, Little Caterpillar seems to shift to this forward register in his letter whenever he professes his commitment to his new faith.

The Pragmatics of Conversion

Haitians' tactical use of conversion as resistance has been discussed in the ethnological and religious literature. Fred Conway's (1978) and Paul Brodwin's (1996) ethnographies of religious and therapeutic pluralism provide important descriptions of contemporary conversion practice. They build upon the research of Alfred Métraux (1953b, [1959] 1972), which was conducted more than half a century ago (before the boom in North American evangelization, which began in the early 1960s). Métraux described how conversion could be pursued as an act of revolt against lwa. Because conversion to Protestantism entails a drastic break and a total, public renunciation of past practices, conversion provides an opportune strategy to disavow relations with lwa. Catholicism, on the other hand, coexists with family-based service to the lwa and is, in any case, a prerequisite for it. As a Marbial person explained to Métraux, "To serve the lwa you have to be a Catholic" (Métraux [1959] 1972:323). Métraux also quotes a Marbial person's advice for liberating oneself from the burden of serving lwa: "If you want the lwa to leave you in peace, become a Protestant" (Métraux [1959] 1972:351–352).[2] Several cases of conversion in Marbial also appear in Métraux's work, including the narrative of one exasperated man whose children died despite their father's generous feedings of the lwa. In words that are echoed in Little Caterpillar's letter to me, the man told him, "No more [lwa] for me, no more *boko* (sorcerers/priests), it's all rubbish" (Métraux [1959] 1972:354).

Catts Pressoir, a leading Protestant intellectual of the early–mid-20th century and the author of the first history of Protestants in Haiti, published a surprisingly frank commentary about the pragmatic approach to conversion. He quotes his colleague Roger Dorsainville, who argued that "true conviction and profound commitment to be saved" were "rarely" the reason Catholics converted to Protestant sects (Pressoir, 1942:5).[3] Dorsainville questioned whether, in light of the continued reality of "spiritual experience" in the lives of the converts, the term "change of religion" was indeed the correct one to describe such action. Converts seemed merely to substitute one set of mediating powers for another without substantially altering their world view. "The Gospel is thus pursued as a superior *ouanga* [magical power], the pastor is like a more powerful sorcerer, simple and good, who commands the key words for deliverance." (*L'Evangile est alors recherché comme un "ouanga" supérieur, le prédicateur est comme un bocor puissant, simple et bénéfique qui connait les maîtres mots de délivrance* [cited in Pressoir, 1942:5].) In spite of the Protestants' aggressive discourse of renunciation of "the Catholic/Vodou other," which they classify as Satan, they do not ultimately deny the reality and force of Satan's powers. Indeed their vilifying rhetoric only affirms that reality. The Protestants simply lay claim to a Puritan *ouanga supérieur*, a more potent, Protestant, magical power.

Catholics who serve their lwa, on the other hand, confront fewer contradictions in openly turning to Protestants in times of crisis. Indeed as Dorsainville (cited in Pressoir 1942:5) keenly observed, a gangan himself will occasionally advise conversion. Having exhausted his own spiritual resources, he may direct a desperate patient to visit a Protestant healer. In the case of the urgent quest to save my late godchild, whose nickname was Alimèt (Matches), a similar ideological flexibility prevailed. Alimèt was 16 when she died in 2000. She grew up in a household headed by her paternal grandparents that included her parents and her siblings. Her father's father, Ilavert, is a gangan ason, and he has been succeeded in the role by his son, Alimèt's father. Her grandmother is a senior ounsi (servitor) who, as "kanzo mother" (*manman kanzo*), oversees women's initiations at the House. Alimèt had been chronically ill for several years, despite the interventions of her grandfather and a series of biomedical doctors, including a surgeon. Thus when her maternal grandmother, who is Protestant, approached her paternal family and asked to take her away "to enter her in Protestantism," they agreed, knowing that conversion was a requisite part of the therapy. When their Protestant in-laws failed to cure her, they bore them no ill will.

This practical logic underpins the apathy of Catholics (who serve their lwa) toward Pentecostals in their midst and also underscores the extent to which the "opposition" to Protestantism is a creation of the Pentecostals themselves (Conway 1978:252). While living in Ti Rivyè, I still unfortunately did not quite understand or respect the residents' tacit acceptance of the ubiquitous North American missionaries, who were well represented in the area, though they had as yet made few converts. I learned the embarrassing lesson at the culminating rite of the women's initiation ritual. The rite took place at the House headed by Alimèt's paternal grandfather (and now her father). (See chapter 5, figures 5.13–5.17.) The final ceremony began in an intensely sacred and solemn mood. The neophytes emerged timidly from their nine-day seclusion, barely visible under their wide-brimmed straw hats and towels. A lay Catholic priest uttered Catholic prayers in French and baptized the "infant" servitors with holy water. The novices then took their places in a great procession of white-clad ounsi (servitors) and their relatives, an immense, white column parading down the path to the beach, stopping at certain trees or house remains—sacred monuments of the lineage's history—and finally congregating at the mouth of Ti Rivyè, where the Little River meets the sea. The lagoon is the watery haunt of the patron spirit of the initiation, Danbala Wedo. In due time, the Water Snake "mounted" three ounsi, who plunged into the pool and slithered around before emerging onto the sandbank to welcome the new members waiting at the edge.

The reincorporation rite now concluded and the mood relaxed, the marchers retraced the route along the beach. At the angle where the parade turned south to follow the dirt path, we suddenly confronted an incongruous spectacle: a "pastor" was standing atop an overturned boat, Bible in hand, preaching at us about God, Jesus, and Satan. None of the marchers, not even Alimèt's grandfather nor the other two professional priests (gangan ason), heeded the intruder. But I was incensed! I challenged the pastor, accusing him of disrespect and demanding rhetorically to know, "Do they 'crash' your Protestant services, singing sacred songs honoring Danbala Wedo?" My self-appointed advocacy and clumsy

9.2. An evangelist castigates the sinners at the final procession at a *kanzo* rite, Ti Rivyè, August 1984.

violation of the norms of public graciousness met silent rebuke from the celebrants. They had muffled the forceful evangelizing of the intruder with equally forceful apathy.

Thus Catholics who serve their lwa do not view conversion to Protestantism as a wholesale rejection of a system of morality. As Conway (1978:251) argues, conversion signifies "a personal adjustment in extreme circumstances." Reconversion is a realistic possibility if the crisis provoking the conversion in the first instance recedes or if the Protestant's vaunted "magic circle" turns out to be impotent. All of these reasons probably figured into the decisions of Little Caterpillar and his wife Maxia, less than two years after trying Protestantism, to "fall out of it." I found out after he returned to Haiti. He was gravely ill.

The Death of the Pwen

Little Caterpillar left for Haiti in June 1993. I visited him in Fort Pierce, Florida, the day before he departed. I did not hear from him for about ten months and, since he called or wrote me when he had a problem, I assumed he was getting along well enough back home. Neither was I thinking about much besides my move to Chicago and the start of my first teaching job. Then in the summer of 1994 I spoke to Yvon, the courier, who had been trying in vain to get in touch with me at my previous address in Virginia, telling me that he had a letter from Little Caterpillar, and that my friend was sick. Caterpillar's tape shocked me with the news that he was bedridden with an incapacitating "gas." I kept in touch through the courier, who forwarded encouraging news that my friend "wasn't too bad." But a few months later, the courier called to say that Caterpillar had taken a turn for the worse. I dispatched some money and a tape, in which I beseeched him to return to the United States, to come directly to Chicago, where I could help him seek medical treatment and help take care of him.

His tape arrived in January 1995. The robust voice I expected from a score of cassette letters was gone. His throat was hoarse and he had to keep shutting off the recorder when his throat filled up, politely excusing himself each time he resumed. He said that if I were to see him, "tears would come to my eyes." He delineated his agonizing condition in detail. The pain running through his body and head wouldn't allow him to sleep either at night or during the day. He felt like he was suffocating. To relieve the pressure from the gas, Maxia occasionally pulled on a rope tied around his chest. He vomited whether he ate or not. And if the discomfort caused by the "gas" weren't enough, he had come down with shingles, too.[4] Because of the shingles, he couldn't stand to put on clothes or to have any fabric contact his skin.

Sorcery was the cause of his suffering. He was attacked when he first returned home. He claimed he had been in good health then, though he didn't appear to be so when I saw him. In any case, he felt well enough to work in his gardens, where he was hit with a poison powder. The malefactor reinforced his/her assault by launching a second attack of powder, and then dispatching two agents, "dead spirits," to hover around him and continue administering the curse. Little Caterpillar "went far away" to seek treatment from a gangan. Since such "trips" and Protestant discipline do not mix, at least not in public, he also mentioned in passing that he had "fallen out" of Protestantism. Yet his increasingly futile quest for relief had primarily engaged biomedical professionals, whom he classed as "a joke." They ordered tests and prescribed pills, but did not offer any relief. He spent all of his resources: cows, pigs, even his bicycle. He was about to sell the piece of land he had bought with his remittances. As if the suffering from his bodily affliction weren't enough, Little Caterpillar had to abide the pain of squandering his material resources.

The ultimate blow, though, was losing the crowning achievement of his sojourn abroad: a four-room cinder-block house with a galerie the size of a room. After 13 years, he had finally succeeded in controlling enough of his remittances ($17,000) to build a home (rather than enhancing the House). He was just about to put (from afar) the finishing touches on the ostentatious galerie, a forged iron enclosure, when his wife's mother "took the house" (*pran kay la*), which was built on her land, and put a guard dog there to keep them out. He had flattened me with the news during our last visit together. I had argued then that Maxia likely had rights in the land, and, since he celebrated a civil marriage with her, he probably had rights in the property as well. Little Caterpillar didn't take up my argument, quoting an English idiom in his Creole response, "I don't care *de sa* [about it]," and vowing not to try set foot there. In my December letter to him, I brought up the crisis again. He responded in this correspondence with the disheartening news that they had yet to reconcile, and he and Maxia were paying to rent two squalid rooms in a structure on the edge of the town (where his sister, Eve, also leased quarters).

Little Caterpillar thanked me for my letter, the money I sent, and my urgent plea for him to come back to the United States to get treated. He offered a half-hearted pledge to travel if he recovered enough strength, and only after the annual rites for the lwa at the House, which were to begin in another two weeks. (The mere mention of these rites was a sign of his "backsliding" out of Protestantism and into the Guinea fold.)

There had been a death watch by his bed. As soon as a person takes the last breath, women begin the ritual wailing. Caterpillar reported that twice they had begun wailing, but then "God said, 'not yet.'" He seemed to be showing me how to accept his death by tenderly describing my anticipated mourning in vivid detail but also by imploring me not to be overcome by the grief. He was obviously not afraid. He stated in a variety of ways that people are born to die. He affirmed his faith in whatever fate God had assigned him. Nor had he abandoned hope that God would resuscitate him as had already happened twice.

Little Caterpillar had prided himself on his style and rhetorical stamina on previous tapes, and he apologized for the inferior production quality of this one. His mood lightened when he talked about cassette oratory, which he had proudly perfected over the years. He said I could measure the gravity of his infirmity by comparing his present delivery to how he used to talk to me on cassettes. He also mentioned that "if you get this tape and I haven't sung [recorded] at least two [ritual] dance pieces on it, you already know there was something wrong with me." In another admission that he had drifted away from the evangelists and back into the Guinea fold, he said he was going to get someone to record the dance at the upcoming ritual at the House. He chided me for failing to fill up my tape. And after a coughing fit interrupted the conclusion of his "letter writing," he resumed the recording to utter the most endearing closing.

Well, I send word to you, Karen, take good care of yourself for me. Tell your husband and your child for me that I say good afternoon to them, and to take very good care of themselves. Karen, when I tell you I'm sick, I'm really sick, you know? Last night, I spent the whole night awake. The thing was eating me up. If I were over there, I would find a remedy for the gas. They would have to operate on me. All of the doctors I have seen here are a joke. These doctors can't do a damn thing for me. They only give me pills and the pills don't do anything for me. Well, I'll accept it with God's protection. [Raspy noise as he clears his throat.] Excuse me for clearing [my throat] on the tape, excuse me for that.

Well Karen, if you see the cassette arriving in the morning, I send 2,000 kisses, 2,000 good days to you and your husband. If you see the cassette arriving in the afternoon, I send 3,000 kisses, 3,000 good evenings to you, your husband, and your child. Karen, take enough care of yourself. Tell your child I say hello to him. Make him—say a big good-day, good evening to him for me, and everyone around you, your friends, all of your people, say a big good day, good evening for me. Thank-you. Good bye.

Anben, m voye di ou, Kalin, konpòte ou tre byen pou mwen anpil. Di misye ou a pitit ou pou mwen m voye bonswa anpil pou yo, konpòte nou tre byen.

*Kalin, lè m di ou mwen malad la, m malad anpil vre, wi? Iyè swa la, m fè nwit
la, m pa dòmi. Bay la ap manje m. Si e te lòt bò a m te ye, m ta jwenn solisyon
a gaz la. Fò yo tap fè m operasyon. Nan tout doktè m mache isi, e blag. Doktè
pa fouti fè anyen pou mwen. Se grenn yap ban mwen, m bwe li, grenn pa fè
anyen pou mwen. Anben, ma pran tout a pwotèksyon Bondye.*

*Anben Kalin, si ou wè kasèt la rive maten, mwen voye 2000 byeze, 2,000
bonjou pou ou a tout misye ou. Si ou wè kasèt la rive apre midi, mwen voye
3,000 byeze, 3,000 bonswa pou ou a tout misye ou a tout pitit la. Di pitit la m
salye l byen. Fè l-di l bonjou bonswa pou mwen anpil. Kalin konpòte ou ase
byen. Ni tout moun kote ou, zanmi ou, tout moun ou yo, di yo bonjou, bonswa
pou mwen anpil. Mwen menm m fè yon bò nèt. Oke. Kalin mwen voye bonjou,
bonswa pou ou. Mèsi. Babay.*

After hearing this distressful cassette letter, I called Yvon, the courier, who was
leaving for Haiti again in a few days. I sent him 100 dollars. Despite his frailty,
Little Caterpillar wrote me one last time. He was intent on respecting the correspondence etiquette of acknowledging a remittance. What is more, he wanted to
say a final good-bye to me. His tender, sad words of farewell are the ultimate gift
of his endearing friendship and a precious record of his dignified and uncommon
eloquence. He had warned me in his previous cassette letter to expect the (collect)
call from Mme. Pierre announcing the dreaded news. I had already received her
call when the tape arrived in the mail. Months passed before I could bring myself
to listen to it (CD, track 6).

Little Caterpillar struggles to understand his imminent, unnatural death. How
could such a cruel fate meet someone who endeavored to lead a dignified, moral
life, who, as a migrant, demonstrated generosity and kindness to his home kin? At
the same time, he is convinced of the etiology of his distress. He faces the standard
punishment of anyone who tries to lift herself or himself out of misery and, as
emissaries of their families' ambitions, migrants are particularly prone. A sorcerer
is slowly "killing him for what he gained": a house, livestock, a small plot of land.
He takes some solace in his belief that the person will ultimately be punished by
God. He does not name the one who did this to him. After adding up the signs of
malfeasance consuming his life, he raises his voice to demand, "What does it look
like to you, Karen?" I don't think he knew for certain who it was, and he left me to
wonder as well.

Yet in the final moments of his life he contends that the evil enemy is not a
discrete person but rather a vast, sorcerous system that turns poor Haitian neighbors against one another. This system, in which suppliers of mobile labor like
Haiti play an unequal and minor part, seems to reserve its cruelest sentences for
migrants who cross nation-states' borders to "pursue livelihood." The migrants

are its fuel and prey. Little Caterpillar closes with a haunting truth about the people of the little nation-state of Haiti. "The nation of Haiti will never be right. It will never be right."

I ask you, how are you, how is your husband, how is your child? Karen, God has held on to me and lifted my voice so I could talk to you. Nevertheless, it's not because I'm healthy that I'm making this tape for you. This morning I got up, and what caused me to revive was that a guy came. I wasn't even here really. They called me. When I went to him, he said, "Here is a letter Yvon gave me that is for you." [I replied,] "Is that for real?" He didn't give me a letter; he gave me $100. Well, Karen, the $100 that I received, it was as if $10,000 had just dropped in front of me. [pause] Karen, my friend, I was talking to you, it's someone at the moment of death who is talking to you. It's someone about to die, Karen, who is talking to you. You see this cassette tape? I'm not going to speak a lot on it. I don't have the energy to speak.

I said to myself that if I recorded a letter to send to you, you would think that what I say in it cannot be true. When you hear my explanation, the way I am speaking to you—I am someone you knew when I was in good shape —you will hear and you will also know, compared to when I was in good shape and we were face to face, or when I spoke to you on tape, you will see if they are the same people. Well, Karen, if you get the news that I died, em hm, that's because last week I was a dead man. The wailing had already erupted; the house had already been cleared out. But God held on to me, resuscitated me, turned me around.

Well, Karen, until now I haven't found a solution [remedy] for my sickness. Despite everything I've tried, I can't find a solution. What I've found is an illness and it is killing me. I'm sitting and waiting for God to take me. Yes. I'm waiting for God to see what S/He will do with me. Nonetheless I have one regret and that is that I'm not near you. I won't see you and you won't see me again. Nonetheless, Karen—ah—this thing is hard for me. Mm hm. This thing is really, really hard for me, Karen. Whatever I had on my right, whatever I had on my left, all of it has been sold; all of it has been sold. Karen, I don't have anything left anymore. Now, if you could see my condition. There is nothing left of me. My illness is one that itches, Karen, and it is killing me, killing me, killing me. I don't sleep during the night and I don't sleep during the day. It itches me on my back. Maxia has to go over my back with a comb, combing, combing my back for me. Hm. And then, my feet— If you could see me while I'm talking to you, my body is marked up as if I were an animal. Well, Karen, I don't know if God is the one who did this to me or if it is a person. In any case, everywhere I've been they tell me that it's human beings who did it to me. They threw a powder on me. The powder is eating me alive, eating me alive. I got hit with powder. Karen, there is nothing left of me anymore.

God was watching, and saw. If I were someone who had done evil/wrong, I wouldn't be living anymore. If, when I had a gourde [20 cents] in my pocket, I saved it and didn't consume it with people, I wouldn't be living anymore. Christ is powerful, nonetheless. And if where I send this tape to you, you get it at the same time you get the news I died, don't regret it. I don't have anything left, Karen. I would take another little trip, but my hands are empty. The hundred dollars you sent me, I gave $8.00 to everyone. With the remainder, I paid for what I lost in the pawn shop but that doesn't mean I got all of it back. Well, that's why God did it. If you hadn't sent the $100 to me, everything would have been lost, everything would have been lost to pawn. Thanks to what you sent me, God caused, the Eternal caused them not to be lost.

Well, Karen, I am going to turn off the tape. I am going to turn it off. I cannot keep going all the way to the end. I don't have the energy. If you were to arrive to see my condition, you know, tears would come to your eyes. Yes. [tenderly] If you were to arrive here you would see that this isn't the same Little Caterpillar you knew. If you were to see my condition, the tears wouldn't dry out from your eyes. I resign myself, nevertheless.

It will be good for that person. After I die, s/he will take what s/he killed me for. You understand? After they killed me off for what they saw I had achieved—Karen, you know, since I was born, since I was born, I have never disrespected people; I have never disrespected people. In any case, the person who did this to me will meet their judgement before God. But I cannot find him/her to judge him/her, neither could I judge him/her. Karen, if this tape arrives during the daytime, I send a good-day to you. And if it arrives in the evening, I send a good evening to you, along with your husband and your child.

You see that even one side of the cassette, I cannot finish filling up. I cannot. Well, take very good care of yourself. Me, I'm a person for whom death and I sleep in the same place, we wake up in the same place. Well my makomè [godmother of my child], my sister, if that is what is meant to take place, it will take place. If it isn't meant to take place, it won't take place. That [premise] is what you are raised with: there is sickness and there is death. A child is born today, a youngster is born today, tomorrow, God willing, he dies by his mother's side. He doesn't know anything yet. Well, if today, at my age, I have to pass away like this, I should be happy. I should be happy. In any case, if it isn't like that either, that it happens, I'll say to God, "thank you." You understand? I'll say "thank you" to God.

Everyone who sees me, those who come to see me, say to me, "Little Caterpillar, you're not going to die yet, no, so take strength from God and you won't die." I don't say "yes" to them, I don't say "no" to them. You see? I don't say "no." They are the ones who know what they see for me in their sleep. You understand? In reality, Karen, considering the paths I've crossed, I should not still be alive, no. Considering the paths I've crossed, its true, I shouldn't be living anymore. Well, Karen, I send word that the hundred dollars you sent me is like ten thousand dollars to me. Well, my sister, my darling, I can't say to you to send to me; I cannot tell you not to send to me. I have problems in any case. I have a ton of problems; I don't have five cents in hand. There is one more road that I could take, that I could still check out, but because of money—I'll accept it with God's protection. I'll accept it with God's protection.

Mm hm. All of it is God. The person who did it to me, who did it to me, if God had not given him/her permission, s/he wouldn't have done it to me. You understand? You might also say that if a person did it to me, God was the one who gave him/her permission to do it to me, s/he could steal from me one day and God knows s/he did it to me. God is aware of it all. Well, look, they killed me over my lousy house. [Forcefully] What does it look like to you, Karen? The nation of Haiti will never be right. It will never be right. Well, I'll do one side of the tape. On the bit that is left Maxia will finish talking to you. Well, Karen, if the tape arrives during the day, I send a good day to you along with your husband and child. If you find that it arrives in the evening, I send good evening to you. Karen, take very good care of yourself. Try to get my response when Yvon arrives over there. Try to get your response back to me, too, when he arrives over there.

M voye mande ou ki jan ou ye, ki jan misye ou, ki jan pitit ou ye? Kalin, se Bondye ki kenbe mwen, ki leve bouch mwen pou m pal avèk ou. Senpman e pa sante m genyen ki fè m fè kasèt la voye ba ou. Maten an la m leve, sak fè m parèt, m wè yon bray ki rive. M pat menm la menm. Yo rele mwen. Lè m vin jwenn ni, li di m kon sa se youn lèt Yvon voye ban mwen pa ou menm. Ou di m kon sa, vre? Lè a li pa ban m lèt la, li ban m $100. Anben, Kalin, $100. sa m jwenn nan, se $10,000. ki kapab tonbe an fas mwen. Monchè, Kalin, mwen tap pal avèk ou la, se yon enstan lamò, k ap pal avèk ou. S'on enstan lamò, Kalin, k ap pal avèk ou la. Ou wè kasèt la, m pap pal anpil ladan, non? M pa gen rezistans pou m pale.

Mwen di si m fè yon lèt m voye ba ou, ou a panse gen konprann sa m voye di ou yo, e pa vre. Depi sou esplikasyon m ou tande jan m ap pal avèk ou, m se yon mounn ou konen jan m te enganm, ou a tande, e ou a konen tou, lè m te enganm anfas ou, lè m pale avèk ou nan kasèt, pou ou wè si se menm bagay. Anben, Kalin, si ou pran nouvèl m mouri, eh heh, sa k fè sa, semen ki sòt pase la, m te yon nèg ki mouri. Rèl gen tan pete pou mwen; kay la te gen tan debarase. Bondye kenbe m, li resisite mwen, li tounen m.

Anben, Kalin, jiska denye moman, m pa ka jwenn solisyon ak maladi a. Tout sa m manyen, m pa sa jwenn solisyon. Mwen jwenn maladi a kap touye m. M ap chita m ap tann Bondye lè l vin pran m nan. Wi. M ap tann Bondye, pou m wè sa li vle fè avè m nan. Senpman, se yon sèl regrèt m pa pre ou. M pap wè ou, ou pap wè m, ankò. Senpman, Kalin—ay—bay la di pou mwen. M hm. Bay la di anpil, anpil pou mwen Kalin. M pa gen a dwat; m pa gen a goch. Tout sa m te genyen, tout fin vann nèt. Tout fin vann nèt. Kalin, m pa gen anyen nan menm ankò. Kouniyè a si ou ta wè pozisyon m. M ap fini debout. M gen yon maladi ki grate sou mwen, Kalin, sa touye m nèt, touye m, touye, m touye m. M pa gen dòmi la nwit, m pa gen dòmi lajounen. L ap grate m nan do. Fo Maxia al nan do m tout tan a peni, ap penyen, penyen do m pou mwen. M hm. Lè fini, nan piye mwen-ou wè jan m p pale av' ou la, kò m ap make kòm yon bèt.

Anben, Karin, mwen pa konen si se Bondye tap fè m, si se "les hommes." Senpman, tout kote m pase yo di se "les hommes" ki tap fè m. Yo voye yon poud sou mwen. Poud la manje m nèt debout, manje m debout. Youn kout poud mwen pran. Kalin, m pa gen nan mwen menm ankò.

Bondye tap gade, wè m. Si m te yon mounn ki tap fè mal, m pa ta la ankò. Lè m gen yon goud nan poch mwen, m sere l m pa manje l a mounn, m pa ta la ankò. Senpman Kris kapab. Menm si kote m voye kasèt la ba ou a ou pran nouvèl menm enstan m mouri, senpman m pa regrèt sa. M pa gen nan menm, Kalin. M ta fè yon lòt ti sòti, m pa gen nan menm. $100. ou voye, m bay tout mounn $8. Rès la m peye sa m genyen nan plann m te pedi. Se pa pou di m fini m pran yo non? Anben, sak fè Bondye fè l. Si ou pat voye $100. ban mwen, tout bay mwen ta pedi, tout bagay pedi nan plann. Granmèsi sa ou te voye ban mwen, Bondye fè, Leternèl fè yo pa t pedi.

Anben, Kalin, m pral fenmen kasèt la. M pral fenmen n. M pa fouti kenbe nèt ale. M pa gen rezistans. M pa gen rezistans, Kalin. Si ou te parèt, ou wè pozisyon m, ou konen, dlo ap sòt nan je ou. Wi. Si ou parèt ou a wè se pa menm Ti Chini ou konen an. Si ou wè pozisyon m dlo pap fin chèch nan je ou. Senpman m ap rezinye m.

La bon pou mounn nan la. Lè m fin mouri pou sa l touye m nan la val pran n. Ou konprann? Lè yo fin touye mwen pou sa yo wè m genyen an, y al jwen ni, ou konen, depi m ne nan lavi, depi m ne nan lavi, m pa janm derespete mounn. M pa janm derespete mounn. [talks to Maxia] Senpman, mounn nan tap fè m nan, la va gen jijman ak Bondye. Men m pa sa jwen ni pou jije l, ni m pa sa jije avè l. Kalin, si kasèt la rive maten, mwen voye bonjou pou ou. Si li rive aswa tou, m voye bonswa pou ou, ak tout misye ou a tout pitit ou.

Ou wè menm yon bò kasèt la, m pa sa fin plen. M pa kapab. Anben konpòt ou tre byen. Mwen menm m se on mounn, mwen a lamò nou kouche menm kote, nou leve menm kote. Anben makomè m nan, sè m nan, si sa pral vin pou fèt, li pral fèt. Si li pa vin pou fèt tou, li pap fèt. E sa ou leve jwenn. E maladi a la mò. Yon ti mounn piti fèt jodi, yon ti mounn fèt jodi, bon, vè demen si Dye vle li mouri anba vant manman n. Li poko kon anyen. Anben. Si jodi a m rive, a laj sa, se nan pozisyon sa m gen pou m vin pase, ma byen kontan. Ma byen kontan. Senpman, si e pa konsa tou sa vin pou pase, ma di Bondye, "mèsi." Ou konprann? Ma di Bondye "mèsi."

Tout mounn ki wè mwen, sak vin wè m, yo di m Ti Chini, ou poko ap mouri, non, pran kouray a Bondye tou pou ou pa mouri. M pa di yo non, m pa di yo wi. Ou kanprann? M pa di yo non. Se yo menm ki konen sa yo wè nan dòmi pou mwen. Ou kanprann? Filyè m pase vre Kalin, m pa yon nèg pou te la ankò, non, pou filyè m pase m pa yon nèg pou te la ankò. Anben, Kalin, m voye di ou, $100 ou voye ban mwen, e $10,000 ou voye ban mwen. Anben, sè mwen, cheri m nan, m pa fouti di ou voye ban mwen, m pa fouti di ou pa voye ban mwen, senpman m gen pwoblèm. M gen dal pwoblèm, m pa gen senk kòb nan menm. M gen wout pou m ta al fè, tcheke toujou, pou tèt kòb-M pran n a pwotèksyon Bondye, wi, m pran n a pwotèksyon Bondye.

M hm. Tout sa se Bondye. Mounn nan tap fè m nan, tap fè m nan, si e pa Bondye ki te ba l lalwa, li pa tap fè m. Ou konprann? Ou kapab byen di tou, si yon mounn tap fè m, se Bondye k ap ba l lalwa fè m, li kapab volè m yon jou li konen li fè m. Li pase sou Bondye. Anben. Gade sa pou mwen, viye kay mwen pou yo touye m pou li. [ap pale fò] Kote ou wè sa sanble, Kalin? Peyi D'Ayiti pap janm bon vre. Li pap bon. En ben, s'on bo kasèt m ap fè. Ti rès ki rete a Maxia ap fin pal avèk ou. Anben Kalin, si kasèt la rive maten, m voye bonjou pou ou a tout misye ou a tout pitit ou. Si ou wè li rive aswa, m voye bonswa pou ou a tout ou menm a tout misye ou a tout pitit ou. Kalin, konpòte ou tre byen. Bat pou lè Yvon ap vin la, pou ou jwenn repons mwen. Bat pou lè Yvon vin la pou m jwenn repons ou.

Epilogue

My return to Ti Rivyè seven years after Little Caterpillar's death was a reckoning. His loss permeated my reunions with his family, including Zo and Menmenn, parents of the renegade migrant, Sergo, whose murder Over There brought fears of his desertion to a definitive end; Menmenn's younger brother, Bo, the would-be migrant whose repeated attempts to sail to Miami came to naught; and Caterpillar's favorite niece, who as a precocious little girl had earned the nickname of "Mrs." and who now awaits notice of her visa to the United States, the fruit of her "business marriage" to a U.S. citizen. Zo's reflection on the death of his confidant was, "that one was too good [to survive this world]," a conclusion Menmenn did not dispute.

When I asked who might take me to see Little Caterpillar's grave, Menmenn appointed her brother. The next day, Bo and I rode our bicycles to the cemetery in upper Miton. We walked between the elaborate, pastel-colored, cinder-block tombs affirming the respectable statuses of those laid to rest inside while trying not to step on the heaps of fading conch shells covering the underground graves of their less fortunate neighbors. We sat down, leaning against the side of a gigantic lavender tomb to talk. Bo surprised me with his admission that he wasn't sure where his friend was buried. He had been too distraught to attend the funeral. "Little Caterpillar was a good, good friend of mine," he said. He pointed to two adjacent tombs, one pink, the other yellow, and said he thought Caterpillar's remains were in one or the other of them.

My longest, private conversations about Caterpillar were with the two persons he loved most and whose enmity well-nigh tore him asunder: Maxia and Se Byen. I asked Caterpillar's niece, Mrs., if she could one day take me to see Little Cater-

10.1. Bo pointed to these two tombs when we talked about Little Caterpillar's burial, Ti Rivyè, June 2003.

pillar's widow. I was surprised when, the following morning, someone told me that "someone who calls herself Mme. Pierre" was at the door. Opening it to see her standing there, emotion overtook me. I tried hard to regain the composure her society would expect at such a moment. All that I shared with my friend's wife, really, was our mutual loss. I didn't know her when I lived in Ti Rivyè. She kept her distance from Se Byen and his family and I foolishly didn't make a concerted attempt to seek her out. Our friendship had begun once I returned to the United States; it unfolded through the many cassette letters and cheerful photographs I exchanged with her husband, Little Caterpillar.

She is strikingly lovely, with penetrating, almond eyes gracing a delicate, round face—more beautiful than in the picture I have of the contented, handsome couple. Mme. Pierre is the name Maxia earned by her civil marriage to Pierre "Little Caterpillar" Dioguy. Even though Pierre is deceased and she has a new partner, everyone, including her parents, close relatives, and her current husband, addresses her by her permanent title, Mme. Pierre.

Little Caterpillar's niece had told me that Mme. Pierre "waited a good little time" after his death before taking a new partner. I wanted to show my departed friend's widow that I supported her decision to take a new husband, so I asked how she and her husband were getting along with one another. "Well," she said. I told her I was happy for her.

We talked, uninterrupted for hours. Her grief and bitterness seemed to have

10.2. Little Caterpillar and Maxia. He gave me this picture after he visited her in Léogane. (Date and place of photo unknown.)

faded after taking their toll. Mme. Pierre remained surprisingly controlled as she described Caterpillar's unbearable suffering and the shocking indifference of his kin. The family had abandoned their devoted emissary once he could no longer provide for them. They did not offer to help him find relief from his affliction, nor did they assist in his care after he could no longer do for himself. As a result, Caterpillar and Maxia had to sell all of their livestock and put their possessions, including her wedding ring and a bicycle, in a pawn shop. She was fortunate to retrieve the ring she now wears after it sat for ten months in pawn.

Little Caterpillar was very close to death, she recounted, when he suddenly resuscitated. His patron lwa, Baron la Croix, was "in his head" (*nan tèt li*). Baron did what Little Caterpillar could not; he demanded an audience with Se Byen. Se Byen did not refuse the spirit. When Se Byen arrived, Baron instructed him, "you are the one to treat Little Caterpillar" (*se ou menm pou ta trete Ti Chini*). Se Byen acquiesced to the spirit's demand. Later, however, he had the gall to tell his sister-in-law that they would have to pay 1,000 Haitian dollars (about US$125) for the treatment. Though his former benefactor was in his darkest hour, Se Byen could think only of money.

Mme. Pierre felt utterly alone with Little Caterpillar in his suffering and in his death. Of course Se Byen did not offer to help pay for the funeral. He accused her of hiding her husband's resources so that she wouldn't have to spend them on the rites. Three of Caterpillar's four sisters lived (and remain still) in Guadeloupe; the fourth, the mother of Mrs., lived next to him in Ti Rivyè. (She migrated to Florida in 2003). One of the Guadeloupe sisters came forward to assist with the costs of the funeral and burial. Caterpillar's body sat in the morgue while his wife awaited word from the others. Another sister in Guadeloupe finally came forward. She told Mme. Pierre that a black butterfly landed on her chest, which she interpreted as a sign that she should send money to help out with the funerary arrangements. (Migrants are expected to finance the death rites of kin back home, and to give unstintingly toward the quintessential reproduction of the family's status. Thanks to this standard, Léogane's mortuary industry appears to be its most thriving business: there are three funeral homes in the town center.) Only the sister who had first offered assistance returned for the funeral. How ironic, Mme. Pierre said, that all three sisters returned for the funeral of their other brother, Adam, several years before. "You see how they preferred Adam?" she noted.

Echoing words that Caterpillar used in his last, desperate letters to me, Mme. Pierre claimed that Little Caterpillar was "killed for what he had" (*touye pou sa li te genyen*). Sorcery almost took her life, too. After burying her husband, she said that she felt a dead spirit hovering around her. It was an agent dispatched by a sorcerer. "It was like a shadow of a person," she said. "It was in front of me and in back of me." In an effort to escape the tormenting shade, she joined the Protestants. Their exorcism apparently worked; the shade left her alone. She soon abandoned the sect because she "lost interest in them." Like her husband, then, she "tried" Protestant conversion. But unlike him, she found tangible relief inside their magic circle, and left it once she recovered. Mme. Pierre resisted identifying the enemy who wielded the "peasant" weapon to strike down those who try to rise above their station and to steal their property. She nonetheless shared her doubt that sorcery killed her husband. His death could have been straightforward or unmotivated, caused by Bon Dye (God). "After all," she said, "you know he had diabetes and hypertension, and then he got shingles on top of them."

My conversation with Mme. Pierre left me reeling. Se Byen had rejected his brother's wife from the outset, I well knew. But I was shocked by her charges of his shameful behavior toward his ailing brother. How could Se Byen have so cruelly abandoned the dying migrant who had been so loyal and generous to him over the years? And when he relented and ultimately agreed to help, how could he have stooped to demanding money from his destitute, dying brother? I spoke to Se Byen next to hear his side of these unforgivable accusations and listen to his explanation of the cause of Caterpillar's affliction and the failure of therapy that could not prevent his death.

Se Byen was in front of the House, leaning back in a low chair under the shade of the red mombin tree. He was expecting me; I had arranged in advance for our third visit that week. Earlier he had showed me around the enlarged House, whose renovation incorporated some splashier elements of urban "voodoo temple" style. Dazzling murals of Ezili Dantò and baby, Baron's cross, and other spirit emblems adorned the front, exterior walls. The professional painter was Se Byen's eldest son, who, as a boy, had painted the eerie white silhouettes on the tangerine walls of the former House. Much had changed inside the House, too. The former arbor is now the peristyle, painted blue and pink, with a huge center post. The old ritual and dance space was partitioned and transformed into Se Byen's residence, which he shares with his wife and youngest son. To the right were three rooms where Se Byen does his "work," including the tiny, dark altar room where he had started recording the aggressive letter to his brother long ago. As we toured the updated House, we talked of the voided plan for Little Caterpillar eventually to assume leadership of the House. Se Byen expected one of his three children—all sons—to step up, but he stated frankly that none compared to Little Caterpillar, a charismatic, masterful performer with conspicuous mystical power—the equal of Se Byen.

10.3. Se Byen sits under the *cirouelle* tree in front of the House, Ti Rivyè, June 2003.

10.4. The painter, Se Byen's son, stands in front of his paintings on the wall of the House. Ti Rivyè, June 2003.

10.5. Inside the House, June 2003. Public rites take place in this room, which was formerly the bower. The original exterior wall is in the background.

10.6. The room inside the House where Se Byen works and heals victims of sorcery, June 2003.

At the age of about 73, Se Byen is yet tall and robust. His twinkling eyes are still his most alluring feature. He does not wear the dentures Little Caterpillar purchased for him, and the absence of teeth distort his eloquent rhetoric with a distinctive, toothless accent. That day, Se Byen was wearing a clean, white undershirt and black pants. He fetched a chair out of the House, placing it close to and facing his. A small crowd of children gathered, as it inevitably does when a blan, or foreigner, visits. Looking into Se Byen's sparkling eyes, I indicated that I wanted to speak to him privately. He dismissed the children, periodically reproaching others who came too close, and when an occasional adult came to observe or join our conversation, he more politely asked them to leave us alone. Nonetheless his eldest son, the painter, parked himself on a nearby porch railing, as if the earphones to his compact disc player, which were dangling around his neck rather than covering his ears much of the time, accorded us privacy.

I told Se Byen there were things I wanted to discuss about losing my friend, Little Caterpillar, questions I had wanted to pose for a long time. "*Wi*," he said calmly, giving me unqualified permission to proceed. I began by asking what caused Little Caterpillar's untimely death. He answered directly: "It came from the woman." (*Sa sòt nan fanm nan*). He wasn't about to mention her name. He and "the woman" do not talk to one another, he added, but if she walks on the road by the yard, which she must pass to get from her residence to her family land, he says "good day." "The woman killed my brother so she could take his property," he stated. "She was poisoning him from the moment he returned here. He couldn't see it. Don't you know that he bought land in her name? And he built a big house on her land. He didn't build a home here" [gesturing toward the maternally inherited yard in which we were sitting]. (*Ou pa wè li achte tè sou non madanm ni? Li bati yon gwo kay pou li nan tè pa l. Li pa bati kay isit*).

I asked about the norm that a husband ought to build a house for his wife on her property, and added, "Didn't you do that for your wives?" "Yes," he replied to both questions, "but you should have your own place on your own [family's] land."

"Afterward," he continued, "they were wed in a civil court. They didn't invite me when they went and did it." (*Lè fini, yo pase ak civil. Yo pa t envite m lè yo te fè l.*) Se Byen again summed up the cause of Little Caterpillar's death: "The woman killed him. She took my brother's property so she could live with another man. Even after he died, she hoarded money my sister [in Guadeloupe] sent home to pay for the funeral." (*Fanm nan touye li. Li pran byen frè m pou l ka viv ak lòt gason. Menm apre li mouri, li te sere kòb sè mwen te voye pou antèman an.*) Se Byen tried to warn his little brother, but Little Caterpillar did not heed his advice. "I am his older brother. My mother died, my father died. I was the eldest. I spoke to him; he didn't listen to me. The woman is the one who turned his head"—implying that she resorted to magical means to influence Caterpillar. (*Se mwen ki gran frè l. Manman m mouri, papa m mouri. Se mwen k pi gran. Mwen te pale li; li pat koute m. Se fi a k te vire tèt li*).

Se Byen went on. "Little Caterpillar died because he abandoned his lwa. He joined the Protestants. He had a lwa in his head, Baron, from the time he was an older child. When he came back he threw away Baron's hat, cane, and clothes—everything. After that, Baron took another older child in the compound, a boy. He is [my sister] Germaine's child—I mean, Germaine's son's child." (*Epi sa k koz lamò Ti Chini se paske li abandonen lwa l. L al nan levanjil. Li te gen yon lwa nan tèt li—Baron—depi li te gran ti mounn. Lè l vini li jete chapo Baron, beki Baron, rad li, tout. Apre, Baron te pran yon lòt gran ti mounn nan lakou a, yon gason. Li se pitit Germaine—pitit, pitit gason Germaine.*)

I asked his name. Se Byen didn't know his "good name," but told me his nickname. He continued, "The lwa didn't kill my brother. He [Baron] withdrew his protection. That is why he died." (*Lwa pa touye li. Li retire pwotèj li. Se sak fè l mouri*.) Se Byen summed up the narrow limits of the lwa's power. In spite of Little Caterpillar's flagrant rejection of his lwa, Baron did not hurt him. The lwa simply abrogated his disaffected servant's "guaranty" and "protection," allowing the sorcerer's powers to penetrate him and extinguish his life.

If Se Byen had believed that Caterpillar was afflicted by a sorcerer (working on behalf of his evil wife), why, I wondered, didn't he try to save him? Se Byen was a formidable gangan, reputed for rescuing victims from the deadly grasp of other sorcerers' powers. The blue altar room in the back of the House, which he allowed me to photograph, holds the implements of his magical trade. Several metal cases are filled with colorful stuffed and bound cloth "packets" for treating a distinct variety of afflictions (the colors indicate different etiologies). Bunches of balled-up cloth hang on a rope, suspended diagonally from a rafter to the floor. They are the garments of people he has treated. The metonymic associations between his patients and the clothes they left behind provide double insurance: for his patients, continued prophylactic protection against sorcery affliction; for Se Byen, indemnity against defection. Should they "forget [to keep paying] him," he can get to them through their clothes and "make them remember."

I asked Se Byen if he had tried to cure Little Caterpillar when he was sick. "Yes," he replied, "When I did the work with another man I saw that the woman was the one who poisoned him." (*Wi. Se lè mwen fè travay la ak yon lòt mounn m wè se fanm nan ki pwazonen li.*) I asked who the other person was. He said it was a gangan. "Someone from around here," I asked? "Someone from far away," he answered. "Why did you solicit another gangan's help?" I asked. "The burden was too much for me," he confessed. "The thing cost me a lot of money, too," he added. (*Chay la twòp pou mwen. Bay la koute m anpil kòb.*)

Hearing his explanation, I recalled Maxia's charge that Se Byen had the gall to ask for 1,000 Haitian dollars to treat his own brother. Perhaps she didn't know that he had to pay the other gangan.

Speaking in an endearing tone, Se Byen said to me, "Look, the one we lost was a good one" (*gade, sa nou te pedi a te yon bon*). Coming from Se Byen, those words were both a surprise and a relief. Se Byen had finally affirmed his confidence in his younger brother. When I first met him, he had stunned me with allegations of the irresponsible migrant's desertion of his piteous family. As though he had no recollection of those accusations, he continued to praise Little Caterpillar as a responsible and generous kinsman. Se Byen recalled how he would ask his brother for sums of two or three hundred dollars and the latter would always pay him directly, without question. Yet as Se Byen uttered these words, Caterpillar's voice sounded in counterpoint in my head: "Se Byen sends word to me, 'Little Caterpillar, I need 300 or 400 dollars for me to do the work for the lwa.' I send it off. 'Little

Caterpillar, I need money to buy a steer for the New Year to sacrifice for the lwa.' I send off the money for the steer." Se Byen's accounting indeed accorded with Caterpillar's, but his grateful tone hardly blended with Caterpillar's sentiments. When Caterpillar recalled those exchanges, his voice had bristled with resentment over Se Byen's stubborn ingratitude and his lwa's utter lack of reciprocity. "I've been doing for the lwa," he added on the 1992 cassette letter denouncing his lwa and defending his conversion, "but instead of being better off, I'm worse."

Little Caterpillar's declining status owed much to the machinations of his other (elder) brother, Adam, who raided the "guaranty" of his migration back home. According to Little Caterpillar, Adam stole his investments and, furthermore, Se Byen was complicit in the theft. So now I asked Se Byen, "Is it true that Adam stole Little Caterpillar's investments?" Se Byen confirmed that Adam not only did sell off the cows he was supposed to be tending on his migrant brother's behalf but also did "the same bad thing" to his migrant sisters, secretly selling the livestock they purchased as guaranties of their migrations.

I asked Se Byen what he did when he found out about Adam's deception and thievery. "Nothing," he replied. Incredulous, I demanded to know, "Why did you do nothing?" He defended his passivity by arguing that because his migrant siblings hadn't informed him of their arrangements with Adam, he didn't feel he could intervene later on. Adam nonetheless was persecuted for his treachery, Se Byen said. "He was a traitor. He would tell you one thing and turn around and do something else. He was persecuted. Bon Dye [God] saw what he did, and he died."

I mentioned that I knew that although Little Caterpillar was back home when Adam died, he refused to attend the funeral. Se Byen concurred that "he had good reason not to go." If Adam had betrayed his three sisters, why, I wondered, did they each fly back from Guadeloupe to attend his funeral? "They are [nevertheless] his sisters," he replied. Earlier Maxia had remarked to me that the attendance of all three sisters at Adam's funeral, in contrast to the presence of only one sister at Little Caterpillar's final rites, was evidence that the family favored Adam. I asked Se Byen about it. He denied that they preferred one brother to another, adding that a second sister sent her son in her place to Caterpillar's funeral. Then, to demonstrate their solidarity, he told me a story.

"You see this tree?" (*Piye sa a?*) he asked, pointing to the trunk of the *cirouelle*, or red mombin, tree whose shade was protecting us from the burning midday sun.[1] "One day I noticed that the tree was bleeding" (*yon jou m wè piye bwa ap senyen*). "It was bleeding. Blood dripped, blood dripped, a lot of blood" (*L ap senyen. San koule, san koule, yon bann san*). He got up and pointed to marks on the tree that seemed to be from machete gashes. "This is Legba's tree." (*Se pou Legba li ye.*) Legba is the oldest and most supreme Guinea spirit, the first lwa summoned at rituals and beseeched to permit the other spirits to attend. "I called the people [in the family] together and said to them, someone [in the family] is about to die. Then I get word that [my sister] Germaine's son in Guadeloupe is gravely ill, near death. I pray for him there. Can you see where I lit the candle? After three days he recovered" (*M rele mounn yo, m di, gen yon moun ki pral mouri. Epi m pran nouvèl pitit Germaine Gwadoub malad, byen mal, li avanse mouri. M priye pou li la. Ou pa wè kote m limen balenn? Apre twa jou li refè*). The sacred tree of the oldest Guinea lwa looks out for whole family; its body is connected to all of theirs, no matter how far they range. Some member of the kin group has to perceive the sensitive tree's language, and that person is Se Byen.

Se Byen's unexpected affirmation of his brother's substantial remittances and generosity opened the door for me to confront him. How would Se Byen defend having falsely accused his brother and trumping up his own resultant decline? I brought up the extraordinary cassette letter that he and other performers had recorded for Little Caterpillar. "When I first came, and you asked me to help you record a letter for Little Caterpillar because you didn't have a radio-cassette player and didn't know his address, you said on the tape that during the three years since Little Caterpillar had been Outside, he never wrote to you, even though none of it was true?" Unfazed, he admitted that he lied. "He had been writing to you, right?" Again, still composed, he acknowledged the truth. Using the very words he had shouted on the tape, I grilled him: "Why did you want me to think that he didn't write to his family in Haiti at all? Why did you want me to be embarrassed to learn that my friend had abandoned his family in Haiti?" (*Poukisa ou te vle fè m konprann ke li pat ekri fanmi ni an Ayiti di tou, pou mwen ta santi wont pou m wè ke zanmi m te abandonen fanmi ni an Ayiti?*) Still composed, he replied, "I said it because the woman took our money. My brother had written to us that he sent the money to her but when we went to get our share, she refused to give it to us. The next time he sent money directly to us through Silien and when she asked me for her money I did the same thing back to her. I didn't give it to her. She went to her boyfriend, the sheriff, and he made me give her the money and pay a fine, too." Indeed Se Byen had complained bitterly about the incident on the cassette letter to his brother, accusing the sheriff and Maxia of deception, but he didn't specifically denounce their affair.

Se Byen's memory of his dissembling about the migrant who abandoned his family exposed not a hint of contrition. His sister-in-law's malfeasance and Caterpillar's apparent tolerance of it justified his tall tale of Caterpillar's desertion. Looking back, I have to admit that the feigned chastisement was effective. Little Caterpillar had told me later (when I visited him in Fort Pierce, Florida), that he sent money to Se Byen to replace what the sheriff took from him. He said that Se

Byen was wrong not to give Maxia her portion of his remittance, but that she, in turn, was wrong to involve the law in a family matter.

During the same conversation I had with Little Caterpillar about the astonishing casette letter from Se Byen and his family, Little Caterpillar explained to me that once Se Byen had started singing pwen-songs, he contradicted his previous speech. The pitiful harangue about his emotional and bodily decline since Caterpillar's desertion was a bluff. Se Byen's opening song sent the message that he didn't need the migrant's money anyway and no matter what happened to his emissary, he would persevere. I wanted to know if the sender of those pwen messages had the same understanding as the target who "picked them up." So I asked Se Byen, "And on the same tape, you sent a pwen in a song whose message was the opposite of what you were saying when you said that three years had passed since Little Caterpillar wrote to his family." Without hesitating, I began singing the call-and-response song:

> The House falls down;
> Ti Jean doesn't fall down.
> The House falls down;
> Ti Jean doesn't fall down.
> Brother Chini, my friend,
> It's for their big mouths, true.

> Little Caterpillar falls down;
> Se Byen doesn't fall down.
> Little Caterpillar falls down;
> Se Byen doesn't fall down.
> Brother Caterpillar, my friend,
> It's for their big mouths, true.

> *Kay la tonbe;*
> *Ti Jean pa tonbe.*
> *Kay la tonbe;*
> *Ti Jean pa tonbe.*
> *Frè Chini, monchè,*
> *Se pou dyòl yo, vre.*

> *Ti Chini tonbe;*
> *Se Byen pa tonbe.*
> *Ti Chini tonbe;*
> *Se Byen pa tonbe.*

Frè Chini,
monchè,
Se pou dyòl yo, vre.

Se Byen joined in, and then took over the lead of the call-and-response song. When we finished, he exclaimed, "You are a priestess!" (*Se manbo ou ye!*). I happily accepted the flattery from the master singer, then promptly gave him the opportunity to retract it by asking, "What pwen did you send him in that song?" Se Byen replied with a challenge, "Where is he?" (*Kote li?*) I stared back in silence. I didn't know how to respond. What was the right answer? Again, Se Byen pressed me, "Where is he?" (*Kote li?*) All of a sudden the anguish of losing my friend swept through me. "He's dead!" (*li mò!*) I blurted out, choking back tears. "Well, . . ." (*Anben . . .*) Se Byen interjected, urging me to complete the answer to my own question. "But you are here" (*Men ou la*), I stated. "Well!" He smiled. Se Byen's pleased expression demonstrated confidence in the authority of his prediction.

Se Byen has indeed held on. In his seventh decade, he is yet in good health and he and his spirit, Ti Jean, direct a formidable, reinforced House, thanks to the migrant's remittances.

Se Byen's narrative validated Guinea's authority to discipline (and pwenify) its migrant "children." Se Byen is the mediator between Guinea and the kin group, or eritaj. He assumes this role as leader of their House. His usual station is, however, outside the House. Unless they are sick or have something to hide, people generally sit, lean, or lie outdoors. Gangan, of course, do their magical "work" inside. If he is not "working" or sick, Se Byen positions himself in a spot in front of the House that offers a metonymic reminder of his Guinea authority. He can reliably be found under the cirouelle tree and we were sitting under it when he explained how its roots and branches embody (and actually feel) the connection between the descendants and Guinea. As Guinea's intermediary for the family, Se Byen bears the responsibility for "protecting" (guarding and disciplining) his brother. Caterpillar readily acknowledged Se Byen's intermediary role, but he ultimately rejected his brother's abuse of that authority. Se Byen could not or would not see that Guinea's—and his—recurrent highhandedness and want of reciprocity had finally driven the dutiful migrant to rebel. In his view, Guinea dealt properly with its migrant child. But the unruly migrant rejected Guinea. The Guinea spirits withdrew their "protection," and the migrant succumbed to a sorcerer's deadly power. Se Byen reported that when Little Caterpillar returned home, he certified his Protestant conversion by desecrating his spirit "master's" sacred things. In response to this glaring insult, Baron la Croix removed his protection. Baron let the poison consume his child.

In Se Byen's eyes, Little Caterpillar was not in full command of his own will when he renounced Guinea. Instead, he was "charmed" by his home-wife, Maxia. She did not love her migrant husband; she loved only the money he sent home. Once he returned, she used sorcery to kill him off so that she could enjoy his wealth with another man. She controlled the entirety of the departed migrant's estate: a substantial, cinder-block house and a small plot of land. Well before her mercenary's utility had waned, she had ensured that titles to the two properties were in her name. Her exclusive possession of these properties was definitive evidence of her steady campaign, over almost two decades, to take ultimate advantage of her husband. Once Caterpillar fell ill, his relatives were not about to let her exploit them, too. Why should they offer him money if she would divert it? After he died, they resisted contributing to costs of the funeral, daring her to spend some of the money she already extorted from their brother. One sister nonetheless relented. But according to Se Byen, some of the money she sent wound up in Mme. Pierre's hands.

Blame a migrant brother's downfall on his scheming home-wife. Misogyny sullies Se Byen's slanderous accusation of his sister-in-law and also absolves him of manipulating his brother. Since I did not ask Se Byen, I can only speculate about how he might have viewed the case if the defeated migrant were a woman and her home-husband remained in control of her land. Especially during 1979 and 1980, the majority of those who "took the Canter" to Miami were men. Many a husband left behind a young wife to submit to her husband's kin's surveillance of her "respect" for her migrant husband, all the while competing with them (and often co-wives, too) over claims to his remittances (Richman 2002). This polygynous society would not put a home-husband in the same impossible position. In fact, I do not know of a single woman from Little River who migrated and left behind a current partner, though many of course left estranged, former husbands in Haiti. Migrating mothers left their children in the care of trusted kin, typically their mothers and sisters, and in some cases, their in-laws.

Deep in-law mistrust is a recurrent theme in sorcery accusations and counter-accusations. The antagonism blows up when the person in the middle is a migrant who lives up to his burden to pursue life for both parties, as Caterpillar, in fact, did. The struggle between a Haitian family and the people their members marry, while hardly unique to them, nonetheless involves the unique social, cultural, and religious meanings of descent and marriage in rural Haiti generally and in this particular, dispersed Ti Rivyè community. Descent is valorized through the concept of eritaj, meaning at once the inherited land, the Guinea lwa, the apical ancestor who links the descent line to Guinea, and all of his or her heirs, living and dead. Especially through their role as protectors against and transmitters of affliction along particular lines of descent, the lwa substantiate this value. Local (meaning this transnational community's) marriage practices reproduce the primacy of kinship over alliance, limiting its threat to descent. These practices assume male polygyny and female serial monogamy and together reflect a pattern common throughout poor rural and urban communities in the Afro-Caribbean (Kerns 1983; Clarke 1957; Smith 1988).

In his analysis of rural Haitian consensual union, called *plasaj* (from French *plaçage*), Ira Lowenthal (1987) demonstrates that children belong foremost to the individual parent and his or her kin line, rather than to the marriage in common. Children extend the kin line, rather than the romantic love of the couple, as in middle-class American culture (Schneider 1968). Everyday language reproduces this norm when co-parents habitually refer to their children in common, even while conversing with one another, as "my children." The well-known proverb "Children are the riches of poor women" (*pitit se richès fanm pov*) connotes struggling single mothers rather than devoted couples facing misery together as an independent unit. The state abets the independent strategies of the parents of children in common by recognizing the legitimacy and bilateral inheritance rights of children born to plasaj unions, and by discounting spouses' claims to one another's estates.

Little Caterpillar and Maxia's celebration of a civil union represented a direct challenge to this delicate relation, tipping the balance against the kin of the eritaj in favor of a permanent, independent couple. Actually, the Creole word for this bourgeois form of union is "marriage" (*maryaj*). "Marriage" is required for full conversion to Protestantism, hence the practice also distinguishes separatist Protestants from the Catholic majority. Se Byen bitterly recalled how Little Caterpillar and Maxia carried out their civil marriage in secret. Their secretiveness only exaggerated the latent threat to the kin line that all marital alliances pose, since a civil union explicitly privileges the interests of the autonomous couple over those of kin. Because the state recognizes the inheritance rights of "married" spouses, the latter can benefit more from "marriage" than from plasaj if one spouse dies leaving a substantial estate. But it is not in the interest of polygynous men who desire and expect to continue to sire children with additional women as long as possible, since children born to "outside wives" after the enactment of the civil union may not legally inherit the estate (Lowenthal 1987:167).

Caterpillar had long expressed his plan to "marry" his (*plase*) wife. He invited me to be the godmother of their wedding years before it actually took place in March 1992. (I was unable to attend the celebration.) Caterpillar's achievement of residency status in the United States created a new rationale for "marriage." The only legal and, therefore, most cost-effective way to sponsor his wife's immigration was to "marry" her, enacting thereby a union sanctioned by the Haitian state that would be "legible" to his host government (Scott 1998).[2] After Maxia became Mme. Pierre, he applied to the Immigration and Naturalization Service to sponsor her immigration to the United States. Mme. Pierre's final approval to immigrate to the United States arrived not long after his death. Indeed he had asked me to help her immigrate, should he die before the documents arrived. But without her husband Over There, she had little motivation to leave. Se Byen disregarded the immigration rationale for the civil union between his brother and sister-in-law. To Se Byen, the formalization of the union was simply Maxia's ploy to wrest all of her husband's property from his family before murdering him through sorcery.

Accusations of sorcery to undermine competitors and to steal someone's property are standard in "peasant" communities. So real is sorcery that competing explanations of the same "murder" can coexist. Se Byen thought Caterpillar's wife contracted with a sorcerer to kill her husband so she could enjoy his property as she pleased. Mme. Pierre, on the other hand, echoed her husband's belief that he was "killed for what he gained." She did not impeach her in-laws, or anyone for that matter. Neither did Caterpillar name his enemy, leaving me to wonder. The message is that those who raise themselves up too high will inevitably be brought down. Zo and Menmenn remain miserably poor despite sending their sole offspring abroad. But they also know well that the humiliating failure of his migration insulates them somewhat from sorcery. Just as fear of sorcery might help some find solace in their miserable station, it prompts others to conceal their minuscule gains. Seemingly, the smaller the assets, the greater the danger. Caterpillar's estate was minuscule: a good but modest house and a tiny plot of land.

Lurking in the background of even modest improvement is the suspicion that the successful person has done something immoral to gain, used sorcery to steal wealth from someone else or bought a pwen. As lowly mobile wage laborers and emissaries of their "peasant" families' morally ambivalent social and economic ambitions, Ti Rivyè migrants are caught—pwenified—by this discourse. Little Caterpillar lived the painful experiences of the migrant: exploited as if he were his family's pwen, accused of buying illicit pwen, and tormented by the lethal repercussions of successfully "sending to do for" (*voye fè pou*) those back home. Some migrants delay returning home for fear of "getting hit" by sorcery. Generous prestations to Guinea, which redistribute resources, serve of course to assuage such suspicions by laundering the illicit money and turning it into a moral gift. Moreover, Guinea reciprocates with "protection" of the person's productive capacity, including thwarting sorcery. As Se Byen explained, had Caterpillar stayed loyal to Baron, the Guinea spirit would not have "let him die" by a sorcerer's hand.

I do not think, in the end, that either Mme. Pierre or Se Byen lied to me. They and I believe in the reality of our complex relationships with Little Caterpillar and, through him, with one another. The rivalry between Se Byen and Mme. Pierre compounded their individual suffering of his wrenching decline and death. Though I stayed far away in Chicago, for reasons that now seem trivial, I meanwhile suffered Caterpillar's distress and the anguish of our losing one another. He was "writing" to me and chronicling his decline with uncommon dignity, "even after the mourning cries erupted but God said, 'no, not yet.'"

I arrived in Caterpillar's yard in Ti Rivyè as the migrant's message—or pwen—to his family, playing an allusive part in an extraordinary transnational performance. My role included recording and interpreting its challenging script. Little Caterpillar trusted me to publish this work. As he "wrote" to me, "Whatever you do, it's fine. However you can do it, do it. You understand? However you can do it, do it." I did do it, Ti Chini, despite my sorrow that you are not here for me to read it to you.

Notes

Chapter 1. The Pwen of Transnational Haitian Migration

1. Around 1980, boom boxes conducive to high-volume public broadcasting, in sizes that were hardly portable, were being aggressively promoted to African Americans; the white middle class, meanwhile, had been targeted for solitary consumption of the "personal portable," which could be unobtrusively attached to the body and connected to light-weight earphones (Bill Mays and Wes Farris, marketers of stereo equipment, pers. comm.). The new Haitian arrivals, who lived in racially segregated areas, appropriated the portable radio-cassette players into a vital means of correspondence. They of course also replayed music tapes and made use of the radio in the device.

Creole radio programs have increasingly connected migrants to the local Haitian ethnic community and to the home nation as well. In large diaspora centers like New York and South Florida, Haitian-owned radio stations broadcast Creole programs, including those first aired in Haiti. (One can also purchase equipment to receive stations broadcasting directly from Haiti.) In such smaller communities as Boston, Chicago, and Washington, Creole speakers host their own shows on public radio stations. See also Peter Manuel's (1993) *Cassette Culture: Popular Music and Technology in North India*. Though his concern is with cassettes and commercial music, he offers a relevant discussion of cassettes as "new media" characterized by decentralized ownership, control, and consumption patterns that offer new potentialities for "autonomy, dissent, and freedom" (Manuel 1993: 2–3).

2. I thank Roy Wagner for inventing this term.

3. See Drexel Woodson's (1992) review of *The Serpent and the Rainbow*.

4. Murray (1984) writes that the religion is a "healing cult." Brown (1991:345) states that "healing is the main purpose of all types of (Vodou) ritualizing." The identification of Haitian religion and healing is treated in a rich medical anthropological literature including studies by Brodwin (1991), Coreil (1979), Farmer (1988b, 1990), Laguerre (1984), Métraux (1953a), Murray (1976), Weidman (1978), and Wiese (1971).

Chapter 2. Migrants, Remittances, and Development

1. There is a growing body of demographic and sociological data on Mexican migrants' remittance transfers and allocations including Cornelius (1990), DeSipio (2000), Orozco (2000, 2002), and Massey et al. (1987). Griffith (1985, 1986a) analyzes the role of Jamaican migrants' remittances in perpetuating their mobile labor force. Earlier views of remittances, primarily negative, can be found in Rubenstein (1982a, 1982b), Brana-Shute and Brana-Shute (1982), Marshall (1985), and Philpott (1970).

2. See Virginia Kerns' (1983) subtle discussion of the morality and symbolism of feeding among Garifuna in *Women and the Ancestors*.

3. The intolerable black republic nonetheless represented a solution to the citizenship question in the first white nation-state in the hemisphere. Colonization of blacks in Haiti (and Liberia) would rid the polity of troublesome and non-assimilable inferior races, all the while preserving black slavery. Haitian President Geffrard (1859–67) invited "all ye negroes and mulattoes who, in the vast Continent of America, suffer from the prejudices of caste ... [to offer] a formal denial, most eloquent and peremptory, against those detractors of our race who contest our desire and ability to attain a high degree of civilization" (cited in Nicholls 1979:84). President Lincoln advocated black emigration until the plan was trumped by the South's desire for cheap, black labor for rebuilding after the war (Plummer 1992:28).

4. The movement of Haitian immigrants from New York, Boston, and Quebec into South Florida has also swelled the population there. Like other Caribbean migrants, they had previously avoided the South because of the dearth of job opportunities and its legacy of segregation. These latter tend to be from higher social and economic echelons than the boat migrants and have achieved substantial economic success in the United States (Stepick 1999:53).

5. Only one larger sailboat (*bato*) was used for a kanntè from Ti Rivyè in 1980. Its owner transported about 50 people, including 14 of his children, 2 of his wives, and numerous in-laws and neighbors. (He returned to Ti Rivyè in 1981 and organized a second kanntè, charging passengers $300.)

6. Challenges to the Bush administration's policy toward the Haitian refugees, including a futile suit before the Supreme Court, mounted during the 1992 presidential election. Candidate Bill Clinton responded to the advocacy of the Congressional Black Caucus by condemning President Bush's cruel policy and promising, if he were elected, to offer Haitian refugees a chance to request asylum here. Predictably, a few weeks before Clinton was to take office, spurious news reports began appearing in American media. Swarms of Haitians were preparing to invade South Florida the moment Clinton was sworn in. Foreign journalists honed in on Ça Ira, Léogane, and published photographs of local boatbuilders at work, implying that the only reason these vessels were being constructed was for migrations to Miami, not for cargo transport or fishing along the Haitian coast.

The propaganda was successful. President Clinton announced that he would not, after all, modify Bush's policy toward the Haitian refugees. His explanation was that he was concerned for their safety and did not want a new policy to tempt them to risk their lives on the Caribbean Sea in desperate attempts to reach the United States. Clinton hoped to add legitimacy to his abrupt change of position by prevailing upon ousted President Aristide to broadcast an address to Haitians imploring them not to attempt the voyage. The approach effectively reduced Haitians' attempts to reach the United States by sailboat.

7. Because these civil proceedings had statutory limits on fines, they amounted to hand-slapping rather than an effective deterrent. Neither did monetary victory in court mean getting paid; government agencies, including the IRS, often had prior liens on the crew leaders' assets. I translated at one of the first cases to invoke the new law, *Bertrand v. Jorden*, 672 F.SUPP. 1417 (M.D. Fla. 1987). Florida-based labor contractor Jimmie Lee Jorden was convicted of 22 violations of the Migrant and Seasonal Agricultural Worker Protection Act against four Haitian members of his crew. Among other torts, Jordan beat Lucien Bertrand, a native of Ti Rivyè, for sitting down in a field to protest a piece rate that was disclosed to the workers after they had begun to work picking squash.

8. Legal guest workers, whose temporary H-2 visas at the discretion of employers also make them a pliant labor force, have also been recruited to replace the overly assertive Haitians. But the H-2 guest worker law prohibits discrimination against native and resident immigrant labor. I served as a translator for migrants from Ti Rivyè at hearings convened in Belle Glade in April 1983 by the Labor Standards Subcommittee of the Labor and Education Committee of the United States House of Representatives, then headed by Representative George Miller. The hearings exposed blatant abuses of the H-2 program, which had been authorizing the recruitment of thousands of Jamaican and other West Indian men to work in the sugarcane plantations around Lake Okeechobee and in tobacco farms and apple orchards up north. The sugarcane firms used various schemes to avoid employing Haitians, including imposing impossibly high productivity standards used as a basis for revoking the new recruits and sharing a blacklist of all workers ever fired from any one firm. The chairman also revealed the Department of Labor's false certification that a local labor shortage made the importation of foreign labor necessary and that such importation would not adversely affect local workers (*Miami Herald*, April 12, 1983).

The broader political context for these hearings was the debate over immigrant, refugee, and guest labor then going on in the United States Congress and which culminated in the 1986 Immigration Reform and Control Act (*Miami Herald*, April 12, 1983). As Attorney Rob Williams of Florida Rural Legal Services explained to me, this law intended to free various categories of alien workers from immigration limbo, including the "entrants," and to stem the extreme exploitation of the "undocumented." To satisfy the demands of the agricultural lobby, the 1986 immigration bill also granted residency status to a large body of undocumented workers. A relatively lenient criterion was applied to qualify as a "special agricultural worker" for temporary residency status: anyone who had worked in U.S. agriculture for at least three consecutive months between May 1985 and May 1986 (Barry 1989:39). The powerful persuasion of the Florida sugarcane lobby decided the definition of "agricultural worker." The person was eligible if s/he worked in the production, harvesting, or processing of any fruits, vegetables, or perishable commodities. This definition included beet sugar and even accommodated Christmas trees, cotton, and tobacco. Sugarcane alone was excluded. The cane cutters from the British West Indies thus remained the only "guest" migrant labor force excluded from immigrant status until 1995, when the sugarcane industry shifted to mechanical harvesters. See *Orlando Sun Sentinel* (Nov. 30–Dec. 4, 1986), McCoy and Wood (1982), Griffith (1986a, 1986b), Wilkinson (1989), and Black (1990).

Attorney Schell pursued several cases involving an apple grower's violations of the guest worker program in Hancock, Maryland. Judgements were entered against the grower in the cases of *Bernett v. Hepburn Orchards, Inc.* 106 LAB CASES (CCH) §34,913 (D. Md. 87), *Caugills v. Hepburn Orchards, Inc.* 108 LAB CASES (CCH) §35,042 (D. Md. 87), both tried in U.S. District Court, District of Maryland, and *Azor v. Hepburn Orchards* 87-JSA-1, tried before an administrative court of the U.S. Department of Labor in Hagerstown, Maryland. I interpreted at the federal trials and was an expert witness for the administrative court.

Chapter 3. Ti Rivyè: Between Home and Over There

1. Descriptions of the town of Léogane and port settlement of Ça Ira can be found in Rémy (1969), Laguerre (1976), Plotkin (1979), and Haïti, Ministère de L'Information (1983).

2. The threshold for mortuary expenditure in Ti Rivyè was apparently established in 1984 by the emigrant son and daughter of Lidya, who treated their deceased mother to a requiem in a major Port-au-Prince cathedral. They furnished transportation for scores of mourners to and from Ti Rivyè. Lidya was buried in an enormous white and royal blue concrete square, with room for others. For 13 days after the burial, the guests were treated to huge meals including enormous quantities of beef, imported beverages, and candies, as well as a dance by the (secular) Dyuba dance society, to which she had belonged. I heard from more than one source that Lidya's son and daughter dispensed $12,000 to pay for the funeral, burial, and feasting. See Murray's (1980:315) and Lowenthal's (1987:228–245) commentaries on the social meanings of funerals in rural Haiti.

3. The tempo of migrant-sponsored home building elsewhere in Haiti during the 1980s was reported by Godard (1984) and Saint-Louis (1988). This trend had an unanticipated impact on the agroforestry development project created and run by anthropologists to redress grave erosion in the Haitian hills. Gerald Murray designed the project to encourage peasants to cultivate fast-growing trees, using the same strategies they applied to produce and market cash crops, and use them to make and sell charcoal (1987). But according to Glenn Smucker (1989), who served as the project director during the mid-1980s, planters were instead using the trees for poles as well as boards for home construction.

4. While some outsiders see calculating remittances as a neutral, rational exercise, many migrants and their home families do not. Their ambivalence effectively repressed my ambitions to quantify remittances. Because I occasionally helped migrants send money, I was able to observe that the amounts migrants send home vary, depending on the migrant's relative employment security, health, and competing responsibilities in the new country of residence, and number of dependents and life crises as well as degree of commitment at

Home. Little Caterpillar sent back several thousand some years and only a few hundred other years. His relative and quasi ward, Sergo, sent nothing to his impoverished parents, even though he was their only child. Pierre had sent his mother only a few hundred dollars a year before he returned for the first time in 1991. He took out a bank loan in order to carry more than $2,000 in addition to a suitcase full of gifts. Returning home requires arriving with symbols of migration success: piles of gifts and ample cash. The value of these gifts should also be considered in assessments of the magnitudes of remittances.

5. Citibank sponsored Josh DeWind's (1987) research into migration behavior in New York City, the largest Haitian diaspora center with approximately half a million Haitians. DeWind's survey reported an average of $1,300 remitted annually by individual Haitians. (Citibank decided not to get into the business of transferring Haitians' remittances at that time.)

Chapter 4. Peasants and Hidden Proletarians in Léogane

1. The Frères Simmonds operated a coffee factory near the town of Léogane (at Bineau) that was connected by a new railway to the Port-au-Prince wharf. The coffee commerce declined in the third decade, however, in response to the world economic crisis and competition from Brazil. Prices declined by two-thirds (Moral 1961:279). A series of hurricanes also devastated the coffee trees and directly contributed to the closing of the Frères Simmonds' factory in 1929 (Rémy 1969:47).

2. I am especially grateful to Herbert Docteur (assistant director and, later, director) of the Usine and to the cartographer Nicolas Guy Jules for giving so generously of their time and sharing data and resources with me, including the factory's cadastral survey.

3. At my recommendation, Marie-Louise and several singers and drummers recorded the songs on a separate occasion. We later delivered a copy of the cassette tape to the director, who by then had been promoted to minister of agriculture. The first song was in the *yanvalo* style; the second in the *zepol* style.

Chapter 5. Discovering the African Traditions

1. Belief in avenging, inherited spirits who are central to the construction and practice of descent is not widespread in the Caribbean but it is found in other Afro-Caribbean societies that, like Haiti, were born in early defiance of European chattel slavery and had limited experience being slaves on colonial plantations. Virginia Kerns (1983) documents Garifuna's worship of ancestors (rather than spirits) who punish heirs with sickness and who, like Haitian lwa, can be propitiated with elaborate food offerings. Members of Saramaka maroon matrilineages similarly collaborate in ritual to lessen their vulnerability to their particular avenging spirits (Price 1975; Van Velzen and Van Wetering 1988).

2. Sales of garden plots financed these costs. Murray (1980) concluded that, by putting land into circulation among members of the same socioeconomic stratum, this religious innovation indirectly resolved the Kinanbwa peasants' land shortage problem. This pattern did not appear to apply to Ti Rivyè a decade later: rituals for the lwa and funerals were financed with cash, provided almost entirely by migrants.

3. His charismatic sons have obviously mastered the same skill in their respective rises to prominent ritual and political positions. One son was a sheriff; another a police agent or "chèf" without portfolio. Having observed them in various interactions with individuals from the urban elites, I can attest to their subtle ways of charmingly confirming the latter in their superiority while at the same time setting them up to discover in a nonthreatening way that their "peasant" is civilized after all.

Aiscar proudly recounted how he secured the job as the trusted manager of the property of a diplomat. When the ambassador came to survey the land he was buying from Joseph Lacombe's heirs, Aiscar pretended to be a simple, illiterate peasant, only gradually letting the diplomat discover that he was literate after all, projecting a model of the ideal competent and deferent caretaker. Diane Wolkstein (1980:184) accurately describes Aiscar as a storyteller with "a commanding presence and a strong forceful voice. He seemed to have incredible energy."

4. Some of Métraux's ([1959] 1972) text appears to have been borrowed from Mennesson-Rigaud (1951) without proper citation.

5. Descriptions of death rites are provided in Lowenthal (1987:231–252), Murray (1977:528–532), Métraux ([1959] 1972:243–265), Deren (1953:41–53), Maximilien (1945: 171–177), and Larose (1975a:112–114).

6. Lowenthal writes that several authors have mistakenly claimed that the secondary mortuary rite transforms the ancestor into a lwa (1987:361). Ancestors, who link the living members of the descent group to their spirits, are clearly distinct from lwa.

7. As for dating the introduction of the kanzo initiation elsewhere in Haiti, Herskovits (1937) writes that initiations of servitors (*ounsi*) were not being carried out in more remote Mirebalais but were taking place closer to Port-au-Prince, in the Cul-de-Sac. Dorsainvil (1931) and Maximilien (1945) describe these rites. (None of these authors specifies a location.) For later descriptions of the kanzo confinement see also Métraux ([1959] 1972:192–212) and Deren (1953: 154–155, 216–224).

8. Novices typically include females of all ages (from young girls to senior women) and an occasional male who is transgendered and performs feminine work such as marketing of produce and buying and preparing food. Métraux ([1959] 1972:69) comments that there are usually more women than men among the ranks of the ounsi and that henceforth in his book he will "speak of the [ounsi] as feminine."

9. A review of various descriptions of the African Prayer in the literature suggests that Misdor employed a version of this prayer mediating urban, congregational, and rural kin-based systems of substantiation. The temple voodoo versions do not present a genealogy linking the participants to the founder while the domestic voodoo examples do not include the temple hierarchy. See Maximilien (1945:98–101), Brown (1976:54–58), Métraux ([1959] 1972:206), and Deren (1953:208). Mennesson-Rigaud (1946) reports on a service sponsored by a trader from Miragoane who lived in the capital and belonged to an urban shrine. The *manbo* (priestess-shaman) rendered the prayer by invoking her own inherited lwa and official temple roles and relied upon the sponsor to recite names of her ancestors and her particular lwa. Mennesson-Rigaud translates *mait'bitation* (*mèt bitasyon*) as "master of the house" (or shrine), rather than founding ancestor of the family's cultivable land.

In contrast to these examples of urban performances of the African Prayer, Lowenthal's (1987:250–251) account from the rural area of Fond des Nègres is a genealogy of all of the remembered "dead" members of the descent group. Names of the lwa are not integrated into the prayer; neither are the ranks of the temple hierarchy since these formalized roles were relatively rare in the region. Larose's (1975b:506) description from a community in Léogane is, as we would expect, the closest to the Ti Rivyè version, with the important difference that a temple hierarchy is not invoked. The Bois L'Etang Prayer includes an enumeration of "all the spirits worshiped by the family" (which he defines as a cognatic descent group), "those of prominent ancestors," the "founding ancestor," and even the "French plantation owners."

Chapter 6. The Dialectic of Guinea and Magic

1. Courlander's (1939, 1960) two volumes on Haitian folklore and music include the first thorough English language analyses of ritual songs and texts. Dauphin's (1984) *Musique du Vaudou: Fonctions, Structures et Styles* is entirely devoted to the genre of ritual music. Interest in interpreting the rich and subtle song texts has occupied Métraux ([1959] 1972), Deren (1953), Brown (1976, 1987, 1989), and Laguerre (1980). Repertoires of sacred song can be found in Mennesson-Rigaud (1946) and Simpson (1940).

2. Larose (1975a:99) cites a version of this song: "When they do not need me, they call me shit. But when they do need me, they call me father."

3. Banana speculation during the first half of the century pitted foreign monopoly capital against small farmers and was a catalyst for the repressive United States Marine Corps occupation of the country. A resurgence of interest in mango production for export revisited this woeful history upon Léogane, in particular, during the 1970s and 1980s. The Bennett family, in-laws of President Jean-Claude Duvalier, appropriated a tract in Ti Rivyè to set up a plantation of the highly desirable *fransis* mango variety found only in Haiti, displacing small and large farmers alike. Mango exports tripled between 1978 and 1983, making Haiti the world's sixth largest producer, third largest in the Americas after Brazil and Mexico (World Bank 1985:29,104). One firm (ASDEM) held a monopoly on raw *fransis* mango exports. Mango puree for export is processed in a factory subsidized by USAID and the Miami-based Latin American Agribusiness Development Corporation (World Bank 1985:28; DeWind and Kinley 1986:114).

4. As for the historical depth of offerings to the foreign lwa, Odette Mennesson-Rigaud (1946) provides a detailed description of the contents, an offering whose sponsor was a Miragoane fruit vendor and ounsi (at a Port-au-Prince shrine). It included "fried eggs, *acassan* [a sweetened maize mush], fried eggs with slices of fried bananas, sweets, melons, watermelons, *ti-figues* [small bananas], pineapples, [white flour] biscuits [rolls], flour and rice pudding . . . water, *sirop de batterie* [unfermented sugarcane juice], chocolate and coffee." (The figure accompanying this text also showed a bowl of raw flour, cookies, and a bottle of Orgeat.) (Mennesson-Rigaud 1946:16–17).

Herskovits (1937:160) describes a similar dessert offering under a white canopy attached to which were chromolithographs of saints identified with the lwa blan (Mater Dolorosa, Our Mother of Perpetual Aid, St. James, St. Anthony, and St. Patrick). It included

"rice cooked in milk, a stew of rice and beans, cooked chicken—and sweetened drinks—
kola, and orange drinks among the rest, together with small drinking-glasses containing
coffee, pineapples, fig-bananas, cassava [bread] and syrup."

5. The method of preparation also figures in the classification of viv and the other main
food groups of "protein," *vyann*, and "vegetables," *legim* (Alvarez and Murray 1981:153–
156). When cornmeal is cooked in a mush, it constitutes one of the most robust viv.
When the whole ear is roasted or boiled, it descends into the class of nonnutritious
"mouth passer." Beans, classed as a viv when cooked in granular form, are assigned to the
"protein" group when prepared in a thick puree or bean sauce (*sos pwa*) that both requires
more beans and renders them a more useful protein by elimination of the bean skins.

6. See Brown's (1976:97–101) description of eating etiquette and its incorporation into
the symbolism of ritual offerings.

7. Although people sometimes confound the terms pwen and *dyab*, they are separate
concepts. A "devil" (*dyab*) is a particular kind of pwen. A client agrees to a contract with a
dyab for a specified number of years during which time the individual controls the hor-
rible powers and hot money provided by the dyab. The dyab, however, controls the next
period. One informant explained, "the devil gives you 40 years; you give it 40 years" (*dyab-
la ba ou karant an; ou ba li karant an*). What one gives the dyab is his or her own life or that
of his or her child, which is why people say of someone suspected of serving a dyab, "he
knows when he/she'll die anyway" (*la konnen ki lè lap mouri kan menm*). Differences between pwen and dyab include that the family can, indeed must one day "pick up" their
ancestor's pwen and that they send the dyab away. Furthermore one can restrain a pwen
from eating children by feeding it; in the case of dyab, "someone will pass no matter what"
(*yon moun ap pase kan menm*).

8. Larose (1975a:106) describes a variety of morally appropriate pwen: the power to
disappear (*pwen disparèt*), the power of ubiquity (*pwen deplase*), the power of immunity to
bullets (*pwen bal*), and a variety of pwen that cause increase of and simultaneously protect
gardens (*pwen jaden*), livestock (*pwen gadinay*), and market sales (*pwen lavant*).

9. I can only speculate about the catalyst for her personal crisis. The embodiment of her
distress in the form of paralysis suggests parallels with the conditions of young Viennese
women that first drew Freud's attention and inspired the founding of psychoanalysis
(Breuer and Freud [1893–95] 1950; Bernheimer 1985). Hysteria was a socially appropriate
means for young women to passively rebel against their insufferable and repressive situations. See also Farmer's (1988b) discussion of poor Haitian woman's diseases, "bad
blood," and "spoiled milk" female diseases.

10. Maximilien (1945:185–191) and Brown (1976:91–97) describe the manufacture of
"bundles" and "beating *gè*" ceremony. Thompson (1978:26–27) attributes the origin of the
bundles to Kongo practices.

11. The names of pantheons vary across Haiti. Port-au-Prince cults classify the lwa as
rada and *petwo* (Métraux [1959] 1972; Brown 1989). In Kinanbwa (fictive name of a community in the Cul-de-Sac studied by Murray [1977]), the lwa belong either to *Ginen* or
petwo. Larose (1975a:100 ff.7) has pointed out that in Léogane, the category zandò is

analogous to what is meant by petwo in Port-au-Prince. Similarly, the term *petwo*, used in Léogane to refer to an undifferentiated "nation" of spirits, corresponds to Port-au-Prince groups' use of the term *zandò*. Mennesson-Rigaud and Denis (1947:13) write that the petwo gods are divided into two groups, the *don petwo* or *petwo blan* (foreign petwo) and the zandò or Kongo Savann (Congo of the Savannah). They do not specify the location.

12. Few historical descriptions of zandò/petwo offerings go beyond the sacrificial victim, typically a pig. Maximilien (1945:156) reports a petwo/zandò offering that included rice, cornmeal mush, sweet potato, plantains, and vegetables, served in a half-calabash, sack, and basket. Mennesson-Rigaud and Denis (1947:16) provide a list of the offerings: a black and white sow, a she-goat, pair of black chickens, a female dog, guinea grass, millet, and boiled starches.

13. The relative significance and positioning of the viv distinguishes even the best Sunday meal in Ti Rivyè from meals consumed in upper-class households. While the lower classes enjoy rice, typically mixed with beans as the center of a "good" one-plate meal, the upper classes consume rice mixed with shrimp, mushrooms, or beans as the last course, after the entrée, and vegetable and starch (e.g., potatoes), before dessert.

Chapter 7. Guarantying Migrants in the Core

1. More extensive commentaries on the magic of writing and linkages between literacy, state power, and modernity are by Benjamin (1968), Godzich (1994), Scott (1998), and Taussig (1993).

Chapter 8. They Will Remember Me in the House

1. In keeping with the absence of a grammar for expressing vagueness and speculation, Creole has no passive voice. In Creole, one must attribute responsibility—or blame—for actions. In my work as a court interpreter in U.S. federal and state courts, I discovered the conflict between the dispositions of American English and Haitian Creole. I also discovered the subtle powers of the interpreter in navigating that divide. Attorneys, especially on cross-examination, typically used the passive voice to "lead" the witness. Since there is no passive voice in Creole, I, as interpreter, was handed the undeserved authority to name the agent.

I developed a strategy of asking the judge to allow me, at the beginning of the trial, to lecture briefly about Creole's lack of a passive voice. Although the attorneys heard my speeches, they were generally unable to refrain from phrasing their questions in the passive voice. I would then ask that they rephrase the given question in the active voice. Some were yet unable to do so, and the power of ascribing agency resorted to the neutral interpreter. Creole speakers tend to be extraordinarily unflappable witnesses, especially as plaintiffs under cross-examination, testifying only to what they personally heard or saw. They would typically respond to hostile questions soliciting their speculation by referring only to their own concrete observations, leaving many a frustrated, bewildered defense attorney in their wake.

2. Fisher's (1976) interpretation of the Jamaican practice of throwing words included a

valuable critique of European and American language philosophers' views of meaning. He suggested that the discourse analysts consider "communication as a *relationship* between individuals rather than a response in an individual" (1976: 232–233). Kochman (1986) similarly highlights the differences between the "white" speaker-based system where social accountability rests with the speaker and "what you say is what you mean," and a "black" "receiver-based" message system where responsibility for interpreting meaning rests with the receiver and "if the shoe fits, wear it."

3. The preference for indirection and communication by means of a sham audience also influences protocol for the conduct of "direct" interpersonal quarrels. Ideally, it takes four people to conduct a verbal dispute, two to argue and two to mediate the noise! To illustrate, A and B are antagonists. A wants to accuse B. A procures a sham (C) and, speaking directly to C in the second person ("Why did you do such and such?") indirectly accuses B. In defense, B will select his/her own sham (D, or C if no one else is available) and respond to A by speaking directly to D (see Richman 2002 and Richman and Balan-Gaubert 2001.)

4. See Larose's (1975a:89–92) discussion of rivalries between Léogane's ritual leaders and their successors.

5. There is another shrine located at the rear of the yard, which is dedicated to the cooler pantheon of lwa vodou and managed by another heir (who is an initiated gangan ason.) The physical separation of the Houses reproduces the dichotomy between the superior, precedent lwa Ginen and the inferior late-comers, the lwa zandò.

6. President Aristide wove this proverb into his rousing, call-and-response inaugural speech as a vivid motif of the entrenched class inequality in Haiti. He inverted the proverb to say, "the donkey will stop working to promote the horse" (*bourik ap sispann travay pou chwal galonen*) (*Haïti Progrès* 13–19 Feb. 1991).

7. Courlander (1960:166) defined the society as "a mutual aid association . . . exclusive . . . but not secret . . . [whose membership] corresponds roughly with the membership of a *hounfor*, or cult temple." Recent discussions of the Bizango bands claim that they function as shadow governments. Wade Davis (1985:257) argued that the Bizango functioned as the real government of Haiti and that the dictator François Duvalier was the "effective head of the secret societies." Davis attributes this idea to an essay by Michel Laguerre (Laguerre 1982). In *Voodoo and Politics in Haiti*, Laguerre (1989:127) cites Davis's research in his recommendations that the Haitian state exercise formal control over the secret societies.

8. The line between these selves is a fine one. Karen McCarthy Brown describes how people shift between them (1976:300–304, 1987:154).

Chapter 9. The Rebellion of the Pwen

1. After mentioning the term God, Little Caterpillar uses the third person pronoun, *li*. Li can mean "it," "he," or "she." I translate the word as "God" to avoid misleading connotations. I have found no evidence that Bondye is conceived of as a male, unlike lwa, who are sexed (and gendered).

2. An extended discussion of Protestant missionization, migration, and conversion can

be found in my forthcoming *The Protestant Ethic and the Spirit of Vodou* (Richman 2005). Fred Conway's (1978) dissertation documents the use of conversion as a rebellion against the lwa. See also Paul Brodwin's (1996) careful analysis of strategic denunciations of the lwa in *Medicine and Morality in Haiti*.

3. Pressoir (1942:5) does not identify this eloquent text, except to say that it was written the previous year, 1941.

4. "Gas" is similar to, but broader than, the concept in English. It can travel to any part of the body, and causes incapacitating pain. Shingles creates its own sort of gas, as well. Here is a description of shingles from *The Medical Advisor* (Time/Life: Alexandria, Va. 1997:746):

> Shingles is a reactivation of the herpes zoster virus in which painful skin blisters erupt on one side of your face or body. Typical shingles begins with a general feeling of malaise accompanied by a slight fever and a tingling sensation or pain on one side of your body. Within days a rash appears in that same area in a line along the affected nerve, and a group of small, fluid-filled blisters crops up. Typically, this occurs along your chest, abdomen, back, or face, but it may also affect your neck, limbs, or lower back. The area can be excruciatingly painful, itchy, and tender. After one or two weeks the blisters heal and form scabs, although the pain continues.
>
> The deep pain that follows after the infection has run its course is known as postherpetic neuralgia. It can continue for months or even years, especially in older people. Shingles usually occurs only once, although it has been known to recur in some people.

Epilogue

1. The tree is called Spanish plum and red mombin in the English-speaking Antilles (Pierre-Noël 1971:142).

2. Like other mobile societies stretched across national boundaries, Haitians creatively exploit their host society's demand for documentation of state-sanctioned civil unions. "Business marriage" with a U.S. citizen or resident is a widely used adaptation. (The going rate in Haiti in 2003, according to Caterpillar's niece, was $5,000.) See Garrison and Weiss's (1987) detailed and engaging account of one extended Dominican family's creative uses of marriage to relocate all of its members to New York.

Glossary

ajan—a person who connects host and home sites. Some *ajan* are independent couriers who deliver money, gifts, and correspondence. Others are associated with large money-transfer firms. Their offices also assist clients with immigration, travel, translation, taxes, and other documents.

ason—sacred bell and gourd rattle covered with beads and snake vertebrae that is used to "call the lwa." "Taking the ason" is the culminating stage in the initiation rite for priests *(gangan)*.

bitasyon—plantation; settlement; estate.

Bizango—secret society whose membership corresponds to the temple society, also called "band" *(bann)*. Bizango symbolizes defensive violence and fearless protection.

blan—foreign/foreigner; white.

Bondye—supreme being. Bondye is otiose and benevolent. Bondye is worshipped in French.

chache lavi—to pursue livelihood, to make a living.

chante—to sing; song.

demwatye—sharecrop.

Deyò—Outside, where migrants are, in contrast to Home.

Dizyèm Depatman—Haiti's external Tenth Province, located wherever Haitians live abroad, represented in Haiti by a cabinet-level minister. "The Tenth" was declared by President Aristide in 1991. The current term is "Haitians Living Abroad," and the top-ranked official is now a secretary of state.

ekri—to write, to correspond, including "writing" a cassette letter; can be used as a metonym for sending money.

eritaj—inheritance, a cognatic descent group claiming descent from a founding ancestor; the inalienable land inherited by members of that unit; can be synonymous with "family" *(fanmi* or *lafanmi).* Members of the eritaj not only share rights in the family land, but also inherit all of the unique anthropomorphic spirits, or lwa, served by the founder. These specific lwa can afflict any member of the eritaj.

fè pou—do for; reproduce. Migrants are supposed to send money to "do for" their families.

fran—authentic; purist.

gangan—male shaman; priest; sorcerer; healer.

Ginen—Guinea; Africa; signifies tradition, mutuality, and moral authority. Ginen refers to the far-off, mythical place "on the other side of the water" where the original ancestors migrated from, and to which all deceased who are honored with proper rites of passage return at death.

govi—clay jar consecrated to spirit; temporary dwelling for ancestor or lwa.

kanntè—euphemism for the sailboats, or "canoes," that were used in a massive clandestine migration to Florida. It appropriates the name of the powerful truck motor, Canter, as a wordplay about the impulsiveness of the migrants.

kanòt—canoe, small sailboat used by fishermen.

kanzo—rite of passage into the temple corps; the name of a ceremony that uses fire and special pots to sacralize persons or objects. This ceremony occurs on the seventh day of the initiation rite.

kawo—square of land equal to 3.14 acres or 1.49 hectares.

kay lwa—spirits' house; shrine; ritual performance space.

lakay—home.

lakou—compound; yard; homestead.

Lapriè Ginen—Guinea Prayer; litany honoring spirits and ancestors at beginning of rituals for the lwa.

Lòt Bò—Over There; where the migrants live.

lwa—anthropomorphic spirits who are inherited through family lines among land-holding descent groups. Lwa have power to help or harm the heirs. They come from Ginen. Their iconography blends African and European influences; some are based on Catholic saints and many have African names.

Maji—Magic, Guinea's Other; a way of being associated with wage labor, the outside, unbridled individualism, and sorcery. The agents of Magic are pwen.

maladi—affliction; sickness. The three types of maladi are attributed to (1) Bondye, (2) lwa, and (3) mounn (person [sorcerer]).

makanda—a rite and genre of music and dance in worship of the spirits of the Bizango cult.

manbo—female shaman; priestess; sorcerer; healer.

manje—food; feeding.

mò—ancestor, deceased.

mounn—person.

ounsi kanzo—a "woman" initiated into the temple corps.

prenmye mèt bitasyon—first owner of the plantation; founder of the eritaj; testator.

pwen—point; mimetic power; power through imitation. A pwen captures the essence of relations or situations. A pwen can be an underdetermined message coded in speech, song, a name or a visual image. A pwen can be a magical power that makes fast money, an appropriation of the essence of wage labor. Such pwen are manufactured and sold by sorcerers.

pwenify—word composed for this book of Creole and English meaning to treat someone as a pwen of Magic (Maji).

ranmase—to pick up; to collect; to gather. One picks up a pwen.

rit—rites in worship of a particular pantheon involving a designated genre of song, drumming, and dance.

sèvi—to serve with food and drink; the term for worship of lwa is *sèvi lwa*.

sèvis—a ceremony or ceremonies involving service of food and drink to lwa.

vann jounen—to sell the day; day labor.

viv—to live; class of high carbohydrate foods that are the backbone of the peasant diet.

vodou/vodoun—a category of Guinea spirits; rit (song, dance, drumming) performed in their worship. Outsiders applied the term to refer to the religion as a whole.

voye—to send; to throw; used in double-verb constructions for designating communication by indirect means or a messenger. Cassette correspondence requires this syntax, as in *voye di* (say or tell) and *voye mande* (ask).

voye pwen—to send or throw an indirect or coded message.

wete mò nan dlo—secondary mortuary rite of passage that transforms the deceased into an ancestor who can be accessible to heirs and placed in a govi jug. The title means "take the ancestor out of the [abysmal] waters."

zandò—an unruly category of spirit that began in Magic and gets incorporated as lower-ranked Guinea lwa.

Bibliography

Law Cases

Azor v. Hepburn Orchards 87-JSA-1, (U.S. Department of Labor).
Bernett v. Hepburn Orchards, Inc. 106 LAB CASES (CCH) §34,913 (D. Md. 1987).
Bertrand v. Jordan 672 F.SUPP. 1417 (M.D. Fla. 1987).
Caugills v. Hepburn Orchards, Inc. 108 LAB CASES (CCH) §35,042 (D. Md. 1987).
Certilus v. Peeples 101 LAB CASES (CCH) §34,587 (M.D. Fla. 84).
Haitian Refugee Center v. Civiletti 503 F.SUPP. 442 (S.D. Fla. 1980).
Louis v. Nelson 544 F.SUPP. 973 (S.D. Fla. 1982).

Memoranda and Letters

United States Embassy, Port-au-Prince
Migrant Interdiction Program, Unclassified Reports.
Numbers of Interdictees, April 24, 1984.
Numbers of Interdictees, December 3, 1984.
Report of July 22, 1983: Interdiction of Boat from Léogane.
Agence Américaine pour la Communication Internationale
Mesures prises par le Président à l'égard des étrangers en situation irrégulière. Le Président ordonne que soit interdite l'entrée aux étrangers en situation irrégulière. October 9, 1981, Bulletin 2.
Letter from U.S. Ambassador to President Jean-Claude Duvalier, Re: Interdiction Treaty, September 23, 1981.

Newspapers

Chicago Tribune
June 6, 2001   Send Money, Pay the Price. By Delroy Alexander.
July 5, 2001   Mexico Asks Emigres to Lend Hand: Expatriates Weight Appeals to Invest in Hometowns. By Oscar Avila.

Eastern Shore (Va.) News
March 6, 1985   Farmers Cited for Migrant Violations. By Cheryl Nowak.

Hagerstown (Md.) Herald-Mail
April 24, 1988   Hepburn Orchards Auctioned Off. By R. Sean McNaughton.

Haïti Progrès
February 13–19, 1991   7 Février 1991: Un Discours Historique.
n.d.   Transcript of Jean-Bertrand Aristide's "Mesaj pou Dyaspora."

Haitian Times
March 12–18, 2003   Haitians Strive for Brighter Days in Delray Beach. By Malco-
                       ville Jean-François.
November 27–December 3, 2002   Census Bureau Lowballs Haitian Count, Experts
                       Say. By Malcoville Jean-François.

Miami Herald
April 12, 1983   Lawmaker Eyes Cane-Field Job Crunch. By Randy Loftis.

New York Times
July 19, 1998   New Immigrant Tide: Shuttle Between Worlds. By Deborah
                       Sontag and Delia Dugger.
December 5, 1990   Even in the '90s Dinner Time Is Family Time.
June 23, 1992   Haiti's Split Seen at a Swearing In. By Howard French.

Orlando Sun-Sentinel
November 30–December 4, 1986   The Cutting Fields (five-part series). By Margo
                       Harakas, Robert McClure, William Gibson and John Ken-
                       nedy.
December 4, 1988   One for the Workers. By Margo Harakas.

Washington Post
August 28, 1985   Virginia to Act on Migrant Workers' Plight. By Molly Moore.

Books, Articles, Dissertations, and Recordings

Abrahams, Roger
1983   The Man-of-Words in the West Indies: Performance and the Emergence of
       Creole Culture. Baltimore: The Johns Hopkins University Press.
Ahlers, Theodore
1979   A Microeconomic Analysis of Rural-Urban Migration in Haiti. Ph.D. disser-
       tation, Fletcher School of Diplomacy.
Allman, James, and Karen Richman
1985   Migration Decision Making and Policy: The Case of Haitian International
       Migration, 1971–1984. Paper presented to the Annual Meeting of the Popula-
       tion Association of America, March 28–30, Boston.
Alvarez, Maria, and Gerald Murray
1981   Socialization for Scarcity: Child Feeding Beliefs and Practices in a Haitian
       Village. Report submitted to USAID/Haiti, Port-au-Prince.

Anglade, Georges

1981   L'Espace Haïtien. Montreal: Editions des Alizés.

Appadurai, Arjun

1986   Introduction: Commodities and the Politics of Value. *In* The Social Life of Things: Commodities in Cultural Perspective. Arjun Appadurai, ed. Pp. 3–65. Cambridge: Cambridge University Press.

1990   Disjuncture and Difference in the Global Cultural Economy. Public Culture 2(2):1–24.

1991   Global Ethnoscapes: Notes and Queries for a Transnational Anthropology. *In* Recapturing Anthropology: Working in the Present. Richard Fox, ed. Pp. 191–210. Santa Fe: School of American Research Press.

Appadurai, Arjun, ed.

1986   The Social Life of Things: Commodities in Cultural Perspective. Cambridge: Cambridge University Press.

Appadurai, Arjun, and Carol Breckenridge

1988   Editor's Comments. Public Culture 1(1):1–4.

Averill, Gage

1997   A Day for the Hunter, a Day for the Prey: Popular Music and Power in Haiti. Chicago: University of Chicago Press.

Bakhtin, Mikhail

1971   Discourse Typology in Prose. In Readings in Russian Poetics: Formalist and Structuralist Views. Matejka, Ladislav and Krystyna Pomorska, eds. Pp. 176–198. Cambridge: MIT Press.

Balch, Emily Greene

1927   Occupied Haiti. New York: Writers Publishing.

Barnett, Steve, and Martin Silverman

1979   Ideology and Everyday Life: Anthropology, Neomarxist Thought, and the Problem of Ideology and the Social Whole. Ann Arbor: University of Michigan Press.

Barry, D. Marshall

1989   The Adverse Impact of Immigration on Florida's Farmworkers. Miami: Florida International University, Center for Labor Research and Studies, Occasional Paper no. 3.

Barry, Tom, Beth Wood, and Deb Preusch

1984   The Other Side of Paradise: Foreign Control in the Caribbean. New York: Grove Press.

Basch, Linda, Nina Glick-Schiller, and Cristina Szanton Blanc

1994   Nations Unbound: Transnational Projects and the Deterritorialized Nation-State. New York: Gordon Breach.

Bastien, Rémy

1961   Haitian Rural Family Organization. Social and Economic Studies 10(4):478–510.

Bauman, Richard

[1977] 1984   Verbal Art as Performance. Prospect Heights, Ill.: Waveland Press.

Beldekas, John, Jane Teas, and James R. Herbert

1986   African Swine Fever and Aids. Letter to The Lancet, March 8:564–565.

Benjamin, Walter
1968   Illuminations, edited with an introduction by Hannah Arendt. Harry Zohn, trans. New York: Schocken Books.
Berman, Morris
1981   The Reenchantment of the World. Ithaca: Cornell University Press.
Bernheimer, Charles
1985   Introduction: Part One. In In Dora's Case. Charles Bernheimer and Clair Kahane, eds. Pp. 1–18. New York: Columbia University Press.
Besson, Jean
1984   Family Land and Caribbean Society: Toward an Ethnography of Afro-Caribbean Peasantries. In Perspectives on Caribbean Regional Identity. Elizabeth Thomas-Hope, ed. Pp. 57–83. Liverpool: University of Liverpool, Centre for Latin American Studies, Monograph Series, no. 11.
Bhabha, Homi
1994   The Location of Culture. London: Routledge.
Black, Stephanie
1990   H-2 Worker. Documentary film. Produced, directed, and distributed by Stephanie Black.
Blandford, Andrew
2002   By Ignoring Island's Suffering, U.S.'s Frivolous Haiti Policy Invites Approaching Catastrophe. Washington, D.C.: Council on Hemispheric Affairs.
Bohannon, Paul
1955   Some Principles of Exchange and Investment among the Tiv. American Anthropologist 57:60–69.
Boruchoff, Judith
1998   The Road to Transnationalism: Reconfiguring the Spaces of Community and State in Guerrero, Mexico and Chicago. Center for Latin American Studies, Mexican Studies Program, University of Chicago.
Boswell, Thomas
1982   The New Haitian Diaspora. Caribbean Review 11(1):18–21.
Brana-Shute, Rosemary, and Gary Brana-Shute
1982   The Magnitude and Impact of Remittances in the Eastern Caribbean: A Research Note. In Return Migration and Remittances: Developing a Caribbean Perspective. William Stinner, Klaus de Albuquerque, and Roy Bryce-Laporte, eds. Pp. 267–290. Washington, D.C.: Smithsonian Institution, Research Institute on Immigration and Ethnic Studies, Occasional Papers no. 3.
Bretell, Caroline
2003   Anthropology and Migration: Essays on Transnationalism, Ethnicity, and Identity. Walnut Creek, Calif.: Alta Mira.
Breuer, Joseph, and Sigmund Freud
[1893–95] 1950   Studies on Hysteria. James Strachey, trans. New York: Basic Books.
Brodwin, Paul
1991   Political Contest and Moral Claim: Religious Pluralism and Healing in a Haitian Village. Ph.D. dissertation, Harvard University.

1996 Medicine and Morality in Haiti. Cambridge: Cambridge University Press.

Brown, Karen McCarthy

1976 The *Vèvè* of Haitian Vodou: A Structural Analysis of Visual Imagery. Ph.D. dissertation, Temple University.

1987 Alourdes: A Case Study of Moral Leadership in Haitian Vodou. *In* Saints and Virtues. J. Hawley, ed. Pp. 144–167. Berkeley: University of California Press.

1989 Systematic Remembering, Systematic Forgetting: Ogou in Haiti. *In* Africa's Ogun: Old World and New. S. Barnes, ed. Pp. 65–89. Bloomington: Indiana University Press.

1991 Mama Lola: A Vodou Priestess in New York. Berkeley: University of California Press.

1997 Presentation to Panel on Translocation and Transcendence: Moving Religious Objects from Sacred Space to Museum Space. Haitian Studies Association, Detroit. October.

Bryce-Laporte, Roy

1979 The United States' Role in Caribbean Migration: Background to the Problem. *In* Caribbean Immigration to the United States. Roy Bryce-Laporte and Delores Mortimer, eds. Pp. 1–15. Washington, D.C.: Smithsonian Institution, Research Institute on Immigration and Ethnic Studies, Occasional Papers no. 1.

1985 Caribbean Immigrations and Their Implications for the United States. Pamphlet, 33 pp. Focus: Caribbean (Series). Sidney Mintz and Sally Price, eds. Washington, D.C.: Woodrow Wilson International Center for Scholars.

Buchanan, Susan

1979a Haitian Women in New York City. Migration Today 7(4):19–39.

1979b Language Identity: Haitians in New York City. International Migration Review 13(2):298–313.

1980 Scattered Seeds: The Meaning of the Migration for Haitians in New York City. Ph.D. dissertation, New York University.

1982 Haitian Emigration: The Perspective from South Florida and Haiti. Unpublished report submitted to USAID.

Carnegie, Charles

1987 A Social Psychology of Caribbean Migrations: Strategic Flexibility in the West Indies. *In* The Caribbean Exodus. Barry Levine, ed. Pp. 32–43. New York: Praegar.

Carsten, Janet

1989 Cooking Money: Gender and the Symbolic Transformation of Means of Exchange in a Malay Fishing Community. *In* Money and the Morality of Exchange. Jonathan Parry and Maurice Bloch, eds. Pp. 117–141. Cambridge: Cambridge University Press.

Castles, Stephen, and Godula Kosack

1985 Immigrant Workers and Class Structure in Europe. Oxford: Oxford University Press.

Castor, Suzy

1971   La Occupación Norteamericana de Haití y sus Consecuencias (1915–1934). Mexico City: Ediciones Siglo Veintiuno.

Certeau, Michel de

1984   The Practice of Everyday Life. Steven Rendall, trans. Berkeley: University of California Press.

Chaffurin, Louis

1954   Le Parfait Secrétaire: Correspondance Usuelle, Commerciale et D'Affaires. Paris: Librairie Larousse.

Chaney, Elsa

1987   The Context of Caribbean Migration. *In* Caribbean Life in New York City: Sociocultural Dimensions. Constance Sutton and Elsa Chaney, eds. Pp. 3–30. New York: Center for Migration Studies.

Charles, Carolle

1990   A Transnational Dialectic of Race, Class and Ethnicity: Patterns of Identities and Forms of Consciousness among Haitian Migrants in New York City. Ph.D. dissertation, State University of New York, Binghamton.

1992   Transnationalism in the Construct of Haitian Migrants' Racial Categories of Identity in New York City. *In* Towards a Transnational Perspective on Migration: Race, Class, Ethnicity and Nationalism Reconsidered. Nina Glick-Schiller, Linda Basch, and Cristina Blanc-Szanton, eds. Pp. 101–125. New York: New York Academy of Sciences.

Chartier, Roger

1997a   Introduction: An Originary Kind of Writing: Model Letters and Letter-Writing in Ancien Régime France. *In* Correspondence: Models of Letter-Writing from the Middle Ages to the Nineteenth Century. Roger Chartier, Alain Boureau, and Cécile Dauphin, eds. Christopher Woodall, trans. Pp. 1–23. Princeton: Princeton University Press.

1997b   Secrétaires for the People? *In* Correspondence: Models of Letter-Writing from the Middle Ages to the Nineteenth Century. Roger Chartier, Alain Boureau, and Cécile Dauphin, eds. Christopher Woodall, trans. Pp. 59–111. Princeton: Princeton University Press.

Chesnut, R. Andrew

2003   Competitive Spirits: Latin America's New Religious Economy. New York: Oxford University Press.

Chierici, Rose-Marie

1985   *Demele*: "Making It," Migration and Adaptation among Haitian Boat People in the United States. Ph.D. dissertation, University of Rochester.

Clarke, Edith

1957   My Mother who Fathered Me. London: George Allen and Unwin.

Clifford, James

1997   Routes: Travel and Translation in the Late Twentieth Century. Cambridge: Harvard University Press.

Colas, Willem

1981   "Canter." Recorded on Gemini All Stars de Ti Manno by Ti Manno and the Gemini All Stars. Recorded by Robert Denis at Audioteck of Port-au-Prince, distributed by Musique des Antilles Records.

Comaroff, Jean

1985   Body of Power, Spirit of Resistance. The Culture and History of a South African People. Chicago: University of Chicago.

Conway, Frederick

1978   Pentecostalism in the Context of Haitian Religion and Health Practice. Ph.D. dissertation, American University.

Cordero-Guzmán, Héctor, Robert Smith, and Ramón Grosfoguel, eds.

2001   Migration, Transnationalism, and Race in a Changing New York. Philadelphia: Temple University Press.

Coreil, Marie

1979   Disease Prognosis and Resource Allocation in a Haitian Mountain Community. Lexington: University of Kentucky.

Cornelius, Wayne

1990   Labor Migration to the United States: Development Outcomes and Alternatives in Mexican Sending Communities. Washington, D.C.: Commission for the Study of International Migration and Cooperative Economic Development, Working Papers no. 38.

Cornelius, Wayne, Leo Chávez, and Jorge Castro

1982   Mexican Immigrants and Southern California: A Summary of Current Knowledge. San Diego: University of California, Center for U.S. Mexican Studies, Research Report Series 36.

Courlander, Harold

1939   Haiti Singing. Chapel Hill: University of North Carolina Press.

1960   The Drum and the Hoe: Life and Lore of the Haitian People. Berkeley: University of California Press.

Danticat, Edwidge, ed.

2001   The Butterfly's Way: Voices from the Haitian Dyaspora in the United States. New York: Soho Press.

Dauphin, Claude

1984   Musique du Vaudou: Fonctions, Structures et Styles. Québec: Éditions Naaman.

Davenport, William

1961   The Family System of Jamaica. Social and Economic Studies 10(4):420–454.

Davis, Wade

1985   The Serpent and the Rainbow. New York: Simon and Schuster.

Debien, Gabriel

1947   Aux Origines de Quelques Plantations des Quartiers de Léogane et du Cul-de-Sac. Revue de la Société d'Histoire et de Géographie d'Haïti 18(64):11–80.

Delatour, Leslie

1983   The Centrifugal Sugar Sector in Haiti. Unpublished report submitted to USAID, Port-au-Prince.

Deren, Maya

1953   Divine Horsemen: The Living Gods of Haiti. New Paltz, N.Y.: McPherson.

DeSipio, Louis

2000   Sending Money Home . . . For Now: Remittances and Immigrant Adaptation in the United States. Washington, D.C.: Working Papers of the Inter-American Dialogue and Tomás Rivera Policy Institute.

DeWind, Josh

1987   The Remittances of Haitian Immigrants in New York City. Unpublished final report prepared for Citibank. In files of author.

DeWind, Josh, and David Kinley

1986   AIDing Migration: The Impact of International Development Assistance on Haiti. New York: Columbia University Center for the Social Sciences, Immigration Research Program.

Diederich, Bernard

1984   Swine Fever Ironies: The Slaughter of the Haitian Black Pig. Caribbean Review 14(1):16–19, 41.

Dinerman, Ina

1978   Patterns of Adaptation among Households of U.S.-Bound Migrants from Michoacán, México. International Migration Review 12(4):485–501.

Dixon, Marlene, Susanne Jonas, and Ed McCaughan

1982   Reindustrialization and the Transnational Labor Force in the United States Today. In The New Nomads: From Immigrant Labor to Transnational Working Class. Marlene Dixon and Susanne Jonas, eds. Pp. 101–115. San Francisco: Synthesis.

Dominguez, Virginia

1975   From Neighbor to Stranger: The Dilemma of Caribbean Peoples in the U.S. New Haven: Yale University Antilles Research Program.

Dorsainvil, Justin

1931   Vodou et Névrose: Etude Médico-Sociologique. Port-au-Prince: Imprimerie de l'Etat.

Douglas, Mary, and Baron Isherwood

1979   The World of Goods: Towards an Anthropology of Consumption. New York: Norton.

Duperval, Blaise

1983   La Canne à Sucre: Son Origine, Sa Culture et Son Industrie. Port-au-Prince: Henri Deschamps.

Dupuy, Alex

1990   Haiti in the World Economy: Class, Race, and Underdevelopment Since 1700. Boulder, Colo.: Westview Press.

Durkheim, Emile

[1915] 1965   The Elementary Forms of the Religious Life. John Swain, trans. New York: Free Press.

Ebaugh, Helen R., and Janet S. Chafetz

2000   Religion and the New Immigrants: Continuities and Adaptations. Walnut
        Creek, Calif.: Alta Mira Press.

Evans-Pritchard, E. E.

[1956] 1974   Nuer Religion. New York: Oxford University Press.

Farmer, Paul

1988a   Blood, Sweat and Baseballs: Haiti in the West Atlantic System. Dialectical
        Anthropology 13:83–99.

1988b   Bad Blood, Spilled Milk: Bodily Fluids as Moral Barometers in Rural Haiti.
        American Ethnologist 15(1):62–83.

1990   Aids and Accusation: Haiti and the Geography of Blame. Ph.D. dissertation,
        Harvard University.

2002   Haiti: Unjust Aid Embargo During Health Emergency. Washington, D.C.:
        Council on Hemispheric Affairs.

Ferguson, Charles

1959   Diglossia. Word 15:325–340.

Fick, Carolyn

1990   The Making of Haiti: The Saint Domingue Revolution from Below. Knoxville:
        University of Tennessee Press.

Fisher, Lawrence

1976   "Dropping Remarks" and the Barbadian Audience. American Ethnologist 3(2):
        227–242.

Foster, George

1967   Peasant Society and the Image of the Limited Good. In Peasant Society: A
        Reader. Jack Potter, May Diaz, and George Foster, eds. Pp. 300–323. Boston:
        Little, Brown.

Fouron, Georges

1985   Patterns of Adaptation of Haitian Immigrants of the 1970's in New York City.
        Ed.D. dissertation, Columbia University.

1990   AIDS and the Implementation of a Transnationalist Identity Among Haitians
        in New York. Paper presented to the Panel on Transnational Identities and
        Cultural Strategies: The Afro-Caribbean and the United States. 89th Annual
        Meeting of the American Anthropological Association, Nov. 28–Dec. 2, New
        Orleans.

Freeman, Gary

1987   Caribbean Migration to Britain and France: From Assimilation to Selection.
        In The Caribbean Exodus. Barry Levine, ed. Pp. 185–203. New York: Praeger.

Garrison, Vivian, and Carol Weiss

1987   Dominican Family Networks and United States Immigration Policy: A Case
        Study. In Caribbean Life in New York City: Sociocultural Dimensions. Con-
        stance Sutton and Elsa Chaney, eds. Pp. 220–238. New York: Center for Mi-
        gration Studies.

Geertz, Clifford

1973   Religion as a Cultural System. In The Interpretation of Cultures: Selected
        Essays. Pp. 87–125. New York: Basic Books.

Geffert, Hannah

n.d.   Tell Them to Stay Home. Unpublished manuscript.

1985   Picking. A Play. Performed at New Dramatists. New York, Dec. 14–15, 1984. Lupa Productions.

Gell, Alfred

1986   Newcomers to the World of Goods: Consumption among the Muria Gonds. *In* The Social Life of Things: Commodities in Cultural Perspective. Arjun Appadurai, ed. Pp. 110–140. Cambridge: Cambridge University Press.

Georges, Eugenia

1990   The Making of a Transnational Community: Migration, Development and Cultural Change in the Dominican Republic. New York: Columbia University Press.

Gerlach, Luther, and Virginia Hine

1968   Five Factors Crucial to the Growth and Spread of a Modern Religious Movement. Journal for the Scientific Study of Religion 7:23–40.

Glick, Nina

1975   The Formation of a Haitian Ethnic Group. Ph.D. dissertation, Columbia University.

Glick-Schiller, Nina, Josh DeWind, Marie-Lucie Brutus, Carolle Charles, Georges Fouron, and Antoine Thomas

1987   All in the Same Boat? Unity and Diversity in Haitian Organizing in New York. *In* Caribbean Life in New York City: Sociocultural Dimensions. Constance Sutton and Elsa Chaney, eds. Pp. 182–201. New York: Center for Migration Studies.

Glick-Schiller, Nina, and Georges Fouron

1990   "Everywhere We Go We Are in Danger": Ti Manno and the Emergence of a Haitian Transnational Identity. American Ethnologist 17(2):329–347.

2001   Georges Woke Up Laughing: Long Distance Nationalism and the Haitian Search for Home. Chapel Hill: Duke University Press.

Glick-Schiller, Nina, Linda Basch, and Cristina Blanc-Szanton

1992   Transnationalism: A New Analytic Framework for Understanding Migration. *In* Towards a Transnational Perspective on Migration: Race, Ethnicity, and Nationalism Reconsidered. Nina Glick-Schiller, Linda Basch, and Cristina Blanc-Szanton, eds. Pp. 1–24. New York: New York Academy of Sciences.

Gmelch, George

1992   Double Passage: The Lives of Caribbean Migrants Abroad and Back Home. Ann Arbor: University of Michigan Press.

Godard, Henri

1984   L'Influence des Transferts de Capitaux des Haïtiens Expatriés sur les Mutations du Paysage Urbain de Port-au-Prince. Collectif Paroles 27:5–11.

Godzich, Vlad

1994   The Culture of Literacy. Cambridge: Harvard University Press.

Gold, Herbert

1991   Best Nightmare on Earth: A Life in Haiti. New York: Touchstone.

Goldin, Liliana, ed.

1999   Identities on the Move: Transnational Processes in North America and the Caribbean Basin. Albany: State University of New York, Institute for Meso-american Studies.

Gould, J. W.

1916   General Report on Haiti to Messrs. Breed, Elliott and Harrison and Messrs. P. W. Chapman and Company. Unpublished report.

Gouldner, Diane

1985   Caught in the LSC Cross Fire. The American Lawyer. December: 83–89.

Grasmuck, Sherri, and Patricia Pessar

1991   Between Two Islands: Dominican International Migration. Berkeley: University of California Press.

Gregory, Christopher

1980   Gifts to Men and Gifts to God: Gift Exchange and Capital Accumulation in Contemporary Papua. Man 15(4):626–652.

1982   Gifts and Commodities. London: Academic Press.

Griffith, David

1985   Women, Remittances and Reproduction. American Ethnologist 12(4):676–690.

1986a   Social Organizational Obstacles to Capital Accumulation among Returning Migrants: The British West Indies Temporary Alien Labor Program. Human Organization 45(1):34–42.

1986b   Peasants in Reserve: Temporary West Indian Labor in the U.S. Farm Labor Market. International Migration Review 20(4):875–898.

Griffith, David, Alex Stepick, Karen Richman, Guillermo Grenier, Ed Kissam, Allan Burns, and Jeronimo Camposeco

2001   Another Day in the Diaspora: Changing Ethnic Landscapes in South Florida. Proceedings of the Meetings of the Southern Anthropological Society. Pp. 82–93. Athens: University of Georgia Press.

Haïti, Institut Haïtien de Statistique et d'Informatique (IHSI)

1980   Analyse du Recensement de 1971.

1981   Etude de la Migration Intèrne, Phase 1: Les Données Démographiques.

1983a   Régulation de la Croissance Démographique Selon la Pression de la Population en Haïti (d'Apres les Recensements de 1950 et 1982).

1983b   Etude de la Migration Intèrne, Phase 2: Aspects Socio-Economiques

1983c   Analyse de Quelques Indicateurs Démographiques Tirés des Recensements de 1950, 1971 et 1982.

1984   Estimation de la Migration Internationale en Haïti au Cours de la Période 1971–1982 (Youssef Courbage, statistician).

Haïti, Ministère de L'Information et des Relations Publiques.

1983   Connaissons Nos Communes: Léogane. 3(29):24–33.

Haiti Insight: A Bulletin on Refugee and Human Rights Affairs

1992   3(5–7), 4(1), October–June.

Haitian Television Network Video Club

1990   Mouvement Lavalas. Miami. VHS.

Hannerz, Ulf

1989a   Notes on the Global Ecumene. Public Culture 1(2):66–75.

1989b   Culture Between Center and Periphery: Toward a Macroanthropology. Ethnos 3–4:200–216.

Heinl, Robert, and Nancy Heinl

1978   Written in Blood. The Story of the Haitian People, 1492–1971. Boston: Houghton Mifflin.

Heppel, Monica

1982   Harvesting the Crops of Others: Migrant Farm Labor on the Eastern Shore of Virginia. Ph.D. dissertation, American University.

Herskovits, Melville

1937   Life in a Haitian Valley. New York: Knopf.

Hocart, A. M.

[1936] 1970   Kings and Councillors: An Essay on the Comparative Anatomy of Human Society. Chicago: University of Chicago Press.

Hooper, Michael

1987   Model Underdevelopment. NACLA Report on the Americas 11(3):32–39.

Huxley, Francis

1966   The Invisibles: Voodoo Gods in Haiti. New York: McGraw Hill.

Jaffee, JoAnn

1987   The Haitian State and Agricultural Development. Paper presented to the Panel on Haiti, Continuity and Change. 86th Annual Meeting of the American Anthropological Association, 18–22 November, Chicago.

Kearney, Michael

1991   Borders and Boundaries of State and Self at the End of Empire. Journal of Historical Sociology 4(1):52–74.

1995   The Local and the Global: The Anthropology of Globalization and Transnationalism. Annual Review of Anthropology 24:547–565.

Kearney, Michael, and Carole Nagengast

1989   Anthropological Perspectives on Transnational Communities in Rural California. Davis: California Institute for Rural Studies, Working Group on Farm Labor and Rural Poverty, Working Paper no. 3:1–42.

Keely, Charles, and Bao Nga Tran

1989   Remittances from Labor Migration: Evaluations, Performances and Implications. International Migration Review 23(3):500–525.

Keene, R.

1991   Death by Firelight. Leatherneck. 74(2):22–30.

Kerns, Virginia

1983   Women and the Ancestors: Black Carib Kinship and Ritual. Urbana: University of Illinois Press.

Kochman, Thomas

1981   Black and White Styles in Conflict. Chicago: University of Chicago Press.

1986   Strategic Ambiguity in Black Speech Genres: The Reality of Social Account-
        ability. Text 6(2):153–170.
Kopytoff, Igor
1986   The Cultural Biography of Things. *In* The Social Life of Things: Commodi-
        ties in Cultural Perspective. Arjun Appadurai, ed. Pp. 64–94. Cambridge:
        Cambridge University Press.
Laguerre, Michel
1976   L'Adaptation Socio-Economique des Pecheurs Haïtiens: Le Village de Ça Ira.
        Montreal: Presses de l'Université de Montréal.
1978a   The Impact of Migration on the Haitian Family and Household Organiza-
        tion. *In* Family and Kinship in Middle America and the Caribbean. Arnaud F.
        Marks and Renée A. Römer, eds. Pp. 446–481. Leiden: Department of Carib-
        bean Studies, Royal Institute of Linguistics and Anthropology.
1978b   Ticouloute and His Kinfolk: The Study of a Haitian Extended Family. *In* The
        Extended Family in Black Societies. Demitri Shimkin, Edith Shimkin, and
        Dennis Frate, eds. Pp. 407–445. The Hague: Mouton.
1980   Voodoo Heritage. Beverley Hills: Sage.
1982   Bizango: A Voodoo Secret Society in Haiti. *In* Secrecy: A Cross-Cultural Per-
        spective. Stanton Tefft, ed. Pp. 147–160. New York: Human Sciences.
1984   American Odyssey: Haitians in New York City. Ithaca: Cornell University Press.
1989   Voodoo and Politics in Haiti. New York: St. Martin's Press.
1998   Diasporic Citizenship: Haitian Americans in Transnational America. New
        York: St. Martin's Press.
Lancet, The Correspondence. April, May, June, July 1983; March, June, October 1986.
Larose, Serge
1975a   The Meaning of Africa in Haitian Vodu. *In* Symbol and Sentiment. J. Lewis,
        ed. Pp. 85–116. London: Academic Press.
1975b   The Haitian Lakou, Land, Family and Ritual. *In* Family and Kinship in Middle
        America and the Caribbean. A. Marks and R. Romer, eds. Pp. 482–512. Cura-
        çao: Institute of Higher Studies and Leiden: Royal Institute of Linguistics and
        Anthropology.
Lebigre, Jean-Michel
1974   La Canne à Sucre dans la Plaine du Cul-de-Sac. Doctorat de Troisième Cycle,
        Université de Bordeaux.
Lemoine, Maurice
1983   Bitter Sugar: Slaves Today in the Caribbean. Andrea Johnston, trans. Chicago:
        Banner Press.
Lessinger, Johanna
1992   Investing or Going Home? A Transnational Strategy among Indian Immi-
        grants in the United States. *In* Towards a Transnational Perspective on M-
        igration: Race, Ethnicity, and Nationalism Reconsidered. Nina Glick-Schiller,
        Linda Basch, and Cristina Blanc-Szanton, eds. Pp. 53–80. New York: New
        York Academy of Sciences.

Lévi-Strauss, Claude

1967 The Savage Mind. Chicago: University of Chicago Press.

1969 The Elementary Structures of Kinship. James Bell and John von Sturmer, trans. Boston: Beacon Press.

Levitt, Peggy

2001 The Transnational Villagers. Berkeley: University of California Press.

Locher, Uli

1977 Rural-Urban Migration and the Alleged Demise of the Extended Family: The Haitian Case in Comparative Perspective. Montreal: McGill University, Center for Developing Area Studies, Working Paper no. 20.

1978 The Fate of Migrants in Urban Haiti: A Survey of Three Port-au-Prince Neighborhoods. Ph.D. dissertation, Yale University.

Loederer, Richard

1935 Voodoo Fire in Haiti. New York: Literary Guild.

Loescher, G., and John Scanlan

1984 U.S. Foreign Policy and Its Impact on Refugee Flow from Haiti. New York: New York University, New York Research Program in Inter-American Affairs, Occasional Paper no. 42.

Lowenthal, Ira

1978 Ritual Performance and Religious Experience: A Service for the Gods in Southern Haiti. Journal of Anthropological Research 34(3):392–414.

1984 Labor, Sexuality and the Conjugal Contract in Rural Haiti. In Haiti—Today and Tomorrow: An Interdisciplinary Study. George Foster and Albert Valdman, eds. Pp. 15–33. Lanham, Md.: University Press of America.

1987 "Marriage Is 20, Children Are 21": The Cultural Construction of Conjugality and the Family in Rural Haiti. Ph.D. dissertation, Johns Hopkins University.

Lundahl, Mats

1983 The Haitian Economy: Man, Land and Markets. New York: St. Martin's Press.

Maguire, Robert

1990 Haiti's Emerging Peasant Movement. Cimarrón 2(3):28–44.

1991 The Peasantry and Political Change in Haiti. Caribbean Affairs 4(2):1–18.

Mahler, Sarah

1995 American Dreaming. Princeton: Princeton University Press.

Maine, Sir Henry

[1884] 1970 Ancient Law. Reprint of Tenth Edition. Gloucester, Mass.: Peter Smith.

Manuel, Peter

1993 Cassette Culture: Popular Music and Technology in Northern India. Chicago: University of Chicago Press.

Marshall, Dawn

1979 "The Haitian Problem": Illegal Migration to the Bahamas. Mona, Jamaica: University of the West Indies, Institute of Social and Economic Research.

1982 Haitian Migration to the Bahamas. In Contemporary Caribbean: A Sociological Reader, 1. Susan Craig, ed. Pp. 110–127. Maracas, Trinidad and Tobago: College Press.

1985 Migration and Development in the Eastern Caribbean. *In* Migration and Development in the Caribbean: The Unexplored Connection. Robert A. Pastor, ed. Pp. 91–116. Boulder, Colo.: Westview Press.

Marshall, Paule

[1959] 1981 Brown Girl, Brownstones. New York: Feminist Press.

Martinez, Samuel

1989 Risk, Reward and Power in the Household: Rural Haitian Women's Perceptions of Male Seasonal Migration. Paper presented to the Panel on Migrants and Refugees, 88th Annual Meeting of the American Anthropological Association, November 15–19, Washington, D.C.

1991 Labor Circulation and Peasant Social Reproduction: Haitian Migrants and Dominican Sugar Plantations. Ph.D. dissertation, Johns Hopkins University.

Marx, Karl

[1857–58] 1973 Grundrisse. Martin Nicolaus, trans. New York: Vintage.

[1843–44] 1975 The Early Writings. Rodney Livingstone, trans. New York: Vintage.

[1867] 1977 Capital, vol. 1. Ben Fowkes, trans. New York: Vintage.

Massey, Douglas, Rafael Alarcón, Jorge Durand, and Humberto González

1987 Return to Aztlan: The Social Processes of International Migration from Western Mexico. Berkeley: University of California Press.

Mauss, Marcel

1967 The Gift: Forms and Functions of Exchange in Archaic Societies. Ian Cunnison, trans. New York: Norton.

Maximilien, Louis

1945 Le Vodou Haïtien: Rite Radas-Canzo. Port-au-Prince: Imprimerie de l'Etat.

Mayard, Louise, and Adeline Moravia

n.d. Tropical Cooking. Port-au-Prince: Henri Deschamps.

McAlister, Elizabeth

1998 Vodou and Catholicism in the Age of Transnationalism: The Madonna of 115th Street, Revisted. *In* Gatherings in Diaspora: Religious Communities and the New Immigration. R. Stephen Warner, ed. Pp. 123–160. Philadelphia: Temple University Press.

2002 Rara: Vodou, Power and Performance in Haiti and Its Diaspora. Berkeley: University of California Press.

McClellan, James III

1992 Colonialism and Science: Saint Domingue in the Old Regime. Baltimore: Johns Hopkins University Press.

McCoy, Terry, and Charles Wood

1982 Caribbean Workers in the Florida Sugar Cane Industry. Gainesville: University of Florida, Center for Latin American Studies, Caribbean Migration Program, Occasional Paper no. 2.

Meillassoux, Claude

1972 From Reproduction to Production: A Marxist Approach to Economic Anthropology. Economy and Society 1(1):93–105.

Mennesson-Rigaud, Odette

1946   The Feasting of the Gods in Haitian Vodu. Alfred Métraux, trans. Primitive
        Man 19(1–2):1–59.

1951   Noël Vodou en Haïti. Présence Africaine 12:37–59.

Mennesson-Rigaud, Odette, and Lorimer Denis

1947   Cérémonie en l'Honneur de Marinette. Bulletin du Bureau d'Ethnologie
        3:13–21.

Métraux, Alfred

1946   Introduction to the Feasting of the Gods in Haitian Vodu, by Odette Men-
        nesson-Rigaud. Alfred Métraux, trans. Primitive Man 19(1–2):1–7.

1953a   Médecine et Vodou en Haïti. Acta Tropica 10:28–68.

1953b   Vodou et Protestantisme. Revue de l'histoire des Religions 144:198–216.

1954–55 Le Noël Vodou en Haïti. Bulletin de la Société Neuchâteloise de Géographie
        51:95–118.

[1959] 1972   Voodoo in Haiti. Hugo Charteris, trans. New York: Schocken Books.

Métraux, Alfred, E. Berrouet, Jean Comhaire-Sylvain, and Suzanne Comhaire Sylvain

1951   Making a Living in Marbial Valley. Paris: UNESCO Occasional Papers in Edu-
        cation, no. 10.

Miller, Jake

1984   The Plight of Haitian Refugees. New York: Praeger.

Millspaugh, Arthur

1931   Haiti Under American Control (1915–1930). Boston: World Peace Foundation.

Mintz, Sidney

1960   Worker in the Cane. New Haven: Yale.

1961   Pratik: Haitian Personal Economic Relationships. Proceedings of the 1960
        Annual Spring Meeting of the American Ethnological Society. V. Garfield, ed.
        Pp. 54–63. Seattle: American Ethnological Society.

1966   Introduction to The Haitian People, by James Leyburn. New Haven: Yale Uni-
        versity Press.

1973   A Note on the Definition of Peasantries. Journal of Peasant Studies 1(1):91–106.

1974a   Caribbean Transformations. Chicago: Aldine.

1974b   The Rural Proletariat and the Problem of Rural Proletarian Consciousness.
        Journal of Peasant Studies 1(3):291–325.

1985   Sweetness and Power: The Place of Sugar in Modern History. New York: Vi-
        king.

Mitchell-Kernan, Claudia

1972   Signifying, Loud-Talking and Marking. In Rappin' and Stylin' Out: Commu-
        nication in Urban Black America. Thomas Kochman, ed. Pp. 315–335. Ur-
        bana: University of Illinois Press.

Moral, Paul

1959   L'Economie Haïtien. Port-au-Prince: Imprimerie de L'Etat.

1961   Le Paysan Haïtien: Etude sur la Vie Rurale en Haïti. Paris: Maisonneuve and
        Larose.

Moreau de St. Méry, Médéric-Louis-Elie

[1791] 1958   Description Topographique, Physique, Civile, Politique, et Historique de la Partie Français de l'Isle de Saint-Domingue, vol. 2. Paris: Librarie Larose.

Morgan, Dan

1979   Merchants of Grain. New York: Viking.

Murphy, Martin

1984   Semejanzas y Diferencias en la Utilización de la Mano de Obra en las Plantaciones Azucareras de la República Dominicana. Ciencia y Sociedad 9(2):242–285.

Murray, Gerald

1976   Women in Perdition: Ritual Fertility Control in Haiti. *In* Culture, Natality and Family Planning. John Marshall and Steven Polgar, eds. Pp. 59–78. Chapel Hill: University of North Carolina Press.

1977   The Evolution of Haitian Peasant Land Tenure. Ph.D. dissertation, Columbia University.

1980   Population Pressure, Land Tenure and Voodoo: The Economics of Haitian Peasant Ritual. *In* Beyond the Myths of Culture: Essays in Cultural Materialism. E. Ross, ed. Pp. 295–321. New York: Academic.

1984   Bon Dieu and the Rites of Passage in Rural Haiti: Structural Determinants of Postcolonial Religion. *In* The Catholic Church and Religion in Latin America. T. Bruneau, et. al, eds. Pp. 188–231. Montreal: Centre for Developing Area Studies, McGill University.

1987   The Domestication of Wood in Haiti: A Case Study in Applied Anthropology. *In* Anthropological Praxis: Translating Knowledge into Action. Robert Wulff and Shirley Fiske, eds. Pp. 223–242. Boulder, Colo.: Westview Press.

Nicholls, David

1970   Politics and Religion in Haiti. Canadian Journal of Political Science 3:400–414.

1979   From Dessalines to Duvalier: Race, Colour and National Independence in Haiti. Cambridge: Cambridge University Press.

Orozco, Manuel

2000   Remittances and Markets: New Players and Practices. Washington, D.C.: Working Papers of the Inter-American Dialogue and Tomás Rivera Policy Institute. May.

2002   Remittances, Costs and Market Competition. Paper presented to the Federal Reserve Bank, Chicago, 14 November.

Orsi, Robert, ed.

1999   Gods of the City: Religion and the Urban American Landscape. Bloomington: Indiana University Press.

Parry, Jonathan, and Maurice Bloch

1989   Introduction: Money and the Morality of Exchange. *In* Money and the Morality of Exchange. Jonathan Parry and Maurice Bloch, eds., pp. 1–32. Cambridge: Cambridge University Press.

Parry, Jonathan, and Maurice Bloch, eds.

1989   Money and the Morality of Exchange. Cambridge: Cambridge University Press.

Péan, Leslie

1985   Le Secteur Privé, le Capital International et le Pouvoir Duvaliériste. Collectif Paroles 32:24–34.

Pessar, Patricia

1988   Introduction: Migration Myths and Realities. *In* When Borders Don't Divide: Labor Migration and Refugee Movements in the Americas. Patricia R. Pessar, ed. Pp. 1–7. New York: Center for Migration Studies.

Philpott, Stuart

1970   The Implications of Migration for Sending Societies: Some Theoretical Considerations. *In* Migration and Anthropology. Proceedings of the 1970 Meeting of the American Ethnological Society, pp. 9–21. Seattle: University of Washington Press.

Pierre-Noël, Arsène

1971   Nomenclature Polyglotte des Plantes Haïtiennes et Tropicales. Port-au-Prince: Presses Nationales d'Haïti.

Plotkin, Donna

1979   Land Distribution in a Lowland Haitian Community: The Case of Ça Ira. Unpublished paper.

Plotkin, Donna, and Suzanne Allman

1984   Haitian Women's Participation in Development. New York and Port-au-Prince: report submitted to the United Nations Development Programme.

Plummer, Brenda

1988   Haiti and the Great Powers, 1902–1915. Baton Rouge: Louisiana University Press.

1990   The Golden Age of Tourism: U.S. Influence in Haitian Cultural and Economic Affairs, 1934–1971. Cimarrón 2(3):49–63.

1992   Haiti and the United States: The Psychological Moment. Athens: University of Georgia Press.

Portes, Alejandro

1978   Toward a Structural Analysis of Illegal (Undocumented) Migration. International Migration Review 12(4):469–508.

1999   Conclusion: Towards a New World: The Origins and Effect of Transnational Activities. Ethnic and Racial Studies 22(2):463–478.

Portes, Alejandro, and Jòzsef Böröcz

1989   Contemporary Immigration: Theoretical Perspectives on Its Determinants and Modes of Incorporation. International Migration Review 23(3):606–630.

Portes, Alejandro, Luis Guarnizo, and Patricia Landolt

1999   Introduction: Pitfalls and Promise of an Emergent Research Field. Ethnic and Racial Studies 22(2):217–238.

Portes, Alejandro, and Rubén Rumbault

1990   Immigrant America: A Portrait. Berkeley: University of California Press.

Portes, Alejandro, and Alex Stepick

1985   Unwelcome Immigrants: The Labor Market Experiences of 1980 (Mariel) Cuban and Haitian Refugees in South Florida. American Sociological Review 50:493–514.

Portes, Alejandro, and John Walton

1981   Labor, Class, and the International System. Orlando: Academic.

Pressoir, Catts

1942   L'Etat Actuel des Missions Protestantes en Haïti. Conférence Prononcée au Dimanche de la Bible, à L'église St. Paul. December 13. (16 pages).

1945   Le Protestantisme Haïtien, 1–2. Port-au-Prince: Imprimerie de la Société Biblique et des Livres Religieux d'Haïti.

Price, Richard

1975   Saramaka Social Structure: Analysis of a Maroon Society in Suriname. Rio Pedras: University of Puerto Rico, Institute of Caribbean Studies, Caribbean Monograph Series, no. 12.

Price-Mars, Jean

[1928] 1983   So Spoke the Uncle. Magdaline Shannon, trans. Washington, D.C.: Three Continents Press.

Ravenscroft, Kent

1965   Voodoo Possession: A Natural Experiment in Hypnosis. International Journal of Clinical and Experimental Hypnosis 13(3):157–182.

Raynolds, Laura

1986   The Importance of Land Tenure in the Distribution of Benefits from Irrigation Development Projects: Findings from the Cayes Plain, Haiti. Unpublished report submitted to USAID.

Reichert, Joshua

1981   The Migrant Syndrome: Seasonal U.S. Wage Labor and Rural Development in Central Mexico. Human Organization 40(1):56–66.

Reisman, Karl

1970   Cultural and Linguistic Ambiguity in a West Indian Village. In Afro-American Anthropology: Contemporary Perspectives. Norman Whitten and John Szwed, eds. Pp. 129–144. New York: Free Press.

Rémy, Raoul

1969   Etude Socio-Economique sur Ça Ira. Port-au-Prince: Presses Nationales D'Haïti.

Richman, Karen

1978   Servitors and Their Masters: An Analysis of Ritual Performance in Haiti. Honors thesis, Wesleyan University.

1984   From Peasant to Migratory Farmworker: Haitian Migrants in U.S. Agriculture. Gainesville: University of Florida, Center for Latin American Studies, Occasional Paper 3:52–65.

1990a   Guarantying Migrants in the Core: Commissions of Gods, Descent Groups, and Ritual Leaders in a Transnational Haitian Community. Cimarrón 2(3): 114–128.

1990b   With Many Hands the Burden Isn't Heavy: Creole Proverbs and Political Rhetoric in Haiti's Presidential Elections. Folklore Forum 2(3):115–123.

1992a   *Lavalas* at Home/A *Lavalas* for Home. Inflections of Transnationalism in the Discourse of Haitian President Aristide. *In* Towards a Transnational Perspective on Migration: Race, Class, Ethnicity and Nationalism Reconsidered. Nina Glick-Schiller, Linda Basch, and Cristina Blanc-Szanton, eds. Pp. 189–200. New York: New York Academy of Sciences.

1992b   They Will Remember Me in the House: The *Pwen* of Haitian Transnational Migration. Ph.D. dissertation. University of Virginia.

1993   Review of Aids and Accusation: Haiti and the Geography of Blame by Paul Farmer. New West Indies Guide 67(3–4):334–336.

2002   Miami Money and the Home Gal. Anthropology and Humanism 27(2):1–14.

Richman, Karen, and William Balan-Gaubert

2001   A Democracy of Words: Political Performance in Haiti's Tenth Province. Journal of the Haitian Studies Association 7(1):90–103.

2005   The Protestant Ethic and the Dis-Spirit of Vodou. *In* Immigrant Faiths: Transforming Religious Life in America. Karen Leonard, ed., with Alex Stepick, Manuel Vasquez, and Jennifer Holdaway. Pp. 165–187. Walnut Creek, Calif.: Altamira Press.

Rocheleau, Dianne

1984   Geographic and Socioeconomic Aspects of the Recent Haitian Migration to South Florida. Gainesville: University of Florida, Center for Latin American Studies, Caribbean Migration Program, Occasional Paper 3:11–51.

Romain, Charles

1986   Le Protestantisme dans la Société Haïtien. Port-au-Prince: Henri Deschamps.

Rothenberg, Daniel

1988   With These Hands: The Hidden World of Migrant Farmworkers Today. New York: Harcourt Brace.

Roumain, Jacques

1946   Gouverneurs de la Rosée. Paris: Editions Messidor.

[1947] 1978   Masters of the Dew. Langston Hughes and Mercer Cook, trans. Oxford: Heineman Educational.

Rouse, Roger

1991   Mexican Migration and the Social Space of Postmodernism. Diaspora 1(1): 8–23.

1992   Making Sense of Settlement: Class Transformation, Cultural Struggle, and Transnationalism among Mexican Migrants in the United States. *In* Towards a Transnational Perspective on Migration: Race, Class Ethnicity, and Nationalism Reconsidered. Nina Glick-Schiller, Linda Basch, and Cristina Blanc-Szanton, eds. Pp. 25–52. New York: New York Academy of Sciences.

Rubenstein, Hymie

1982a   The Impact of Remittances in the Rural English-Speaking Caribbean: Notes on the Literature. *In* Return Migration and Remittances: Developing a Caribbean Perspective. William Stinner, Klaus de Albuquerque, and Roy Bryce-

Laporte, eds. Pp. 237–265. Washington, D.C.: Smithsonian Institution, Research Institute on Immigration and Ethnic Studies, Occasional Papers 3.

1982b   Return Migration to the English-Speaking Caribbean: Review and Commentary. *In* Return Migration and Remittances: Developing a Caribbean Perspective. William Stinner, Klaus de Albuquerque, and Roy Bryce-Laporte, eds. Pp. 3–34. Washington, D.C.: Smithsonian Institution, Research Institute on Immigration and Ethnic Studies, Occasional Papers 3.

Saint-Louis, Loretta

1988   Migration Evolves: The Political Economy of Network Process and Form in Haiti, The U.S. and Canada. Ph.D. dissertation, Boston University.

Sassen-Koob, Saskia

1981   Exporting Capital and Importing Labor: The Role of Women. *In* Female Immigrants to the United States: Caribbean, Latin American and African Experiences. Delores Mortimer and Roy Bryce-Laporte, eds. Pp. 203–234. Washington, D.C.: Smithsonian Institution, Research Institute on Immigration and Ethnic Studies, Occasional Papers 2.

1982   Recomposition and Peripheralization at the Core. *In* The New Nomads: From Immigrant Labor to Transnational Working Class, Marlene Dixon and Susanne Jonas, eds. Pp. 88–100. San Francisco: Synthesis.

1998   Globalization and Its Discontents: Essays on the New Mobility of People and Money. New York: New Press.

Schmidt, Hans

1971   The United States Occupation of Haiti, 1915–1934. New Brunswick, N.J.: Rutgers University Press.

Schneider, David

1968   American Kinship. Englewood Cliffs, N.J.: Prentice- Hall.

Schneider, Jane

1978   Peacocks and Penguins: The Political Economy of European Cloth and Colors. American Ethnologist 5(3):413–448.

Schwarz-Bart, Simone

1987   Ton Beau Capitaine. Play in One Act. Paris: Editions du Seuil.

Scott, James C.

1990   Domination and the Arts of Resistance. New Haven: Yale University Press.

1998   Seeing Like a State : How Certain Schemes to Improve the Human Condition Have Failed. New Haven: Yale University Press.

Segal, Aaron

1987   The Caribbean Exodus in a Global Context: Comparative Migration Experiences. *In* The Caribbean Exodus. Barry Levine, ed. Pp. 44–67. New York: Praeger.

Shacochis, Bob

1999   The Immaculate Invasion. New York: Viking.

Sherman, Amy

1997   The Soul of Development: Biblical Christianity and Economic Transformation in Guatemala. New York: Oxford University Press.

Silverman, Martin
1979   Gender and Separations in Precolonial Banaban and Gilbertese Societies. *In* Ideology and Everyday Life: Anthropology, Neomarxist Thought, and the Problem of Ideology and the Social Whole, by Steve Barnett and Martin Silverman. Pp. 85–165. Ann Arbor: University of Michigan Press.

Simpson, George
1940   The Vodun Service in Northern Haiti. American Anthropologist 41:236–254.
1980   Religious Cults of the Caribbean: Trinidad, Jamaica and Haiti. Rio Pedras: University of Puerto Rico, Institute of Caribbean Studies.

Siskind, Janet
1978   Kinship and Mode of Production. American Anthropologist 80(4):860–872.

Smith, Jennifer
2001   With Many Hands: Community Organization and Social Change in Rural Haiti. Ithaca: Cornell University Press.

Smith, M. P., and Luis Guarnizo, eds.
1998   Transnationalism from Below: Comparative Urban and Community Research, vol. 6, New Brunswick, N.J.: Transaction Publishers.

Smith, Raymond
1988   Kinship and Class in the West Indies. Cambridge: Cambridge University Press.

Smucker, Glenn
1982   Peasants and Development Politics: A Study in Haitian Class and Culture. Ph.D. dissertation, New School for Social Research.
1984   The Social Character of Religion in Rural Haiti. *In* Haiti—Today and Tomorrow: An Interdisciplinary Study. George Foster and Albert Valdman, eds. Pp. 35–56. Lanham, Md.: University Press of America.
1989   Myth and Reality in Haitian Agroforestry: Applications of Anthropological Knowledge in Project Implementation. Unpublished paper presented to the Panel on Applications of Social Science to Rural Development: Experiences in Haiti. 88th Annual Meeting of the American Anthropological Association, November 15–19, Washington, D.C.

Société Française de Réalisation, d'Etudes et de Conseil
1982   Etude de la Culture de la Canne à Sucre Dans la Plaine de Léogane. Evaluation des Superficies Cultivées en Cannes. Unpublished report.

Solien, Nancy
1960   Household and Family in the Caribbean: Some Definitions and Concepts. Social and Economic Studies 9(1):101–106.

Stepick, Alex
1982a   Haitian Boat People: A Study in the Conflicting Forces Shaping U.S. Immigration Policy. Law and Contemporary Problems 45(2):163–196.
1982b   (with Dale Swartz) Haitian Refugees in the U.S. New York: Minority Rights Group, report no. 52.
1984   Haitians Released from Krome: Their Prospects for Adaptation and Integration in South Florida. Miami: Florida International University, Latin Ameri-

can and Caribbean Center, Occasional Papers Series, Dialogue no. 24.

1986   Flight into Despair: A Profile of Recent Haitian Refugees in South Florida. International Migration Review 20(74):329–350.

1987   The Haitian Exodus: Flight from Terror and Poverty. *In* The Caribbean Exodus. Barry Levine, ed. Pp. 131–151. New York: Praeger.

1992   The Refugees Nobody Wants: Haitians in Miami. *In* Miami Now!: Immigration, Ethnicity and Social Change. Guillermo Grenier and Alex Stepick, eds. Pp. 57–83. Gainesville: University Press of Florida.

1999   Pride Against Prejudice: Haitians in the United States. Boston: Allyn and Bacon.

Stepick, Alex, and Carole Dutton Stepick

1990   People in the Shadows: Survey Research among Haitians in Miami. Human Organization 49(1):64–76.

Streit, Rev. Thomas

2003   About the Haiti Project. http://www.nd.edu/~hcahaiti/HaitiaAbout.html.

Sutton, Constance

1987   The Caribbeanization of New York City and the Emergence of a Transnational Socio-Cultural System. *In* Caribbean Life in New York City: Sociocultural Dimensions. Constance Sutton and Elsa Chaney, eds. Pp. 15–30. New York: Center for Migration Studies.

Sutton, Constance, and Elsa Chaney, eds.

1987   Caribbean Life in New York City: Sociocultural Dimensions. New York: Center for Migration Studies.

Taft, Edna

1938   A Puritan in Voodoo-Land. Philadelphia: Penn Publishing.

Taussig, Michael

1980   The Devil and Commodity Fetishism in South America. Chapel Hill: University of North Carolina Press.

1993   Mimesis and Alterity. London: Routledge.

Teas, Jane

1983   Could AIDS Agent be a New Variant of African Swine Fever Virus? Letter to The Lancet, April 23:923.

Thome, Joseph

1978   Land Tenure Insecurity in Haiti. Report submitted to USAID, Port-au-Prince.

Thompson, E. P.

1967   Time, Work-Discipline, and Industrial Capitalism. Past and Present 38:56–97.

Thompson, Robert Farris

1978   The Flash of the Spirit: Haiti's Africanizing Vodun Art. *In* Haitian Art. Ute Stebich, ed. Pp. 26–37. Brooklyn: Brooklyn Museum.

Toren, Christina

1989   Drinking Cash: The Purification of Money through Ceremonial Exchange in Fiji. *In* Money and the Morality of Exchange. Jonathan Parry and Maurice Bloch, eds. Pp. 142–165. Cambridge: Cambridge University Press.

Trouillot, Michel-Rolph

1981 Peripheral Vibrations: The Case of Saint-Domingue's Coffee Revolution. *In* Dynamics of World Development. Richard Robinson, ed. Pp. 27–41. Beverly Hills: Sage.

1982 Motion in the System: Coffee, Color, and Slavery in Eighteenth Century Saint-Domingue. Review 5(3):331–388.

1990a The Odd and the Ordinary: Haiti, the Caribbean and the World. Cimarrón 2(3):3–12.

1990b Haiti: State Against Nation. New York: Monthly Review Press.

Turner, Victor

1957 Schism and Continuity in an African Society. Manchester: Manchester University Press.

1967 The Forest of Symbols: Aspects of Ndembu Ritual. Ithaca: Cornell University Press.

1969 The Ritual Process: Structure and Anti-Structure. Ithaca: Cornell University Press.

United Nations Industrial Development Organization

n.d. Haiti's Sugar Industry.

[USAID] United States Aid for International Development.

2004 Strategic Plan (Fiscal Year 1999–2006). Unpublished report.

Valdman, Albert

1975 The Language Situation in Haiti. *In* The Haitian Potential: Research and Resources of Haiti. Vera Rubin and Richard Schaedel, eds. Pp. 62–83. New York: Teacher's College Press.

Valdman, Albert, Sarah Yoder, Craige Roberts, Yves Joseph, Francia Laborde Joseph, and Josiane Hudicourt

1981 Haitian Creole–English–French Dictionary. Bloomington: Indiana University, Creole Institute.

Van Velzen, H. U. E., and Van Wetering, W.

1988 The Great Father and the Danger: Religious Cults, Material Forces, and Collective Fantasies in the World of the Surinamese Maroons. Dordrecht, Holland: Foris.

Visser, Margaret

1991 The Rituals of Dinner: The Origins, Evolution, Eccentricities, and Meaning of Table Manners. New York: Penguin.

Wagner, Roy

1978 Lethal Speech. Daribi Myth as Symbolic Obviation. Ithaca: Cornell University Press.

1986 Symbols that Stand for Themselves. Chicago: University of Chicago Press.

Wallerstein, Immanuel

1974 The Modern World System I: Capitalist Agriculture and the Origins of the European World-Economy in the Sixteenth Century. New York: Academic.

1980 The Modern World System II: Mercantilism and the Consolidation of the European World-Economy, 1600–1750. New York: Academic.

1989   The Modern World System III: The Second Era of Great Expansion of the Capitalist World-Economy, 1730–1840s. New York: Academic.

Warner, R. Stephen, and Judith G. Wittner, eds.

1998   Gatherings in Diaspora: Religious Communities and the New Immigration. Philadelphia: Temple University Press.

Waters, Mary C.

1990   Ethnic Options: Choosing Identities in America. Berkeley: University of California Press.

Weber, Max

[1905] 1958   The Protestant Ethic and the Spirit of Capitalism. New York: Charles Scribner's Sons.

Weidman, Hazel

1978   Miami Health Ecology Project Report: A Statement on Ethnicity and Health, 1–2. Miami: University of Miami School of Medicine.

West India Management and Consultation Company

1916   Haitian Investigation: Plains of Cul-de-Sac and Léogane. Unpublished report.

Wiese, Helen J.

1971   The Interaction of Western and Indigenous Medicine in Haiti in Regard to Tuberculosis. Ph.D. dissertation, University of North Carolina.

Wilèk Film

1991   Titid Ak Dizièm Depatman an. Brooklyn. VHS.

Wilentz, Amy

1989   The Rainy Season: Haiti Since Duvalier. New York: Simon and Schuster.

1990   Foreword to In the Parish of the Poor: Writings from Haiti, by Jean-Bertrand Aristide. Amy Wilentz, trans., ed. Pp. ix–xxiv. Maryknoll, N.Y.: Orbis Books.

Wilkinson, Alec

1989   Big Sugar: Seasons in the Cane Fields of Florida. New York: Knopf.

Woldemikael, Telkemariam

1980   Maintenance and Change of Status in a Migrant Community: Haitians in Evanston, Illinois. Ph.D. dissertation, Northwestern University.

Wolf, Eric

1966   Peasants. Englewood Cliffs, N.J.: Prentice Hall.

1982   Europe and the People Without History. Berkeley: University of California Press.

Wolk, Daniel

2000   The Futile Exodus of Assyrians from Persia: Extravagance and Organized Charity. Paper presented to the Panel on Transnational Ties and Cultural Conflict in Middle Eastern Communities, 99th Annual Meeting of the American Anthropological Association, San Francisco.

Wolkstein, Diane

1980   The Magic Orange Tree and Other Haitian Folktales. New York: Schocken Books.

Wood, Charles, and Terry McCoy

1985   Migration, Remittances, and Development: A Study of Caribbean Cane Cutters in Florida. International Migration Review 19(2):251–277.

Woodson, Drexel

1990   Tout Mounn se Mounn, Men Tout Mounn Pa Menm: Microlevel Sociocultural Aspects of Land Tenure in a Northern Haitian Locality. Ph.D. dissertation, University of Chicago.

1992   Review of Passage to Darkness: The Ethnobiology of the Haitian Zombie, by Wade Davis. Africa 62(1):151–154.

World Bank

1985   Haiti: Agricultural Sector Study, 1–3.

1987   Haiti: Public Expenditure Review.

Zéphir, Flore

1996   Haitian Immigrants in Black America: A Sociological and Sociolinguistic Portrait. Boulder, Colo.: Westview Press.

2001   Trends in Ethnic Identification Among Second-Generation Haitian Immigrants in New York City. Boulder, Colo.: Westview Press.

Index

ports of, 48, 51, 92, 157, 295n.3; guinea grass, 297n.12; and imports, 47; and income, 101–2; peasant, 47; sharecroppers and, 101–2; sisal, 44; tobacco, 291–92n.8; transportation of, 55. *See also* Foods and beverages; Sugarcane

Cuba: and Canter migration, 57; Haitians in, 27, 38, 47, 53, 185; Jamaicans in, 100; mentioned, 58; National City Bank of New York and, 43; and sugar imports, 48; U.S. activities in, 19, 27, 43; wage labor in, 43, 100

Cul-de-Sac Plain, Haiti: Charles Lacombe in, 94; foods in, 160; gangan ason in, 119–20; Haytian American Sugar Company in, 44, 91, 103, 105; location of, 65; lwa pantheons in, 296–97n.11; ounsi initiations in, 294n.7; railroads in, 100, 103; scholarship on, 89; sharecropping in, 100; sugarcane production in, 86; Tancrède Auguste in, 94

Currency, 78, 87, 98, 268. *See also* Money

Dada, Grann (Ti Rivyè resident), 175

Dame Marie, Haiti, 93

Danbala Wedo (lwa): and affliction, 132; in African/Guinea Prayer, 145; characterization of, 155; flour blazons of, 136; and Karen Richman, 197; mentioned, 90, 186, 190; and ounsi, 130–44, 145, 155, 168, 177, 178, 190, 197, 262; and possession-performance, 140–41, 152, 262; songs of, 155, 156–57; and water, 140, 152, 157, 262. *See also* Lwa

Dancing: Banda, 122; and beating gè ceremonies, 173; and feedings, 247; and funerary rites, 292n.2; mentioned, 157, 200; and ounsi initiations, 132, 178; photos of, 138; and possession-performance, 129–30, 187, 198; recording of, 265; as ritual component, 23, 144

Danticat, Edwidge, 28, 29

Darbonne, Haiti, 67, 106–7, 236

Darius, Richelieu, 53, 105

Dash, J. Michael, xiv

Dauphin, Claude, 295n.1

Davis, Wade, 22, 298n.7

Death rites. *See* Funerary rites

Debts: "coffee," 95, 98; Haitian national, 43; lwa and, 126, 187, 188, 196

Dedine, Frankel, 7, 8, 10, 238

Dediscar, Nelio, 10, 50

Delatour, Leslie, 108–9

Delray Beach, Fla., 64, 77, 78, 79, 199, 200

Demwatye. See Sharecroppers; Sharecropping

Denis, Lorimer, 296–97n.11, 297n.12

Deren, Maya, 122, 126, 150, 294n.5, 294–95n.9, 295n.1

Descent groups: and affliction, 132, 285–86; and African/Guinea Prayer, 294–95n.9; and Bizango societies, 237, 239; and *dyab* (devil), 296n.7; and feedings, 143, 144, 157, 182–83, 185–86; and first testaments, 89, 117–18, 285; and gangan ason, 119, 121, 198; history of, 118; inheritance by, 117–18; lands of, 85, 95–96, 118, 285, 294–95n.9; and lwa, 41, 90, 117–18, 120, 126, 188, 193–94, 207, 285–86, 293n.1; and lwa blan, 162; and lwa zandò, 174, 176–77, 182–83; and Magic, 154; 19th-century, 118; and protection, 223, 285–86; and pwen, 169–71, 187, 189, 296n.7; and rituals, 117, 143, 176–77; roles of, 185; sacred sites for, 148; scholarship on, 117; and shrines, 148; spiritual legacy of, 128, 143, 144, 177, 147; and temple voodoo traditions, 144

DeSipio, Louis, 290n.1

Desisier Plantation, 98

Desmesmin, Mozart, 91, 96

Dessalines, Jean Jacques, 52, 89

Devil and Commodity Fetishism in South America, The (Taussig), 19

DeWind, Josh, 46, 293n.5

D'Haïti, Mercina, 34, 35, 59, 150, 227

D'Haïti, Pierre, 5, 11, 34–36, 37

Diaspora, xiii, xiv, 16–17, 28–29, 219, 289n.1

Diasporic Citizenship: Haitian Americans in Transnational America (Laguerre), xiv

Diet, 42, 46, 48–49, 50, 51. *See also* Foods and beverages

Dieu Grace (Mika Jean-Jacques' daughter), 146

Dioguy, Adam (Adan): death of, 74, 251; as farmer, 74; funeral of, 275, 281; and Karen Richman, 5–6; and Little Caterpillar, 6, 236, 250–51, 281; mentioned, 3; and Se Byen, 250, 281

Dioguy, Eve: children of, 74; in Florida, 74; and Karen Richman, 6; in Léogane, 264; and Little Caterpillar, 236, 250; mentioned, 3, 5; photo of, 35; and Se Byen, 250; as vegetable trader, 74

Dioguy, Germaine, 279, 282

Dioguy, Maxia (Mme. Pierre): application for migration by, 76, 77; boyfriend of, 282; and cassette-letters, 269; children of, 74; civil marriage of, 264, 273, 279, 286–87; and conversion to Protestantism, 263, 275; description of, 273; and family lands, 264, 279; illnesses of, 254; and Karen Richman, 272–75, 272, 288; as landowner, 279, 285; in Léogane, 264; and Little Caterpillar, 74, 76, 77, 233, 236, 250, 263, 267, 266, 279, 281, 285, 286–87, 288; mentioned, 231, 232; mother of, 264; photos of, 274; and reconversion, 263; remarriage of, 273–74, 285; residence of, 233, 250, 279, 285; and Se Byen, 273, 274–75, 279, 280, 282–83, 285, 287; and sorcery, 275; sponsorship of immigration of, 286–87; as trader, 2, 39

Dioguy, Pierre (Little Caterpillar): and Adam Dioguy, 6, 236, 250–51, 281; beating and stabbing of, 2, 230; burial of, 275; and cassette-letters, 216, 217, 218, 230; on cassette oratory, 265; children of, 74; civil marriage of, 264, 273, 279, 286–87; and conjugal unions, 231; and conversion to Protestantism, 251–57, 258–59, 275, 279–80, 281, 283; death of, 266, 272, 275, 276, 278–80, 281, 283, 287–88; and descent group, 258; description of, 1–2; and Dioguy shrine, 231, 237, 251, 276; and divination, 2, 231; and Eve Dioguy, 236, 250; extended family of, 18; as farmer, 74; as farm laborer, 2, 39, 62, 229, 230, 231, 237, 242, 251, 253, 258; feedings sponsored by, 247; final illness of, 263–71, 274–75, 276, 278–80, 283, 285, 287–88; in Florida, 2, 5, 74, 217, 230, 233, 236, 237, 250, 251, 258, 259, 263, 282; funeral of, 275, 279, 281, 285; grave of, 272, 273; on Guinea, 18, 153; on Haiti, 267, 269; and home kin, 231, 274, 275; illnesses of, 2, 230–31, 251; and immigration status, 59, 233, 246, 250, 286; inju-

ries of, 3, 231, 237, 251, 258; investments of, 250, 264, 266, 274, 281; and Karen Richman, xvii, 3–4, 5, 34, 60, 216, 230, 232, 233, 234, 236–37, 241–42, 247, 251–57, 258, 259, 263–71, 273, 281, 282, 283, 286, 287, 288; at Krome detention center, 59; as landowner, 76, 250, 264, 266, 279, 285, 287; and literacy, 2, 74, 236, 258; and Lucien Bertrand, 258; and lwa, 172–73, 174, 175, 182, 190–91; on Magic, 18; and Maxia Dioguy, 74, 76, 77, 233, 236, 250, 263, 267, 266, 279, 281, 285, 286–87, 288; in Michigan, 2; and migration by, 2, 39, 192; patron lwa of, 190, 237, 247, 274, 279–80, 283, 287; and Pepe Michel, 242; as performer, 16; photos of, 1, 34, 217, 258, 259, 274; and possession-performance, 247, 274; and poverty, 269; on protection, 184; and pwen, 2, 16, 153, 168–69, 172–73, 175, 230, 232, 242, 258, 287; and reconversion, 263, 264; remittances by, 3, 6, 231, 232–33, 234, 236–37, 241, 242, 252, 253, 257, 264, 280–81, 282–83, 292–93n.4; as representative of Guinea, 230; residence of, 3–4, 232, 233, 237, 250, 264, 266, 285, 287; and Se Byen, 5, 6–15, 16, 17, 18, 26, 231–47, 248–49, 250, 251, 252, 254, 257, 258, 274–76, 278, 280–81, 282–85, 288; and Sergo Guerrier, 229–30, 232; as shaman, 276; and sharecropping, 2, 74, 250; as small-business owner, 76, 250; songs by, 212; and sorcery, 264, 266, 267–68, 275, 283, 287; and Ti Rivyè, 2, 3–4, 6, 74, 233, 246–47, 250, 254, 263, 264, 292–93n.4; in Virginia, 1, 3, 5, 11, 230, 236, 247; as "the voodoo man," 231; and workman's compensation, 3, 231, 258; and worship, 2; and Yvon, 267, 269; and zandò song texts, 232; and Zo Guerrier, 229–30, 232, 233, 242. *See also* under Cassette-letters

Dioguy, Se Byen: and Adam Dioguy, 250, 281; as business owner, 74, 231; descriptions of, 6–7, 278; eldest son of, 276, 277; and Eve Dioguy, 250; extended family of, 6; as farmer, 39, 74, 231; and Frankel Dedine, 238; as gangan ason, 2, 6–7, 74, 231, 232, 280; and healing, 282; illness of, 233; and Karen Richman, 6–11, 235, 236, 238, 272, 276–85,

France: and Haiti, 21, 38, 52, 86; Haitians in, 54, 95, 97; literacy in, 215

French language, 2, 23, 24, 28, 56, 214–16

Frères Simmonds, 93, 293n.1

Freud, Sigmund, 296n.9

Funerary rites: burials, 124, 225; burning pots, 126, 128; caskets for, 68; and Catholic texts, 124; clothing for, 68; costs of, 124, 125, 292n.2; and feasts, 292n.2; and feedings, 124; and final prayers, 124; financing of, 125, 225, 275, 293n.2; funerals, 124, 171; mourning periods, 42, 124; objects for, 125, 126, 127; requiems, 292n.2; retrieving the dead from the water, 121, 147, 170–73, 176–77, 186–87, 188; scholarship on, 294n.5; as social drama, 125; and status, 275; wailing, 264–65, 267. *See also* Rituals

Gangan ason: and African/Guinea Prayer, 144, 145–46; at Agwe's Barge, 161; authority of, 154–55; and beating gè, 174; and Bizango societies, 239; and burning pots, 126; Camolien Alexandre on, 120–21, 152; and changes in ritual practices, 128; and communication with ancestors, 119, 121, 147; and communication with lwa, 119, 120, 129, 130, 147, 186, 187, 193, 196, 197, 198; and control of clients, 196; and conversions to Protestantism, 261; credentials of, 120–21; definition of, 90; and descent groups, 119, 145, 176, 185; diagnoses by, 126, 170, 171, 193, 194, 196, 197–98; and dreams, 120–21; on first testaments, 89; and foreign clients, 208; and genealogy, 144, 145–46, 189; and healing, 24, 126, 194, 219, 264; initiation of, 119, 121, 129, 147; and liturgy, 119; and Loko, 145, 147, 154–55; and lwa blan feedings, 182–83; and migration, 119, 198, 199; numbers of, 127; and oral history, 90; and ounsi, 119, 124, 126, 129, 130, 132, 144, 152, 176; photos of, 25, 136; and possession-performance, 129; power of, 121; and pwen, 165–66, 167–68, 172, 184; and retrieving the dead from the water, 124–28, 186–87; rise of, 118–21, 185; and ritual idioms, 144; as ritual specialists, 24, 119, 121, 126, 176, 185; rivalries between, 298n.4; and

scheduling conflicts, 178; as shrine managers, 119, 121, 298n.5; skepticism about, 120–21, 127, 197–98; and sorcery, 207; and trances, 120–21; women as, 129

Gardens: Adam Dioguy's, 6; Haytian American Sugar Company and, 103, 104; and intercropping, 67, 103, 104; as investments, 76, 77; and irrigation, 104; in Ka Pè, 86, 88; migrants and, 76, 77; ownership of, 111; and pwen, 165, 296n.8; sales of, 293n.2 (ch.5); and sharecropping, 99, 101, 104, 111, 112; sizes of, 67, 86, 99; wage laborers and, 103

Garifuna, 290n.2, 293n.1

Garrison, Vivian, 299n.2

Geffert, Hannah, 62

Geffrard, Fabre Nicholas, 290n.3

Gemini All Stars de Ti Manno, 56

Genealogy. *See* African/Guinea Prayer; Descent groups

Georges Woke Up Laughing: Long Distance Nationalism and the Search for Home (Glick-Schiller and Fouron), 31

Gérard (Ti Rivyè native), 70, 199–201, 206, 208

Gerlach, Luther, 260

Germaine (Se Byen's sister). *See* Dioguy, Germaine

Getting Haiti Right This Time: The U.S. and the Coup (Chomsky, Farmer, and Goodman), xiv

Gifts and Commodities (Gregory), 20

Ginen. *See* Africa

Glick-Schiller, Nina, 28–29, 31

God, 153, 298n.1. *See also* Lwa

Godard, Henri, 292n.3

Godzich, Vlad, 297n.1 (ch. 7)

Gold, Herbert, 21–22

Goodman, Amy, xiv

Gouverneurs de la Rosée (*Masters of the Dew*, Roumain), 27–28, 53

Government, Haitian: Aristide administrations (1991, 2000–2004), xiv, 29–30, 51, 58, 64, 82, 209–10, 290–91n.6, 298n.6; and Bizango societies, 298n.7; Boyer administration (1818–43), 86–87; constitution of, 103; and corruption, 66, 81, 92; and coups d'etat/juntas, 29, 82, 93; Dessalines administration (1804–06), 52; and eminent domain, 87; Duvalier

(François) administration (1957–71), 29, 45, 298n.7; Duvalier (Jean-Claude) administration (1971–86), 29, 45, 49, 51, 58, 85, 106; administration (1971–86), 29, 45, 49, 51, 58, 85, 106; Estime administration (1946–50), 45; and extermination of Haitian black pigs, 49; Geffrard administration (1859–67), 290n.3; and grain enterprises, 48; and Haytian American Sugar Company, 106–7; Hyppolite administration (1889–96), 87; and infrastructure improvements, 85; and inheritance, 286; and Joseph Lacombe, 91; and laborers' wages, 113; and land, 87, 91; Magloire administration (1950–56), 122; and marriage, 287; and migrants, xiv, 29–30; military dictatorships, 46; minister of agriculture, 293n.3; and National City Bank of New York, 43; and national debt, 43, 48; and peasants, 19, 86; Petion administration (1807–18), 87–88; Sam administration (1915), 93; Simon administration (1908–11), 43; and sugarcane prices, 108; surveys by, 67; Tenth Province (Dizyém Depatman), xiv, 29–30, 209, 210; and Usine Sucrière Nationale de Darbonne, 106, 108; Vincent administration (1930–41), 53

Grande Rivière, Haiti, 91; district, 66; river, 66

Grand Goâve, Haiti, 65, 97

Grandparents, 72, 190, 208

Gran Rivyè, Haiti, 121

Gran Rivyè (river), 66

Graves, 96, 103, 170, 272. *See also* Cemeteries; Tombs

Gregory, C. A., 20, 144

Greif, A. J., 103

Gressier, Haiti, 65

Griffith, David, 37, 290n.1, 291–92n.8

Guadeloupe, 208; Antoinne Edouard in, 78; Haitians in, 29, 54, 189; Meyze in, 69; and Tenth Province of Haiti, 29; Ti Rivyè natives in, 2, 72, 73, 74, 189, 275, 279, 282

Guantanomo Bay, 59

Guaranty. *See Lwa:* and protection

Guerrier, Joseph (Zo), 237; description of, 226; as drummer, 10, 238, 247; and Karen Richman, 272; and Little Caterpillar, 229–30, 232, 233, 242, 247; on lwa, 184, 190; photos of, 10, 227; and poverty, 287; on pwen, 166, 184, 190; and Se Byen's letter to Little Caterpillar, 238; and Sergo Guerrier, 229–30, 232, 247, 248, 292–93n.4; as singer, 238, 247, 249; and sorcery, 287; and throwing pwen, 226, 229–30

Guerrier, Lorius (Little Spider), 65, 69, 219

Guerrier, Sergo: and Menmenn Bien-Aimée and Zo Guerrier, 226–30, 231, 247, 248, 287, 292–93n.4; murder of, 272; photo of, 227

Guinea, 185, 220, 225; and ancestors, 153; calabash trees of, 152; definitions of, 150; gangan ason and, 120–21; and inheritance, 17; lack of power of, 153; and legitimization of power, 150; lwa associated with, 152–53; and lwa blan, 154–63; and lwa zandò, 176–77; and Magic, xv–xvi, 18–21, 22, 26, 150, 163, 170–71, 176–77, 189, 208, 213; morality of, 150, 152, 172; objects associated with, 152–53; and pwen, 18, 153, 176–77; ritual numbers for, 173; support of, 153; traditions associated with, 152–53; and water, 152

Guinea Prayer. *See* African/Guinea Prayer

Hacking, Ian, xiii

Hagerstown, Md., 291–92n.8

Haiti: and AIDS, 50; black colonization in, 290n.3; and Caribbean Basin Initiative, 46; civil wars in, 170; class prejudice in, 28; Creole radio broadcasts in, 289n.1; economy of, 39; embargo against, 82; and food aid, 48; as French colony, 19, 21, 38, 39, 86; geography of, 65; literary depictions of, xiv, 21–22; migration within, 38; population in, 44; Protestants in, 260; resistance to neocolonialism in, 19, 21–22; scholarship on, xiv–xv; total remittances to, 40; and tourism, 21, 50, 158, 209; unemployment in, 53; U.S. occupation of (1915–34), xiv, 19, 21, 22, 38, 43–45, 47, 53, 91, 93, 103, 104, 105–6, 295n.3; and world systems, 39–42. *See also* Government, Haitian

Haitian-American Development Company, 44

Haitian Americans, The (Zephir), xv

Haitian Bureau of Ethnology, 122

La Place (Ti Rivyè native), 139

Larose, Serge: on African/Guinea Prayer, 294–95n.9; on creation of pwen, 165–66; on descent groups, 117; on funerary rites, 294n.5; on gangan ason, 298n.4; on Guinea-Magic dialectic, 150; on lwa zandò, 172, 296–97n.11; on pwen, 18, 177, 296n.8; on religious and social change, 116; on "When they do not need me," 295n.2

Latin America, 260

Latin American Agribusiness Development Corporation, 295n.3

Lawless, Robert, xiv

Legal Services Corporation, 63

Legal systems, 57, 90, 95–98

L'Eglise Sainte Rose, 66

Lejena (Mika Jean-Jacques' granddaughter), 146

Lemoine, Maurice, 66

Lenin, 110

Léogane (commune), Haiti, 65

Léogane (district), Haiti, 65, 93, 97

Léogane (town), Haiti: cemeteries in, 66, 78, 87; Charles-Mitan Marie's tomb in, 87; Démosthène Lacombe in, 94; description of, 66, 67, 68, 83, 292n.1; diseases and illnesses in, 67; distilleries in, 66–67, 78; electricity in, 250; elites in, 99; factories near, 293n.1; and Haytian American Sugar Company, 91; and labor conscription, 66; Little Caterpillar and, 250; mayors of, 97; migrant recruitment in, 54; missions in, 66; mortuary industry in, 68, 275; and railroad, 293n.1; rented lodgings in, 264; roads and streets in, 66, 83, 106–7; Usine Sucrière Nationale de Darbonne in, 106–7

Léogane Plain, Haiti: agriculture in, 2, 67, 86–87, 102, 295n.3; cemeteries in, 103; communication with, 4; elites from, 2–3, 231; gangan ason in, 120–21; Haytian American Sugar Company in, 44, 91, 97, 103, 105; Joseph Lacombe and, 91, 92, 93–94, 95; landholding in, 67, 97, 98–99; lawyers in, 97; location of, 65; Little Caterpillar in, 2; lwa in, 296–97n.11; mills in, 108; notaries in, 97; ounsi initiations in, 141–42; and Port-au-

Prince, 99; railroads in, 100, 103; religious change in, 116; residents of, xv, 2; Serge Larose in, 150; sharecropping in, 100–102, 112; surveyors in, 97; surveys of, 37; U.S. agribusiness in, 184; Usine Sucrière Nationale de Darbonne in, 49

Lerose (Ti Rivyè native), 179

Letters, 214–16. See also Cassette-letters

"Levering Migrants' Remittances" (USAID program), 30

L'Hôpital St. Croix, 66

Liberia, 290n.3

Lidya (Ti Rivyè native), 292n.2

Lina (Ti Rivyè native), 201

Lincoln, Abraham, 290n.3

Literacy: Aiscar and, 294n.3; and cassette-letters, 214, 218; in France, 215; Little Caterpillar and, 2, 74, 236, 258; Lucien Bertrand and, 258; migrants and, 4, 66, 230; and modernity, 297n.1 (ch. 7); peasants and, 4, 97; scholarship on, 297n.1 (ch. 7); of scribes, 214–15; and sorcery, 191; and state power, 297n.1 (ch. 7)

Literature, xiv, 21–22, 27–28, 201

Little, Cheryl, 58

Little Caterpillar. See Dioguy, Pierre

Little Haiti (Miami, Fla.), 80

Little Spider. See Guerrier, Lorius

Loans: collateral for, 96; for financing migration, 166, 167–68; Haitian government and, 43; Joseph Lacombe and, 95–96, 97; Little Caterpillar and, 292–93n.4; livestock as, 96; seeds as, 96

Loederer, Richard, 22

Loremi (Ti Rivyè native), 194, 195, 196, 197

Louima, Abner, 16

Louis (Ti Rivyè native), 73–74

Lovingston, Va., 62

Lowenthal, Ira: on affliction, 193–94; on African/Guinea Prayer, 294–95n.9; on descent groups, 117; on funerary rites, 292n.2, 294n.6, 294n.5; on Haitian consensual union, 286; on lwa, 118

Lundahl, Mats, 53

Lwa: and affliction, 22–24, 119, 126, 130, 132, 141, 155, 157, 170, 176, 179, 182–83, 184,

Manuel, Peter, 289n.1

Marbial, Haiti, 260

Mardi Gras, 222

Marie, Charles-Mitan, 87–88, 90

Mariel, Cuba, 57

Markets, marketing, 2, 67, 68, 294n.8

Marriage: business, 272, 299n.2; Catholics and, 286; civil, 264, 279, 286, 287; costs of, 299n.2; and descent groups, 286; and divorce, 73; Haitian consensual union (*plasaj*), 286; meanings of, 285, 286; and migration, 286–87, 299n.2; polygynous, 73, 77, 285, 286; prohibited, 147; and Protestantism, 286; requirements of, 250; and status, 73; transnational nature of, 77

Marshall, Dawn, 290n.1

Martinique, 54, 73–74, 182–83, 193–94, 208

Marx, Karl, 16, 69

Maryland Legal Aid, 63

Massey, Douglas, 290n.1

Masters of the Dew (*Gouverneurs de la Rosée*, Roumain), 27–28, 53

Mathieu, Haiti, 91

Maurice (Mme. André and Tonton Ogoun heir), 96

Mauss, Marcel, 144

Maxia. *See* Dioguy, Maxia

Maximilien, Louis, 294nn.5, 7, 294–95n.9, 296n.10, 297n.12

McCoy, Terry, 291–92n.8

McDonald, James P., 43

"Meaning of Africa in Haitian Vodu, The" (Larose), 18, 150

Medical Advisor, The, 299n.4

Medicine and Morality in Haiti (Brodwin), 298–99n.2

Medicines, 196, 224, 264, 265

Men: ailments of, 131; and Canter migration, 2, 55, 285; economic activities of, 67–68, 69; marital roles of, 186; as migrants, 72; as ounsi, 294n.8; and polygyny, 73, 77, 286; ritual roles of, 129; and social rank, 161–62; transgendered, 294n.8. *See also Gangan ason*

Menmenn. *See* Bien-Aimée, Germaine

Mennesson-Rigaud, Odette: on African/Guinea Prayer, 294–95n.9; Alfred Métraux and,

294n.4; Harold Courlander on, 122–23; on lwa pantheons, 296–97n.11; on offerings to lwa, 295–96n.4, 297n.12; on ritual songs, 295n.1

Mercerie, Haiti, 78

Mercina. *See* D'Haïti, Mercina

Merger, Haiti, 92, 206

Météllus, Joseph (Malgre Sa): on Antoinne Edouard, 78; on children's obligations, 42; on "Do for me" song, 226; in Florida, 111; on foods, 160, 181; on lwa blan, 154; on migrants, 226; on pwen, 220; origin of nickname for, 16, 219; on sharecropping and wage labor, 111–12; sponsorship of migration by, 76

Métraux, Alfred: on African/Guinea Prayer, 294–95n.9; on Catholicism, 23; on conversion to Protestantism, 260; on funerary rites, 294n.5; on Haitian religion and healing, 289n.4; on maji service, 123, 294n.4; and Odette Mennesson-Rigaud, 123, 294n.4; on ounsi initiations, 294n.7, 294n.8; on Protestantism, 259–60; on ritual songs, 116, 144, 295n.1; on Voodoo types, 117

Mexico, 30, 40, 49, 295n.3

Meyze (Ti Rivyè native), 69

Miami, Fla.: and Canter migration, 55, 56, 72, 272, 290–91n.6; cassette-letters in, 229; Haitian companies in, 82; Jean-Bertrand Aristide in, 29; Krome detention center in, 58, 59; Latin American Agribusiness Development Corporation in, 295n.3; Little Caterpillar in, 231; Little Haiti, 80; mentioned, 113; Meyze in, 69; Pierre D'Haïti in, 37; as synonym for southeastern U.S., 69, 193, 252; and Tenth Province of Haiti, 29; Ti Rivyè natives in, 69, 72, 199

Michel, Pepe (Ti Rivyè gangan ason): and descent group's shrine, 237; description of, 191–92; on Guinea-Magic dialectic, 18; Little Caterpillar and, 242; on lwa, 166, 208; and migrants, 192, 208; on ounsi, 141; photos of, 191; on possession-performance, 242; on pwen, 163, 166; and Se Byen's cassette-letter to Little Caterpillar, 238; as singer, 150, 238

Michèl, Tonton. *See* Pè, Michel

Michigan, 2

Michou (Ti Rivyè native), 133–34

Migrant and Seasonal Agricultural Worker
Protection Act (MSAWPA), 63, 291n.7

Migration: and agroindustrial development, 46;
Caribbean, 30–31, 54; costs of, 40; European,
47; and Protestantism, 298–99n.2; and world
systems, 39

—Haitian: costs of, 40, 41, 82; Clinton administration and, 290–91n.6; within Haiti, 38, 53,
99, 111; historical overview of, 52–59; in-
creases in, 53, 57; interpretation of, 223; le-
gality of, 56–57, 105, 114; Little Caterpillar
on, 266–67; loans for, 166, 167–68; lwa and,
186, 192; to Miami, 290–91n.6; from New
York to South Florida, 80; occupation administration and, 43–44, 47; from Port-au-
Prince to New York, 55; sponsorship of, 225;
as strategy, 41, 71–72, 77, 82, 114

Migrants: and assimilation, 248; Caribbean, 40,
54–55, 63, 290n.4; Cuban, 57, 58; Dominican, 299n.2; and home kin, 247–49; Indochinese, 57; Jamaican, 100, 290n.1, 291–92n.8;
Latin American, 30, 40, 55, 63; Mexican, 30,
40, 41, 63, 290n.1; in Papua New Guinea, 20;
and protection, 209; as pwen, 19; and residency status, 291–92n.8; West Indian, 291–
92n.8

—Haitian: arrests and detention of, 58, 59, 199,
228; blacklisting of, 291–92n.8; characteris-
tics of, 71–72; and class prejudice, 28; at congressional hearings, 291–92n.8; conscription
of, 66; deportation/repatriation of, 53, 55, 57,
58, 59, 228; and Dominicans, 105; and diaspora, xiii–xiv; expectations for/obligations
of, xvi, 3–4, 26, 41, 42, 26, 71, 74–76, 118,
210, 225, 233, 275; and Haitian government,
xiv, 29–30, 209–10; and home kin, 26, 185,
208–9, 211, 213, 224; massacre of (Dominican Republic, 1937), 53; occupations of, 26,
54, 59, 66, 78, 80, 199; productivity of, xvi,
198–99, 208; and Puerto Ricans, 105; as
pwen, 26, 185, 199, 208, 209, 224–25, 233,
252, 257, 258, 283, 287; recruitment of, 40,
53; resistance by, 62, 63, 291n.7, 291–92n.8;
return of, 69, 73, 76, 207, 210, 287, 292–

93n.4; and separation of life and work, 69;
as small-business owners, 76, 80; and smugglers, 56, 57; and socioeconomic status, 28,
248, 290n.4; sponsorship of migration by, 70,
73, 76, 83; and stereotypes, 21; and tourism,
209; transnational character of, 4, 25, 28–30,
39, 77; treatment of, xv, 34, 57, 59, 113, 291–
92n.8; and U.S. government, xv, 54, 55, 57–
59, 73, 76, 290–91n.6; U.S. homeownership
by, 64; and U.S. legal system, 34, 57, 63,
290–91n.6, 297n.1 (ch. 8), 291n.7. See also
Canter migration; Farm laborers; Service
jobs

Military: Haitian, 45, 51

Miller, George, 291n.8

Mills: colonial, 106–7; and distilleries, 108;
elites and, 108; government seizure of, 106–
7; Haytian American Sugar Company and,
103, 105; Joseph Lacombe and, 92, 95, 101;
in Léogane, 3; in Northern Plain, 106–7;
remains of, 106–7; small, 105, 108; steam-
powered, 92; taxes on, 108; Usine Sucrière
Nationale de Darbonne and, 108; water-
powered, 92

Millspaugh, Arthur C., 38, 47

Mimesis, 16, 163, 218

Min (Ti Rivyè ounsi), 161

Ministère de L'Information, Haiti, 292n.1

Minister of the Diaspora (Haiti), 29

Mintz, Sidney, 46, 52, 109–11

Miracia (Ti Rivyè native), 238

Miragoane, Haiti, 294–95n.9, 295–96n.4

Mirebalais, Haiti, 294n.7

Misdor (Ti Rivyè gangan ason): and African/
Guinea Prayer, 294–95n.9; and communication with lwa, 198; death of, 122, 147;
descriptions of, 121, 122, 147; and foreign
ethnologists, 122–24; and introduction of
urban temple practices, 121–22, 147; and liturgy, 172; mentioned, 125, 132, 165–66; and
other gangan ason, 122, 129, 178; and ounsi,
122, 143; and retrieving the dead from the
water, 126–28, 171–72

Missionaries, 260, 261–63

Missions, 66, 85, 92. See also Croix des Pères

Miton, Haiti, 272

Saint-Louis, Loretta, 292n.3
St. Michèl (church), 167
Saints, 23, 295–96n.4
Sanon, André, 60
Saramaka maroons, 293n.1
Schell, Gregory, 60, 63, 291–92n.8
Schneider, David, 148
Scholarship: on affliction, 193–94; on African/
Guinea Prayer, 294–95n.9; on beating gè,
296n.10; on Bizango societies, 298n.7; on
cassettes in India, 289n.1; on child feeding,
49; on Colombia peasantry, 19; on Cul-de-
Sac Plain, 89; on descent groups, 117; on
diaspora, xiv; on eating etiquette, 296n.6; on
European peasants, 46; on expropriation of
peasant lands, 86; on feedings, 290n.2; on
foods and beverages, 160; on French letter
writing, 215; on funerary rites, 292n.2,
294n.5; on grandparent-grandchild relationship, 190; on Guinea-Magic dialectic, 150;
on Haiti, xiv–xv, 90; on Haitian consensual
unions, 286; on Haitian folklore, 295n.1; on
Haitian music and musicians, 28, 155, 222,
295n.1; on Haitian religion, 116–17, 119–20,
122–23, 129, 289n.4; on Haitians in New
York, 293n.5; on house construction, 292n.3;
on indirect communication, 219, 297–98n.2;
on Jamaican cane cutters, 291–92n.8; on
Kinanbwa, 89, 119; on lactation, 42; on landless proletarians, 109–11; on land tenure, 90;
on literacy, 297n.1 (ch. 7); on lwa, 23, 172,
296–97nn.11, 12; on manufacturing bundles,
296n.10; on Mexican-U.S. migration, 41; on
migration to South Florida, 80; on mimesis,
16, 163; on modernity, 16; on offerings, 295–
96nn.4, 6; on ounsi initiations, 294n.7; on
peasant organizations, 222; on possession-
performance, 242, 298n.8; on production of
labor for export, 40; on Protestantism, 259–
60, 298–99n.2; on pwen, 15–16, 18, 163, 165–
66, 177, 218, 220, 296n.8; on religious conversion, 260–61; on remittances, 41, 290n.1;
on rituals, 90; on second *caco* war, 43; on
sharecropping, 101; on social construction of
reality, xiii; on substance and contract, 148;
on theology, 90; on transformation of

money and wage labor, 20; on transnational
communities, 30–31, 247; on vodou, 289n.4;
on Voodoo, 117; on world systems, 39
Schools, 66, 76, 99
Schwarz-Bart, Simone, 212, 247
Scott, James C., 297n.1 (ch. 7)
Se Byen. *See* Dioguy, Se Byen
Second *caco* war, 43
Serpent and the Rainbow, The (book and film),
22
Service jobs, 54, 63–64, 79, 80, 99
Shaman, 119, 121, 146. *See also Gangan ason*
Sharecroppers, 67, 89, 99, 101–2, 103, 231
Sharecropping, 2, 100–101, 102, 111–13, 250
Shrines: altars in, 170, 237, 238; and arbors, 237,
276, 277; bundles placed in, 174; and communication with lwa, 130; descent groups
and, 118, 148; descriptions of, 6, 7, 237–38,
276, 280; of Dioguy descent group, 231, 232,
236, 237–38, 251, 264, 276–78, 283, 298n.5;
feedings in, 157; gangan ason and, 119, 121,
164; of Ilavert's descent group, 261–62; locations of, 200; losses of, 96; and lwa, 176–77,
186, 232, 298n.5; performance space in, 10;
photos of, 8, 10, 134, 276–78; in Port-au-
Prince, 294–95n.9, 295–96n.4; in pwen, 8–
15; rooms in, 126, 130–44, 134, 152, 186, 196,
197, 200, 232, 276, 277–78, 280; and sorcery,
207; and temple staffs, 145, 146–47; of Yvon's
descent group, 143
Silien (Ti Rivyè native), 253, 282
Silverman, Martin, 148
Simmonds Brothers, 93, 293n.1
Simon, Antoine, 43
Simpson, George, 295n.1
Singers, 123–24, 150, 238, 247
Singing, 23, 25, 173. *See also Pwen:* throwing;
Songs
Sirina, 167
Slavery, 21, 52, 158, 290n.3, 293n.1
Slaves: African, 21, 85, 86; African-Creole, 86;
as ancestors, 185; in Colombia, 19; on Croix
des Pères, 86; emancipation of, 21, 38, 52,
85; and food production, 52; and French
colonists, 52; Lacombe family and, 94; and
sugarcane, 85; and trade, 52

Karen E. Richman is assistant professor of anthropology and Fellow at both the Kellogg Institute for International Studies and the Institute for Latino Studies at the University of Notre Dame.